Nourishing Daily Devotions

Homily Grits 7

"Snack Food for the Soul"

By Robert W. VanHoose

Homily Grits Daily Devotions
are also
available
or the internet at
www.homilygrits.com
(free daily email subscription available

Other Books by Robert VanHoose
Homily Grits (2003)
Homily Grits 2 (2003)
Homily Grits Daily Devotions and Proactive Prayer (2004)
Homily Grits 4 (2005)
Homily Grits 5 (2006)
Homily Grits 6 (2007)
Let's Walk (2008)
Manage Well (2009)
Memories Do Matter (2010)
Enjoying God's Pleasure (2010)

Most of these books are available from Amazon.Com

Introduction

We are blessed to share another book of insights and hope that they will be a source of spiritual growth, encouragement, and blessings for all who read them.

I marvel at and praise the amazing grace of God that has permitted me to share the Good News of His love with people all over the world through these devotions.

My prayer is that these meditations will be pleasing in God's sight, and that these grits will feed and nourish the souls of all who feed on them.

In Christ's Love,
Robert W. VanHoose

Dedication
To Lorna, my beloved bride of almost 60 years through whom the Lord graced me with love, beauty, companionship, faithfulness, 6 wonderful children, and a wonderful life.

You Deserve a Break Today

""Ah, God, listen to my prayer, my cry—open your ears. Don't be callous; just look at these tears of mine. I'm a stranger here. I don't know my way— a migrant like my whole family. Give me a break, cut me some slack before it's too late and I'm out of here." Psalm 39:11 MSG

God knows that you need a break today. This is why He renews his mercies every day. This is why He sent the Helper to come live in your heart. Our all knowing, ever loving God knows exactly what kind of break you need and exactly when you need it.

> **"He who diligently seeks good seeks [God's] favor, but he who searches after evil, it shall come upon him"**
> **Proverbs 11:27 AMP**

God may give you a break through circumstances that bless you. He may comfort you with His love through His Word or through a friend or loved one. He may heal an illness, or lift a burden of worry, guilt, or shame. He may answer a prayer. He may help with financial or marital problems. He delights in making His strength perfect in your weaknesses

The feedback from many people the Lord has blessed through these grits makes me confident that if you feed on His Word in these devotions on a daily basis you will find yourself getting some of the breaks God loves to give those who love Him and take the time to get to know Him better.

If we are to receive our break today we may need to take a break to spend some time in prayer or meditation with the giver of every good and perfect gift. Scripture tells us that God is a rewarder of those who seek Him. Jesus says that if we seek we will find, and that if we ask we will receive.

> **"It was a case of Christ's strength moving in on my weakness. Now I take limitations in stride, and with good cheer, these limitations that cut me down to size—abuse, accidents, opposition, bad breaks. I just let Christ take over! And so the weaker I get, the stronger I become"**
> **1 Corinthians 10:9 MSG**

Sometimes we need to brake and take a broken spirit and contrite heart to the Lord and confess and repent before we can receive our break.

We also need to remember that the blessing of God's all surpassing peace is promised when we rejoice with a grateful heart regardless of our circumstances.

Father, I pray your goodness and mercy today and every day for this reader who abides and grows in You. In Jesus' name, Amen

Can God Trust You?

"This is a trustworthy saying, and I want you to insist on these teachings so that all who trust in God will devote themselves to doing good. These teachings are good and beneficial for everyone." Titus 3:9 NLT

"Then the LORD asked Satan, "Have you noticed my servant Job? He is the finest man in all the earth. He is blameless—a man of complete integrity. He fears God and stays away from evil."
Job 1:8 NLT

We hear a lot about trusting God, but perhaps not enough about God trusting us. Seeking God's trust in every area of our lives might well be the highest calling of every believer.

The parable of the talents illustrates that God rewards those He can trust to be good stewards of the lives they have been given. God's supreme confidence that Job would continue loving Him in spite of anything the devil could throw at him speaks volumes about God's trust in Job.

When I think of God's promise to never give us more than we can handle with His help, I think of friends and acquaintances who God trusts with much more sorrow, pain, and suffering than I could ever imagine persevering through, and I thank and praise God for their strength and for sparing me such testing.

When we read of the problems of many lottery winners and heirs to great fortunes, we can better understand why God chooses not to trust a lot more people with wealth because it would ruin them instead of blessing them.

The moral meltdowns of David, Peter and the other disciples, and leaders in our churches, governments, and other areas of life seem to indicate God finds a lot of untrustworthy people in His kingdom.

"Therefore let anyone who thinks he stands [who feels sure that he has a steadfast mind and is standing firm], take heed lest he fall [into sin]."
I Corinthians 10:12 AMP

How much God can trust us is directly related to how well we wear the armor He has provided when temptations and tests come our way. This is what we need to avoid the pitfalls of ego, anger, pride, greed, lust, and envy that make us untrustworthy.

Father, teach me to trust in your strength instead of my own that I might be found trustworthy. In Jesus' name, Amen

Self Confidence

"I have told you these things, so that in Me you may have [perfect] peace and confidence. In the world you have tribulation and trials and distress and frustration; but be of good cheer [take courage; be confident, certain, undaunted]! For I have overcome the world. [I have deprived it of power to harm you and have conquered it for you.]"John 16"33 AMP

Self confidence is a valued character and personality trait in most areas of life. It is closely akin to self reliance which is one of the traits many people admire most.

"In peace I will both lie down and sleep, for You, Lord, alone make me dwell in safety and confident trust. "Psalm 4:8 AMP

In a larger than life perspective, our nation is putting man confidence over God confidence and promoting the religion of secular humanism in our schools, government, and judicial system.

When we put self confidence over God confidence we are sure to get into trouble. When we try to do life trusting in ourselves and our own abilities we are sooner or later going to find ourselves coming up lacking.

When we are full of ourselves and our own abilities we leave no room for God to manifest His glory and abilities in our lives. We take credit for all our successes and good fortunes and rob God of the praise and glory He deserves.

Self Confidence versus low self esteem has to do with how secure we are in how well our self image matches what we think it should be.

"Don't be so naive and self-confident. You're not exempt. You could fall flat on your face as easily as anyone else. Forget about self-confidence;" 1 Corinthians 10:11 MSG

When our self confidence and security is based on our confidence in God, who we are in Christ. and the peace and joy that this provides we can be self confident, indeed.

Nothing should ever be able to separate us from God's love and good plans and purposes for our life.

Father, help me to keep my confidence in You and your wonderful promises. In Jesus' name, Amen

Children at Risk

"The promise is for you and your chiildren and for all who are far off—for all whom the Lord our God will call."Acts 2:38

There are organizations, study groups and focus groups concentrating on children at risk. Related topics including, human trafficking, food, insecurity, and the quality of public education.

"We will not hide these truths from our children;we will tell the next generation about the glorious deeds of the Lord,about his power and his mighty wonders. Psalm 78:3-NLT

As bad as these problems are, they are trumped by thieves in the night disguised as public school educators, college professors, judges, TV and movie producers, internet, music, etc. that are robbing our children of their faith and Christian heritage in alarming numbers.

We need to know that latest estimates predict that *75 to 80% of our Church's children will leave our churches* by their second year of college. (Many believe we have lost them during middle school but that it doesn't show until later.)

It is almost unbelievable but true that our children's faith has been put at risk by schools that have taken faith in God out and put faith in man in.

As the church and parents have basically been engrossed in other things and sat idly by and let the secular humanists take over, our children have been brainwashed into believing that not believing is cool and that man, not God, holds the keys to happiness and fulfillment.

"No prolonged infancies among us, please. We'll not tolerate babes in the woods, small children who are an easy mark for impostors. God wants us to grow up, to know the whole truth and tell it in love—like Christ in everything." Ephesians 4:14 MSG

Only when our churches and parents get serious about modeling their faith and making the spiritual growth of their children priority one, can we hope to reverse this trend and save more children at risk.

Father, Help us to equip our children at risk to become children of faith to enjoy the abundant life you promise to all who will trust and obey.In Jesus' name, Amen.

Entitlements

"All of us also lived among them at one time, gratifying the cravings of our flesh and following its desires and thoughts. Like the rest, we were by nature deserving of wrath." Ephesians 2:3 NIV

In case you haven't noticed, we are living in an age of entitlements. There are those who believe that the government should entitle us with cradle to the grave security, while others who preach that our faith in Christ entitles us to material prosperity.

> **"As your name deserves, O God, you will be praised to the ends of the earth. Your strong right hand is filled with victory."**
> **Psalm 48:10 NLT**

Children are growing up feeling that the world owes them a living and that they are entitled to have whatever they want whenever they want it.

There is seldom any reason given as to why they believe this, but over indulgent parents spoiling them rotten is a big factor in many instances.

Jesus' disciples thought that following Him was going to entitle them to rule with Him in high places in an earthly kingdom.

Welfare recipients make demands as though they deserve the gracious provision God has made for them through a generous government.

Everyone seems to have a list of entitlements. Whether it's checking our retirement, insurance, or medicare policies or employment manual, we all want that to which we believe we are entitled.

In all the self centered preoccupation with our entitlements, it is easy to forget about God's death on the cross for our sins that entitles us to a life forever in a sin free heaven.

> "And I saw a strong angel announcing in a loud voice, Who is worthy to open the scroll? And [who is entitled and deserves and is morally fit] to break its seals?"
> Revelation 5:2 AMP

Although our salvation is a free gift and requires nothing on our part other than belief, we should always be mindful that God is entitled to our obedience and love for Him and for others in appreciation of the great thing He has done for us.

Father, help me appreciate the entitlement I have received from my Savior and to show my appreciation by sharing it with others. In Jesus' name, Amen

Playground or Battleground

"You're addicted to thrills? What an empty life! The pursuit of pleasure is never satisfied." Proverbs 21:17 MSG

A.W. Tozer was probably one of God's best messengers of the 20th Century and even today. His sermon on "Playground or Battleground" is the thought for today's grit.

"For You are not a God Who takes pleasure in wickedness; neither will the evil [man] so much as dwell [temporarily] with You.
Psalm 5:4 AMP

Tozer writes: "*The idea that this world is a playground instead of a battleground has now been accepted in practice by the vast majority of fundamentalist Christians. They might hedge around the question if they were asked bluntly to declare their position, but their conduct gives them away. They are facing both ways, enjoying Christ "and the world, gleefully telling everyone that accepting Jesus does not require them to give up their fun- Christianity is just the jolliest thing imaginable. The "worship" growing out of such a view of life is as far off center as the view itself—a sort of sanctified nightclub without the champagne and the dressed-up drunks.*"

We probably don't have to look beyond ourselves or our own families to realize the truth of Tozer's preaching.

The prosperity gospel, the lack of fear of God, and the pursuit of pleasure in all the wrong places and ways is evident all around us. The idea that God wants us to be happy instead of Holy is one of the devil's favorite ploys in winning the battle for our souls.

"For the weapons of our warfare are not physical [weapons of flesh and blood], but they are mighty before God for the overthrow and destruction of strongholds,
2 Corinthians 10:4 AMP

May God help us all to remember that we are not living on a playground but on a battleground and we are going to lose the battle if we do not wear the full armor of God as we do life daily.

Father, forgive me for too much playing and not enough praying or taking sin seriously in this battleground called life. In Jesus' name, Amen

Experiencing God's Best

"But without faith it is impossible to please and be satisfactory to Him. For whoever would come near to God must [necessarily] believe that God exists and that He is the rewarder of those who earnestly and diligently seek Him out." Hebrews 11:6 AMP

It is remarkable that many have to be at their worst to experience God's best. The testimonies of thousands of redeemed Saints attest to the fact that God showed up big time at their worst time and gave them a new life worth living to replace the old one in which they were dying.

"Delight thyself also in the LORD: and he shall give thee the desires of thine heart." Psalm 37:5 KJV

There are also thousands of Saints who have experienced God's best from the day they were born. They have been initiated into the family of God through infant baptism and nurtured and admonished in the Lord by loving parents who modeled the love of Christ and sincerely confirmed their faith and became model disciples without having to experience the refiner's fire.

The parable of the Prodigal Son reflects to some degree on both of these experiences.

While those who have been rescued from wandering aimlessly lost in a life of sin may seem to appreciate God's grace more, those who have been spared the misery and enjoyed God's favor from birth may have even more reason to appreciate what God has done for them.

"Everything that goes into a life of pleasing God has been miraculously given to us by getting to know, personally and intimately, the One who invited us to God." 2 Peter 1:3 MSG

Regardless of how we came to experience God's best gift of eternal life and a new birth in Christ we should never lose sight of the fact that God has so much more of His best He wants to give us.

We need to understand that obeying and abiding in God's Word are the channels of God's best blessings. The more like Jesus we become the more abundance of love, peace, and joy we will experience.

Father, help me to experience Your best by living a fruitful life fully pleasing to you. In Jesus name, Amen

Franchise Players

"For the eyes of the Lord run to and fro throughout the whole earth to show Himself strong in behalf of those whose hearts are blameless toward Him." 2 Chronicles 16:9 AMP

Professional Sports take advantage of rules that allow them to protect and keep a player they consider essential to their success. The designated "franchise players" are given every inducement to remain with that team and in some cases even excluded from becoming free agents.

"But this is the man to whom I will look and have regard: he who is humble and of a broken or wounded spirit, and who trembles at My word and reveres My commands."
Isaiah 66:2b AMP

God initiated the Franchise Player System. Noah, Abraham, Joseph, and David are prime examples of Old Testament heroes who were major players for God.

Jesus selected His own "franchise players" that all played an essential role in bringing His New covenant of grace to the World. Even Judas was an essential franchise player in fulfilling prophecy by betraying Christ.

The idea that a rag tag largely uneducated group of 12 men could change the world is almost incomprehensible, but it happened not by their ability and strength, but by their availability and the strength and power of the Holy Spirit who fell upon and transformed them at Pentecost. The World has never been the same.

We need to be ever mindful that God is still looking for "franchise players" who are essential for God to successfully carry out the Great Commandment and Great Commission.

Then Jesus said to His disciples, If anyone desires to be My disciple, let him deny himself [disregard, lose sight of, and forget himself and his own interests] and take up his cross and follow Me [cleave steadfastly to Me, conform wholly to My example in living and, if need be, in dying, also].
Matthew 16:24 AMP

May we all pray for the heart to say "send me, send me" when God comes knocking. He is still looking for "Franchise Players" at His local church franchise locations.

Father, help me to be one of your franchise members. In Jesus' name, Amen

Without Realizing

"Don't pick on people, jump on their failures, criticize their faults— unless, of course, you want the same treatment. Don't condemn those who are down; that hardness can boomerang. Be easy on people; you'll find life a lot easier. Give away your life; you'll find life given back, but not merely given back—given back with bonus and blessing. Giving, not getting, is the way. Generosity begets generosity."Luke 6:37 MSG

We all need to be aware of our ability to hurt feelings and give offense without even realizing or meaning to. Many of these hurts come while making "cheap conversation" about nothing in particular. Others are caused when we fail to listen to what some one is saying.

An offended friend is harder to win back than a fortified city. Arguments separate friends like a gate locked with bars. Proverbs 18:19 NLT

We also need to beware of taking offense when none is intended.

Insensitive remarks about someone's weight, looks, or dress can be hurtful to others. Often we are making the remarks about someone else forgetting that the one we are making them to may be sensitive about the issue in their own lives.

Others may feel excluded when we ignore them while fellowshiping with another person.

Some of us have forgotten the sensitivity of adolescents and teen-agers and will find out years later that something we said or did offended them.

"For the rest, brethren, whatever is true, whatever is worthy of reverence and is honorable and seemly, whatever is just, whatever is pure, whatever is lovely and lovable, whatever is kind and winsome and gracious, if there is any virtue and excellence, if there is anything worthy of praise, think on and weigh and take account of these things [fix your minds on them]." Philippians 4:8 AMP

Pushing too hard for our own will or way can often cause a lot of needless offense. Ridiculing others' political views is not productive.

As imperfect people living in an imperfect world, we should realize that these things can easily happen, and do all that we can to avoid them by guarding our hearts, tongues, thoughts and conduct.

Father, help me to be sensitive to the feelings of others and not knowingly or unknowingly give needless and unintended offense. In Jesus' name, Amen

The Learning Curve

"[That you may really come] to know [practically, through experience for yourselves] the love of Christ, which far surpasses mere knowledge [without experience]; that you may be filled [through all your being] unto all the fullness of God [may have the richest measure of the divine Presence, and become a body wholly filled and flooded with God Himself]!" Ephesians 3:18 AMP

We sometimes forget that following also means learning. Our call to discipleship is a life long call to learning more about who we are following, and the more we learn, the more like them we will become.

"Learn to do good. Seek justice. Help the oppressed. Defend the cause of orphans. Fight for the rights of widows." Isaiah 1:17:NLT

It starts with our parents and much of what we learn by imitating them become life long habits and personality traits. Studies show that most parenting skills or faults are learned from our parents.

Our wonderful walk of faith is much like one giant learning curve. Learning about Jesus as our Savior starts a life long process of learning more about Him as friend, brother, and companion.

As He *"walks with us, talks with us, and tells us that we are His own"* through His Word, we find ourselves abiding in Him and experiencing His friendship, joy, and encouragement more and more.

When we become true disciples by surrendering our hearts and wills to His control, we put all of His teachings we have learned and continue to learn into practice by knowing and doing His will more and better until we become an extension of His love to others.

'Don't copy the behavior and customs of this world, but let God transform you into a new person by changing the way you think. Then you will learn to know God's will for you, which is good and pleasing and perfect.' Romans 12:1 NLT

Our learning curve will have become a full circle when we see Him face to face and behold His glory in Heaven. The more we learn in this life, the better prepared and more we will enjoy the life that is to come.

We would all do well to learn and apply the greatest lessons ever taught by the greatest Teacher Who ever lived.

Father, give me a teachable spirit and seeking heart that I may enjoy a life of learning in and from You In Jesus' name, Amen

The German Church Tax

"However, we don't want to offend them, so go down to the lake and throw in a line. Open the mouth of the first fish you catch, and you will find a large silver coin. Take it and pay the tax for both of us." Matthew 17:27 NLT

"In addition, we promise to obey the command to pay the annual Temple tax of one-eighth of an ounce of silver[b] for the care of the Temple of our God."
Nehemiah 10:32

Living in a country where our government seems intent on removing all references to God out of our schools, courtrooms, and legislative assemblies, makes it is almost inconceivable that there are governments throughout the world that collect church taxes for the benefit of their churches..

On our last tour of Germany we visited several beautiful but virtually empty churches and cathedrals and made the amazing discovery that the German Government collects over 65 billion dollars yearly in contributions from church members for the benefit of most German Churches. This tax deductible tax amounts to 8 or 9% of the member's gross income tax. The churches pay the government for collecting this tax.

Average church attendance at taxing countries is less than 10% of the people paying the tax in Germany, Denmark, Sweden, Austria, Switzerland, or Finland.

"And I know it is important to love him with all my heart and all my understanding and all my strength, and to love my neighbor as myself. This is more important than to offer all of the burnt offerings and sacrifices required in the law."
Mark 12:33

Whether this is a continuation of the temple tax law of the Old Testament or based on an old pre Christian tribal tradition, God is obviously not pleased with it. It appears that the people's hearts have not followed their taxes into Christ's Churches in Germany.

Most of the churches receiving tax money seem to have lost their way in seeking and saving the lost.

Father, may I never forget that you want my offerings from the temple of my heart. In Jesus' name ,Amen

Open Handed Christianity
"But you shall open your hands wide to him and shall surely lend him sufficient for his need in whatever he lacks" Deuteronomy 15:8 AMP

Whether in love forgiving or giving we are called to be open handed Christians.

"When you supply it, they gather it. You open your hand to feed them, and they are richly satisfied." Psalm 104:27

The right hand of friendship should be extended to all. The cup of kindness that reflects the love of Christ in us should always be filled and ready to be poured out. Our grace of giving should be growing as in order to not only increase our capacity to give, but also to inoculate us against greed.

In spite of how much forgiveness we have received we sometimes find it to be as generous with our forgiveness of others.

Generosity is something not only taught but caught. In commanding us to be generous God wrote the book on generosity and we have all benefited from the examples He set. His generosity to us should beget our generosity to Him and to others.

When we have caught the generosity of God, we will become like the Israelites who gave so much to build the temple they actually had to be told to give no more. We will catch the spirit of the Macedonians who inspite of their extreme poverty begged to be allowed to contribute to the Lord's work.

The truth is that God doesn't need or want our money. He owns it all and can bring it home at any time. God wants our hearts to be stayed on Him and to reflect our love for Him and others that we have received through Christ.

"You hold your hand up high, God, but they don't see it. Open their eyes to what you do, to see your zealous love for your people" Isaiah 26:11 MSG

We are never going to look anyone in the eye who does not matter to Christ. Our love of Christ compels us that they should also matter to us. We need to be as open handed with our love, time, talents, and resources to them as God has been with us.

May everyone know we are Christians by our open handed love.

Father, may your open handedness show through me as I seek to live a life fully pleasing to You. In Jesus' name, Amen.

Un Holy "Scamimony"

"But I fear that somehow your pure and undivided devotion to Christ will be corrupted, just as Eve was deceived by the cunning ways of the serpent."
2 Corinthians 11:2

"What if my father touches me? I would appear to be tricking him and would bring down a curse on myself rather than a blessing."
Genesis 27:12 NIV

Scams and con artists have been deceiving others since the beginning of time. Satan deceived Eve and there has been hell to pay ever since. Jacob scammed Esau's blessing. Joseph's brothers scammed their father. The Trojan Horse was one of the greatest cons ever recorded.

Police blotters in many communities have been overfilled with sad tales of mostly elderly people who have been taken in by the wide spread Nigerian internet scams.

The sale of indulgences that triggered the protestant reformation was one of the cruelest and most shameful scams ever perpetrated on faithful believers. Being told they could buy gain time out of purgatory for themselves or their dearly beloved was the cash cow for the church for many years.

Today we have charities playing on our heartstrings to make donations that mostly go to pay the operating expenses and salaries of those raising the money. We have ministries that have out lived their effectiveness but continue to sustain the large hierarchy that is in place.

'[But] without are the dogs and those who practice sorceries (magic arts) and impurity [the lewd, adulterers] and the murderers and idolaters and everyone who loves and deals in falsehood (untruth, error, deception, cheating"
Revelation 22:15 AMP

The growing demand for funds to operate sometimes make funding and raising money the main priority of some churches. The exorbitant life styles of some of the prosperity gospel advocates gives great cause to ponder.

We also need to be careful not to let the devil discourage our giving by worring about the possibility of being scammed.

Father, give me wisdom and discernment to recognize and avoid scams but let me never fail to recognize and respond cheerfully to help supplyfor real needs. In Jesus' name, Amen.

13

Abused Churches
"Then on the next day he suddenly appeared to some who were quarreling and fighting among themselves, and he urged them to make peace and become reconciled, saying, Men, you are brethren; why do you abuse and wrong one another?"Acts 27:26 AMP

We often hear of abused children, spouses, parents. We also hear of or experience being in an abused church often without realizing it.

"This is what God, the Master, says..." when God hasn't said so much as one word. Extortion is rife, robbery is epidemic, the poor and needy are abused, outsiders are kicked around at will, with no access to justice."
Ezekiel 22:29b MSG

We have abusive pastors who try to impose their agendas and passions upon us which often have nothing to do with our spiritual growth or the upbuilding of God's Kingdom.

We have abusive traditions that are not relevant to today's world that have led millions to leave their churches.

Some pastors and members of Christ's church are being abused by "boss elders" or polity that seeks to impose human will and preferences above God's will and purposes for the church.

Many of the perpetrators of the above described examples of church abuse don't even realize the harm they are doing. Many of the participants of abuse committed in the name of Christ during the Spanish inquisition, crusades, and burnings at the stake thought they were serving the cause of Christ and building up His kingdom

The deceiver of our souls is always working overtime to undermine Christ's church and its mission. He would have us all be stumbling blocks instead of the building blocks we are called to be in Christ.

"But now put away and rid yourselves [completely] of all these things: anger, rage, bad feeling toward others, curses and slander, and foulmouthed abuse and shameful utterances from your lips! "
Colossians 3:7 AMP

There is a fine line between a critical and judgmental spirit and wisdom and spiritual discernment with which we can recognize, avoid, and work to correct any Church abuse that may be harming our mission to love one another and to seek and to save the lost.

Father, let me never be part of any abusive gossip, agenda, or group within my Church body. In Jesus' name, Amen

Heart Spam

"But take heed to yourselves and be on your guard, lest your hearts be overburdened and depressed (weighed down) with the giddiness and headache and nausea of self-indulgence, drunkenness, and worldly worries and cares pertaining to [the business of] this life, and [lest] that day come upon you suddenly like a trap or a noose;" Luke 21:34 AMP

Before the internet, "spam" was best known as the canned meat that fed our troops during World War II, and is still popular with many people today. Now it is the unrelenting emailing of unwanted letters from unknown people offering all sorts of things and conducting all sorts of scams.

"Guard your heart above all else, for it determines the course of your life." Proverbs 4:22 NLT

We really need to be wary of all spammed emails because these can sometimes spam thoughts into our hearts that don't need to go there.

TV advertisers and marketing gurus and sometimes the devil himself spam unwanted subliminal messages below the threshold of our conscious perception. These spams allowed to pass from our thoughts to our hearts can do a lot of damage before we even realize it.

Too many of us have been too easily lulled into acceptance of cultural changes effected by the constant depictions of immoral life styles that have filled the daytime soaps and evening sit coms for over half a century. The commercials that link products with status, happiness, and pleasure have done their share of spamming our hearts.

"I'm not asking that you take them out of the world But that you guard them from the Evil One." John 17:15 MSG

Like the frog in the kettle as the garbage continues to flow we become victims of a spammed heart that is no longer guided by a clear conscience, but by a so called enlightened conscience that no longer believes and obeys God's truths but buys into relative truth and the wisdom of man.

We need to perhaps have more wisdom and spiritual discernment now than ever before to protect us from "heart spam".

Father, protect me from those trying to play tricks with my mind that can damage my heart. In Jesus' name, Amen

Are You All In?

"Come near to God and he will come near to you. Wash your hands, you sinners, and purify your hearts, you double-minded. James 4:7 NIV

TV and Internet have made Texas Holdem Poker and being "all in" popular among a lot of people. When you put everything you have in the pot you can declare that you are "all in" and share in any winnings up to the amount of the pot at that time.

"For I have kept the ways of the LORD; I have not turned from my God to follow evil."
Psalm 18:21 NLT

Jesus didn't play poker, but He did tell everyone who listened that they needed to get "all in" with God by following Him. No going home to bury the dead, and no preferring mother, father, money, etc.

This begs the question of whether we are "all in" with Jesus or holding back in some area of our lives. We may be holding back our money, time, or talents. We may be holding back forgiveness or repentance. We may be holding back in growing into the fullness of Christ by not growing in the Word.

Early church members held back nothing in sharing what they had with other believers. Ananias and Sapphira were struck dead on the spot for saying they were "all in" while holding back some of the proceeds from the sale of their property.

The Lord told the Laodicean Church that He was going to spit them out of His mouth because they were only lukewarm and not "all in".

Many of us are often guilty of not living like followers who have really decided to follow Jesus. Many believe that receiving eternal life is all that matters. The idea of becoming all in disciples and surrendering control of their lives in obedience to the Great Commandment and Great Commission has never entered their heart.

And he who does not take up his cross and follow Me [cleave steadfastly to Me, conforming wholly to My example in living and, if need be, in dying also] is not worthy of Me.
Matthew 10:38 NLT

Father, help me to remain "all in" by being conformed into the image of Your Son by the daily renewing of my mind. In Jesus name, Amen

The View from the Top
"So we have stopped evaluating others from a human point of view. At one time we thought of Christ merely from a human point of view. How differently we know him now!" 2 Corinthians 5:15

"Roll your works upon the Lord [commit and trust them wholly to Him; He will cause your thoughts to become agreeable to His will, and] so shall your plans be established and succeed."
Proverbs 16:3 AMP

Viewing life from our perspective instead of God's will usually result in faulty vision. We need to put on the eyeglasses of God's revealed Word and draw our view of living as modeled for us by our Lord Jesus Christ.

We sometimes get so caught up in our own enthusiasm for loving and serving God that we forget checking things out with Him. We all too often presume the Lord's will to mask our own by setting arbitrary conditions to confirm our will as God's will.

We may have targeted a deadline as to when we will proceed if God sends no objections. We may view random circumstances as God's will. We too often presume to know the minds of others.

When we view our past through perfect hindsight we will often see that God was flashing red lights all over the place which we ignored and chose not to heed.

Devastated spouses will remind themselves of God's warning not to be yoked with an unbeliever. Broken relationships resulting from loaning or co signing a note for a friend contrary to Scripture, and putting too much trust in people instead of God will often come back to bite us.

"Jesus turned to Peter and said, "Get away from me, Satan! You are a dangerous trap to me. You are seeing things merely from a human point of view, not from God's."
Matthew 15:23 NLT

The Good News is that nothing can stand in the way of God's love for us in Christ Jesus and that He can and will turn our worst into His good purpose of conforming us into the likeness of Christ.

Father, help me to concentrate on knowing and doing Your will instead of mine to the praise of Your glory. In Jesus' name, Amen

The Sincerity of Repentance
"Wash yourselves and be clean! Get your sins out of my sight. Give up your evil ways.." Isaiah 1:16 NLT

"Don't tear your clothing in your grief,but tear your hearts instead."Return to the LORD your God,for he is merciful and compassionate, slow to get angry and filled with unfailing love.He is eager to relent and not punish."
Joel 2:13 NLT

John the Baptist recognized the hypocrisy of the Scribes and Pharisees. As he baptized with the baptism of repentance he reminded them that they needed to bear fruits as proof of the sincerity of their repentance.

Jesus had little patience with the hypocrisy and insincerity of the Scribes and Pharisees. He said they were like white washed tombs which looked beautiful on the outside, but were full of dead men's bones, and everything impure. We should all pray that He never say the same about us.

Whether we are confessing and repenting of our sins in order to be saved, or for receiving the forgiveness we need for the sins we commit on a daily basis, we also need to bear fruits worthy of our repentance. When it comes to faith or sorrow for our sins our actions speak louder than our words.

Jesus' call to faith and repentance is first and foremost an interior call to our hearts. The outward expressions of sorrow and apology mean nothing if they do not come from a sincere heart.

True internal repentance should always be accompanied by an external expression of the fruit of righteousness. Whether it is prayer, fasting or giving true repentance, it should always be accompanied by outward signs that signify an inward change.

Sincere love expressed in loving others by forgiving ,praying, and helping them in any way will always cover a multitude of sins when done out of a broken spirit and contrite heart.

"Bear Fruit worthy of repentance"
Matthew 3:8 KJV

When we approach God's throne of grace to confess, repent, and seek forgiveness for our sins, may we never forget to approach with sincerity and truth and offer and correct our ways to validate our true repentance.

Father, help me to prove the sincerity of my repentance. In Jesus' name, Amen

The Right Call

"If you decide that it's a bad thing to worship God, then choose a god you'd rather serve—and do it today. Choose one of the gods your ancestors worshiped from the country beyond The River, or one of the gods of the Amorites, on whose land you're now living. As for me and my family, we'll worship God."Joshua 24:15 MSG

From Little League umpire manuals to beer commercials, making the "right call" has become a catchy phrase for every day life.

"LORD, who may dwell in your sacred tent? Who may live on your holy mountain?" Psalm 15:1 NIV

A lot of our quality of life is going to depend on making the right calls. There are right calls about education, jobs, mates, morality, and faith that are a lot more important than the beer we call out for, or whether we call a player safe or out in a baseball game.

Prisons. rehab centers. divorce courts, and bankruptcy courts are full of people who have made some wrong calls.

The truth is that we are all born with a sin DNA that guarantees we will all make some wrong calls. (*"For all have sinned and fall short of the glory of God"* Romans 3:23)

How exciting it is to know that all of our wrong calls can be erased when we make the right call to God. Although there may be some consequences, when we confess to God that we are sinners who need a Savior and ask Jesus to come into our hearts, God takes all of our bad calls and buries them in His sea of forgetfulness.

"Seek, inquire for, and require the Lord while He may be found [claiming Him by necessity and by right]; call upon Him while He is near." Isaiah 55:6 AMP

Conversely, it is also exciting to know God is never going to forget and will bless and reward our right calls in loving and serving Him and others.

Our God of free will never forces, but will always help us make the right calls when our hearts are right with Him. We can never strike out with God when we worship Him in spirit and in truth.

Father, help me to make the right calls that will earn your "well done" when I stand before you to give an account of my life on judgment day. In Jesus' name, Amen

Culture Shock
"He went on in this vein for a long time, urging them over and over, "Get out while you can; get out of this sick and stupid culture!"Acts 2:40 MSG

Many parents and grandparents are shocked at the prevailing standards of today's culture.

"The counsel of the Lord stands forever, the thoughts of His heart through all generations."
Psalm 33:11 AMP

The Bible was written in a culture where slavery was condoned and women were barely regarded as more than slaves. There were no prisons because those who broke the law were stoned to death along with juvenile delinquents. Adulterers were subject to the death penalty.

Marriages took place close to the age of puberty and there was no sexual activity before marriage. Children were required to memorize the first five books of the Old Testament even though there were no schools as we know them. People who couldn't repay loans were made slaves.

Today sexual activity outside of marriage and same sex marriages are becoming accepted practices among many living in today's culture.Some of today's churches even condone such evil.

Whether what many perceive to be the moral decline of our country and its people points to the impending destruction of the world or is just part of a cultural revolution called "age of enlightenment", it is good to know that God is still on the throne.

"Embracing what God does for you is the best thing you can do for him. Don't become so well-adjusted to your culture that you fit into it without even thinking"
Romans 12:1 MSG

That everyone who does not know God should seek Him while He can still be found is perhaps now more than ever before the best advice we can give to anyone who would escape the real culture shock of eternal torment in hell.

Father, thank you for the blessed assurance I have in knowing that nothing can separate me from your love and that you are continuing to work all things for my good and your glory. In Jesus' name, Amen

The Prosperity Gospel
"Enjoy prosperity while you can, but when hard times strike, realize that both come from God. Remember that nothing is certain in this life." Ecclesiastes 7:14 NLT

The "name it and claim it" proponents of the prosperity gospel are

"Let me share in the prosperity of your chosen ones. Let me rejoice in the joy of your people; let me praise you with those who are your heritage."
Psalm 106:5 NLT

inferring that we can have wealth and healing by believing, praying, and often by giving them a donation. They overlook the poverty, pain and suffering of the apostles and disciples.

The cruelest of false teachings blames lack of healing on lack of faith.

Instead of bringing that peace that surpasses all understanding, it brings poverty, guilt, and discouragement to people around the world who buy into this popular theology. In trying to discredit the prosperity Gospel there is a tendency among many to "throw out the baby with the bathwater" and rob a lot of believers of the prosperity God offers and promises to those who tithe.

In Malachi 3:9. God clearly challenges us to "give to get", while many teach that this is a wrong motivation, and that we should only give out of gratitude for what Jesus did on the cross for us.

The true prosperity gospel is that God is working all things for our good in conforming us to the image of Christ. This "good may often include pain, suffering, and material poverty as God does whatever it takes to give us the prosperity of our souls. The all surpassing peace and security in knowing Jesus as Savior and Lord, is the prosperity we should all seek.

"I have told you all this so that you may have peace in me. Here on earth you will have many trials and sorrows. But take heart, because I have overcome the world."
John 16:32-NLT

God does answer prayers for healing according to His good will. He pours out financial, relational, physical, and spiritual blessings from His overflowing cup of blessings as we trust, obey, ask, and depend on him .

Father, help me to enjoy the prosperity You give my soul that can only be found through abiding in You and Your Word. In Jesus' name, Amen

Are You Being Withheld?

"For the Lord God is our sun and our shield. He gives us grace and glory. The Lord will withhold no good thing from those who do what is right." Psalm 84:11 NLT

"Withhold not Your tender mercy from me, O Lord; let Your loving-kindness and Your truth continually preserve me!"
Psalm 40:11 AMP

Anyone who draws a pay check is aware of State, Federal, and in many cases local tax withholding. There is really not a whole lot we can do about this except vote for those who will cut spending and taxes.

We sometimes hear of problems caused by withholding information or help.

There is a much larger and more important withholding going on that we all need to be aware of and can do something about.

When we seek first the kingdom of God and His righteousness we can be sure that the Lord will not withhold the blessings He promises.

We are promised rewards in this life and the next, and that all of our needs will be met when we seek Him first.

Although God pours out some general blessings to all, He reserves many others for those who love, serve, and obey Him.

There is nothing wrong with seeking the Lord's blessings. There is great reward and joy in finding God's way of opening the floodgates and pouring out bountiful blessings that have been withheld pending our getting our hearts right with God.

"Seek the Kingdom of God[d] above all else, and live righteously, and he will give you everything you need."
Matthew 6:33 NLT

Anytime we feel we are not experiencing God's best, or that He is holding out on us, we need to honestly and earnestly judge our hearts, thoughts, and conduct to make sure there are no "deal breakers" which might cause God to be withholding all that He wants to give us.

Father, may your grace and mercy flow in me and through me that I might enjoy all of the abundant life you died to give me on this earth as you prepare me for my eternal life in heaven. In Jesus' name, Amen

God's Unemployed
"What I've done, you do. I'm only pointing out the obvious. A servant is not ranked above his master; an employee doesn't give orders to the employer. If you understand what I'm telling you, act like it—and live a blessed life." John 13:17b MSG

As bad as economic unemployment is, it is nothing compared to the spiritual unemployment rampant throughout the world.

"Don't shove me into the same jail cell with those crooks, With those who are full-time employees of evil."
Psalm 28:3 MSG

The people of God have left their Great Commission and Great Commandment jobs in record numbers leaving far too few to help harvest the souls who desperately need the Lord.

The deceiver of our souls has promoted a consumer mentality among many church goers. They expect to be ministered to and have their needs met rather than become involved in the church's mission of seeking and saving the lost.

If we are not actively working to build the kingdom of God in our every day life, we are most likely among God's unemployed.

When we consider that God gave us this air we are breathing and the life we are living for His pleasure and purposes we should be aware of Who we are working for and what we should be doing.

Obeying God in every area of our lives should be our first priority in life. As God's employee, we should be seeking His kingdom and His righteousness so that we can receive all of the wonderful work and retirement benefits He promises.

"Don't just do what you have to do to get by, but work heartily, as Christ's servants doing what God wants you to do. "
Ephesians 6:7 MSG

When we choose to opt out of our employment in God's service, we are choosing to serve our own selfish interests. Working the world's way is not working God's way. How sad it will be for a believer to stand before the Lord with nothing left to earn His well done, after all the wood hay and stubble of our trivial pursuits of unemployment are burned away.

Father, may I always find gainful employment in loving and serving You and others. In Jesus' name, Amen

Beware of the Border Bullies

"Keep on loving your friends; do your work in welcoming hearts. Don't let the bullies kick me around, the moral midgets slap me down. Send the upstarts sprawling flat on their faces in the mud."Psalm 36:10 MSG

In "The Prayer of Jabez" best selling author and friend Dr. Bruce Wilkinson talks about "border bullies" that keep us from expanding our territories for ministry and service.

"God, these bullies have reared their heads! A gang of thugs is after me— and they don't care a thing about you." Psalm 86:14 MSG

The "fear bully" that caused the children of Israel to wander in the wilderness for 40 years before entering the promised land is still probably agent number one in holding us back. Pride, doubt, indifference, pleasure, discouragement, expense, disagreements, and self centeredness are also often big obstacles to overcome.

These agents of the devil are always at work discouraging us and giving us reasons not to reach out beyond our comfort zones into the promised land of blessings of doing the things God created us to do.

We need to remember that God has defeated the border bully and his agents on the cross, and that we have nothing or no one to fear other than God.

God will see us through the crisis of belief that almost always accompanies us when we step out of our comfort zones into fulfilling God's purpose and mission for our lives.

"Don't be bluffed into silence by the threats of bullies. There's nothing they can do to your soul, your core being. Save your fear for God, who holds your entire life—body and soul—in his hands. Matthew 10:27 MSG

When Jesus Christ died on the cross to unchain us from our bondage to sin, He also died in order that the Holy Spirit come to dwell within us giving the boldness and power to make disciples.

We must never let the "border bullies" keep us from being on mission for the Great Commission.

Father, by the power of Your Spirit, help me to overcome the "border bullies" that are keeping me from being and doing all that I an and should be and do in loving and serving You and others. In Jesus name, Amen

If God Doesn't Mind, It Doesn't Matter
"Blind guides! You strain your water so you won't accidentally swallow a gnat, but you swallow a camel!" Matthew 23:24 NLT

The deceiver of our soul's favorite past times seems to be creating division and conflict with a body of Christ's believers. He knows that any time he can get us arguing among ourselves, it's time taken away from building up the kingdom of God.

"The Spirit of the Lord GOD is upon me; because the LORD hath anointed me to preach good tidings unto the meek; he hath sent me to bind up the brokenhearted, to proclaim liberty to the captives, and the opening of the prison to them that are bound;"
Isaiah 61:1 KJV

Churches have become conflicted and even split over choice of choir robes, color of carpet, dress codes, and style of worship.

The fact that there are now literally thousands of denominations comprising the body of Christ give cause to ponder how the simplest truth in the world could become so complicated.

Somehow the truth that Jesus Christ died to set us free not only from the bondage of sin, but also the bondage of the mosaic law and so many of the trivial requirements thereof is forgotten as men try to make their own rules as to how the people of God should conform.

Jesus reserved His severest condemnation for the Scribes and Pharisees and their hypocrisy should teach us all that it's not HOW we worship, but WHO we worship that really matters.

When we focus our minds on things that don't really matter to God the main thing of seeking and saving the lost gets side tracked.

"let us therefore make every effort to do what leads to peace and to mutual edification."
Romans 14:19 NIV

Our freedom in Christ also brings the Christian liberty to observe many beliefs and practices that are neither condoned nor forbidden by God.

We have more than enough real sins to worry about than pursuing arguments and conflicts over things that don't matter to God.

Father, help me stay focused on the things that really matter to You. In Jesus' name, Amen

Living Life for a Living

"For through the law I died to the law so that I might live for God. [20] I have been crucified with Christ and I no longer live, but Christ lives in me. The life I now live in the body, I live by faith in the Son of God, who loved me and gave himself for me." Galatians 2:19 NIV

When we ask someone what they do for a living, we usually expect to hear about their job, profession, or occupation.

Actually this can also be a very challenging philosophical question.

"You make known to me the path of life; you will fill me with joy in your presence, with eternal pleasures at your right hand."
Psalm 16:11 NIV

We should all be doing a lot more living than working to make a living. Most people have at least 16 non job related hours in most days, with 24 on week ends..

Every day is a gift wrapped day for living life to the fullest. We may be living for our families, friends, recreation, occupation, and hopefully for our faith. These are all excellent ways to help us living life well.

The evidence of what are we living for is demonstrated by the time and effort we put into something. Some seem to be living to eat rather than eating to live and even living to work other than working to live. We can get so caught up in a particular activity that we become slaves to it at the expense of other areas of our lives.

Jesus came that we might have life and have it more abundantly. This is never going to happen unless we are living to love and serve Him and others according to His purposes for creating us.

When we start living with Christ in us as our hope of glory we will start sinning less and loving more. As we grow in Christ by getting to know him better through His Word we will find ourselves enjoying the blessings of His joy and friendship and more answered prayers as the abundance of His grace overflows into every area of our lives.

"In this way they will lay up treasure for themselves as a firm foundation for the coming age, so that they may take hold of the life that is truly life."
1 Timothy 6:19 NIV

May God help us all to live like Christ in living a life worth living.

Father. help me to practice living in You for a a living. In Jesus' name, Amen

26

Misgivings

"For we take thought beforehand and aim to be honest and absolutely above suspicion, not only in the sight of the Lord but also in the sight of men." 2 Corinthians 8:21 AMP

Doubts, suspicions, and uneasy consciences abound in our imperfect world filled with imperfect people. To be *"wise as a serpent and harmless as a dove"* (Matthew 10:16) as commanded, we should pray for spiritual discernment and wisdom from on high.

"Preserve my life, for I am godly and dedicated; O my God, save Your servant, for I trust in You [leaning and believing on You, committing all and confidently looking to You, without fear or doubt]."
Psalm 86:2 AMP

In spiritual and moral matters we need to carefully consider the source of our misgivings. If they are based on our knowledge of God's Word or our knowledge of right and wrong we have every reason to be concerned.

When we look back with our perfect hindsight we will often see where our doubts and suspicions proved well founded but others where we should have given the benefit of any doubts we might have had. We can often spend a lot of worrisome hours with misgivings that never happen.

The deceiver of our souls who wants us to curse God and die continually tries to create doubt and suspicions about our salvation in order to bring us back under his control. We should have an uneasy conscience when we surrender to sin.

We need to fully confess our sin and ask for the strength and power of the Holy Spirit to help us overcome the sins we don't have the power to overcome in our own strength.

There should never be any misgivings about God's love. He works all things for our good in conforming us into the image of Christ. Our saving faith is the sustaining faith that will overcome our misgivings when we learn and claim the wonderful promises of God as taught in Scripture.

"Be on your guard against the yeast of the Pharisees, which is hypocrisy."
Luke 12:1b AMP

Father may I take seriously any misgivings I might have, and filter them through my conscience and your Word, so that I can best know how to respond in a way that pleases You. In Jesus' name, Amen.

The Chasm

"And besides all this, between us and you a great chasm has been set in place, so that those who want to go from here to you cannot, nor can anyone cross over from there to us." Luke 19:25 NIV

There is an everlasting division and separation between heaven and hell. Jesus Christ died on the cross to pay our way of escape from the destination we were headed for under the curse of original sin.

"For there is nothing trustworthy or steadfast or truthful in their talk; their heart is destruction [or a destructive chasm, a yawning gulf]; their throat is an open sepulcher; they flatter and make smooth with their tongue."

As we cross over the divide by faith and become dead to sin and alive in Christ we are clothed in the righteousness of Christ in God's sight. We escape separation from God in the eternal torment of hell and enter into the abundant eternal life with God now and forever.

Make no mistake about it! Hell is a terrible place. No one should choose to go there. As we pray for, beg and plead with those we love to receive God's wonderful gift of salvation we must remember never to give up while they are living.

We need to understand that our God is a God of love. He does not force anyone to love Him or receive Him. He has revealed His love and his character through Scripture. He came to earth as a man to welcome and receive all who would freely and willingly receive Him.

He offers clear choices of life or death, so there can be no excuse for anyone perishing except by their own choice to reject Jesus.

"But Abraham said, 'If they won't listen to Moses and the prophets, they won't listen even if someone rises from the dead.'"
Luke 19:31 NLT

Knowing that there is no way back after death closes the escape route should encourage us all to take more seriously Christ's commands for us to make disciples and be His sermons in shoes. The eternal future of someone we know and love may depend upon our testimony.

Father, may no one remain lost because I have remained silent about your wonderful gift of eternal life and how to receive it. In Jesus' name, Amen

Nothing to Wear?

"I delight greatly in the LORD; my soul rejoices in my God. For he has clothed me with garments of salvation and arrayed me in a robe of his righteousness, as a bridegroom adorns his head like a priest, and as a bride adorns herself with her jewels." Isaiah 61:9 NIV

Of all the lame excuses for not attending church having nothing to wear is perhaps the lamest of all.

"In that day of battle, your people will serve you willingly. Arrayed in holy garments, your vigor will be renewed each day like the morning dew."
Psalm 110:3 NLT

Although there may be many churches where tradition and practice dictate that we be dressed up in our "Sunday Best" for coming into the presence of the King, we also need to think about the hypocrisy of the Scribes and Pharisees who were always dressed to the hilt in fine robes and trappings which did nothing to clean up their hearts.

There is a story about church members who welcomed a poorly dressed family to church one Sunday, and immediately went out and bought them nice clothes to wear when they came back.   When the family didn't return and they went out to check on them, they found that they looked so good they decided to go to a better and bigger church.

There is nothing humorous about this parable. It is about God sending John the Baptist and Jesus to invite the children of Israel to the wonderful celebration of Gods New Covenant of Grace only to have them refuse the invitation.

There are some commentaries that teach that it was the custom of the day that the king holding the feast also provided suitable wedding garments for all attendees who might not have them and that the inappropriately attired guest who was thrown out had no excuse for not being properly clothed.

When the king entered and looked over the scene, he spotted a man who wasn't properly dressed. He said to him, 'Friend, how dare you come in here looking like that!' The man was speechless. "
Matthew 22:11,12 MSG

We need to understand that when we are clothed by faith with the robe of Christ's righteousness we are always royally dressed..

Father, May I never approve or disapprove of what others wear on their backs but always pray that they are wearing the righteousness of Christ in their hearts. In Jesus name, Amen

What's on Your Bucket List?
"So, dear brothers and sisters, work hard to prove that you really are among those God has called and chosen. Doing this, you will never stumble or fall away. And God will open wide the gates of heaven for you to enter into the eternal Kingdom of our Lord and Savior Jesus Christ." 1 Peter 2:10,11

The movie about a couple of old geezer's setting out to complete their list of things they wanted to do before they

"The desire accomplished is sweet to the soul: but it is abomination to fools to depart from evil." Proverbs 7:13 KJV

"kicked the bucket" stimulated a lot interest and generated a lot of ideas and suggestions

The older we get, the more aware we become that the time for seeing the world, writing that book, driving that dream car is getting shorter and shorter. Time seems to fly faster and faster. We would do well to ask what's on God's bucket list for us before He calls us home.

When we understand and believe by faith that God has created us for His good purposes we can't help but wonder what these purposes might include, and above all seek to know and do the Lord's will.

We know that God wants us to become more like Christ, so we need to pursue the holiness and humility of Christ. We know that Christ has called us to make disciples. This is generally accomplished by reflecting Christ's love among the sphere of family and friends. We may need to follow the Lord's leading outside our comfort zones to seek and save the lost where they might be found.

"For we must all appear and be revealed as we are before the judgment seat of Christ, so that each one may receive [his pay] according to what he has done in the body, whether good or evil [considering what his purpose and motive have been, and what he has achieved, been busy with, and given himself and his attention to accomplishing]." 2 Corinthians 5:10 AMP

Rick Warren's story about his father's last desire to "win one more soul for Jesus" should encourage us all to make this the desire of our heart.

Father, as you hold my future let me hold loving and serving you and others more be at the lop of my "bucket list". In Jesus' name, Amen.

The More That Really Matters
"When you grab all you can get, that's what happens: the more you get, the less you are." Proverbs 1:1b MSG

We are a nation of people obsessed with getting more. Whether it's more car, house, money, food, sex, pleasure, drugs, or approval many of us are wanting and sometimes willing to do anything to get more.

"Day by day the LORD takes care of the innocent,and they will receive an inheritance that lasts forever. **¹⁹ They will not be disgraced in hard times;even in famine they will have more than enough."** **Psalm 37:18,19 NLT**

As we read the history of God's people we find that grumbling and complaining for more has been an age old problem.

It started with Adam and Eve who wanted more equality with God. Although being well fed with manna from heaven, the Israelites wanted more variety of food.

The insatiable demand for more toys, games, and gadgets among our children is getting bigger and more expensive all the time. The more they get, the more they want, and the less satisfied they become with what they have.

Amidst all of the desires of our flesh that fuel our perceived needs satisfaction, we too easily forget about wanting the more that really matters.

We forget that becoming more like Jesus is the plan and purpose toward which God is working all things for our good.

.   The Bible calls it being transformed and we achieve it by the ongoing renewing of our minds by abiding in and becoming imitators of Christ on a day by day, year to year process of growing into spiritual maturity.

"Therefore, my dearly beloved, shun (keep clear away from, avoid by flight if need be) any sort of idolatry (of loving or venerating anything more than God)." **1 Corinthians 10:14 AMP**

Seeking to become more like Jesus is the only more that can really satisfy. When "I would be happy if only I had more" turns into "I am happy because I have eternal peace and joy in Christ" we will find that all surpassing peace and joy.

Father, keep me ever mindful that wanting more of Jesus should be the number one priority of my life. In Jesus' name, Amen

Making a Name for Ourselves

"The good person is generous and lends lavishly; No shuffling or stumbling around for this one, But a sterling and solid and lasting reputation. Unfazed by rumor and gossip, Heart ready, trusting in God, Spirit firm, unperturbed," Psalm 112:6 MSG

Whether we realize it or not, we all start making a name for ourselves from the day we are born. We will become to be known as good babies, cry babies, etc., to start with, and go on from there up until the day we die.

"A GOOD name is rather to be chosen than great riches, and loving favor rather than silver and gold." Proverbs 22:1 AMP

We would all like to make a good name for ourselves, and act accordingly. Sometimes we carry a reputation acquired in our youth that haunts us forever. Sometimes we lose a good reputation built up over a lifetime in one mistake later in life.

Corporate executives, movie stars, recording artists and politicians spend millions trying to make a good name for themselves in the public arena.

Others spend even more trying to do damage control and protecting a good name.

Ego is usually accompanied by a certain amount of self promotion that calls attention to how great we are in case someone doesn't know

The truth is that when we are good people notice and will do all the PR work needed to help us gain a good name.

"Do you want to be counted wise, to build a reputation for wisdom? Here's what you do: Live well, live wisely, live humbly."

When we are living to make a good name for Jesus people will notice and respond to this also. This is still by far the most effective way God can use us to be instruments of bringing others into a saving relationship with Jesus Christ.

God has created us and written our names in the Lamb's book of life. We need to be ever faithful in making a name for Him and His kingdom rather than worrying about making a name for ourselves.

Father, when my name is called in heaven may I be remembered as one who honored and glorifed Your name by living a fruitful life fully pleasing to You while here below. In Jesus"name, Amen

The United Way

"I am in them and you are in me. May they experience such perfect unity that the world will know that you sent me and that you love them as much as you love me."John 17:22

"BEHOLD, HOW good and how pleasant it is for brethren to dwell together in unity!" Psalm 133:1 AMP

Sports teams, event organizers, businesses, families, soldiers, and especially churches can all attest to the success and satisfaction that comes from working together to accomplish a common goal.

Most people will always remember the thrill of being on a winning team or participating in a successful project. The bonding that takes place among the participants often results in lifelong friendships.

Sometimes going through some tough times together produces the same effect.

Great things happen when people buy into a team or concept and commit to doing all they can to help make it succeed.

Championships and battles are won, buildings get built, and all sorts of other goals get accomplished when people unite.

The United Way charity organizations in most communities use this concept to get people and businesses contributing together to fund many worthwhile causes within their cities that could never be funded individually.

Scripture gives many good examples of the great things that were accomplished the United Way. God's people gave so much to build the temple that they were told to give no more. Nehemiah got the people united to rebuild the wall around Jerusalem. The early church thrived and survived by being united,

"fulfill my joy by being like-minded, having the same love, *being* of one accord, of one mind." Philippians 2:2 KJV

When it comes to seeking and saving the lost we should all be united in heart and soul, always being building blocks and never stumbling blocks to help accomplish God's greatest purpose.

Father, help me to always be united in purpose with all who are committed to building up your kingdom. In Jesus' name, Amen

34

The Power of Joy

"Don't be dejected and sad, for the joy of the Lord is your strength!"
Nehemiah 8:10b NLT

The deceiver of our souls is constantly working to rob us of our joy because he knows it is a source of some of our greatest power.

**"For his anger lasts only a moment, but his favor lasts a lifetime! Weeping may last through the night, but joy comes with the morning."
Psalm 30:5 NLT**

The Lord is continually filling our cups of joy so that we can find the strength we need to overcome discouragement and depression and to be able to comfort and encourage others.

When we consider the joy of our salvation in being called, claimed, and redeemed by the Lord we are filled with a bright hope for now and forever.

As we add Jesus' joy to our own we grow in friendship with Him through abiding in His Word.

The joy of knowing that God is our refuge and strength and very present help in time of trouble is priceless.

The joy of having the Holy Spirit's presence within us to guide, guard, and lead us into all truth is joy indeed.

Joy is a fruit of the Spirit which is being continually produced within us to bear in every area of our life.

**"I have told you these things, that My joy and delight may be in you, and that your joy and gladness may be of full measure and complete and overflowing.
John 15:10-12**

As we pass on our joy in the Lord and the great things he has done and continues to do for us we will experience even more joy.

When we understand that God is working all things (including our problems and failures) for our good as part of His plan to conform us into the image of Christ, we can rejoice and receive the peace and joy of the Lord that surpasses all understanding.

Father, help me to live my life as a celebration of the joy you have given me. In Jesus' name, Amen

In Praise of Angels
"Are not the angels all ministering spirits (servants) sent out in the service [of God for the assistance] of those who are to inherit salvation?" Hebrews 1:14 AMP

As we live pursuing life, liberty, and happiness we often overlook and forget to thank God for His holy angels He has sent to watch over us every day of our lives.

"For he will order his angels to protect you wherever you go." Psalm 91:11 NLT

Were it not for the divine intervention of our guardian angels, few of us would be alive today. When we see how our children are spared harm from what could have been fatal accidents, when we think about all the near misses we have had on the highways, and when we think about how blessed we are that some purchases were never completed or that some were made, we have every reason to thank and praise God for our angels.

As we see the heartbreaks, tragedies, and problems of our friends and acquaintances, we have even more reason to be thankful for God's angels that may have kept the same disaster from befalling us.

Scripture mentions angels over 300 times and teaches that they are ministering spirits who worship God and Christ, serve as His messengers, and have charge over us.   They are wise, mighty, holy, and there are millions of them.

It is wise to note that the devil also has legions of angels and that we should always be on guard and ask for wisdom and spiritual discernment to recognize and avoid being misled or deceived by them.

"He made it known by sending his angel to his servant John, [2] who testifies to everything he saw—that is, the word of God and the testimony of Jesus Christ." Revelation 1:1b.2 NLT

We can sometimes meet angels disguised as people. They can work through others and our selves to deliver God's instruction and counsel and accomplish their good purposes.

How comforting it is to know that we have someone watching over us and our loved ones protecting, encouraging, and making God's will known.

What a sight that will be when we see the angels in heaven rejoicing with us whenever a sinner is saved. We should never worship angels, but we should always thank God for blessing us through them.

Father, help me to recognize and always be thankful for the divine intervention of my guardian angel that has watched over me all the days of my life. In Jesus' name, Amen.

Drive Out Price

" Fear not, for I have redeemed you [ransomed you by paying a price instead of leaving you captives]; I have called you by your name; you are Mine." Isaiah 43:1b AMP

"For the ransom of a life is too costly, and [the price one can pay] can never suffice—"
Psalm 49:7-9

Most experienced car buyer know when buying a car that the drive out price is usually quite a bit higher than the agreed upon purchasing or trading price. After interest, taxes, extended warranties, title processing fees, etc are added, we find ourselves driving out with a lot more debt or a lot less cash than we expected. It's always a good idea to ask for the drive out price before deciding to buy.

There seems to be some confusion among many as to whether the price Jesus paid to drive out our sins was is subject to some extra effort on our part.

The vanity of man to suggest that we need to add anything to the perfect sacrifice of our Lord and Savior to receive His righteousness in God's sight by faith is a cruel insult to Christ that suggests that His death on the cross was not enough.

We need never doubt that Jesus' blood and righteousness was more than enough to assure our mansion in heaven. Scripture makes it abundantly clear that salvation is by grace alone through faith alone and not of works of which we might boast.

Although the hour we first believed "seals the deal" with God as far as our eternal life in heaven is concerned, He does graciously offer the means for us to show our appreciation for the great thing Christ has done by honoring Him in all that we do as God works all things for our good in conforming us into the image of His Son so that we can drive out of this world as righteous as we can be before going into the presence of our perfect Lord.

"Yes, furthermore, I count everything as loss compared to the possession of the priceless privilege (the overwhelming preciousness, the surpassing worth, and supreme advantage) of knowing Christ Jesus my Lord and of progressively becoming more deeply and intimately acquainted with Him "Philippians 3:8 AMP

God's life long character development process offers many opportunities to drive out of this world with a lot of treasures stored up for the next as we obey God's commands to help the widows and orphans, visit the prisoners, and seek and save the lost, etc.

Jesus makes promise after promise of rewards we can send ahead before we drive out when all the wood, hay and stubble of our lives are burned away at the judgment seat of Christ. May we all drive out seeking to hear "well done, thou good and faithful servant", when we see Him face to face in glory.

Father, help me to drive out of this life with a treasury of good works sent ahead that truly reflects how much I appreciate the price you paid for me In Jesus' name, Amen.

Hybrid Religion
"As we said before, so say I now again, if any man preach any other gospel unto you than that ye have received, let him be accursed."Galatians 1:8-

The increasing popularity of hybrid automobiles is much more pleasing than the increasing popularity of hybrid religion.

Blessed (happy, fortunate, to be envied) is the man who makes the Lord his refuge and trust, and turns not to the proud or to followers of false gods.
Psalm 40:4 AMP

As the man made religion of secular humanism takes over in our schools, court rooms, and government, it becomes harder and harder to pass on the faith of our fathers to our children.

As teen agers go on into college their biblical faith is further eroded by so many non believing professors. Many are left with a hybrid faith of mixed beliefs, or no faith at all.

Some mainline churches seem to be developing a hybrid religion that ignores clear teachings of Scripture. In the name of tolerance and love some churches and pastors teach a hybrid faith trying to please everyone that ends up destroying everyone as they fall away into apostasy.

This hybrid faith may show up in many of us at some time or another. We tend to fall into worship of the idols of this world in our flesh while trying to worship God at the same time in our spirit.

The thousands of different professing Christian denominations throughout the world further attest to the popularity of hybrid religions. They usually want to add something to the Gospel of grace with the legalism of tradition, rituals, and conduct which will supposedly give more miles to the gallon much like a hybrid car.

"But since you are like lukewarm water, neither hot nor cold, I will spit you out of my mouth!"
Revelation 3:16 NLT

Jesus makes it very clear that there is no room for hybrid religion in the Kingdom of God. He is the only way, truth, and life through which anyone can hope to live forever.

Father, help me to avoid the false teachings of a hybrid faith that denies your deity and that you alone can save. In Jesus' name, Amen

In It to Win It
"All athletes are disciplined in their training. They do it to win a prize that will fade away, but we do it for an eternal prize." 1 Corinthians 9:25 NLT

From movie to game show to popular usage the phrase "In it to win it" sums up a good motto for living life.

"Wise living gets rewarded with honor; stupid living gets the booby prize. Proverbs 3:33b MSG

Whether its athletic, academic, social, political, or spiritual activity, we should all be giving our all to win whatever we pursue.

There is competition in every endeavor and how well we succeed will depend largely on how well we prepare.

We are often going to find ourselves competing with others more gifted than we are, but no one should have an advantage when it comes to how hard we are willing to work to achieve our goals.

Every goal should have a game plan for success. We need to clearly define the goal and what it will take for us to achieve it. It may be studying or working out an extra hour a day, or gaining more experience. Our success in any endeavor will often depend on how well we develop an action plan and the discipline to follow it.

Even though we have been given our greatest win of all through faith in Jesus Christ as our Savior, we still need to stay "in it to win it."

There is a roaring lion looking to devour us if he can, and knows and uses every dirty, deceitful trick in the world to tempt us and take us back into bondage to sin from which Jesus rescued us.

God knows all about this, and has given us all an action plan to escape or overcome the temptations that come our way. When we get into the full armor of God we can win the battles of life.

"But God's truth stands firm like a foundation stone with this inscription: "The LORD knows those who are his,"[a] and "All who belong to the LORD must turn away from evil" 2 Timothy 2:19 NLT

When we put on the helmet of salvation, breastplate of righteousness, belt of truth, sandals of Gospel peace, and the Sword of the Spirit of God's Word, we are going to be equipped to live the victorious life in Christ and receive the crown of Glory that awaits all who are "in it to win it."

Father, help us all live to validate our faith that we receive what you have already won for us by your death on the cross. In Jesus' name, Amen

Unholy Volatility

"Not to allow your minds to be quickly unsettled or disturbed or kept excited or alarmed, whether it be by some [pretended] revelation of [the] Spirit or by word or by letter [alleged to be] from us, to the effect that the day of the Lord has [already] arrived and is here." 2 Thessalonians 2:2 AMP

There is a lot of talk about the volatility of the stock market these days. With stocks rising and falling many investors have been left with frayed emotions and thinner wallets.

> "But as for me, I know that my Redeemer lives, and he will stand upon the earth at last."
> Job 19:25 NLT

The volatility of our Christian faith is also evidenced by the intensity of millions of the faithful falling away. Surveys show a vast majority of our children losing their faith before they get out of college. The intense persecution of Christians is growing throughout the world.

It seems that many churches are embracing relative truth instead of proclaiming God's unchanging truths as they make concessions in the name of love and tolerance instead of changes for the better in the name of revival, renewal, and restoration.

Just when we think sin can't get any worse we see more foundations of faith shaken among Christians on both a personal and corporate basis.

As family values plunge, and historically banned alternative lifestyles flourish it is easy see that Un Holy volatility is setting new standards for what "fallen" means in a fallen world.

It's through volatile times like these that we need to pray that our anchors of faith hold as we traverse the deep waters of doubt and despair that seem to be surrounding us.

> "Now all glory to God, who is able to keep you from falling away and will bring you with great joy into his glorious presence without a single fault"
> Jude 1:24 NLT

We can all take comfort in knowing that we know Who has won the final victory for us and that no amount of un holy volatility can ever separate us from His love and His good purposes for us.

Father, as I ride this roller coaster of life, let me never lose sight of the fact that you are in Control and that you are working all things for my good and Your glory. In Jesus' name, Amen

Knowing Truth that Really Matters
"Jesus said to the people who believed in him, "You are truly my disciples if you remain faithful to my teachings. 32 And you will know the truth, and the truth will set you free." John 8:13 NLT

"Truthful words stand the test of time, but lies are soon exposed"
Proverbs 12:19 NLT

When Pilate asked Jesus: "what is truth", he did not wait for or expect to get an answer. The truth of truth has been sought after and written about by some of the greatest minds down through the ages, and is still an unsolved mystery to many people.

We have questions and theories about absolute truth, relative truth, moral truth, logical truth, scientific truth, and whether truth is subjective or objective.

Today's emphasis on relative truth leaves people free to believe anything as they're sincere.

We Christians are blessed to know everything we will need to know about truth when we know Jesus as "the way, the truth, and the life," The revealed will of God should always be our standard of truth,

The Holy Spirit will "guide us into all truth" as it pertains to knowing and doing the will of God. As we seek God's revealed truth in His Word, we will find that His truth never changes and that we should find our truth in Jesus.

"I write to you not because you are ignorant and do not perceive and know the Truth, but because you do perceive and know it, and [know positively] that nothing false (no deception, no lie) is of the Truth."
1 John 2:21 AMP

Above all, we should not get carried away by the relative truths of man but anchor deep in the truth of God and not only believe it, but also live by it.

Only when we have the eternal truths of God as modeled and taught by Jesus will we ever have the freedom to live above the false truths of the world, our flesh, and the devil and be free from even death itself.

Father, help me to be ever mindful of the truth that you died on the cross to save a wretch like me. Thank you for giving me truth I can believe and trust. In Jesus' name, Amen

Experiencing God Smile

"GOD bless you and keep you, GOD smile on you and gift you, [26] GOD look you full in the face and make you prosper." Numbers 6:24-26 MSG

Sometimes we get so caught up in awe of the holiness, power, and majesty of God we forget that He is a God of love, peace, and joy who loves to smile.

"He led me to a place of safety; he rescued me because he delights in me"
2 Samuel 22:20 NLT

We are all continually experiencing God's blessings without even realizing that they are accompanied by His smile. Our Father loves to bless, and delights in granting us the desires of our heart.

We often experience God's smile in little things that happen that make us know in our hearts that God is smiling upon us. It may be an answered prayer, an unexpected blessing, an exceedingly good outcome of a concern or effort.

There is no limit to experiencing God's smiles when our hearts are right with Him. I have personally experienced God's smile when I have followed His leadings to be generous, when I have stepped out in faith to accomplish something to please Him, and when I have gone out of my way to be a blessing to someone else, etc.

We can be sure that God is smiling right in the middle of the choir of angels who are rejoicing when a sinner is saved.

"Blessed (happy, [a]to be envied, and [b]spiritually prosperous--[c]with life-joy and satisfaction in God's favor and salvation, regardless of their outward conditions) are the poor in spirit (the humble, who rate themselves insignificant), for theirs is the kingdom of heaven!"
Matthew 5:3 Amp

When God poured out His wrath for our sins on Jesus when He died on the cross for them, there is no longer any enmity between us and God. There is only sadness or joy.

God would have none of us perish, and still hurts when we disobey and dishonor Him. We need to do all that we can do and be all that we can be in Christ in order to make sure that we will always be able to experience the sacred delight of His smile.

Father, thank you for the blessing of experiencing Your joy as I abide in You. In Jesus' name, Amen

Old Time Religion
"MY SON, forget not my law or teaching, but let your heart keep my commandments; For length of days and years of a life [worth living] and tranquility [inward and outward and continuing through old age till death], these shall they add to you." Proverbs 3:1,2 AMP

The old hymn is still being sung and timeless faith continues secure in Jesus' promise that He has built His church on the rock of our trust in him for salvation, and that *"the gates of hell shall not prevail against it."*

"Even in old age they will still produce fruit;they will remain vital and green." Psalm 92:14 NLT

There is another facet to old time religion to which we all need to pay more attention. What do we do with our religion when we get old?

God is building a great reservoir of seniors to use for His purposes thamls tp ever increasing life expectancy and retirement benefits.

He is not only doing this for His benefit but in order to make the "golden years" more truly golden for us.

The retirement years are not meant for becoming couch potatoes or retiring from kingdom work.

Many people have found that God has equipped them for a fruitful and fulfilling retirement life spent in loving and serving the Lord and others with gladness.

For the first time many find that they have the time to be willing servants to do whatever and wherever God leads. Whether it's volunteering in the community hospitals, nursing homes, or schools, or in our church on going outreach, visitation, or other ministries, there is something that God has equipped you to do to honor and serve Him and bless others.

"That the aged men be sober, grave, temperate, sound in faith, in charity, in patience." Titus 2:2 KJV

If you but look around, you will see that the healthiest and happiest people you know are the ones who are making their golden years golden by serving the Lord.

Father, help make my golden years golden by blessing others through me as I continue to live and work for You. In Jesus' name, Amen

Whitewater Rafting

"If God hadn't been for us when everyone went against us, We would have been swallowed alive by their violent anger, Swept away by the flood of rage, drowned in the torrent; We would have lost our lives in the wild, raging water."Psalm 124:1 MSG-

Therefore, let all the godly pray to you while there is still time,that they may not drown in the floodwaters of judgment.
Psalm 36:6 MLT

Millions of people travel near and far to ride the rapids on rivers in some 25 states. The higher rated faster and rockier rapids have made this an extremely dangerous sport . This sport is also a good illustration of our journey down the river of life. Sin and evil are like rapids threatening to sink us as we go through the rough waters.

While cruising down the river, we can find ourselves running into physical, relational, financial, and spiritual storms that can turn the gentle current into raging waves and whirlpools that threaten to sink us at any instant.

When we are getting "tossed about by many conflicts and doubts" how good it is to know that we have a life saver on board who has promised to see us through or make a way of escape through the raging waters.

Jesus died and lives so that we will never have to worry about being swept away by the rough waters of life.

Jesus invites us all to come to the waters of Baptism and stand by His side in faith. He promises that when we do, we will never be denied full access to His throne and grace when we come in true repentance with a broken spirit and contrite heart.

Just as safety dictates that all white water rafters wear life jackets, our safe passage through the rapids of life dictate that we are wearing our eternal life saver in our heart.

"The disciples went and woke him up, shouting, "Lord, save us! We're going to drown!"
Matthew 8:25 NLT

Father, sometimes the waves are too high and currents too strong for me to survive in my weakness. Give me your strength to overcome. In Jesus' name, Amen

Easy Street

"And he who does not take up his cross and follow Me [cleave steadfastly to Me, conforming wholly to My example in living and, if need be, in dying also] is not worthy of Me."Matthew 10:37

The idea that becoming a Christian is the key to living a healthy, trouble free life is a lie right out of the devil's handbook.

We should always remember that the Via Dolorosa on which Jesus carried His cross was called "the way of sorrow" not "Easy Street".

"My health may fail, and my spirit may grow weak, but God remains the strength of my heart; he is mine forever." Psalm 73:26 NLT

If we need further proof that "the Way" is often a way of pain and suffering, we need not look any further than the Apostles and early followers of Christ and the cost of their discipleship.

Although Jesus' yoke is much lighter than the yoke of the law, and our burdens are lighter because we have the power and presence of the Holy Spirit to strengthen and guide us, we can all be sure that we can expect troubles in this life.

The truth is that we can usually expect more troubles and trials in this life than those who reject Christ because the devil already owns them and doesn't have to waste his time capturing them.

Even though we receive the gift of eternal life and the abundance of God's grace to see us through the difficulties of this life when we accept Jesus as Savior and Lord, we are still imperfect people living in an imperfect world under the curse of sin.

God will give us a new birth and pour out relational, financial, and spiritual blessings upon us as we trust and obey Him.

Although we have been set free from sins bondage and condemnation we are still going to suffer the consequences of our own sins, and the consequences of the sins of a sin cursed world in which we live.

"and to keep you from being shaken by the troubles you were going through. But you know that we are destined for such troubles." 1 Thessalonians 3:2

We should never be surprised when the troubles come, but rejoice in knowing that God can and will use them for His purpose of conforming us into the image of Christ.

Father, thank You for promising your all sufficient grace to see me through or help me escape the dangers of living in this fleshly body in a sin sick world .In Jesus' name, Amen

Expensive Disobedience

"You are under a curse—your whole nation—because you are robbing me."
Malachi 3:9 NLT

"Even from the days of your fathers you have turned aside from My ordinances and have not kept them."
Malachi 3:7 AMP

If current tithing statistics are correct 95% of professing Christians in this country are robbing God. This may be the most wide spread example of rebellion and disobedience in the world today. It is certainly the most expensive.

All who believe that God's Word is true should realize that His promises are also true. When He promises those who tithe to *"open up heaven itself to you and pour out blessings beyond your wildest dreams"* and to: *"defend you against marauders, protect your wheat fields and vegetable gardens against plunderers."*, He is making a promise that only our unbelief and disobedience keep us from receiving.

Although the Mosaic law is no longer the means of our salvation it is still a guide. When God challenges us to test Him by tithing it is a challenge we ignore at our own loss. We simply cannot afford not to afford giving God 10% right off the top of what He Has given us.

There are many blessings associated with tithing that go beyond prosperity. Tithing is also a great antidote and inoculation against greed, a wonderful act of thanksgiving, praise and worship, and helps us better distinguish between needs and wants. There is also the wonderful promise that the more God finds He can trust us the more he is going to trust us with

"So now finish doing it, that your [enthusiastic] readiness in desiring it may be equalled by your completion of it according to your ability and means.
2 Corinthians 8:11 AMP

Does it really make sense not to trust and claim God's promises by tithing? How much longer can we afford not to afford giving God His full share. Tithing should not even be the maximum but the minimum of what we should give back to God.

Lord, help me to quit leaving many of the blessings You want for me on the table of my disobedience in refusing to tithe. In Jesus' name, Amen

Can God Trust America?

"Then if my people who are called by my name will humble themselves and pray and seek my face and turn from their wicked ways, I will hear from heaven and will forgive their sins and restore their land."2 Chronicles 7:14 NLT

> "When GOD heard that, he was furious— his anger flared against Jacob,he lost his temper with Israel."
> **Psalm 78:21:MSG**

There is a lot of consternation and objection to "In God We Trust" being taken off our coins and mottoes in this country, which is only a symptom of what should be giving great cause for concern among all who love this country.

The secular humanists and freedom from religion advocates have been trying to replace trust in God to trust in man and in the god of Washington DC for decades, and are beginning to succeed.

As trust in God diminishes in this country and the question should be not can we trust God, but rather can God trust us.

From our humble beginnings as a faith based Chistian country right up to a generation ago God's divine providence has generally been recognized as the major reason for our prosperity as a nation.

It seems that the more economic and material prosperity the Lord has trusted us with, the more our idol worship and pursuit of pleasure has diminished our trust in and obedience to God.

Instead of using our excess wealth and leisure time in glorifying God by loving and serving others, we seem to have bought into the "one with the most toys wins" philosophy and use our surplus time and money to buy more status and pleasure for ourselves. We forget that God has provided this improved standard of living to improve our standard of giving of ourselves and our resources for His good pleasure and purposes.

> "Come close to God, and God will come close to you. Wash your hands, you sinners; purify your hearts, for your loyalty is divided between God and the world.
> **James 4:7 NIV**

Can it possibly be that our economic, social and international problems are increasing as a result of God's distrust in us a nation. Has it been decreasing because of our replacing trust in Him and His commandments with the Godless philosophy of secular humanism?

Father, help us all to do whatever possible to restore your faith in us as a country and as individual believers. In Jesus' name, Amen

Sharing Life

"God, who got you started in this spiritual adventure, shares with us the life of his Son and our Master Jesus. He will never give up on you. Never forget that."1 Corinthians 1:7 MSG-

A life well lived is a life well shared. The idea that God created us to share our lives with Him is foreign to many people. That He made us in His image and put us in paradise to share the beauty of it with us is verified by the relationship He established with Adam and Eve in the Garden of Eden.

"And let the beauty and delightfulness and favor of the Lord our God be upon us; confirm and establish the work of our hands-- yes, the work of our hands, confirm and establish it." Psalm 90:17 AMP

We are all bearing the pain of Adam and Eve's disobedience that brought the curses of the sins of the flesh and evil of the world into a perfect paradise. The sin and rebellion got to be too much for the Holiness of God to the point that He even expressed sorrow over ever creating man, and destroyed all except Noah and his family.

God came to earth as Jesus to share life with all who would live their lives in a close and personal relationship with Him. When we, by faith and a conscious act of our will, make Jesus Christ the Lord of our life, we are supernaturally enabled to become imitators of Christ by living life the way He came to show to live it.

As we share our lives grow closer to Christ by abiding in Him, we enjoy the incredible blessings of Jesus' friendship, joy, prayers, and more of the love of God and of others,

"If we claim that we experience a shared life with him and continue to stumble around in the dark, we're obviously lying through our teeth—we're not living what we claim." ! John 1:6 MSG

The life we choose is the life we will be sharing with our children and others and may well determine whether God's wonderful gift of salvation and the abundant life will be passed on to them.

May we all seek to live a life of faith with God so that He will share and eternity of peace and joy with us.

Father, help me to enjoy the blessings of a life well lived and well shared in love with others. In Jesus' name, Amen

New and Enriched
"He who is of a greedy spirit stirs up strife, but he who puts his trust in the Lord shall be enriched and blessed."Proverbs 28:25 AMP

We buy a lot of "new and enriched" products almost everytime we go to the store. When we look at the prices, we are sometimes prone to wonder whether the product or the manufacturer is the one getting enriched.

"A little that a righteous man has *Is* better than the riches of many wicked."
Psalm 37:16 NKJV

As improved as many "new and enriched" products may be, they are nothing compared to "new and enriched" people who have become so by experiencing the new birth in Jesus and enriched by the joy of their salvation.

When we become new in Christ we become Saints instead of sinners. We are set free from the bondage of sin and free to live as children of our living God and heirs to all His wonderful promises.

The enrichment that begins when we receive and accept saving faith continues day by day, week by week, and year by year as we are nourished by His Word, our prayers, and the encouragement of others.

An abundance of material riches may come our way, but they are nothing compared to the riches of God's grace that are poured out on us daily as we abide in our new lives with Christ.

We are promised the supernatural power to move mountains of fear and doubt, and to stand firm and resist the temptations that come our way. We are enriched by God's forgiveness and the security of knowing that nothing can ever separate us from His love that is ours through faith in Jesus.

[So] that in Him in every respect you were enriched, in full power and readiness of speech [to speak of your faith] and complete knowledge and illumination [to give you full insight into its meaning].
1 Corinthians 1:5
- - - -

As the "new and enriched"children of God we experience the joy of our salvation that enables us to rejoice even in our sufferings to receive even more enrichment through all surpassing peace.

Jesus did not come to make us poor, but to make us rich in the love that really matters. We have no excuse for continuing to live in the povertyof doubt, depression, or despair.

Father, help me to live like the "new and enriched" person You have made me to be by the blood of Jesus. In Jesus' name, Amen

49

Our X Factors

"Come—all of you who have skills—come and make everything that God has commanded:" Exodus 35:10a MSG

God gave us all one or several X Factors or special talents as part of His wonderful process of creating us.

"He gave five bags of silver to one, two bags of silver to another, and one bag of silver to the last—dividing it in proportion to their abilities. He then left on his trip.
Matthew 25:15 NLT

As we see more and more of the world through TV and the internet we cannot help but be amazed at the incredible skills and talents of so many people.

We enjoy watching talented musicians, athletes, magicians, and other skilled performers exercise their X factors in a variety of venues.

New scientific discoveries, drugs, and medical procedures show up on almost a daily basis. Smart Phones, Ipads, Ipods,Ie and other electronic devices change the way we do life.

A whole new generation of young millionaires continue to increase as their X Factors lead them to develop Face Book, You Tube, Groupon, Google, and a host of other internet based programs and electronic products that gain world wide popularity and acceptance.

In spite of the fact that most of us are probably never going to achieve fame and fortune on a global or even local scale, we need to know that we can achieve favor and blessings in this world and the next by using our God given X factor for edifying Christ and building up the kingdom of God.

" Now, dear brothers and sisters, regarding your question about the special abilities the Spirit gives us. I don't want you to misunderstand this."
I Corinthians 12:1 NLT

Whether our X Factors are physical, mental, or spiritual Jesus came to give us all something special to offer to the praise of His Glory.

Father, give me the self discipline and focus to find, use, and never abuse my X Factors by wasting them. In Jesus' name,Amen

Unpopular Promises
"We're here! We've come back to you. You're our own true God! All that popular religion was a cheap lie, duped crowds buying up the latest in gods" Jeremiah 3:22 MSG

God's promises of eternal life, and temporal blessings for every area of our life are a source of great inspiration and purpose for living.

"People hate this kind of talk. Raw truth is never popular.But here it is, bluntly spoken:" Amos 5:12 MSG

When we feed on God's promises by learning them through His written, preached, or taught Word we can get filled to overflowing with great expectations. It is certainly exciting and comforting to know that God promises to love us and be with us always, to provide a means of escape or strength to overcome temptations, to be our very present help in time of trouble, etc.

The promises of good things are easy to accept and claim by faith. There are many other promises that are much harder to accept and very unpopular to many.

Amazing Grace is too amazing for some people. The idea that we are saved solely by the grace of God apart from our own performance and conduct seems too good to be true to many. Many insist on adding other conditions as though we could add anything to Jesus living a perfect life and dying so that we would not have to do either.

The concept of hell is also very unpopular, else there would be a lot more professing Christians who live like Christians instead of more and more people who mock God by promoting what God calls abominations as respectable practices and life styles.

'**We, of course, have plenty of wisdom to pass on to you once you get your feet on firm spiritual ground, but it's not popular wisdom, 1 Corinthains 2:6 MSG**

The whole idea that we are going to have crosses to bear when we become disciples of Jesus is very unpopular among the prosperity gospel advocates. Those who seem to think they are promised a rose garden without thorns.

Even God's promise to work all things for our good becomes very unpopular when it includes suffering as part of being conformed into the image of Christ.

Father give me the faith to rejoice in all Your precious promises. In Jesus' name, Amen.

51

Whatever's Out There
""I have told you these things, so that in me you may have peace. In this world you will have trouble. But take heart! I have overcome the world." John 16:33 NIV

Raising children is ultimately about equipping them to meet the challenges of life which seem to be getting more and more challenging for each new generation.

"God is our refuge and strength, always ready to help in times of trouble." Psalm 46:1 NLT

The world continues to get smaller and smaller with instant information and communication through the internet and media. Knowledge of a lot of the bad stuff that's out in the world comes into our homes on a daily basis.

We can hardly go anywhere or do anything without running into some of the by products or problems of a sin sick world. Whether we run into financial, relational, physical, or spiritual issues we need a Christ centered faith to overcome or escape.

We need to be ever mindful and ever thankful that we have a king sized God who is a very present help in time of trouble. We have the King of Kings, Lord of Lords, who is almighty, all knowing, ever present, and ever loving.

He has called us by name into becoming His brother or sister and children of the most high God. When we accept His wonderful invitation to become part of His family, we receive the blessed assurance of His love, grace, mercy and presence that enables us to go out and deal victoriously with whatever's out there in the world.

Best of all we have the promises of a God who cannot lie and who has never broken a promise that He can and will work our worst into His best, and that nothing can ever separate us from His love that is ours through faith in Jesus Christ.

"Who is it that overcomes the world? Only the one who believes that Jesus is the Son of God" 1 John 5:5 NIV

We and our children need to know that because He lives we can face tomorrow and the problems of whatever's out there knowing that the Great Problem Solver has our backs wherever we go.

Father, Thank you for enabling me to face whatever's out there in security, peace, and joy of Your love. In Jesus' name, Amen

The Rock of Our Salvation

"And they all drank the same spiritual (supernaturally given) drink. For they drank from a spiritual Rock which followed them [produced by the sole power of God Himself without natural instrumentality], and the Rock was Christ." 1 Corinthians 10:4 AMP

The shifting sands of time, turmoil, and circumstances leave a trail of broken hearts and broken dreams and remembfrances as we find many things we held dear not so dear after all.

"The LORD is my rock, my fortress and my deliverer; my God is my rock, in whom I take refuge, my shield and the horn of my salvation, my stronghold." Psalm 18:2 NIV

When we build our future and hope on anything other than Jesus Christ being the Son of God who died on the cross for our sins and for our salvation we are building on sinking sand.

There is nothing wrong with possessions, popularity, or so called "good things of life" unless they possess us and become idols.

Idols of materialism, pleasure, popularity, beauty and pride will sooner or later come up short. -We need an anchor for our souls that will not be washed away by the rip tides of life.

The idols of this world can never satisfy the inner longing we have for the peace and security of God's love that He makes available to all who will receive.

"It is like a person building a house who digs deep and lays the foundation on solid rock. When the floodwaters rise and break against that house, it stands firm because it is well built. Luke 6:48 NLT

How good it is to know that In Jesus Christ we have a firm foundation we can not only lean on but build on. When we put the rock of our salvation first in our lives we will see all of our other needs being satisfied more abundantly than we could ever dare hope for or ask.

Father, may I never be found trusting in any thing or any one more than I trust in You. In Jesus' name, Amen

Close Mindedness
"They know nothing, they understand nothing; their eyes are plastered over so they cannot see, and their minds closed so they cannot understand." Isaiah 44:18 NIV

A prayer for wisdom and spiritual understanding might well include a

"Cynics look high and low for wisdom—and never find it;the open-minded find it right on their doorstep!"
Proverbs 14:6 MSG

plea for open mindedness as to what is a true understanding of the revealed truth of God based on His infallible Word.

We have generation after generation of Christians worshipping doctrines based on tradition and faulty interpretations rather than truth, and waging doctrinal wars from within and without.

God and God's Word does not change, but people and people's understanding of God's Word obviously does or there would have been no Reformation nor thousands of denominations of Christian Churches.

While we need to be firm in our faith and know what we stand for and not fall for anything, we need to be open to the fact that God continues to reveal His truths to us through the Holy Spirit and through prophets He continues to raise up to proclaim His truth.

We are often amazed at discovering a new meaning from passages of Scripture that we may have read many times before as we grow in our knowledge and understanding of God through His Word.

The only thing we need to be close minded about is the centrality of the Gospel that teaches we are saved by grace alone through faith in Jesus Christ alone, and that the Bible is the inerrant Word of God.

" And the people of Berea were more open-minded than those in Thessalonica, and they listened eagerly to Paul's message."
Acts 17:11 NLT

What joy there is in growing in our relationship with the Lord by abiding in His Word and continually discovering new truths and better understandings of old truths by being open minded.

Father, thank you for the new understandings you continue to give me as I grow in my relationship with You and Your Word. In Jesus' name, Amen

A Better Understanding
"But he was angry and would not go in. Therefore his father came out and pleaded with him.Luke 15:28 NKJV

I am indebted to Rev. Tim Keller's book ,"The Prodigal God",for providing the insight for a better understanding of what Jesus was really teaching in the Prodigal son parable.

"I dwell in the high and holy place, but with him also who is of a thoroughly penitent and humble spirit, Isaiah 57:15b AMP

We often overlook the significance of the other son in this story. When we realize that Jesus was telling this story to both sinners and the self righteous religious leaders of the day, we can better understand.   We can all identify with the grace and forgiveness which the Father extended to his wayward son. It is the grace He extends to all of us who are convicted of our need for a Savior.

The Scribes and Pharisees in the audience ,did not realize that their self righteousness and rejection of Jesus' was robbing them of the joy of true salvation by grace and leaving them absent from the feast because they rejected the Father's invitation.

Instead of rejoicing with the saints in heaven over one sinner who was lost but found, the pharisee that dwells in the flesh of all of us wants to harbor a critical and judgmental spirit against the fairness of God in allowing such bad people to enjoy all of the rights and privileges of us good people who have been long time children of the King.

The sooner we realize that God does not judge by outward appearances but by one's heart, we should not resent or doubt but seek, save, and rejoice over the lost when they are found.

**"for this my son was dead and is alive again; he was lost and is found.' And they began to be merry."
Luke 15:24 NKJV**

Most of all, we need to always remember never to question the fairness of God, but rather rejoice in the fact that our salvation did not depend on fairness, but on the unmerited favor and grace of God in coming to die on the cross so that we would never die.

Father, forgive me for my self righteous tendencies that generate the hypocritical glory of the Scribes and Pharisees that You despised. In Jesus' name, Amen

Thank God for Tim Tebow

"When a man's ways please the LORD, he maketh even his enemies to be at peace with him."Proverbs 16:6 AMP

Is Tim Tebow a loser? Is he a nerd? Is he "not cool"? I would suggest that no one could rightfully make those claims against arguably one ot he most admired young men in America if not the world.

"I, yes I, am God. I'm the only Savior there is. I spoke, I saved, I told you what existed long before these upstart gods appeared on the scene. And you know it, you're my witnesses, you're the evidence."
Isaiah 43:9 MSG

Could it be that Tim might be God's "poster child" for showing what a faith worth living should look like in the 21st Century.

Tim never flaunts his faith but certainly wastes no opportunity to give God the glory whenever asked about the talents and successes with which he has been blessed.

As Tim lives out his faith on the football field and off, He lives a sermon in shoes that baffles his detractors and made liars out of a lot of college professors while raising the bar for all who earnestly seek to be the salt and light we are called to be.

When we hear "every one is doing it" as rationalization and justification for immoral conduct or behavior, we might remember that Tim Tebow is living proof that everyone doesn't have to be doing it to find true pleasure, peace, and joy in life.

I not only praise God for Tim Tebow and the witness he brings to millions, I earnestly pray for the full armor of God to protect Tim knowing that the devil is going to do everything within his considerable power to bring Tim's faith and witness down.

"Fight the good fight of the faith; lay hold of the eternal life to which you were summoned and [for which] you confessed the good confession [of faith] before many witnesses."
1 Timothy 6:13 AMP

In the meantime let's use Tim Tebow to show our young people that it is really cool to "be like Jesus".

Father, help me to be a good sermon in shoes by reflecting your love and lordship by the way I live my faith. In Jesus name, Amen

I Want it Now!

"No, I want it now. If you won't give it, I'll take it." It was a horrible sin these young servants were commiting—and right in the presence of God!—desecrating the holy offerings to God.1 Samuel 2:12 MSG

I don't know J.G. Wentworth, but his "I Want it Now" commercials have been very effective. His offer to give a lump sum cash settlement now for rights to future benefit payments mirrors the mindset of much of today's culture.

"Because you hated Knowledge and had nothing to do with the Fear-of-God, Because you wouldn't take my advice and brushed aside all my offers to train you, Well, you've made your bed—now lie in it; you wanted your own way—now, how do you like it?
Proverbs 1:29 MSG

Today's youth seem to be growing up thinking they are entitled to instant gratification of their every desire. It seems it there is no thought of the loss of future benefits physically, emotionally, financially or spiritually – getting what they want when they want it seems to be the number one priority of today's youth and many adults under the age of 50.

It probably started with the marketing on Saturday morning cartoon shows and fueled by parents who want to give their little darlings all the things they didn't have when they were children.

The "I want it now" mindset has led to maxed out credit cards at horrid interest rates, and literally millions of foreclosed homes and broken marriages.

So let's keep focused on that goal, those of us who want everything God has for us. If any of you have something else in mind, something less than total commitment, God will clear your blurred vision—you'll see it yet! Now that we're on the right track, let's stay on it.
Philippians 3:14 MSG

Sex has become merely a handshake in a lot of "I want if now" mind sets.

The thing we should be wanting now is the Kingdom of God and His Righteousness so that we can have the things that make for a truly fulfilling and satisfying life now and forever..

Father, help me to adjust my "wanter" to want what You want for me and when You want it. In Jesus' name, Amen

57

Staying In the Loop
For I know the plans I have for you," declares the LORD, "plans to prosper you and not to harm you, plans to give you hope and future."Jeremiah 29:11 NIV

We all like to stay in the loop about what's going on in our family, workplace, school, country etc. We should also all like to stay in the loop of God's will and purpose for our lives.

**"And it will be accounted as righteousness (conformity to God's will in word, thought, and action) for us if we are watchful to do all this commandment before the Lord our God, as He has commanded us.
Deuteronomy 6:25 AMP**

The circle of God's will is a loop that helps inspect, correct and direct us as we are being transformed into the the likeness of Christ.

Living within the circle of God's will is the best way to be sure of receiving the plans God has made for giving the abundant life that Jesus came to give us.

Living within the loop of obedience channels God's blessings reserved for those who are obedient. Living within the loop of faith gives us God's all sufficient grace to forgive, strengthen, sustain, protect, comfort, and encourage us

When we stay within the loops of humility, patience, kindness, gentleness, love, and self control, there we will find no room for the pride, anger, envy and lust of the flesh to consume us.

When we stay in the loop of a good church and community of believers we will find joy in growing in our relationship with Christ as we grow in our relationship with others.

**"Patient endurance is what you need now, so that you will continue to do God's will. Then you will receive all that he has promised."
Hebrews 10:36 NLT**

The bottom line is to stay looped into the friendship, joy, and peace of Jesus by abiding in Him and His Word, so that the deceiver and destroyer of our souls cannot get a toe hold inside our loop.

Father, help me to live each daywith in the circle of Your good and gracious will. In Jesus name, Amen

God's Half Way House
"Take heed to yourselves, lest your [minds and] hearts be deceived and you turn aside and serve other gods and worship them," Deuteronomy 11:16

Half Way houses have proven a good means of making the transition from prison to society. They give ex convicts a better chance to adjust to their freedom, and seem to reduce the repeat offenses.

> "GOD met me more than halfway, he freed me from my anxious fears."
> Psalm 34:4 MSG

This is almost exactly what happens at Christ's Church, which is also God's half way house.

When we receive God's gift of eternal life through faith in Jesus Christ, we are let out of sin prison and are set free to begin a new life of freedom to grow into the likeness of Christ without sin reigning over us.

Growing into the fullness of Christ doesn't happen the instant we are saved. It's a life long process of Holy Transformation in which we surrender more and more of our heart and soul to the Lordship of Jesus Christ and control of the Holy Spirit.

There is no better half way house for our faith than a Christ centered, Bible believing community of believers. They help us make the transition from sinner to saint and become in reality what Christ has already made us to be theologically.

When we assemble ourselves together to receive the grace of God through hearing the Word and partaking of the Lord's Supper we receive a lot of the sustaining grace needed to grow into the fullness of Christ. The encouragement and support of fellow believers is also a great benefit.

> "We have also a more sure word of prophecy; whereunto ye do well that ye take heed, as unto a light that shineth in a dark place, until the day dawn, and the day star arise in your hearts:
> 2 Peter 1:17 KJV

Receiving Jesus Christ as Savior puts us half way to heaven, and letting God's half way house help guide and sustain us as God continues to work all things for the good of our becoming conformed into the image of Christ.

Father, thank you for giving me such a great half-way house to help me grow into fullness Christ. In Jesus' name, Amen

59

Reaching Out by Reaching In
"Stoop down and reach out to those who are oppressed. Share their burdens, and so complete Christ's law. If you think you are too good for that, you are badly deceived." Galatians 6:2 MSG

A body of believers that are not reaching out in love to others are not being faithful to their calling as ambassadors for Christ. It is so easy to get focused inwardly among our fellow members and forget that our mission field is the world at large and the city, street, workplace, golf course or other recreational activities where we live.

"Be generous: Invest in acts of charity. Charity yields high returns. Don't hoard your goods; spread them around. Be a blessing to others." Ecclesdiastes 11:1,2 MSG

Every church worthy of the name of Christ should be reaching out to make disciples by spreading the Good News of God's love and gift of eternal life through faith in Jesus Christ.

We sometimes need to reach in our pocketbooks in order to reach out to help others. We can be sure that God is not going to forget the kindness and compassion we show in allowing Him to provide for the needs of the widows, orphans, poor, and hungry through us.

Before we came to Christ, many of us were like beggars begging for bread until the Lord came in to fill us with the bread of life. When we make sharing this bread with others a priority for our lives, we can be sure that God will be pleased and bless our efforts.

Reaching out not only takes a lot of faithfulness and character. It also takes money. We often have the privilege of reaching in to the material resources with which the Lord has entrusted us to provide funds for outreach ministries and projects as well as pressing needs of others as the Lord lays them upon our hearts.

"Real religion, the kind that passes muster before God the Father, is this: Reach out to the homeless and loveless in their plight, and guard against corruption from the godless world. James 1:26 MSG

We need to be ever mindful that we sometimes need to reach in in order to reach out and touch someone.

Father, help me to extend my outreach by increasing my in reach. In Jesus' name, Amen

Can't We Just Get Along?

"Don't we all come from one Father? Aren't we all created by the same God? So why can't we get along? Why do we desecrate the covenant of our ancestors that binds us together? Malachi 2:9 MSG

Agreeing to disagree and moving on is often the best way to resolve a conflict of irreconcilable differences. This worked for Paul and Barnabas and it can work for us.

"How wonderful, how beautiful, when brothers and sisters get along!" Psalm 133:1 MSG

Unfortunately, there is something about our sin nature or competitive spirit that makes us feel that we would rather be right than reconciled. We insist on getting in the last word, and that often escalates the conflict and makes it harder to get along.

I have very dear family and friends with whom I strongly disagree on some tenets of the Christian Faith. It is hard to have a discussion without it leading to an argument, We do much better by agreeing to disagree and concentrating on the centrality of the Gospel that we all agree on..

It may come as a shock to know that we are going to see a lot of people in heaven with whom we disagreed here in earth. There won't be any disagreements there. We need to beware of displaying a judgmental and unforgiving spirit towards someone that may keep us out.

In this age of political correctness and enlightened new age thinking we are unfortunately finding more and more people and conduct and Ideas with which we disagree.

Bless your enemies; no cursing under your breath. Laugh with your happy friends when they're happy; share tears when they're down. Get along with each other; don't be stuck-up. Make friends with nobodies; don't be the great somebody. Romans 12:13 MSG

Getting along does not mean appeasing others and giving in to their beliefs and unholy practices but it may mean to allow them the freedom to choose what they believe and agree to disagree and move on.

We can pray for them and ask God to change their hearts, but we need to leave judging to our Righteous Judge.

Father, help me to pursue peace and try to get along with everyone, but never compromise my faith in so doing. In Jesus' name, Amen

.

Whose Handiwork?

"Imitate God, therefore, in everything you do, because you are his dear children. Live a life filled with love, following the example of Christ. He loved us and offered himself as a sacrifice for us, a pleasing aroma to God. Ephesians 5:1,2a NLT

The United States Marines have been turning out men of courage

Do not bring shame on my holy name, for I will display my holiness among the people of Israel. I am the Lord who makes you holy.
Leviticus 22:32 NLT

and valor for hundreds of years. Many colleges are recognized for turning out great lawyers, engineers, or businessmen.

Good parents are dedicated to turning out good children who display the results of the workmanship of the parents in raising them.

We sometimes lose sight of the fact that the world is dedicated to turning out followers of the devil who employs legions of angels to seek and destroy us.

This handiwork is evidenced by prisons being overfilled, and people falling into every sort of temptation and sin in ever increasing numbers and more and more people dying in their sins.

God sent Jesus into the world not to seek and destroy but to seek and save sinners from the power of the devil and the curse of sin.

It is not too hard to see whose handiwork someone is by the fruits they bear.

When we see pride, anger, envy, lust, jealousy, selfishness, bitterness, and hate displayed we can pretty well see the handwork of the devil on display.

When we see love, joy, peace, longsuffering, kindness, goodness, faithfulness, and self control displayed we are seeing someone who is being transformed into the image of Christ.

This is exactly the handiwork of God we were created to be that God is working to accomplish in us for our good. .

The question we should all be asking is whether we are evidencing enough of the handiwork of God in our lives to ever be arrested and convicted for being a Christian?

"For we are His workmanship, created in Christ Jesus for good works, which God prepared beforehand that we should walk in them."
Ephesians 2:10 NKJV

Father, let my life be a living example of the good works that are evidence of your handiwork in me. In Jesus' name, Amen

Without A Trace

"Now the Spirit expressly says that in latter times some will depart from the faith, giving heed to deceiving spirits and doctrines of demons,"1 Timothy 4:1

Back door losses continue to plague most mainline churches at an alarming rate. Unfortunately many members are allowed to fade away without a clue.

"For the scepter of wickedness shall not rest upon the land of the [uncompromisingly] righteous, lest the righteous (God's people) stretch forth their hands to iniquity and apostasy. Psalm 125:2 AMP

The pastor charged with shepherding a flock is going to have to give an account for them amd should make every effort to at least find out why people leave and where they go.

The back door losses decline In churches that actively assimilate new members and get them plugged into a small group or other ministries.The communion of saints becomes real to a small community group of believers who fellowship in the Word.

The alarming vanishing rate among young people does not bode well for the future of Christ's church as we know it. Even many parents who earnestly seek to teach a child the way they should walk are seeing their children disappear from their faith as soon as they are out on their own.

That the world, the flesh and the devil is winning so many battles for the souls of men, women, and children cannot be denied.

Whether the apostasy that is taking place around the world is a sign of the end of time rapidly approaching, or just a bump in the road in the history of civilization, it is a real and present danger.

**"Let no one deceive you by any means; for that Day will not come unless the falling away comes first, "
2 Thessalonians 2a KJV**

Thanks be to God that He is in control and not surprised by any of this, and that He has promised that the powers of hell shall never prevail against His church.

In the meantime we should lock the back door of our church by praying for, encouraging and building up all in our body of believers and do and be whatever else we can to keep our children in the faith.

Father let me never be a stumbling block causing anyone to leave your church or forfeit your wonderful gift of the abundant life. In Jesus' name, Amen

Heeding the Warnings

"He said to him, If they do not hear and listen to Moses and the Prophets, neither will they be persuaded and convinced and believe [even] if someone should rise from the dead."Matthew 16:31 AMP

There seems to be a rebellious streak that comes with our sin nature that makes us ignore warnings. Whether it's the idea that no one is going to tell us what to do, no one else knows what they are talking about, or it can never happen to me, too many people go through life ignoring warnings to their great sorrow.

"They are a warning to your servant, a great reward for those who obey them."
Psalm 19:11 NLT

People seem to want to walk on the grass just because the sign says not to. Warning labels have been on cigarettes for over 50 years but each year thousands of people continue to die terrible deaths caused by smoking. (On a personal note, I have been living with impaired breathing for over 10 years as a result of smoking, even though I had quit 15 years earlier)..

It sometimes seems that warnings about the dangers of drugs have advertised and popularized their use rather than slow it down.

Warnings about hell have all but disappeared from most sermons In the rush to preach about the love and grace of God. Unfortunately, when the fear of hell is gone so is the desire of a lot of people to be saved.

The Ten Commandments are not only a guide for how we should live, they are warnings for how we should not live.

These warnings went unheeded for so long, God finally had to come to the earth as a man to keep the commandments so that we would not have to die for not keeping them.

"Don't let him find you sleeping when he arrives without warning. I say to you what I say to everyone: Watch for him!"
Mark 13:36,37 NLT

May we do everything possible to warn others about the torments of hell and teach them how to not only avoid it, but to have an abundant life in Christ for the here and now and forever.

Father, forgive me for not obeying so many warnings, and for the consequences this has caused for myself and others. In Jesus' name, Amen.

God's Love Index

" Don't tear your clothing in your grief, but tear your hearts instead." Return to the Lord your God, for he is merciful and compassionate, slow to get angry and filled with unfailing love. He is eager to relent and not punish."Joel 2:12-14

Of all the great attributes of God, that He is love is by far the greatest. His "*unselfish, loyal, and benevolent concern*"for our good knows no bounds.

"Love the LORD, all you godly ones! For the LORD protects those who are loyal to him, but he harshly punishes the arrogant."
Psalm 31:23 NLT

As you review the ways you might have experienced God's love please take time to acknowledge and thank him.

God's love is abiding, abundant, admonishing, all knowing, amazing, all powerful, and beautifying. He shows us His love by chastening, cleansing, and comforting. He is compassionate, confident, and complete.

God's love Is empowering, encouraging, ever present and ever lasting. He is fatherly, forgiving, fulfilling, and gentle . His love is healing, giving, joyful and kind. His love is patient, personal, protective, sacrificial, unchanging, unconditional and unfailing.

And so faith, hope, love abide [faith--conviction and belief respecting man's relation to God and divine things; hope--joyful and confident expectation of eternal salvation; love--true affection for God and man, growing out of God's love for and in us], these three; but the greatest of these is love.
1 Corinthians 13:13 AMP

In His love, God came to earth as Jesus Christ to model and reveal His love to us so that we might become channels of His love to others.

What joy there is for all who will receive the fullness of God's love by faith in Jesus and following in His footsteps into the perfect love of heaven that awaits all who believe.

Father, thank you for your boundless love which you poured out for me through the blood of Jesus. In Jesus' name, Amen

"That Dog Won't Hunt"

"Down-and-outers sit at God's table and eat their fill. Everyone on the hunt for God is here, praising him. "Live it up, from head to toe. Don't ever quit!" Psalm 22:25 MSG

Thomas Edison admitted finding over 900 things that didn't work before he found one that did. As we go through life seeking significance and security we are also going to find things that don't work.

**"That's right—if you make Insight your priority, and won't take no for an answer, Searching for it like a prospector panning for gold, like an adventurer on a treasure hunt,"
Proverbs 2:3 MSG**

If I had a kennel for all my dogs that didn't hunt, I couldn't buy enough feed for all of them. (They include a lot of show horses that wouldn't show and race horses that wouldn't race).

On a personal level, we pursue romances and finances that often didn't work as intended, but worked as God intended in making us realize that we needed a Savior.

We go hunting for significance and satisfaction in drugs, sex, possessions, and the approval of others and end up leading a dog's life.

Jesus pointed out that the Scribes and Pharisees were hunting for God with the dog of hypocrisy. That dog didn't hunt.

Generation after generation of Abraham's descendents tried living with keeping the law they couldn't or wouldn't keep and some still have not realized that that dog won't hunt.

When we hunt for The way, The truth, and The Life through a personal relationship with Jesus Christ we are sure to find it. He is a rewarder of those who seek Him.

**"Or, God's kingdom is like a jewel merchant on the hunt for excellent pearls. Finding one that is flawless, he immediately sells everything and buys it.
Matthew 13:45 MSG**

When it comes to hunting for comfort, forgiveness, encouragement, strength, and all surpassing peace we don't need a dog.We need the Holy Spirit.

Father, forgive me all my trivial pursuits and help me to hunt where true treasures can be found. In Jesus' name, Amen

Fault Finder's Delight
"Overlook an offense and bond a friendship; fasten on to a slight and—good-bye, friend!" Proverbs 17:9 MSG

Sports, TV,and Food may be some of the world's favorite past times, but they pale in comparision to the delight too many people seem to find in finding fault.

**"He will delight in obeying the Lord. He will not judge by appearance nor ake a decision based on hearsay.
Isaiah 11:3 NLT**

Our critical and judgmental spirits seem to take root and grow as we feed on the failures and shortcomings of our spouses, churches, co workers, neighbors, governments, automobiles, restaurants, etc, ad infinitum.

Whether finding fault elsewhere or with others instead of ourselves is to make us feel better about our own faults or to fill some other emotional need, too many of us seem to delight in fault finding.

One thing is certain, if we are looking for faults we are sure to find them. As imperfect people living in a very imperfect world, we never have to look very far to find something or someone to fault.

The Scribes and Pharisees of Jesus' day were great fault finders. Instead of praising healing, they found fault with it being done on Sunday. Instead of embracing the wonderful new covenant of grace Jesus taught and validated by His miracles, they found fault with all He said and did.

Martha found fault with Mary instead of finding joy in Jesus.

Although the pursuit of excellence is an admirable pursuit, the perfectionism that often accompanies it leads to often finding fault and stressing out over too many things that don't really matter.

**"Do not judge others, and you will not be judged. Do notcondemn others, or it will all come back against you. Forgive others, and you will be forgiven."
Luke 6:37 NLT**

With regard to stoning the woman caught in adultery, Jesus said: ""He who is without sin among you, let him throw a stone at her first." When we find ourselves finding fault we might first think about our own faults before delighting in finding fault elsewhere.

Father, Give me the grace to overlook faults in others as I need You and others to overlook mine. In Jesus' name, Amen

Til Death Do Us Part

"Great gifts mean great responsibilities; greater gifts, greater responsibilities! Luke 12:48 B MSG

Disposable marriages and "significant other" relationships seem to indicate that there is not a lot of belief that marriage is until death anymore. Unmet expectations financially, emotionally, sexually, or spiritually separate a lot of partners before death.

> **We are merely moving shadows,and all our busy rushing ends in nothing.**
> **We heap up wealth,not knowing who will spend it.**
> **Psalm 39:7 NLT**

Jim Elliott's famous quote "a man is no fool to give up something he cannot keep for something he cannot lose" speaks about salvation, but might well be applied to our thoughts about possessions.

Although bankruptcy and foreclosure rates indicate that much of a lot of people's wealth is parted before they even acquire it, the commitment to being married to money 'til death do us part seems to be stronger than married to spouses for some.

If some could see what happened to their money when death departed it from them, they would literally roll over in their graves. Inheritance rights and estate tax laws are probably as old as civilization.

The desire to pass something on to family and loved ones is probably just as old. Unfortunately the devil's ability to turn what we mean for good into evil sometimes lets greed split families apart forever. The inheritance that enables some to live indulgent life styles can turn some of our best intentions into the devil's worst.

The idea of parting with our money before it's too late is well worth considering.Scripture makes it very clear that although we can't take it with us, we can send it ahead by storing up treasures in heaven.

> **"But store up for yourselves treasures in heaven, where moth and rust do not destroy, and where thieves do not break in and steal."**
> **Matthew 6:20 NIV**

If God has trusted us with an abundance of wealth beyond our needs, it may well be so that we can be channels of His provision for kingdom building purposes.

Father, give me the grace of giving and generosity I need to store up more treasures in heaven before I depart. In Jesus' name, Amen.

Beware of Being Broad Minded

""You can enter God's Kingdom only through the narrow gate. The highway to hell is broad, and its gate is wide for the many who choose that way." Matthew 7:13 NLT

In this day of political correctness where relative truth reigns It is very easy to become very broad minded. Any questions about what God calls sin are met with sharp rebuke and identifies us as self righteous hypocrites, bigots, zealots, or crazy.

"There is a way that seems right to a man and appears straight before him, but at the end of it is the way of death."
Proverbs 16:25 AMP

We are called intolerant by those who believe that anything goes, and who are the most intolerant of all when it comes to someone expressing faith based beliefs,

We need to beware of sliding down the slippery slope of broad mindedness that can lead us to watch those we love go straight to hell as we silently see them get sin burnt and blinded into believing that there is no such thing as sin, "if It feels good do it", and there's no such place as hell.

We should be broad minded enough to love the sinner just as God loves us, but never broadminded enough not to hate their sins or pray that their spiritual eyesight be restored.

When we become broad minded enough to believe that we are ok without the favor of God that is ours only through faith in Jesus Christ, or that there is some other name except or in addition to Jesus

"And there is salvation in and through no one else, for there is no other name under heaven given among men by and in which we must be saved.
Acts 4:12 AMP

whereby we can be saved, we have become too broad minded.

Father, help me to be broad minded in love but narrow minded in believing what Scripture says. In Jesus' name, Amen.

69

Who's Got the Power?

"But those who wait for the Lord [who expect, look for, and hope in Him] shall change and renew their strength and power; they shall lift their wings and mount up [close to God] as eagles [mount up to the sun]; they shall run and not be weary, they shall walk and not faint or become tired."Isaiah 40:30 AMP

There are all sorts of philosophies and beliefs about power.

"Be exalted, Lord, in Your strength; we will sing and praise Your power." Psalm 21:13 AMP

The power of position, authority, wealth, personality, and control are Just a few that come to mind.

Parents, bosses, teachers, etc. all have power by virtue of position. Judges, police, elected officials, etc have power based on authority. Wealth and personality can also generate power.

Although He delegates much of it to others and allows some to misuse it, we can take great comfort in knowing that all power Is ultimately controlled by the Lord God Almighty, Creator and Ruler of the universe.

When man disobeyed God in the Garden of Eden, he not only brought the curse of sin into the world, but also surrendered authority and dominion over man to satan by the permissive will of God.

The power of free will is the one power God gives to all. We may choose to use this power to accept or reject the call of God to salvation when He gives it by the power of the Holy Spirit.

Although we were set free from the power of sin the hour we first believed, we still have the power to choose to be controlled by our sinful flesh instead of by the Holy Spirit.

"And then at last, the sign that the Son of Man is coming will appear in the heavens, and there will be deep mourning among all the peoples of the earth. And they will see the Son of Man coming on the clouds of heaven with power and great glory. Matthew 24:29

How comforting it is to know that greater is He who is living within us than the forces of evil working against us in our flesh, or the world kingdom of darkness in which we live.

May we never underestimate or forget that God is the source of all power and promises to supply enough of it for all our needs when our hearts attention and minds affection is on Jesus.

Lord, help me to harness Your resurrection power for living a fruitful life fully pleasing to you. In Jesus name, Amen

Will our Children and Grand Children be There?

If your children will keep My covenant and My testimony that I shall teach them, their children also shall sit upon your throne forever." Psalm 132:12 AMP

One of the first songs I learned from my mother was *"When the roll is called up yonder, I'll be there"*. How good it is to have the faith to know that my name is written in the Lamb's book of life and I'll be there when the roll is called.

"Place these words on your hearts. Get them deep inside you. Tie them on your hands and foreheads as a reminder. Teach them to your children. Talk about them wherever you are, sitting at home or walking in the street; talk about them from the time you get up in the morning until you fall into bed at night. Inscribe them on the doorposts and gates of your cities so that you'll live a long time, and your children with you, on the soil that God promised to give your ancestors for as long as there is a sky over the Earth."
Deuteronomy 11:17 MSG

It is also good to know that all of our children will also be there, thanks to the grace of God and the nurturing they received at home and in a Christian school.

With current predictions that over 75% of today's children will not be saved, the future of some of our children and especially our great grand daughter is very much at risk.

As public schools and especially colleges have not only kicked God out, but replaced Him with a false religion called Secular Humanism and God is mocked and made a joke of on TV, in movies and music our children are being robbed of their faith right before our very eyes.

What a shame that gang memberships are growing some times faster than Sunday School and Church rolls because they often offer a better sense of acceptance, community, and significance.

"How happy I was to meet some of your children and find them living according to the truth, just as the Father commanded"
2 John 1:4 NLT

Until we wake up to what is going on and become intentional about doing a better job of modeling and teaching true Christianity in our homes and churches we are going to have to wonder more and more if our children and grand children will be there *"when the roll is called up yonder."*

Father, help me to do a better job in helping children survive the attacks of today's faith robbers. In Jesus' name, Amen

71

Who's Your Designated Driver?

Then Jesus went to work on his disciples. "Anyone who intends to come with me has to let me lead. You're not in the driver's seat; I am Matthew 16:23 MSG

**"Then the LORD told him, "I have certainly seen the oppression of my people in Egypt. I have heard their cries of distress because of their harsh slave drivers."
Exodus 3:7 NLT**

The highway of life is a dangerous road. There are out of control drivers of every description. Forces of evil seek to rob us, and we come under the influence of the slave driver of sins that can wreck us and hurt those we love the most. We all need designated drivers.

Having a close friend and brother or sister in Christ to hold us accountable can do wonders for keeping us on the right road to the abundant life God wants to give us.

Someone who knows our faults and still loves us enough to come along side to encourage and support us can be a big help in escaping or overcoming the damages caused by our sin wrecks.

God has provided us with the best designated driver of all Who has come to live with us and is better than the best chauffeur we could ever hire.

When we allow The Holy Spirit to take control of our lives He promises to keep us on the highway of righteousness and help us escape or survive any sin wrecks that might occur.

**"And I will ask the Father, and He will give you another Comforter (Counselor, Helper, Intercessor, Advocate, Strengthener, and Standby), that He may remain with you forever-"
John 16:14 AMP**

The sooner we realize that we need help to make it on the highway to heaven, the sooner God's designated driver can take charge and drive us beside the still waters and onto the green pastures.

Father, thank you for sending the Holy Spirit to guide, protect, and clean me up from the road dirt and wrecks in my life. In Jesus' name, Amen

Exercises that Pay Big Dividends
"The generous soul will be made rich, And he who waters will also be watered himself.´Proverbs 26:25 NKJV

We sometimes seem to be better at exercising futility than anything else. How good it is of God to give us worthwhile spiritual exercises to help make us more like Jesus.

"Test me in this and see if I don't open up heaven itself to you and pour out blessings beyond your wildest dreams"
Malachi 3:8 MSG

As we exercise our spiritual muscles, everyone will begin to notice a big improvement in the way we do life. When we exercise our joy muscle it becomes contagious. When we exercise our grace muscle by extending it to others we find more and more grace growing within us. Most of our patience muscle needs a lot of extra exercise, and thr self control muscle is not far behind.

If we think of our grace of giving as a muscle we can understand why we should be exercising it as often as possible. We will never become really strong in the Lord if we neglect developing a strong giving muscle.

Although this exercise may hurt for a little while the more we exercise it the better it will feel as God's pleasure filters back in many different ways, just as we give in many different ways.

Only when we no longer need God to bless us physically, materially, relationally or spiritually should we ever quit exercising our giving muscle.

Although we should never forget giving in appreciation of what God has done for us in Christ, God also tells us to give to get. Giving is the only way we are allowed to test God.

You will be enriched in every way so that you can be generous on every occasion, and through us your generosity will result in thanksgiving to God.
2 Corinthians 9: NIV

I   The more we exercise our giving muscle, the stronger it becomes and the more capacity it receives. The more God can trust us with what He blesses us, the more He will bless. Are you ready to start enjoying the dividends of a strong giving muscle?

Father, thank you for the joy I have found in the privilege of exercising my grace of giving muscle. In Jesus' name, Amen

Getting Mud in Your Face

"They're mud-spattered head to toe with the residue of sin. I see who they are and what they've done." Hosea 7:2b MSG

We all can probably think of several embarrassing experiences of getting mud in our face. The humiliation of being caught in the act of doing something we shouldn't have been doing, being shown up or disgraced, and jumping to wrong conclusions are just a few of the many ways we can end up with mud in our face.

"My very own Temple, mind you— mud-spattered with their crimes." God's Decree."But they won't get by with it. They'll find themselves on a slippery slope," Jeremiah 23:11 MSG

One of the greatest concerns for any Christian should be getting the mud of hypocrisy on our face. Those moments when we lose God control and revert to the control of anger, pride, greed, jealousy, or lust can instantly wipe out years of good witness. As bad as it is for us unknowns, Christian leaders can devastate churches and tear down instead of build up the kingdom of God when they get dragged through the mud.

The mud of greed can blind us to the blessings and joys of giving. The mud of vengeance can often be worse than the offense itself. The mud of vanity can turn our beauty into blight.

The deceiver of our souls is constantly trying to muddy the living water of God's love with temptations of every description Pride is probably our biggest cause of getting mud in our face. When we try to get "too big for our britches" the mud will usually come flying.

David, the Prodigal Son, and Peter give us great comfort and cause for hope in the midst of our worst mud.

Peter said to Him, Even if I must die with You, I will not deny or disown You! And all the disciples said the same thing. Matthew 26:35 AMP

We never have to wallow in the mud forever. God will wash away the mud of all our sins with the blood of Jesus when we confess with godly sorrow and true repentance.

Father, thank you for washing away my mud. In Jesus' name, Amen

What's it Going to Take?
You learned deep in your heart that God disciplines you in the same ways a father disciplines his child."Deuteronomy 8:1b MSG

As good as it is to know that God loves us unconditionally and forgives us forever, we need to always remember that He loves us too much

Turn away my reproach which I dread, For Your judgments *are* good. Psalm 119:39 NKJV

to let us stay the way we are, and is committed to doing whatever it takes to work all things for our good in being conformed into the image of Christ.

For some of us slow learners God has to dish out some pretty harsh discipline to break us of our pride, anger, envy, lust, and bad habits that keep us from becoming like Christ, and we should be happy that He loves us enough to correct us.

We need to know that it takes surrendering our will to God and control of the Holy Spirit for God to be able to work all things for our good. We cannot be fixed until we realize we are broken.

As we begin to worship Jesus not only as our Savior, but as Lord of our life, the Holy Spirit begins producing more and more love, joy, peace, patience, kindness, goodness, faithfulness, and self control in us to bear as we are transformed, renewed, and conformed to become like Christ.

We can make it easier on ourselves. When we learn to cooperate with the Holy Spirit by obedience and abiding in Christ and God's Word, the less painful will be our discipline and chastening we will have and the more peace and joy to share.

My son, do not make light of the Lord's discipline, and do not lose heart when he rebukes you, Hebrews 12:5 NIV

We need to know that God is doing whatever it takes to work all things for our good and His glory. He can even take our worst and turn it into His best. This is why we can rejoice in our sorrows and troubles.

Father, help me to avoid as much of your discipline and chastening as possible by helping me to guard my thoughts, my heart, my tongue and my conduct. In Jesus' name, Amen

The Great Stabilizer

"Establish my steps and direct them by [means of] Your word; let not any iniquity have dominion over me" Psalm 139"33 AMP

Cruise ships are getting bigger and bigger and more and more people are enjoying them. Rough seas could turn any cruise into a very unpleasant experience which leads ship designers to build in giant stabilizers to smooth out the rough seas as much as possible.

"And let the beauty of the LORD our God be upon us: and establish thou the work of our hands upon us; yea, the work of our hands establish thou it. Psalm 90:17 KJV"

The rough seas of life can turn our world upside down in a hurry. Whether our own fault or the curse of sin and evil that still roams the world we can all expect troubles.

It's not a matter of if troubles come, it's a matter of when troubles come we need a stabilizer to keep us afloat during the storms of life.

If we didn't have troubles, we wouldn't need a Savior and Jesus would not have had to die on the cross to establish our righteousness with God and to give us the strength and power of the Holy Spirit to help us maintain stability through the deep waters.

God's stabilizer is also known as armor. When we put on the breastplate of righteousness, sandals of peace, helmet of salvation, belt of truth, shield of faith, and sword of the spirit God promises the strength and power to resist or flee any temptations or storms that may come our way.

"And He will establish you to the end [keep you steadfast, give you strength, and guarantee your vindication; He will be your warrant against all accusation or indictment so that you will be] guiltless and irreproachable in the day of our Lord Jesus Christ (the Messiah)." 1 Corinthians 1:8 MSG

Cruise ship stabilizers may prevent sea sickness, but only God's stabilizers can prevent sin sickness.

Father, thank you for establishing my faith on the solid rock of your Word, and don't let me sink into the muck and mire of the sin in this world. In Jesus' name, Amen

We've Been Robbed!

"The God-haters are living it up; They're plotting to do your people in, conspiring to rob you of your precious ones. "Let's wipe this nation from the face of the earth," they say; "scratch Israel's name off the books." And now they're putting their heads together, making plans to get rid of you. Psalm 83:1-5 MSG

One of the most successful hijackings of all time has taken place while God's people have been too engrossed in pursuing their own agendas to even notice, much less resist.

"You rescue the poor from those too strong for them, the poor and needy from those who rob them."
Psalm 35 10b NIV

Statistics confirm that we are no longer a Christian nation, and that our faith based values have been replaced by the man made values of secular humanism.

The roaring lion has invaded our schools and kicked prayer and eternal truth out and replaced it with condoms, alternative life styles. Scientific theories taught as facts have stripped a whole generation of their Christian heritage of faith in God and His wonderful gift of eternal life.

This so called "age of enlightenment" is based on the false premise that man is born good instead of evil, that there is no such thing as sin and therefore no one really needs a Savior.

The "big bang" has replaced God as our Creator and Father and God is no longer the author and finisher of many faiths. God is blamed for all the evil and suffering in the world as proof that He does not exist.

"You say, 'I am rich. I have everything I want. I don't need a thing!' And you don't realize that you are wretched and miserable and poor and blind and naked"
Revelation 3:17 NLT

The Good News for those who have read the rest of the book is that although the devil may be temporarily robbing the world, our God is the Almighty, All Knowing, Ever Present, and Ever Loving Supreme Ruler of the universe and is coming again to restore what has been stolen in a new home in heaven for all who call upon His name in spirit and in truth.

Father, help us to help our loved ones keep from getting robbed of their birthright by the false teachings that deny God and undermine their faith. In Jesus' name, Amen

Wilted Faith

"But the plant soon wilted under the hot sun, and since it didn't have deep roots, it died."Mark 4:6 NLT

Just as some plants wilt under heat, our faith is subject to wilting under the heat of living in the pressure cooker of life. We have relational,

"He remembered us in our weakness. His faithful love endures forever."
Psalm 136:23 NLT

vocational, financial, and physical challenges that often lead us to the brink of doubt and despair.

One of the devil's favorite ploys is to get us to mistakenly blame God for all of our suffering and problems. We should never forget that it was not God, but Adam and a fallen angel who brought sin and suffering into the world   . If it were not for God holding back the forces of evil, there would be much more sin and suffering.

The only known cure for wilted faith is the living water of God's strength and power being poured out by the Holy Spirit to all who will call upon the name of the Lord. God knows that we are all prone to wilt in our own strength at times, and graciously provides His all sufficient grace to sustain us or provide us with a means of escape when we trust and obey Him.

Job probably had more cause to wilt than any man who ever lived. The Lord allowed any testing or suffering outside of death itself to prove that Job's faith would not wilt. It was so bad that even Job's wife told him to "curse God and die", but Job never wilted.

"At this point many of his disciples turned away and deserted him. [67] Then Jesus turned to the Twelve and asked,"Are you also going to leave?"
John 6:66,67 NLT

Our Lord Jesus had every reason to wilt under the temptations of the devil and the horrible pain and suffering He had to endure to pay our sin debt in full by dying on the cross for us. Knowing this should be more than enough for us to pray for a faith that will not wilt.

Father, keep me ever mindful of my need to drink daily from your well of grace that never runs dry. In Jesus' name, Amen

Why Have they Gone?
"Train up a child in the way he should go [and in keeping with his individual gift or bent], and when he is old he will not depart from it." Proverbs 22:6 AMP

It is a sad commentary that apparently a vast majority of today's youth have gone outside the home and church to find the community, acceptance, and discipline they crave.

"Turn us back to You, O LORD, and we will be restored; Renew our days as of old," Lamentations 5:21 NKJV

The fact that gangs are apparently growing more than Sunday Schools throughout our country is truly alarming. The estimated 75% drop out rate among youth who leave home with faith and have it stolen from then in college is staggering.

Why is our Christian faith based life style that offers more security, acceptance, and joy than anything on this planet being abandoned?

We can probably start with God being kicked out of our schools and replaced by secular humanism offering theories as facts designed to destroy faith in God and causing all to question their faith.

We find another big reason when we look at the divorce rate and preponderance of single parent families. It is hard to model faith as a family value in a dysfunctional family.

Many drop off their children at youth groups and think their job is done. Many youth groups are world and flesh driven instead of Spirit driven and cannot compete with the devil in either of these areas. Surely our churches and God's people can offer more love and community than a street gang or a peer posse of losers. We all need to earnestly seek God's help in doing or being whatever it takes to stop the bleeding.

And not many days after, the younger son gathered all together, journeyed to a far country, and there wasted his possessions with prodigal living. Luke 15:13 NKJV

Father, your covenant has been and is being broken into the second generation. Help us to help our children discover and keep the joy of your salvation. In Jesus' name, Amen.

A Lesson from the Salmon

'When you go through deep waters,I will be with you. When you go through rivers of difficulty, you will not drown. Isaiah 43:2a NLT

The breath taking sight of salmon swimming upstream and jumping up river rapids to reach the place where they were spawned to die is mind boggling.

But me he caught— reached all the way from sky to sea; he pulled me out Of that ocean of hate, that enemy chaos, the void in which I was drowning.
Psalm 18:15a MSG

They not only have to jump the rapids, but also survive all the fishermen and bears trying to catch them as they run. This natural phenomenon is a great lesson of true grit and determination for us all.

As we swim the rivers of life, we often find ourselves swimming upstream against the current physically, financially, relationally, or spiritually.

Thanks be to God that we never have to swim alone, or without a paddle when we have God's power living within us through our faith in Jesus Christ.

Fighting the good fight of faith in a world that's headed for hell is a battle we must continue to fight. Even though our victory was won on the cross, the mortally wounded roaring lion can be like a man eating shark when we are having to swim upstream.

We may never know what drives the salmon to swim upstream and home to die, but we need to know that we have already died to sin and become alive in Christ by being born again so that we can go home not to die but to live forever in the perfect bliss of heaven.

"But those who desire to be rich fall into temptation and a snare, and into many foolish and harmful lusts which drown men in destruction and perdition.
1 Timothy 6:8

God not only gives us a paddle and a life preserver, but also teaches how to swim upstream through His Word.

Lord, the water is often deep and the currents are swift. Give me the strength and power I need to get back home to you. In Jesus' name, Amen

Class Acts

"Recalling unceasingly before our God and Father your work energized by faith and service motivated by love and unwavering hope in [the return of] our Lord Jesus Christ." I Thessalonians 1:10 MSG

Life is designed as a process for "getting our acts together." It's all a part of God's great design in helping us to act like Christ. It is not hard – it's impossible without the transforming power of the Holy Spirit working in us.

"Then you will win favor and a good name in the sight of God and man" Proverbs 3:4 NIV

God has given us a lot of hard acts to follow in the Bible and in our world. When I think of the class acts in the Bible I think of Ruth and Joseph. There are undoubtedly a whole lot more, but these are ones who stand out to me. Their humility and faithfulness in persevering through pain, suffering, and injustice should be an inspiration and model for us all.

How thankful we should be for the few class acts we have left in this world to encourage and model class in an increasingly classless world.

Class Acts are cleaned up acts that please God who makes even their enemies be at peace with them. Billy Graham has been the most admired man in the world for over half a century and has been a class act for all to emulate.

If we will look around, we will find "class acts" within our churches and neighborhoods as well as among the rich and famous.

"THEREFORE BE imitators of God [copy Him and follow His example], as well-beloved children [imitate their father]. Ephesians 5:1 AMP

When we see someone who reminds us of Jesus, we are seeing a "class act" because we are seeing humility and love.

There is no higher compliment we can give anyone than to say they are a "class act."

Father, thank you for the blessing of so many "class acts" who have enriched and encouraged me in my walk of faith. In Jesus' name, Amen

Scam Artists

" And the crooks? Underhanded sneaks they are, inventive in sin and scandal, Exploiting the poor with scams and lies, unmoved by the victimized poor. But those who are noble make noble plans, and stand for what is noble." Isaiah 32:1b MSG

Nigerian internet scams have become so common in our area they are no longer considered newsworthy. The newspaper reports scams going on in parking lots or wherever people congregate.

"That you may exercise proper discrimination and discretion and your lips may guard and keep knowledge and the wise answer [to temptation]."
Proverbs 5:2 AMP

We who are amazed at how people could be so gullible often need to ask ourselves the same question, as satan, the greatest scam artist in the world continues to try to rob us of our identity in Christ.

The deceiver of our souls is without a conscience and has no decency. He is a liar, cheat, and master impersonator determined to do whatever it takes to get us to mock God and die.

He cons us into pursuing our pleasure instead of God's glory and we lead self centered lives controlled by our flesh and the pride, anger, envy, and lust of our sin nature.

He cons us into falling in love with the world he rules as the pathway to happiness and we find the consequences of shame, guilt, pain and misery instead of the happiness he promised.

When we start suffering the consequences of our bad choices, or from the evil of this world, satan tries to scam us into blaming God instead of him whose disobedience and rebellion brought the curse of evil into this world.

The temptations in your life are no different from what others experience. And God is faithful. He will not allow the temptation to be more than you can stand. When you are tempted, he will show you a way out so that you can endure.
1 Corinthians 10:13 NLT

Our only hope is in God, the only power greater than the power of evil in this world. He comes as the Holy Spirit to arm us with the power to resist the temptations of the roaring lion who is constantly seeking to devour us today.

Father, give me the wisdom, spiritual discernment, and power to recognize and resist the scams of the devil. In Jesus' name, Amen

Asking Amiss

"Ye ask, and receive not, because ye ask amiss, that ye may consume it upon your lusts." James 4:3 KJV

One of the greatest blessings of every child of God is immediate access to God's throne of grace through prayer. Millions of healings, saved marriages, restored relationships, saved lives, and other blessings have been poured out and continue to be poured out as a result of the fervent prayers of righteous people.

"O Israel, stay away from idols! I am the one who answers your prayers and cares for you." Hosea 14:8 NLT

There seems be some sort of idea that God is a giant vending machine who delivers whatever we ask for when we ask for it. When we pray with self will instead of God will He is going to deny our requests every time.

It's a good thing that God knows our heart and our motives and loves us too much to give us not what we selfishly want but what we need to become more like Jesus.

We can probably all look back on a lot of inappropriate unanswered prayers and often, in retrospect, thank God that they were not answered.

God hears and answers all our prayers. He answers, "yes", "no", or "not now". The keys to the getting good answers are faith and praying just like Jesus taught us - in submission to God's good and gracious will – and continuing to pray without ceasing.

We will never get an answered prayer if we don't pray. We should not expect positive answers to prayers prayed with an unforgiving or unrepented heart.

"And this is the confidence that we have in him, that, if we ask any thing according to his will, he heareth us:" 1 John 5:14 KJV

We should all beware of "asking amiss".

Father help me to abide more in You so that I can pray more in accordance with your will. In Jesus' name, Amen

The Judging God Allows
" For by the grace given me I say to every one of you: Do not think of yourself more highly than you ought, but rather think of yourself with sober judgment, in accordance with the faith God has distributed to each of you." Romans 12:3 NIV

Although we are warned *"to judge not that we be not judged"* and to leave judgment to God, we are also told to judge ourselves.

We need to judge our consciences, but also to judge ourselves

"Let us test and examine our ways, and let us return to the Lord!"
Lamentations 3:40 AMP

according to Scripture to see in how well we are obeying God and carrying out His will for our lives.

We often wear coveralls to hide our sins and weaknesses and are often reluctant to talk about them with others because we are afraid they might not like us if they knew the truth.

Although the deceiver of our souls can fill us with rationalization and denial that might cloud our judgment, it is refreshing to know that God knows all about us and still loves us.

Best of all we can be totally honest with Him because He knows it all anyhow so there is no need for any pretense or coverup.

The old saying that an *"ounce of prevention is worth a pound of cure"* is a truth worth thinking about when it comes to judging ourselves. .

"Examine yourselves to see if your faith is genuine. Test yourselves. Surely you know that Jesus Christ is among you ; if not, you have failed the test of genuine faith."
2 Corinthians 13:5 NLT

We can avoid a lot of pain and suffering that God has to allow when we refuse to judge and deal with our sinful ways before God has to use some more drastic measures to discipline and conform us into the image of Christ.

"It is a fearful thing to fall into the hands of the living God" and we should seek the strength and power of the Holy Spirit to help us avoid this at any cost. Judging ourselves and dealing with our sins before God has to is one of the best ways to do this.

Father, restore me and renew my mind daily, as I judge, apologize, and repent of my sins. In Jesus' name, Amen

Freedom of the Will
"Wherefore the rather, brethren, give diligence to make your calling and election sure: for if ye do these things, ye shall never fall:" 2 Peter 1L10 KJV

Adam and Eve used the freedom of their will to disobey God in the Garden of Eden and the curse of sin and our bondage to it has been going on ever since

"I posted watchmen over you who said, 'Listen for the sound of the alarm.' But you replied, 'No! We won't pay attention!'"
Jeremiah 6:17 NLT

As painful as it has been for God to see His children lose their innocence and sinless perfection, He obviously thought giving us a free will worth it so that no one would be forced to love or obey Him unless they cheerfully and willingly desired to.

There has been a misunderstanding among Christians for centuries over whether anyone has free will to receive salvation from their own volition, or by the predestination of God to supply the grace to exercise this will.

There are verses in Scripture that seem to support both understandings. There are a lot of understandings we will never fully understand this side of heaven.

Unfortunately the curses from the devil and man's disobedience were not washed away by the flood, and God finally had to wash them away by the blood of His one and only Son.

We should never forget the price that Jesus paid to save us from the wages of death our sins deserve and to assure that all who believe will live forever in the freedom of sinless perfection of the new earth when Jesus comes again.

"Wherefore, my beloved, as ye have always obeyed, not as in my presence only, but now much more in my absence, work out your own salvation with fear and trembling."
Philippians 2:12 KJV

At the resurrection of the just all who have received eternal life will receive a new sin free heart. They will no longer be under the curse of sin but will freely love and obey God and be able to live with Him forever in the sin free paradise of the new earth.

Father, thank you for choosing me before I was ever born to become one of your elect and giving me the grace to open the door when you knocked. In Jesus' name, Amen

The Way it Is

"Then he put another parable before them. "The kingdom of Heaven," he said, "is like a man who sowed good seed in his field. But while his men were asleep his enemy came and sowed weeds among the wheat," Matthew 13:34 NIV

In spite of the fact we believe and are taught that if we bring up a child in the way he should walk, he will not depart from it, it seems that many of the good seeds of faith we planted in our children too often get crowded out by the weeds of the world as they go through adolescent rebellion or young adulthood.

> Neighborhoods and families are falling to pieces. The closer they are—sons, daughters, in-laws— The worse they can be. Your own family is the enemy.
> Micah 7:3 MSG

The sad story of so many children having been brought up in the Lord and then losing their faith in college or earlier is told over and over by parents who are left feeling guilty and disappointed and blaming themselves.

Although some parents may have been guilty of teaching it but not modeling it the truth is that the world is out to devour our children, and is doing a very good job.

When our children's faith gets choked out by the temptations and pleasures of this world, it is very comforting to know that it has not been because of our failing to bring them up right, but in spite of our best efforts.

There is also great comfort and hope in knowing that sooner or later the good seed of faith will re seed and outgrow the weeds of sin and that we often see our children's faith restored.

> "And you must show mercy to[h] those whose faith is wavering. Rescue others by snatching them from the flames of judgment. Show mercy to still others, but do so with great caution, hating the sins that contaminate their lives."
> Jude 1:22 NLT

We should pursue every opportunity to help our children grow in their faith than the devil and the world are doing in trying to choke it out, and pray that God will answer our prayers for renewal and restoration.

Father, thank you for renewing and restoring us and our children who may have fallen into the clutches of the deceiver of our souls. In Jesus'name, Amen

Digging Deeper

"The secret [of the sweet, satisfying companionship] of the Lord have they who fear (revere and worship) Him, and He will show them His covenant and reveal to them its [deep, inner] meaning" Psalm 25:14 AMP

The incredible depths oil rigs drill to find oil is amazing. Having to case through surface water to get down deeper to the good water is not uncommon in drilling water wells.

"Now therefore, I pray You, if I have found favor in Your sight, show me now Your way, that I may know You [progressively become more deeply and intimately acquainted with You," Exodus 33:13a AMP

We need to be mindful that many of the treasures of God are buried and will be found only by those who dig deep enough to find them.

Our relationship with the Lord grows and grows as we dig deeper and deeper into His Word and we find more and more of the peace and joy that comes only from abiding in Him.

God sometimes has to allow major disappointment and hurts in order to get us anchored deeper in Him. When we get so full of ourselves and our own power and ability we tend to stay in the shallowness of a shallow faith and see no need to go deeper.

The abundant life that Jesus came, lived, and died to bring us all who believe is fueled by a living faith that grows in direct proportion to how we grow in our knowledge of Him and His will for our lives as revealed in His Word.

If we believe the Bible that says that "God is a rewarder of those who seek Him", we should also believe that our relationship with Jesus should be growing deeper and deeper so that we can become more spiritually mature and more like Him every day of our lives.

"Then he added, "Pay close attention to what you hear. The closer you listen, the more understanding you will be given[c]—and you will receive even more." Mark 4:24 NLT

As we dig deeper and deeper through prayer, fellowship, worship, and growing in the Word, the more peace, security, and joy we will have in the new eternal life in Christ we have been given.

Father, help me to keep digging deeper and deeper into your well of love that will never run dry. In Jesus' name, Amen

Be Careful for What You Pray

"But, on the contrary, as the Scripture says, What eye has not seen and ear has not heard and has not entered into the heart of man, [all that] God has prepared (made and keeps ready) for those who love Him [who hold Him in affectionate reverence, promptly obeying Him and gratefully recognizing the benefits He has bestowed].1 Corinthians 2:9 AMP

As a senior citizen of some 82 years as of this writing, I become more and more aware of how many professing Christians are scared of dying, especially for their loved ones dying.

"My son, forget not my law; but let thine heart keep my commandments: 2For length of days, and long life, and peace, shall they add to thee."
Proverbs 3:1,2 KJV

I can well understand concern for unsaved people who are still wandering aimlessly lost toward the eternal torments of hell. but it is hard for me to see people praying for the Lord to keep saved people here instead of trusting Him to take them home to all the joys of heaven according to His good purposes and will.

How much better to let someone go peaceably and with no suffering rather than see them go through pain for several years to where we are begging the Lord to take them home to spare them anymore suffering.

It almost seems that some people are so in love with this world that God has to bring a lot of pain and suffering to make them more willing to leave it behind for the green pastures and still waters of heaven. God does have a plan to do whatever it takes to conform all who believe into the image of Christ, and if it takes allowing pain and suffering, He will certainly allow it.

"So when this corruptible shall have put on incorruption, and this mortal shall have put on immortality, then shall be brought to pass the saying that is written, Death is swallowed up in victory."
1Corinthians 15:54 KJV

As I see the lights of that great city of God shining brighter and brighter, how comforting it is to be able to put my days totally in the hands of my Lord and my God and surrender to His good and perfect will. I never want anyone to pray that God extend my days, but only that His good will be done for me.

Father, our time is in your hands, and there is no better place for it to be when our heart's attention and minds affection is stayed on You. In Jesus' name, Amen

What are We Worth

"And turn not aside after vain and worthless things which cannot profit or deliver you, for they are empty and futile." 1 Samuel 12:21 AMP

How much are we worth? Due to inflation, the value of the chemical elements in our body and the value of our skin on a square foot basis, we are now worth about $4.50

"Turn away my eyes from looking at worthless things, And revive me in Your way."
Psalm 119:37 MSG

Lawyers specializing in death and injury cases add estimates of earning power, value of companionship, and other considerations and convince juries that we are worth millions upon millions of dollars.

Thank God our real worth is not based upon our monetary value, but rather on God's believing that we were worth coming to earth and dying for in order for us to have the priceless gift with a priceless value if we would believe in His Son.

There is nothing wrong in trying to become the best that God has created us to be and to enjoy the success and feeling good about ourselves that usually follows. It is good to have others think well of us. Money and possessions are nice to own, but they should never own us.

Instead of valuing our self worth on others opinion of us, performance and achievements, appearance, or possessions, we should find our significance in knowing that we are unconditionally loved, forever forgiven, and have a friend who will never forsake us.

"What's the price of two or three pet canaries? Some loose change, right? But God never overlooks a single one. And he pays even greater attention to you, down to the last detail—even numbering the hairs on your head! So don't be intimidated by all this bully talk. You're worth more than a million canaries.
Luke 12:6 MSG

When we have the security of God's love and the peace that surpasses all understanding that comes only through a right relationship with Him through faith in Jesus Christ we have all the true worth we will ever need.

Father, help me to seek and treasure the true worth I have in Christ. In Jesus' name, Amen.

Boundaries for Abounding

"For I know the thoughts and plans that I have for you, says the Lord, thoughts and plans for welfare and peace and not for evil, to give you hope in your final outcome." Jeremiah 29:11 AMP

We sometimes confuse happiness and holiness and believe that they cannot coexist. The truth that God wants our happiness to be rooted in loving Him and obeying the guidelines He has set is contrary to our sin nature that tells us that we can be happy by living on our terms instead of God's.

"Oh, the joys of those who trust the LORD, who have no confidence in the proud" Psalm 40:4 NLT

God does not warn us not to be yoked with unbelievers to make us unhappy, but to avoid the dangers this involves. "I thought he (or she) would change" are famous last words of too many shattered lives and broken marriages from believers who found out the hard way that the oil of God's grace and presence needs to be upon both spouses if a marriage is to truly abound.

God does not tell us to avoid the pride, anger, envy, and lust of the flesh to break us, but to brake us from sinful conduct that makes it impossible for God to bless us with the fullness of His blessings based on obedience.

Just as earthly children need boundaries to teach them the way they should walk, we, as children of the heavenly father, need the same.

God's boundaries are His guard rails that He has set to instruct us how we should live our new lives in Christ filled with the abounding abundance of His love, grace, and mercy that makes life worth living now and forever.

"This foolish plan of God is wiser than the wisest of human plans, and God's weakness is stronger than the greatest of human strength." I Corinthians 1:25 NLT

He has given us the Holy Spirit to do whatever it takes to get us back into the sheep fold of God's boundaries when we stray, if we will but confess and repent.

Father, help me to learn and live within the boundaries you have set that I might enjoy my abundant life in Christ to the fullest. In Jesus name, Amen

The Triple Whammy

" Jesus said, "The voice didn't come for me but for you. At this moment the world is in crisis. Now Satan, the ruler of this world, will be thrown out." John 12:31 MSG

We often talk about our war with our flesh, the world, and the devil without realizing how we all became cursed and under their power.

"The curse of the Lord is in and on the house of the wicked, but He declares blessed (joyful and favored with blessings) the home of the just and consistently righteous."
Proverbs 3:33 AMP

We understand that Adam and Eve disobeyed God and brought the curse of sin into our lives. We need to know how one of God's favorite angels did the same thing and ended up bringing the evil of satanic oppression into the world.

It is often overlooked that Adam and Eve gave up their God given authority over the world and everything in it to the devil when they were seduced by him in the garden. And this is why we are in a daily battle against this "triple whammy" curse.

Although the war was won on the cross of Calvary, the battle rages on and we must put on the full armor of God daily in order to survive the temptations from any or all of these forces of evil seeking to get us to give up our salvation and eternal glory for the momentary pleasures, counterfeit happiness, and self control of our lives.

The deceiver of our souls is a liar and a thief, and lower than the snake which he became. He is also a lot more cunning and powerful than we think, and we dare not take him too lightly.

"It can never happen to me", "I can handle it", "God wants me to be happy" are just a few of the last words of millions who have fallen before they realized what was happening.

"Therefore put on the full armor of God, so that when the day of evil comes, you may be able to stand your ground, and after you have done everything,"
Ephesians 6:13 NIV

God is still on the throne and working all things for our good and His glory and will still sustain or provide a means of escape when our hearts are stayed on Him.

Father, help me to keep armor ready. In Jesus' name, Amen

91

Missing Children Epidemic
"Tell your children of it, and let your children tell their children, and their children another generation." Joel 1:3 AMP

"The LORD looks down from heaven upon the children of men, To see if there are any who understand, who seek God."
Psalm 14:2 NKJV

There is widespread child abduction going on in this country with hardly a concern being raised. Parents, judges and schools in our country have conspired to steal our children's Christian heritage.

In the name of freedom from religion, the false religion of secular humanism has taken out prayer, Easter, Christmas, and the Ten Commandments, and replaced them with the man made God of enlightenment. self sufficiency, condoms, and big bang evolution.

Surveys indicate that 75 to 80% of children from church homes will be missing from their faith before their junior year of college.

Unfortunately the Christian Faith that is supposed to be modeled by and caught from parents is also missing in too many homes broken by divorce, lack of faith, pursuit of worldly pleasure and insidious TV, movies and games taking the place of worship.

Churches who have neglected the spiritual growth and welfare of their children must also share much of the blame.

Whether this is all part of the great falling away that precedes Christ's return, or just a sad commentary on the increasing depravity of man remains to be seen. The one thing for sure is that we need a Holy Ghost revival in this world, and it needs to begin with us.

We all need to remember that God is the same yesterday, today and tomorrow and purposely pray, live, and do everything possible to keep the children in our families and churches from coming up missing out on the true joy and blessing of a life in Christ now and forever.

"The promise is for you and your children and for all who are far off— for all whom the Lord our God will call."
Acts 2:39 NIV

Father, guard the hearts affection and minds attention of all children that they be grounded in You. In Jesus' name, Amen

Help My Unbelief

"And straightway the father of the child cried out, and said with tears, Lord, I believe; help thou mine unbelief." Mark 9:24 KJV

If any of us believers have not often echoed this honest plea of this father, we are a rarity, indeed.

[What, what would have become of me] had I not believed that I would see the Lord's goodness in the land of the living! Psalm 27:12

The truth is that often the more faith we have, the more aware we become of our unbelief and ashamed of it.

We are sometimes surprised by answered prayers that we never really believed God would answer. There is no telling this side of heaven how many miracles have not happened and how many prayers have been unanswered because of our unbelief.

The deceiver of our souls loves to create doubt and unbelief to cause us to fall away and lose the security of God's love. Our repeated sins will often cause us to doubt whether we were really saved rather than believe that we can confess, repent and be freed from them. The fact that our hearts are heavy instead of hardened is strong evidence that we are still under the shelter of God's grace.

We all should be painfully aware of our inability to always apply our belief to our daily circumstances. We worry needlessly, stress frequently, and sin daily as we continue to live as imperfect people in an imperfect world.

"And Jesus said unto them, Because of your unbelief: for verily I say unto you, If ye have faith as a grain of mustard seed, ye shall say unto this mountain, Remove hence to yonder place; and it shall remove; and nothing shall be impossible unto you." Matthew 17:20 KJV

The proper perspective for any doubts or unbelief we might be struggling with is to do as this father did. We need to ask God to help our unbelief by increasing our faith to overcome it by the power of the Holy Spirit.

God will always hear when we come with broken spirit and contrite heart even with our unbeliefs.

Father, I believe. Help my unbelief. In Jesus' name, Amen

God's Grace Umbrella

"The Lord is my strength and shield. I trust him with all my heart. He helps me, and my heart is filled with joy. I burst out in songs of thanksgiving." Psalm 28:6 NLT

My dear wife usually takes an umbrella with us wherever we go. They have come in handy often to provide shelter from the rain.

But let all who take refuge in you rejoice; let them sing joyful praises forever. Spread your protection over them, that all who love your name may be filled with joy.
Psalm 5:10-12 NLT

God has an umbrella of grace over all of us which goes every where with us. It protects us not only from the storms of life, but from the heat of evil that is all around us.

God's protective grace covered Shadrach, Meshach, and Abednego in the fiery furnace. It covered Joseph in the prisons, the children of Israel as they escaped Egypt.

God's grace is our only protection against sin, death, and the devil. He has covered all by pouring out His blood on the Cross for our sins, and making it possible for us to live grace covered fruitful lives fully pleasing to Him.

God is our refuge and strength, and our very present help in any kind of trouble. He continues to grace us with His goodness and mercy all the days of our lives as He works all things for our good in making us more like Christ.

We can't find this umbrella at Wal Mart or Target. It can only be found by faith. It comes with the best guarantee ever given built right in.

The Holy Spirit has been given with it as a deposit guaranteeing that all who truly believe will see Jesus face to face.

"Now I am departing from the world; they are staying in this world, but I am coming to you. Holy Father, you have given me your name; now protect them by the power of your name so that they will be united just as we are."
John 17:11 NLT

If you do not yet have your grace umbrella, we invite you to get yours by confessing to God that you are a sinner who needs a Savior and inviting Jesus to come into your heart.

Father, thank you for the shelter of your grace that is more than sufficient for my every need. In Jesus' name, Amen

94

Magnetic Attraction
"Trustworthy messengers refresh like snow in summer. They revive the spirit of their employer." Proverbs 25:13 NLT

"The mark of a good leader is loyal followers; leadership is nothing without a following." Proverbs 14:28 MSG

Some people are gifted with looks, talent, personality, or other qualities that draw others to them in remarkable ways.

Concert Halls and stadiums are filled to overflowing when a super star comes to town. Sold out movies, races, and ball games attest to the magnetic attraction of some people.

The Bible has many examples of the magnetic attraction of Moses, Solomon, David, and John the Baptist who preceded Jesus.

Jesus was the greatest magnet for the souls of men the world has ever known. As his ministry grew He drew great crowds wherever He went and fed them all with miracles, signs, and wonders that gave all who would believe in Him the power to become the children of God.

The disciples were filled with the magnetic attraction power of the Holy Spirit at Pentecost where Christ's church was launched, and became the greatest attraction of all time.

Starting perhaps with the apostle Paul, the Lord has gifted many of His Saints with magnetic attraction. Constantine, Martin Luther, Calvin all served God's purposes to attract and capture the souls of men for Christ.

Dr. Billy Graham has been one of the greatest magnetic attractions for Christ the world has ever known. The Lord has used him to draw the hearts of millions of people from every continent.

"Live a lover's life, circumspect and exemplary, a life Jesus will be proud of: bountiful in fruits from the soul, making Jesus Christ attractive to all, getting everyone involved in the glory and praise of God." Philippians 1:8-10

Although we won't attract as many as Billy Graham, we are all called to be magnetic attractions drawing others around us into a saving relationship with Jesus Christ.

As we let our light shine by imitating Christ in our daily life we will find others being drawn by our own magnetic attraction.

Father, help me to be a soul magnet. In Jesus' name, Amen

Estate Planning
"Tell those rich in this world's wealth to quit being so full of themselves and so obsessed with money, which is here today and gone tomorrow. Tell them to go after God, who piles on all the riches we could ever manage—to do good, to be rich in helping others, to be extravagantly generous. If they do that, they'll build a treasury that will last, gaining life that is truly life."
1 Timothy 6:16-

"And make the Almighty your gold and [the Lord] your precious silver treasure, Then you will have delight in the Almighty, and you will lift up your face to God. Job 25,26 AMP

Who will get what we leave behind is a question that almost everyone will have to deal with sooner or later. Failure to deal with this question has caused feuds that break up families, and allows lawyers and state or federal governments to end up with far too much of the estate.

We hear a lot about we can't take it with us but the truth that we can send it ahead doesn't sink in as well.

Scripture does not say that we will be made rich so that we can leave a lot to our loved ones. It says that we will be made rich so that we can be generous on every occasion just as God has been to us.

We should be thinking about our inheritance in heaven as much as the one we are going to leave behind. We need to understand that wealth used for doing good is treasure laid up in heaven.

We have nothing but what we have been given by God who has given it to us for His purposes. He has not given us wealth to corrupt us but to test us, and to make sure our heart is upon him and not upon our wealth.

"Then he said to them,"Watch out! Be on your guard against all kinds of greed; life does not consist in an abundance of possessions." Luke 12:15 NIV

The day we stand before Christ to give an account of what we have done with the lives and treasures we have been given is the day we all need to plan for. Our treasure in Heaven will be what remains after all the wood, hay, and selfish pursuits of our lives have been burned away. May we all incorporate this truth into our estate planning.

Father, may I never short change you or myself when I consider any estate planning. In Jesus' name, Amen

Have You Been Crucified?
"I have been crucified with Christ; it is no longer I who live, but Christ lives in me; and the life which I now live in the flesh I live by faith in the Son of God, who loved me and gave Himself for me." Galatians 2:20

If we are to become the imitators of Christ we are all called to be, we must become dead to our trespasses and sins by laying them at the Cross of Jesus so that His crucifixion can be ours.

"The high and lofty one who inhabits eternity, the Holy One, says this: "I live in that high and holy place with those whose spirits are contrite and humble. I refresh the humble and give new courage to those with repentant hearts."
Isaiah 57:15 NLT

If there had been any other way, God would never have had His beloved Son suffer and die as payment in full for every sin we have ever or will ever commit.

Just as with Jesus, there can be nothing held back nothing short of total surrender in dying to self so that we may experience our own resurrection into the newness of life in Christ by the transforming power of the Holy Spirit.

The joy of Easter is in knowing that Jesus conquered sin, death, and hell for us so that we might live forever in the true peace and joy that only our right relationship with God through faith in Jesus Christ can afford.

Because Jesus rose from the grave and lives, we have the blessed assurance that we too will live forever in this world and the next free from slavery to sin and free to grow into the fullness of the joy of our salvation.

"Therefore we were buried with Him through baptism into death, that just as Christ was raised from the dead by the glory of the Father, even so we also should walk in newness of life."
Romans 6:4 NLT

How good it is to know that when we become alive in Christ through our spiritual death and resurrection we can stay afloat through the good times and the bad knowing that God is working all things in and through us for our good and His glory.

Lord, thank you for the affirmation of Easter. In Jesus' name, Amen

Where Did He Go?
"And at once the curtain of the [sanctuary of the temple was torn in two from top to bottom; the earth shook and the rocks were split." Matthew 27:51 AMP

There is a very profound but often overlooked significance in the

"And you shall put in it the ark of the Testimony and screen the ark [of God's Presence] with the veil: Exodus 40:3 AMP.

above passage that I believe to be true. (Although Scripture does not specifically detail this, I know of no Scripture that contradicts it.)

The presence of God was manifested in a cloud by day and pillar of fire by night during the exodus.

God then manifested His presence in the holy of holies in the temple separated by a veil through which no one could pass except the priest on special occasions.

The instant Jesus died the veil was torn signifying that all who believe have direct access to God. We no longer sacrifice the blood of animals or make other burnt offerings to the temple....WE ARE THE TEMPLE!

God manifests His presence and power in the lives of every one of us who call upon His name.

The more we feed upon His Word, pray, and worship Him in spirit and in truth, the more His presence manifests Christ in us, and the more like Him we become.

As we are filled with God's presence we are given the power from on high to overcome the temptations and wiles of devil and able to live as the salt and light God created us to become.

If we are not aware of God's presence in our lives, we need to go back to the throne of grace in sincere prayer and repentance and truly submit to the Lordship of Jesus and receive the fullness of God's presence and power that Jesus promised to send us.

"So all of us who have had that veil removed can see and reflect the glory of the Lord. And the Lord—who is the Spirit—makes us more and more like him as we are changed into his glorious image." 2 Corinthians 3:18 NLT

Father, thank you for moving your presence into my life. Keep me ever mindful that I have become your temple in mind, body, and spirit. In Jesus name, Amen

Who's Your "Go To"?
"But where shall Wisdom be found? And where is the place of understanding?" Job 28:11 NLT

"Go To" people are some of God's greatest blessings and gifts. How great it is to have a bank of dependable resources to go to with our problems.

"But the Comforter (Counselor, Helper, Intercessor, Advocate, Strengthener, Standby), the Holy Spirit, Whom the Father will send in My name [in My place, to represent Me and act on My behalf], He will teach you all things. And He will cause you to recall (will remind you of, bring to your remembrance) everything I have told you."
John 14:26 AMP

We have "go to" people for hair cuts, car or household repairs, financial planning, legal affairs, or to buy a car or borrow money.

Every church or successful business has some good "go to" people who can be depended upon to get the job done.

If we are wise and very blessed the Lord has given us godly friends to whom we can go to multiply our joys and divide our sorrows. To have support resources to go to when struggling with a problem often makes a great difference in how well we resolve a problem.

Knowing who to go to is as important as having someone to go to. It is generally not a good idea to go to someone who has been divorced 3 times for marital advice. It would be unwise to go to someone who has been bankrupt for financial advice.

A lot of big mistakes and heart aches can be avoided if we get to know the Holy Spirit as our "Go To" resource for every area of our life. When we received Jesus Christ as our Savior the Holy Spirit moved into our hearts to comfort us and guide us in all truth. We are promised wisdom if we pray for it, forgiveness if we apologize and ask for it, and the comfort of God's love if we believe.

When we go to God in prayer, we are going to the one who knows our every weakness, has suffered our every pain, and who is always working all things for our good.

"Simon Peter answered, Lord, to whom shall we go? You have the words (the message) of eternal life"
John 6:68 AMP

There is no better place to go than to our "go to" God. *Father, help me to come to You first. In Jesus' name, Amen*

Custom Made Suffering

"No temptation has overtaken you except what is common to mankind. And God is faithful; he will not let you be tempted beyond what you can bear. But when you are tempted, he will also provide a way out so that you can endure it."1 Corinthians 10:12-14 NIV

The amazing fact that every human ever born has DNA that matches no other is mind boggling. It gives great credence to David's observation that we are truly wonderfully made.

"My brethren, count it all joy when ye fall into divers temptations;" James 1:2 KJV

God creates us all with distinct physical, mental, and spiritual attributes to equip us to accomplish his purposes. He gives some great physical strength and athletic ability. Others get mental prowess to invent, teach, learn, and excel in these areas. It is amazing to see so much talent in this world.

We all have different thresholds of strength and weakness, pain and suffering. We can take heart in knowing that God delights in providing strength to cover our weakness.

How comforting it is that the God who created us and knows our every weakness has promised that He will never allow any more pain and suffering than he has equipped us to bear without providing His strength to endure it or a means of escape.

"I have told you these things, so that in me you may have peace. In this world you will have trouble. But take heart! I have overcome the world." John 16:33 NIV

In my own weaknesses, I stand amazed at the strength, courage and grace with which so many seem to be able to go through suffering that I hate to think having to go through. How comforting to know that my custom built pain and suffering will never be more than I can endure or escape with God's help.

Father, thank you for sparing me from more pain and suffering than you know I could bear. In Jesus' name, Amen

EPS

" Be glad in the Lord and rejoice, you [uncompromisingly] righteous [you who are upright and in **right standing** with Him]; shout for joy, all you upright in heart!" Psalm 32:10-11

For You, Lord, will bless the [uncompromisingly] righteous [him who is upright and in right standing with You]; as with a shield You will surround him with goodwill (pleasure and favor)."
Psalm 5:11-12" AMP

GPS systems can show you how to get anywhere except heaven or hell, if you learn to use them. The satellite maps anywhere in the world bring a bird's eye view to your smart phone or computer.

It is remarkable that people spend so much money trying to find their way everywhere except to the ultimate destinations of us all.

Our God is an equal opportunity God and He gives everyone the free choice of where they want to spend the thousands of years of their eternal life.

God provides His own version of GPS which I like to call EPS for Eternal Position System. EPS (also known as Christianity) can pinpoint sure routes to either heaven or hell.

How anyone would freely choose to go to a place of eternal torment is beyond my understanding. The ruler of darkness has done a great job of infecting millions with spiritual blindness in which there is no hope except for life to only get worse in the here and now and in the hereafter.

Once any one chooses to open the door of faith when Jesus' comes knocking, they immediately position themselves as children of God. He no longer sees us as sinners, but as saints clothed in the righteousness of Christ.

"[All] are justified and made upright and in right standing with God, freely and gratuitously by His grace (His unmerited favor and mercy), through the redemption which is [provided] in Christ Jesus,"
Romans 3:23-25

God also positions the Holy Spirit into our hearts to see that - although we may occasionally take some wrong terms and lose our way – we will reach our heavenly home when we die, and enjoy the abundant life that can only be found in God's grace will we live on this earth.

God's EPS system comes complete with detailed instructions to keep us positioned for eternal love, joy, peace and security. You can find out more at millions of EPS branches around the world.

Father, let me never go anywhere without my EPS. In Jesus' name, Amen.

Painting Inside the Lines

"For I know the plans I have for you," says the Lord. "They are plans for good and not for disaster, to give you a future and a hope".
Jeremiah 29:11 NLT

"Paint by numbers" art was a big hit for many years. As long as you put the right color inside the lines, you painted a nice picture.

"The lines have fallen for me in pleasant places; yes, I have a good heritage.
Psalm 16:6 AMP

Painting inside the lines is often the key to success in any organizational structure. There are always written and unwritten lines of acceptable conduct.

Board and committee members who undermine, second guess, and criticize the actions of the committee and boards are painting outside the lines and will seldom be successful.

Scripture warns us to discipline "*those who cause divisions among you*" While it is sometimes necessary to go against the flow and not compromise principles or Scripture, members of the body should always seek to have no divisions among members of the body.

When a spouse paints outside the lines by flirting or consorting with someone else the results can be painful and disastrous for a lot of people.

We seem to have a whole generation painting outside the lines by redefining acceptable standards of conduct according to man's standards instead of God's.

We should always keep in mind that God has printed boundary lines for our good and His glory. God has not drawn lines to hurt us, but to help us enjoy the abundant life Christ died to give all who would call upon His name and be saved.

We keep getting reports on your steady faith in Christ, our Jesus, and the love you continuously extend to all Christians. The lines of purpose in your lives never grow slack, tightly tied as they are to your future in heaven, kept taut by hope.
Colossians 1:3 MSG

When our life's picture is completed, may it show that we painted it inside the lines of God's will and purpose for our lives.

Father, help me to enjoy the abundant life by painting inside the lines of your perfect will and pleasure. In Jesus name, Amen

What's Your Weakly Offering?

" What can I give back to GOD for the blessings he's poured out on me?"
Psalm 116:12 MSG

We generally think of our offering in terms of how much money we contribute to the Lord's work every week, and if statistics that show that the average Christian gives less than 3% of a tithe are correct, we are generally giving very weakly.

"My sacrifice, O God, is[b]a broken spirit; a broken and contrite heart you, God, will not despise."
Psalm 51:17 NIV

As important as our giving is, God says that our being is even more important. We are no longer required to offer a sacrifice but rather to be one by the washing of regeneration through the blood of Jesus.

When we become a sacrifice by offering ourselves to the Lord by the power of the Holy Spirit, we are going to become true disciples of Jesus Christ by experiencing holy transformation through the daily renewing of our minds in subjection to God's will and purposes.

Being involves making the Kingdom of God first in our lives, and seeking it in every area of our lives. Our God is a jealous God, and he deserves our stongest and best instead of our weakest and worst.

As we become more and more like Jesus by giving more and more of ourselves to the control of the Holy Spirit, we are going to become and accomplish all that God has created us and purposed to be.

So here's what I want you to do, God helping you: Take your everyday, ordinary life—your sleeping, eating, going-to-work, and walking-around life— a"Meanwhile, live in such a way that you are a credit to the Message of Christ."
Philippians 1:27a MSG

We need to take a daily inventory of what we are surrendering to be an offering this day. It may be surrendering our pride, lust, ego, or envy, or our time, treasures, or talents, but knowing that these are the sacrifices with which the Lord is well pleased should encourage us all to seek the Holy Spirit's help in giving up what we cannot give up on our own.

Father, keep me ever mindful of what I am gaining instead of giving up as I live to become a living sacrifice to You. In Jesus' name, Amen

103

Do You Have a Credit Problem?
"If you live upright and well, you get the credit; if you live a wicked life, you're guilty as charged." Ezekiel 18:19b MSG

Maintaining a good credit rating has become increasingly difficult for more and more people during the financial

"And that was credited to him for righteousness (right doing and right standing with God) to all generations forever."
Psalm 106:31-AMP

turmoil of these times. Job loss, unexpected illness and other expenses, coupled with over spending have left millions on the verge of bankruptcy.

There is another type of credit that is much more important than finances. This kind of credit is not about owing or borrowing, but about giving and being. We should always be giving God credit for the great thing He has done for us in Christ, and we should always try to be a credit to His glory.

Obedient children are a credit to their parents. We hear a lot about people who are a credit to their family, school, team, club, community, company, or church.

Christians who not only "walk the walk" but "talk the talk" by living out their lives in thanksgiving and praise to God are a credit to Christ's church.

We are given credit for Christ's righteousness when our names are written in the Lamb's book of life. Although God forgives and forgets our sins, He never forgets any good thing we do to the praise of His Glory. What a great day that will be when Jesus judges what kind of credit

"Meanwhile, live in such a way that you are a credit to the Message of Christ."
Philippians 1:27a MSG

we have been to Him when He says "well done, thou good and faithful servant", at the final judgment and resurrection of the just.

This is why there is no higher calling than being a credit to Christ by living fruitful lives fully pleasing to Him.

Father, may I never be guilty of shaming your name. In Jesus' name, Amen

Our Sin Scanner
" Your eye is the lamp of your body; when your eye (your conscience) is sound and fulfilling its office, your whole body is full of light; but when it is not sound and is not fulfilling its office, your body is full of darkness."
Luke 11:34 AMP

Today's computers have sophisticated scanners to detect, block, and destroy or isolate viruses that come in to damage our programs and systems and even steal our identity.

"On a good day, enjoy yourself; On a bad day, examine your conscience. God arranges for both kinds of days So that we won't take anything for granted"
Ecclesiastes 7:14 MSG

God has given all who call upon His name our own personal scanner to identify, isolate, and dispose of our sins. It's called a conscience!

As our conscience scans our thoughts, words, and conduct, the alarm sounds and we are given the strength and privilege of righting any wrongs and removing the stains of sin through apology, repentance and restoration at God's throne of grace.

I personally prefer apology to confession because when we apologize we not only admit a sin, but express our sorrow for it. Repentance does not always come easy for some sins but we are promised God's forgiveness, strength, and grace when we are truly sorry.

To experience our computers working quicker and better after a virus has been removed is nothing compared to experiencing the renewing of our minds that gives restoration and peace when we unburden our consciences after our daily activities have been scanned and our failures identified.

"They show that the requirements of the law are written on their hearts, their consciences also bearing witness, and their thoughts sometimes accusing them and at other times even defending them.)"
Romans 2:15 NIV

Our consciences are continually growing as our knowledge of God's Word and our relationship with Jesus Christ grows. We will find more and more of the road dirt of life being scanned out and replaced by wanting to do and be more and more in Christ.

Father, help me to keep my sin scanner working better and better as I get to know You and your will better and better. In Jesus' name, Amen

Armed and Dangerous
"The night is far gone and the day is almost here. Let us then drop (fling away) the works and deeds of darkness and put on the [full] armor of light." Romans 13:12 AMP

The pilgrims who settled this country could never be considered armed and dangerous in the conventional sense, but they came armed and dangerous with faith and the power of God's Word.

> "The arrogant cannot stand in your presence. You hate all who do wrong;
> Psalm 5:5 NIV

The spiritual warfare being waged by the forces of evil against Christ and His Church is unrelenting and has been going on for centuries with no end in sight.

It started with casting doubt about what God really said and meant and continues as forces within and without Christ's church seek to discredit God's truth, character, power, and purposes.

God's truth is being replaced by relative truth in about every area of life. He is blamed for all calamities and the consequences of sins. He is being mocked as never before.

We can be sure that all of this comes as no surprise to God. He knew from the beginning that giving us free will would lead to free style sinning and demeaning His Holy Name.

How gracious and kind of God to give each of us our own personal arsenal to stand firm and be victorious on the battlefield of our soul. We are all armed and dangerous when we put on the full armor of God.

> Put on the full armor of God, so that you can take your stand against the devil's schemes."
> Ephesians 6:11 NIV

When we are armed with the helmet of salvation, sandals of peace, breastplate of righteousness, shield of faith and sword of the spirit we can stand firm. Even the devil and forces of evil will flee when we wear the full armor of God.

The full armor of God is able to turn that roaring lion into a meowing pussy cat. We dare not leave home without it.

Father, help me to keep my guard up and my armor on until I am safely at home in heaven with you. In Jesus' name, Amen

Conflicted

"For the flesh desires what is contrary to the Spirit, and the Spirit what is contrary to the flesh. They are in conflict with each other, so that you are not to do whatever you want." Galatians 5:17 NIV

The conflict of being tossed about by doubt is also known as worry. In its worst stages, it's also known as depression. From Scripture's perspective it is a sin, and at some time we are all guilty.

"Hatred stirs up conflict, but love covers over all wrongs." Proverbs 10:12 NIV

The devil sometimes uses conflicts with people, emotions, and faith to bring out our worst while God uses them to bring out His best.

Conflicted relationships run the gamut from love to hate. God's command to forgive and be reconciled falls on deaf ears as we lash out in anger and pride and try to prove that we are right.

The ongoing battle between our flesh and our spirit in the bodies we co-inhabit often find us conflicted and diseased in an emotional roller coaster that often leads where we should not go.

With all of the false teachings by Christians, secular humanists, agnostics, atheists, and believers in other religions abounding and being promoted in the media and from some pulpits, it is no wonder that Christ's church is probably more conflicted than it has ever been.

Worship wars, conflicts over fornication, homosexuality, abortion, same sex marriages, and scriptural inerrancy abound. Our own conflict between believing what the Bible says and living in selective disobedience to it is prevalent.

"Let him search for peace (harmony; undisturbedness from fears, agitating passions, and moral conflicts) and seek it eagerly. [Do not merely desire peaceful relations with God, with your fellowmen, and with yourself, but pursue, go after them!] 1 Peter 3:11 AMP

We need to understand that a spiritual battle rages, and although the war has been won for us by Jesus' death on the cross, we need to trust and obey and pray for the amazing grace of God to lead us into His all surpassing peace.

Father,. Your grace has brought me safe this far, May you lead me safely home. In Jesus' name, Amen

Learning to Lean

"And they who know Your name [who have experience and acquaintance with Your mercy] will lean on and confidently put their trust in You, for You, Lord, have not forsaken those who seek (inquire of and for) You [on the authority of God's Word and the right of their necessity]." Psalm 9:10 AMP

Leaning into the wind is one of the best ways to keep from getting blown away. It is amazing that a slight degree in the angle of our stance can make so much difference in withstanding the force of the wind.

"Trust in the LORD with all your heart, And lean not on your own understanding; Proverbs 3:5 NIV

We are born leaning towards the natural tendency of our sin nature. When we learn by faith to lean upon the all sufficient grace of God we are able to withstand or escape the temptations that blow our way on a regular basis.

When we start leaning on God instead of our own understanding, we receive transforming power from the Holy Spirit that conforms us into the image of Christ and opens the door to the abundant life He died to give all who worship Him in spirit and in truth.

The more we lean on God, the more patience, love,joy, faithfulness, gentleness, and self control we will have to bear to others.

As we learn to lean on God by the daily renewing of our minds, we become more usable and more blessable. As our leaning leads to abiding, we experience the blessings of of Jesus' friendship, joy, and more being and receiving more answered prayers.

'For we have heard of your faith in Christ Jesus [the leaning of your entire human personality on Him in absolute trust and confidence in His power, wisdom, and goodness] and of the love which you [have and show] for all the saints (God's consecrated ones), Colossians 1:2 AMP

When we learn to lean we will no longer be blown to and fro by every conflict and doubt but stand firm and stand tall as one of the much loved and most favored sons or daughters of the living Lord.

Lord help me to keep learning to lean more and more on you in every area of my life. In Jesus' name, Amen

Whose Answered Prayer Are You?

"While you also cooperate by your prayers for us [helping and laboring together with us]. Thus [the lips of] many persons [turned toward God will eventually] give thanks on our behalf for the grace (the blessing of deliverance) granted us at the request of the many who have prayed."
2 Corinthians 1:11 AMP

Answered Prayers are some of the greatest blessings any believer can experience. The privilege of being able to take our needs and concerns to the Lord in prayer is one of our greatest blessings as children of God. To know that God hears and answers our prayers that are in conformity with His will and prayed in the name of Jesus should give us confidence in praying.

"I've thrown myself headlong into your arms— I'm celebrating your rescue. I'm singing at the top of my lungs, I'm so full of answered prayers Psalm 13:5 MSG

Many of us have received eternal life as answered prayers to others. As blessed as we may be to receive an answered prayer, we should never lose sight of the fact that we can be even more blessed by being an answered prayer.

God probably answers more prayers through people than any other means. When we ask God to be an answered prayer to someone, we can confidently start looking and experience the sacred delight of being God's answered prayer.

The Answered Prayer
"Most assuredly, I say to you, he who believes in Me, the works that I do he will do also; and greater *works* than these he will do, because I go to My Father. 13 And whatever you ask in My name, that I will do, that the Father may be glorified in the Son. 14 If you ask[c] anything in My name, I will do *it.*"
John 10:12,13 NKJV

I pray every day that the Lord will use me and let me be a blessing to someone, and often hear from people who read these devotions how a particular one has blessed them, and thank God for using me to be an answered prayer in this way.

My bride of 59 years has been my biggest answered prayers, second only to Jesus becoming the Lord of my life, and I know that I am a big answered prayer to her. The more we abide in Christ and His Word, not only the more answered prayers we will receive, but the more answered prayers we will become.

Father, help me to be an answered prayer for someone today. In Jesus' name, Amen

109

God's Credibility

"Yours, O LORD, is the kingdom; you are exalted as head over all."
1 Chronicles 29:11b NIV

God's credibility is about His power to inspire belief in the minds and hearts of His children. His credibility as all powerful, all knowing, ever present, and ever good God and Creator of the universe is on the wane throughout most of the world.

"And do not forget the things I have done throughout history. For I am God – I alone! I am God, and there is no one else like me. "
Isaiah 46:9 NIV

The world and the deceiver of our souls has done a good job of creating doubt as to what part of Scripture is true, and supplanting rock solid truths of God with the relative truth of a man made secular human religion or no religion at all.

The devil caused Eve to doubt God meant what he said when he forbid partaking of the tree of good and evil and he continues to try to make us doubt the same way today.

Casting doubt on God's power, omniscience, goodness, and His Word has always been the favorite ploy of the devil and the devil's advocates who promote beliefs and conduct contrary to the revealed commands of God.

God's divine attributes and character have been validated through the ages and never proven false. There are some things about God and His higher ways we are never going to fully understand this side of heaven, but that in no way means they are not true.

"but now revealed and made known through the prophetic writings by the command of the eternal God, so that all the Gentiles might come to the obedience that comes from faith—"
Romans 16:26 NIV

Above all, we need to believe in God and what He stands for so that we do not fall for anything that the world, our flesh, or the devil might use to impugn God's credibility and create doubt within us.

"Father, thank you for revealing yourself to me in all of your fullness and protect me from all doubt and disobedience by the strength and power of Your Word and the Holy Spirit. In Jesus' name, Amen

How's Your Credibility?

"Leaders who know their business and care keep a sharp eye out for the shoddy and cheap, For who among us can be trusted to be always diligent and honest?" Proverbs 20:8 MSG

> **"Trustworthy messengers refresh like snow in summer. They revive the spirit of their employer."**
> **Proverbs 25:13 NLT**

Having others believe in us is a blessing we should all seek. Doing what we say we will do when we say we will do it is not too much for anyone to ask of us, and yet we sometimes fail in both counts and lose our credibility.

Politicians all too ofen lose the credibility that got them elected by their conduct once they get in office.

I have a good friend that I have had to set a time a half hour before I really wanted to meet so that he would be there on time.

Our actions speak much louder than our words, and is a real test of our credibility. Saying what we believe and not living like it really gives the cause of Christ a bad name and makes our testimony lose credibility.

While credibility is a character trait we should seek to develop and maintain with others, it is even more important that we seek to develop and maintain it with God.

There are a lot of people God has blessed financially but they have proven that God could not trust them with money as they have wasted it on selfish wants and have not been generous to God or to others.

God has poured out His love and goodness upon us and we have responded by pouring out our love on the pleasures and things of this world and put these things above God.

There are other blessings God is waiting to pour out upon us as soon as we establish better credibility with Him by trusting and obeying Him in every area of our life.

> **"But there's far more to him than popularity. He's rock-solid trustworthy"**
> **2 Corinthians 10:18 MSG**

Lord may my credibility with you grow as I grow in your grace by growing in my relationship with Jesus. In Jesus' name, Amen

No Better Dwelling Place
"How lovely is your dwelling place, LORD Almighty!" Psalm 89:1 NIV

When God moved His earthly dwelling place from the Temple into the hearts of men when Jesus won our victory over sin and death on the cross, He gave us a new dwelling place.

My people will dwell in a peaceful habitation,In secure dwellings, and in quiet resting places,"
Isaiah 32:18 NKJV

No longer do we have to dwell on our past or stay in bondage to sin, death, and the devil. We are free to enjoy an abundant new life in Christ and to enjoy Jesus' friendship, joy, and love when we allow the Holy Spirit to come into our hearts.

When we allow the Holy Spirit to conrol our hearts, He begins the work of holy transformation by renewing our minds to make us more like Christ in the ongoing process of sanctification.

We begin to dwell more and more on God's love and abide more and more in Christ. As we get to know Him better by abiding in His Word, we grow in our friendship with Him and experience more and more of His joy, and the other blessings of dwelling or abiding.

That any of us would choose to lose the blessings of having the Holy Spirit's indwelling power and presence controlling us by continuing to dwell controlled by our own flesh should be a great cause for sorrow and mourning.

There is nothing excellent about dwelling in a cesspool of sin and all of the consequences that will follow in this life or the next. The judgment of God is upon us all, and we dare not face it without being covered by the righteousness of Christ.

"Jesus answered, If a person [really] loves Me, he will keep My word [obey My teaching]; and My Father will love him, and We will come to him and make Our home (abode, special dwelling place) with him
John 14:23 AMP

May we all come to know how excellent the dwelling place of God is now and forever.

Father, keep me ever mindful of and rejoicing in the excellence of your dwelling place. In Jesus' name, Amen

Something God Can't Do

"Whoever receives His testimony has set his seal of approval to this: God is true. [That man has definitely certified, acknowledged, declared once and for all, and is himself assured that it is divine truth that God cannot lie]"
John 3:33 AMP

Through all the turmoil, troubles, and disappointments of life there is a great truth that we need to appropriate if we are to

"I have sworn an oath to David, and in my holiness I cannot lie:"
Psalm 89:35 NLT

enjoy life to the fullest. To know that it is impossible for God to lie should preempt our fears and worries and strengthen us when the going gets rough.

How encouraging it should be for all of us to know that the all powerful, all knowing, ever present and ever loving God of the universe who cannot lie tells us that He is with us always, that He will never forsake us, and that He is working all things for our good.

To have the unbreakable Word of our God who cannot lie that He remembers our sins no more, will never allow us to be tempted beyond what we can handle with His help, and that He has plans to bless us, not harm us should help us through any times of doubt or depression.

The more we think about God's inability to lie, the more excited we should get about getting into and growing in His Word and appropriate His truths into our every day lives.

How can we help but want to abide in Him when He promises His friendship, joy, love, and answered prayers?

Before we get carried away with all the good things God promises to those who trust and obey, we also need to know that God is not lying about the consequences of sin and misery awaiting those who reject God's wonderful offer of eternal life or disobey His commandments.

" God has given us both his promise and his oath. These two things are unchangeable because it is impossible for God to lie"
Hebrews 6:18a AMP

The sooner we surrender control of our lives to the Lordship of Jesus Christ, the more we will appreciate and enjoy the blessings and truths of our God who cannot lie.

Father, I believe, help my unbelief. In Jesus' name, Amen

The Testings of Life

"He tests the good and the bad alike; if anyone cheats, God's outraged. Fail the test and you're out, out in a hail of firestones, Drinking from a canteen filled with hot desert wind'." Psalm 11:4b MSG

Being conformed into the image of Christ is an ongoing process that begins the hour we first believed and continues until we are glorified with Christ in heaven.

"Investigate my life, O God, find out everything about me; Cross-examine and test me, get a clear picture of what I'm about; See for yourself whether I've done anything wrong— then guide me on the road to eternal life "
Psalm 139:23 MSG

God knows our hearts, and everything we will do before we do it. He still lovingly allows pain suffering and other challenges to squeeze our comfort zones as part of His refining or sanctification process to make us holy in actuality as we were made holy theologically when we were made righteous in God's eyes by the blood of Jesus.

God knows our every weakness, and we should all continually thank and praise Him that He accepts and loves us in spite of them and cares enough to help us overcome them by the power of the Holy Spirit.He has even promised that He will allow no temptation to come our way that we cannot endure or escape with His help.

God will test our faith, our courage, love, commitment, obedience, patience, purity, self control, and every other character attribute and help us stand tall when we fall so short.

"Dear friends, don't be surprised at the fiery trials you are going through, as if something strange were happening to you."
1 Peter 4:12 NIV

It's not a matter of 'if " testings come. It's a matter of "when" they come and how to be ready for them.

Even when we learn to rejoice in our testings and receive that peace that surpasses all understanding, we need to remember that we may well fail some of the tests and must be prepared to persevere until God is satisfied.

Father, thank you for reminding me of your incredible love, grace, and mercy you have poured out upon me to sustain me through my testings. In Jesus' name, Amen

Terms and Conditions

"Then God said to Abraham, "Your responsibility is to obey the terms of the covenant. You and all your descendants have this continual responsibility" Genesis 17:9 NLT

Everyone who has or has used a computer has had to check that they have read and accept the terms and conditions for gaining access to some web sites, or for downloading some program or feature.

For the Lord will judge and vindicate His people, and He will delay His judgments [manifesting His righteousness and mercy] and take into favor His servants [those who meet His terms of separation unto Him]. Psalm 135:14 AMP

It may do us all well to read and accept God's terms and conditions for eternal and abundant life.

God forgives all who confess and repent in the name of Jesus. This forgiveness that gives eternal life is not based on what we have done, but on the unconditional love of God expressed through the death of Jesus on the Cross for these sins.

Although our salvation is not based on our performance much of the abundance of God's grace and many of His blessings are based upon our obedience to His commands.

These obedience based terms and conditions basically come down to how well we live like Christians once we believe.

Do we seek to be filled by the Holy Spirit by surrendering our lives to the Lordship of Jesus Christ, and bearing the fruit of the Spirit, or do we insist on living self centered lives bearing the pride, anger, envy, and lust of the flesh?

"But for you who welcome him, in whom he dwells—even though you still experience all the limitations of sin— you yourself experience life on God's terms" Romans 8:9b MSG."

When we fail to learn and obey the clear teachings of Scripture we are going to miss out on God's best promised and reserved for those who trust and obey.

Father, by the power of the Holy Spirit, help me to live my life according to your terms instead of mine. In Jesus' name, Amen.

Free Home Delivery

"The spacious, free life is from God, it's also protected and safe. God-strengthened, we're delivered from evil— when we run to him, he saves us."
Psalm 37:39 MSG

" He who sends a message by the hand of a fool cuts off the feet [of satisfactory delivery] and drinks the damage."
Proverbs 26:6 AMP

There are getting to be fewer and fewer of us who remember the good old days of free home delivery. Milk, bread, and dry cleaning routes thrived.You could even call up your neighborhood grocer or midwife and get it delivered.

There are still a lot of deliveries going on in an amazingly efficient system of stocking grocery shelves with fresh milk, produce and fruit from around the world.

It isn't free, but you can actually get a letter or package delivered any where in the world within 24 hours.

God has some great free home delivery services available to all who call upon His name. He has a band of angels and willing workers through which He delivers strength in times of weakness, healing in times of illness, help in times of trouble, provision in times of need, forgiveness in times of repentance, and comfort in times of sadness.

God has a whole lot more miracles, grace and blessings to deliver than He has obedient, willing drivers to deliver them through.. He continues to search to and fro for people who will say."here I am send me." Unfortunately the deceiver of our souls sometimes seems to have more delivery agents than God.

God calls us all to join in delivering the Good News of salvation through faith in Jesus Christ to our friends and neighbors and people in our local, national, and global communities throughout the world.

"and he has identified us as his own by placing the Holy Spirit in our hearts as the first installment that guarantees everything he has promised us."
1 Cointhians 122 NLT

The best free home delivery ever offered was Jesus promise to send to us the Holy Spirit as our heavenly Fed X carrier to deliver us safely home to heaven when we put our trust in Him. He comes as a deposit and with a guarantee of what He has promised.

Father, help me not only to be delivered, but also to deliver your love, grace, and mercy to others. In Jesus' name, Amen

The Big Roll Over

"Oh, that you had listened to my commands! Then you would have had peace flowing like a gentle river and righteousness rolling over you like waves in the sea." Isaiah 48:18 NLT

"He'll take over the running of the world. His names will be: Amazing Counselor, Strong God, Eternal Father, Prince of Wholeness. "
Isaiah 9:3 MSG

From finances to car wrecks to computer lingo, roll over has become a popular topic. Movies have been made and songs written about rolling over. We have read and even been instructed to roll over and play dead in some situations.

From a spiritual perspective rolling over from death to life is the greatest thing that can happen to anyone. When we answer God's call to eternal life when it comes by the power of the Holy Spirit, we roll over from wandering aimlessly lost to living a life filled with meaning, and joy.

We roll over from bondage to sin to freedom to righteousness and find our real joy in living fruitful lives fully pleasing to God as He sends the Holy Spirit to take control and produce the fruits of love, joy, peace, patience, kindness and self control in us.

When we start paying as much attention to our ERA (eternal retirement account) as we do to or IRA (individual retirement account)we will seek ways to store up more treasures in heaven by making more deposits in our righteousness account down here.

We can never earn our big rollover down here. It is a free gift of God's love, grace, and mercy in coming to die as Jesus Christ to earn it for us. We can only show our appreciation by trying to please Him by becoming more like Christ every day of our lives.

While we need to always remember is that while we cannot earn our way to heaven, we should also remember the many promises of Scripture regarding rewards in heaven that we earn from the good works we do here below.

"But thank God! He gives us victory over sin and death through our Lord Jesus Christ.
1 Corinthians 15:57 NLT

May we all go to heaven with a fully funded eternal retirement account that we can roll over into the currency of heaven.

Father, thank you for giving me the big rollover into my abundant life in Christ. In Jesus' name, Amen

117

MECOMP

"You're blessed when you can show people how to cooperate instead
of compete or fight. That's when you discover who you really are, and your
place in God's family" Matthew 5:9 MSG

**"⁴Whoever is simple
(easily led astray and
wavering), let him turn
in here! As for him who
lacks understanding,
[God's] Wisdom says to
him,"
Proverbs 9:4 AMP**

Competition is what makes our economic, relational, and vocational
lives thrive. Every successful endeavor seeks to
Meet Competition.

From automobiles to cell phones there is
intense competition to get there first with the most.

Maybe its because the devil is more
wordly minded, or that the church is too heavenly
minded, but the sad truth is that most churches are
not meeting the competition in today's world.

Too many churches are being built at the
expense of other churches. We now have thousands of denominations
competing with each other for the hearts of believers, instead of competing
with the world, flesh, and devil in seeking and saving the lost.

Although salvation and eternal life are the greatest pleasures,
happenings, and life enrichment experiences ever offered, The world
is making beer, movies, and sex and physical beauty, and the wisdom of man
counterfeit substitutes for the real thing.

Boring sermons, uninspired and
uninspiring worship, hypocrisy of pastors,
priests, and members alike, doctrinal wars, and
casual Christianity have too often neutered the
excitement and enthusiasm for finding and
proclaiming the only real security, peace and
joy that can only be found in the living Lord.

"Because of our faith, Christ
has brought us into this place
of undeserved privilege where
we now stand, and we
confidently and joyfully look
forward to sharing God's
glory"
Romans 5:2 NLT

Although the war was won on the
cross, we are in a battle for the souls of all people, and we all must do a
better job of MECOMP.

*Father, help me to be an authentic contagious Christian who You can use
to meet and beat the competition for the souls of the lost. In Jesus' name,
Amen*

Deal Breakers

"I will sing to the Lord, because He has dealt bountifully with me."
Psalm 13:6 AMP

'"For the mountains may move and the hills disappear, but even then my faithful love for you will remain. My covenant of blessing will never be broken,"says the LORD, who has mercy on you."
Isaiah 54:10 NLT

Every real estate broker or salesman has encountered some sort of deal breaker that kills a sale prior to closing. It may be a credit turndown, defective title, buyer's remorse, or failure to pass inspection, but it kills the deal.

Every business transaction and relationship can fall apart as the result of some sort of deal breaker.

Infidelity, financial irresponsibility, in-law problems and sexual incompatability are deal breakers that have ended marriages.

Disobedience and idolatry have been deal breakers with God. Down through the centuries through covenant after covenant, God made wonderful deals with His children based on their obedience only to have them broken.

God's New Covenant of grace is the greatest deal anyone is ever going to get. When we think about His wonderful gift of eternal life we are tempted to think that it is too good to be true.

We grow up being taught that there is no free lunch, and that we have to work for what we get. The , idea that someone would come down from on high, live a perfect life and die so that we could live forever is beyond all human understanding.

The fact that this gift is freely given to all who call upon the name of the Lord in true faith by the power of the Holy Spirit is amazing. The fact that the gift is irrevocable and guaranteed by the same Holy Spirit who calls us is astounding.

"God didn't put angels in charge of this business of salvation that we're dealing with here."
Hebrews 2:5a MSG

The only deal breakers to this wonderful offer are unbelief and unforgiveness which sometimes separates the truly saved from the unsaved, and from believers whose faith was too shallow to survive.

Lord, may unbelief or unforgiveness never become deal breakers in the wonderful faith based relationship I have with You In Jesus' name, Amen

The Challenge

"So, my dear brothers and sisters, be strong and immovable. Always work enthusiastically for the Lord, for you know that nothing you do for the Lord is ever useless." 1 Corinthians 15:58 NLT

Some of the most encouraging words I have heard in a long time came from my 6 year old grandson last week when he came to the breakfast table on Tuesday morning and said: "Tell me I'm not dreaming, that I really do get to go to vacation bible school again this morning"!

"What a joyful and enthusiastic procession as they enter the king's palace!"
Psalm 145:15 NLT

I don't know who wrote the content or executed the program, but I do know that they successfully met the challenge of what should be the goal of every church and Sunday school in the world today.

If we could all get up on Sunday mornings with enthusiasm and excitement for enjoying God at church and Sunday school we wouldn't be seeing more and more of the empty pews and chairs most are seeing too many of these days.

Worship has diminished as awareness of the presence of the living Lord has dulled through dull traditions and sermons, and lack of enthusiasm among worshippers and worship leaders alike. Even God would fall asleep in some of our churches.

Today's technology savvy and sophistically entertained youth too often find church and Sunday school boring and almost as bad as going to the dentist.

When we get as serious about making our churches and Sunday schools experiences we can't wait to get to and hate to leave as we are about raising money, seeking and saving the lost, or advancing political or denominational agendas, we might just bring back the the excitement of our romance with God back into the main stream of our Christ centered lives through living Christ centered contagious Christianity.

"I know your record and what you are doing; you are supposed to be alive, but [in reality] you are dead."
Revelation 1:3b AMP

Lord help us all to become contagious Christians conveying the blessings of our love, peace, and joy when we gather in your name. In Jesus' name, Amen

Hard Conformation

"[Suffering for Being a Christian] Dear friends, do not be surprised at the fiery ordeal that has come on you to test you, as though something strange were happening to you" 1 Peter 4:12 AMP

Romans 8:28 is probably at or near the top of everyone's favorite Bible verses. To know that God has promised to work all things for our good is one of the most reassuring truths we can learn.

"He was despised and rejected—a man of sorrows, acquainted with deepest grief.We turned our backs on him and looked the other way.He was despised, and we did not care."
Isaiah 53:3 AMP

When we fully understand and believe this truth we are fully armed for whatever the world, our flesh, or the devil can throw at us

The problem is in understanding in terms of what God considers good, or what we consider good.

Notwithstanding the fact that God wants us to be happy and loves to give good gifts to us, we need to understand that God wants us first of all to become like Christ and is committed to working all things for our good to accomplish this purpose.

When we think of being conformed into the image of Christ, we must never forget that Christ was a *"man of sorrow, acquainted with grief,* and we can expect to become the same as part of God's Holy Conformation godly character program.

Instead of being shocked or surprised and running out on God when pain and suffering come, we need to obey Scripture's exhortation to rejoice so that all surpassing peace will come along with God's all sufficient grace to strengthen and endure or way to escape.

"And if we are [His] children, then we are [His] heirs also: heirs of God and fellow heirs with Christ [sharing His inheritance with Him]; only we must share His suffering if we are to share His glory."
Romans 8:17 AMP

We can escape a lot of pain and suffering by proactively surrendering our will to the control of the Holy Spirit

Father, keep me ever mindful of the pain and suffering Jesus went through in dying for me as I struggle through my troubles in this life. In Jesus' name, Amen

121

The Prodigals
"Do not remember the rebellious sins of my youth. Remember me in the light of your unfailing love, for you are merciful, O Lord." Psalm 25:6

In many ways these are the best of times for young people. We are raising some of the smartest, best educated and overachieving young people in history.

Heaven forbid they should be like their parents, bullheaded and bad, A fickle and faithless bunch who never stayed true to God. Psalm 78:8 MSG

Unfortunately adolescent rebellion is alive and well. With parents being divorced, absent or presented as inept in so many TV sitcoms and movies no wonder it's getting worse.

Today's culture of entitlement, relative truth, and instant gratification has produced a generation of prodigals whose moral compass has been skewed and conduct conflicted by the absence of faith based morals. The spiritual future of our children looks dim indeed.

The problems of our children are probably some of the most painful experiences we will ever have. We can all find comfort and strength from the parable of the prodigal son and the faithfulness of God during those dark days of worry and concern.

Even God-fearing undivorced parents who have brought their children up in the fear and the admonition of the Lord are not spared the heartbreak of rebellious youth. The curse of sin can cause even the best to fall.

Parents need to look back on the worst of their adolescent behavior and remember that as God was gracious and merciful to us, He can and will also be merciful and gracious to our prodigal children.

"I will arise and go to my father, and will say to him, "Father, I have sinned against heaven and before you" Luke 15:18 NKJV

How good it is to know that God is still in control and His arms are never too short to embrace, forgive, renew, and restore the worst of sinners, young or old.

We need to thank Him daily from having spared us and our children from even worse consequences as He continues to perfect His strength in our weaknesses.

Father, thank you for covering us by your grace. In Jesus' name, Amen

Minimum Compliance

"I wrote to you as I did to test you and see if you would fully comply with my instructions." 2 Corinthians 2:8-10 NLT

There is a lot of compliance required in business, travel, homes, military, construction, etc. Detailed regulations abound and often spell out in detail what is required for compliance. Often there are ideal and minimum compliance requirements.

Seek the Lord [inquire for Him, inquire of Him, and require Him as the foremost necessity of your life], all you humble of the land who have acted in compliance with His revealed will and have kept His commandments; seek righteousness, seek humility [inquire for them, require them as vital]. It may be you will be hidden in the day of the Lord's anger.
Zephaniah 2:2 AMP

One of the biggest problems with "cheap grace" is that it misleads people into settling for the minimum blessings of their faith instead of the abundant life that Jesus came to give all who believe in Him.

Eternal life is a free gift of grace given to all who accept Jesus Christ as Savior. It is not merely a "get out of jail" card to get us into heaven when we die. Eternal life begins the instant we believe and the abundance of God's grace becomes available every day of life on this earth.

This raises the question of whether we want to live the abundant life with maximum blessings or the life with minimum blessings.

It is interesting to note how often those who say that they don't have to go to church, Bible study, or give their money are really saying that they don't want to.

The call to salvation is a call to bearing the fruit of repentance the fruit of righteousness which is the evidence that we are really saved.

furing the
I write to you
[perfectly] confident
of your obedient
compliance, knowing
that you will do even
more than I ask.
Philemon 1:21 AMP

In view of the great price Jesus paid for our salvation we should live to show our true appreciation by complying with God's commands to love Him and others, and to make disciples.

We should never devalue the amazing and generous grace of God by minimum compliance with the way He taught us to live.

Father, help me to seek to always do more to thank and glorify you, and never less. In Jesus' name, Amen.

Desertion, Desertion

"Enjoy the wife you married as a young man! Lovely as an angel, beautiful as a rose— never quit taking delight in her be body. Never take her love for granted!" Proverbs 5:16,19 MSG

Marriage is a growing relationship that requires spouses to grow together to keep from growing apart. Desertion of every kind should be avoided.

Emotional, Intellectual, recreational, and spiritual desertions probably cause or precede more divorces or relational breakups than physical desertion.

When one spouse deserts the other by emotionally tuning them out and fails to communicate, problems are sure to follow.

Because God was there as a witness when you spoke your marriage vows to your young bride, and now you've broken those vows, broken the faith-bond with your vowed companion, your covenant wife. God, not you, made marriage. His Spirit inhabits even the smallest details of marriage.
Malachi 2:13b MSG

Outgrowing a spouse intellectually seems to happen more and more as people pursue careers and enlarge their territories and areas of interest.

Recreational desertion may be more widespread than we think. When either spouse's passion for a sport, hobby, or recreational pursuit exceeds their passion for their marriage and family, there are going to be problems.

Spiritual desertion can be a big problem in many marriages. When men desert their responsibility for their children's spiritual welfare and leave it up to their wives or the world's wicked way there may be Hell to pay for the guilty and innocent alike.

"And because of this, a man leaves father and mother and is firmly bonded to his wife, becoming one flesh—no longer two bodies but one. Because God created this organic union of the two sexes, no one should desecrate his art by cutting them apart."
Matthew 19:3b MSG

Our oneness in marriage should not rule out pursuing any other interests, but it does mean that we should not pursue any other interest to the point that it rules over our marriage.

Father help me stay connected physically, emotionally,recreationally and spiritually with the love of my life. In Jesus' name, Amen.

When Greed is Good

Are you going to continue this craziness? For only crazy people would think they could complete by their own efforts what was begun by God. If you weren't smart or strong to begin it, how do you suppose you could perfect it? Galatians 3:3 MSG

When any greedy person is asked: "how much is enough"? the answer most often heard involves meaning: "just a little bit more"!

Who can list the glorious miracles of the LORD? Who can ever praise him half Enough"? Psalm 106:2 NLT

I would like to suggest that there is only one really good motivation for greed, and this is for: "just a little bit more of Jesus"!

Too many people are getting robbed blind by the deceiver of their souls making them believe that "just enough to get to heaven when I die", is getting enough of Jesus.

As wonderful as this gift of eternal life is, it doesn't do a whole lot to give the abundant life on this earth God wants to give us.

When we stop short of being transformed by the renewing of our minds and seek to know better, become more like, and get more of the love, grace and mercy of God through a living faith in Jesus Christ every day of our lives, we are short changing ourselves, and robbing a lot of others we love of blessings we can't give if we don't have.

God has promised to always give us not just a little bit more, but all of the grace we will need to help us escape any temptation.

As we get more and more of Jesus we are promised more and more of His joy, His friendship, answered prayers that are ours through abiding in Jesus and His Word.

"So I tell you, don't worry about everyday life – whether you have food, drink, and clothes. Doesn't life consist of more than food and clothing?" Matthew 6:35

As amazing as God is and as amazed as we are at His loving and blessing us in spite of our sins, we must never forget that a lot of His blessings are conditional on our blessability.

Is it time for you to get greedy for Jesus?

Father, help me to hunger and thirst for your righteousness all the days of my life. In Jesus' name, Amen

Seeking God's Pleasure

"Carefully determine what pleases the Lord. Take no part in the worthless deeds of evil and darkness; instead, expose them" Ephesians 5:10 NLT
.

Jesus Christ did not just come to earth as God to die for us. He came to show us how to live a God pleasing life. He said that He always did what pleased His father. God said that this was His beloved Son in whom He was well pleased.

> "And now, Israel, what does the Lord your God require of you? He requires only that you fear the Lord your God, and live in a way that pleases him, and love him and serve him with all your heart and soul."
> Deuteronomy 10:12 NIV

Most of us start out life wanting to please our fathers and seek to imitate and respect them until adolescent rebellion sets in.

As parents, we do our children no favors by becoming preoccupied with wanting them to be happy instead of holy.

Trying to shower them with all the material things we didn't have as children and modeling the love of the world, the flesh, and the devil will never bring them up in the fear and admonition of the Lord from which they will not depart when they grow older.

If our children do not learn God pleasing behavior and faith at home, where are they going to learn it? It certainly isn't being modeled or taught in a vast majority of our schools and a once a week dose at Sunday School is barely better than nothing.

How sad it is that we too often become preoccupied with wanting our children to have all of the material things we never had, and pay so little attention to wanting them to have the faith we have and the peace,joy and security, of our salvation.

> "Everything that goes into a life of pleasing God has been miraculously given to us by getting to know, personally and intimately, the One who invited us to God".
> 1 Peter 1:3 MSG

We are into our second generation of covenant breakers robbing our children and children's children of their birth right of blessings that can only be found through a right relationship with Jesus.

Father, work in the hearts of our children that they come to know and love you. In Jesus' name, Amen

How to Raise Your Standard of Living

" I will deal with them according to their conduct, and by their own standards I will judge them. "'Then they will know that I am the LORD.'"
Ezekiel 7:27b NIV

The level of material comfort as measured by the goods, services, and luxuries available to an individual, group, or nation is used to measure the standard of living for that country.

"False weights and unequal measures the LORD detests double standards of every kind" Proverbs 20:10 NLT

From this perspective, most of us are doing very well. We have more labor saving devices, more leisure time, and more "toys" than ever before. Even the poorest among us materially are in the upper 10% of the world's population.

We all want our children to have a better standard of living than we have, but unfortunately don't know what the real standard of living should be. The real standard of living should be measured by the standard of giving with which we use our time, talents, and treasures. A lot of us professing Christians would probably be in the lower 10% if measured by this standard.

God's standard of giving starts with the minimum 10% and goes up from there. When we short change God in the area of giving money, time, or talents we are lowering our standard of living to the standards of the world.

So that the righteous and just requirement of the Law might be fully met in us who live and move not in the ways of the flesh but in the ways of the Spirit [our lives governed not by the standards and according to the dictates of the flesh, but controlled by the Holy Spirit]. Romans 8:3-5 AMP

God raised His standard of giving to new heights of glory by giving His life for us on the Cross of Calvary. In light of this, should we not seek to raise our standard of giving by living to please and serve Him with the time, talents, and resources he has provided?

Father, help me to raise my standard of giving love to you and to others. In Jesus' name, Amen

A Recipe for Living

"And know this day--for I am not speaking to your children who have not [personally] known and seen it--the instruction and discipline of the Lord your God: His greatness, His mighty hand, and His outstretched arm;" Deuteronomy 11:1-3 AMP

We grow in our relationship with Christ by getting to know Him better and better through His Word. The life long process of being conformed to His image goes on right up until we see Him face to face.

"He must always keep that copy with him and read it daily as long as he lives. That way he will learn to fear the Lord his God by obeying all the terms of these instructions and decrees." Deuteronomy 17:18-20 NLT

It is often more meaningful to think of apologizing instead of confessing. Confessing reflects admitting, while apologizing reflects not only admitting but also being sorry for what we have or have not done.

We need to start every day asking God to help us have less to apologize for and more to appreciate. As we add this request to our prayer that God will help us guard our heart, thoughts, tongue, and conduct, we can be confident that God will answer this prayer because this is in accordance with His will.

We will discover that the more we abide in Christ, the more like Him we will become, and our spiritual growth index will get higher and higher as we appropriate more and more of His teachings and examples into our every day life.

The more intentional we become about wanting to have less to apologize for, the more the Holy Spirit will help us head off the sinful thoughts before they take root in our hearts. We will find it easier and easier to simply just not "go there".

Do not conform to the pattern of this world, but be transformed by the renewing of your mind. Then you will be able to test and approve what God's will is—his good, pleasing and perfect will." Romans 12:2 NIV

When we choose not to "go there" and focus our hearts and minds on appreciating God's love and blessings, we are going the discover the real joy of our salvation.

Father help me to remember to apologize and appreciate daily.In Jesus' name, Amen.

Watch Out for Those Side Effects

"A prudent person foresees danger and takes precautions. The simpleton goes blindly on and suffers the consequences." Proverbs 27:11-13 NLT

Of the billions of dollars spent advertising prescription drugs about half the money is spent announcing the possible side effects.

> **"Because they've practiced their blasphemous worship, mocking me at their hillside shrines, I'll let loose the consequences and pay them in full for their actions.**
> **Isaiah 65:3 MSG**

I don't know about you, but I can't get too excited about running out to buy or to get a prescription for something that might cause me to faint, vomit, gain weight, become drowsy, keep me awake, or suffer any of the numerous possible side effects.

The cigarette ads have all virtually disappeared since no cigarette maker wants to mention that cigarette smoking might kill you.

I wonder how many beer commercials we would be watching if they had to include warnings against the side effects of arrest for drunk driving, car wrecks, or other consequences of drunkenness from drinking too much.

The Bible does a pretty good job of warning against the side effects of sin but the warnings seem to be going unheeded..

We seem to gloss over the depressing statistics for divorce, STD's, erosion of moral values, and many other side effects of living in sin in today's world.

> **God wasn't at all pleased; but he let them do it their way, worship every new god that came down the pike—and live with the consequences, consequences described by the prophet Amos:**
> **Acts 7:42 MSG**

The Gospel of Jesus Christ offers the only truly liberating life. Jesus Christ came to set us free from the bondage and guilt of sin and give us His all sufficient grace that allows us to trade our sorrows, wash away our sins, and live in the true peace and joy He died to give us. These are side effects worth seeking.

Lord, keep me ever mindful of the side effects of sin, and give me your all sufficient grace to avoid them by following your example how to live my life. In Jesus' name, Amen

Spiritual Obesity

"He went on: "What comes out of a person is what defiles them. For it is from within, out of a person's heart, that evil thoughts come—sexual immorality, theft, murder, adultery, greed, malice, deceit, lewdness, envy, slander, arrogance and folly. All these evils come from inside and defile a person." Luke 7:20 NLT

Even our government is waging war on obesity, and for good reason. The staggering costs of health care of illnesses and disabilities caused by over eating continue to mount.

"The LORD regretted that he had made human beings on the earth, and his heart was deeply troubled."
Genesis 6:6 NIV

As bad as physical obesity is, it doesn't even come close to the spiritual obesity of sin. Over sinning is the number one problem in the world today!

Ever since the fall of man in the Garden of Eden, man's propensity to exercise his free will to sin has broken God's heart, wrecked havoc in every heart, and been the root cause of all disease, suffering and death.

It was so bad thousands of years ago that God became sorry he ever created us. He destroyed the world and all of mankind except Noah and his family with a flood as a means of starting over.

Although God Himself came down and dwelt among us and fulfilled the righteousness demands of the law for us, Sin obesity continues to tax the very limits of God's grace right up to this very day.

How much longer God is going to put up with the obesity of sin among his followers and rejecters throughout the world is a question that has been asked down through the centuries, and being asked with greater urgency as the "over sinning" index continues to rise throughout the world.

"Therefore, get rid of all moral filth and the evil that is so prevalent and humbly accept the word planted in you, which can save you."
James 1:21 NLT

It's time we all stopped over eating from the tree of evil and started feeding more on the nourishing Word of God.

Father help me to overcome my besetting sins by helping me to guard my heart, my thoughts, my tongue and my conduct. In Jesus' name, Amen

Swallow Hard
"A man's wisdom gives him patience; it is to his glory to overlook an offense" Proverbs 19:11

We are sometimes going to have "hard to swallow" difficult errors and distortions of facts that we need an extra measure of grace, spiritual wisdom and discernment in order to swallow and digest.

"In your anger do not sin; when you are on your beds, search your hearts and be silent. Selah"
Psalm 4:4 NIV

As imperfect people living in an imperfect world, we and others are going to make mistakes that adversely affect others and that often cause our judgmental and vindictive spirits to rise and cry out to set the record straight and hold other people accountable for their mistakes.

Regardless of the cause and motives behind the mistakes, we need to know how best to react in a way that helps minimize instead of increasing the consequences and damage that the mistake or distortion causes.

Before we make rash rushes to judgment and begin trying to bring down others by bringing up their mistakes, we had best remember that our own errors, imperfections and mistakes make us just as vulnerable and subject to the criticism and judgmental attitude of others. We cannot experience forgiveness and mercy without extending it.

We also need to consider whether our finger pointing will make the problem better or worse.

"Don't pick on people, jump on their failures, criticize their faults— unless, of course, you want the same treatment. That critical spirit has a way of boomeranging"
Matthew 7:1 MSG

We need to know that we cannot unscramble eggs, or put toothpaste back in the tube, and that we had best "swallow hard" and seek to make the best of the bad situation. We must never let vindictiveness drown out the needs for grace and mercy that God extends to us and requires that we extend to others.

Father, grace me with the grace of forgiveness that I might swallow the hard. In Jesus' name, Amen

Your Resume

"And so, dear brothers and sisters, I plead with you to give your bodies to God because of all he has done for you. Let them be a living and holy sacrifice—the kind he will find acceptable. This is truly the way to worship him." Romans 12:1 NLT

Whether it is written out or filled out as a job application, a summary of past experience and education is essential for finding a job.

"If you do well, will you not be accepted? And if you do not do well, sin lies at the door. And its desire is for you, but you should rule over it."
Genesis 4:7
(Please read Matthew Henry or another good commentary on Genesis 4)

The fact that we are all writing resumes to be presented to God should give us all pause to consider how we should live the life we have been given to do the Lord's business until he comes.

When it comes to a relevant spiritual education, how would you grade yourself? Have you "quit school" as soon as you received God's wonderful gift of salvation, or have you pursued holiness by seeking to know God better and better in a life long study of His Word? Have you worshiped weakly instead of daily?

If you were to write a 2 column list today on your past and present experiences, how many would go under the "irrelevant" or "trivial" column, and how many under "relevant" and "meaningful"?

When the time comes that we must give an accounting of how we have spent our time, talents, and treasures, we are all going to have cause to blush as we see all the wasted hours, selfish pursuits, and shallow activities go up in smoke.

The resumes of the Heroes of the faith are readily available for us to study and seek to emulate in Hebrews 11 so that we too will earn our Lord's "well done good and faithful servant" when we offer our resumes to Him.

"It is not that we think we are qualified to do anything on our own. Our qualification comes from God
2 Corinthians 3:5 NLT

Father, by the power of the Holy Spirit, help me to grow into the fullness of your Son through the life long process of sanctification. In Jesus' name, Amen

God Has No Grandchildren

"God alone made it possible for you to be in Christ Jesus. For our benefit God made Christ to be wisdom itself." 1 Corinthians 1:30 NLT

We can never ride our parents coat tails to glory!. They can teach and encourage us, but parents can never go to the cross for us, and they can only birth us once.

"But those who desert him will perish, for you destroy those who abandon you."
Psalm 73:27 NLT=

We can only become children (never grandchildren) of the living God by being born again through faith in Jesus Christ.

Salvation is not bestowed upon us through the faith of our fathers. It is a gift given directly to us through a personal faith encounter through which the Holy Spirit convicts us of our sin and need for a Savior.

No one can receive Jesus Christ for us. We must invite Him into our hearts and enter into His kingdom as his brothers and sisters and sons and daughters of God.

As parents, we are all given the command and responsibility of bringing our children up in the fear of the Lord and model Christ to them so they will learn to be like Him.

Hopefully, our children will see the happiness and joy we have in the Lord and want to know how to have it for themselves and be receptive to God's invitation when He comes knocking at the doors of their hearts.

"For you have been born again. Your new life did not come from your earthly parents because the life they gave you will end in death. But this new life will last forever because it comes from the eternal, living word of God"
1 Peter 1:23 NLT

The prodigals that all too often grow up in many Christian families are grim reminders that we only inherit our sin natures and that no one ever inherits eternal life from their parents.

The blessings God promises to our children are conditional promises based on them becoming children and not grandchildren of God.

Father, thank you for inviting us all to become your children and joint heirs with Christ. In Jesus' name, Amen

133

God's Selective Amnesia
' "And I will forgive their wickedness, and I will never again remember their sins." Hebrews 8:12 NLT

"He has removed our sins as far from us as the east is from the west."
Psalm 103:12 NIV

How sweet it is that God chooses to not only forgive, but to forget our confessed and repented sins! To have them blotted out of our book of life by the blood of Jesus is the greatest thing that can ever happen to anyone.

This is available to everyone who calls upon the name of the Lord in faith with a broken spirit and contrite heart.

Oh that we, the devil, and others might have the same amnesia! We often say we forgive, but we hold the offense in our memory bank and have a hard time forgetting the sins we have committed and the sins others may have committed against us.

To make matters worse, the devil never forgets our sins. He is always standing by to throw them up in our face to discourage and depress us and try to make us doubt the reality of our salvation.

Outside of Jesus' death on the cross, the love of God is probably the most amazing in his willingness to forget our failures and shortcomings, and yet remember even the smallest of our random acts of kindness and good works that we do in response to His love and mercy to us.

All this being true (and the Bible certainly says that it is) should give us all cause to consider what is going to be left of our book of life after our sins have been forgotten, and all of our trivial pursuits have been burned away at the judgment seat of Christ.

What have we done that Christ will remember when we stand to give account of the time, treasures, and talents we have been given to accomplish the purposes for which God created us?

"God is not unjust; he will not forget your work and the love you have shown him as you have helped his people and continue to help them."
Hebrews 6:10 NIV

We know that he remembers when we forgive and forget, and that he highly prizes obedience.

Father, help me to be a good steward so that I may have something to show for the life God has given me. In Jesus' name, Amen

Factory Recalls

"and have put on the new self, which is being renewed in knowledge in the image of its Creator." Colossians 3:10 NIV

It seems that everything manufactured or sold these days is subject to factory recalls for defective parts or repairs. Manufacturers spend billions of dollars annually recalling automobiles, toys, appliances, medications,meats, vegetables and dairy products.

> "I have listened attentively, but they do not say what is right. No one repents of his wickedness, saying, "What have I done?" Each pursues his own course like a horse charging into battle."
> Jeremiah 8:6 NIV

Even though God doesn't make any junk, the defect of our inherited sin nature becomes more obvious and crippling the older we get.

This is why God, in His mercy, has given us the option of a recall through faith in Jesus Christ that will give us a new birth in the spirit with the sin defect removed.

Once we are remanufactured into becoming new creatures in Christ, God comes as the Holy Spirit to give us daily reminders through our conscience and His Word.

God issues these recalls by the power of the Holy Spirit to bring us back under the shelter of His wings through confession, godly sorrow, and true repentance.

When we disregard God's recalls, we suffer the fate of a hardened heart, dulled conscience and the consequences of unforgiven sin, and will never know true peace and joy.

> "So now we can rejoice in our wonderful new relationship with God because our Lord Jesus Christ has made us friends of God.
> Romans 5:11 NLT

Is today a good day to make a sober estimate of ourselves and concentrate on taking our defects back to God's recall center? We can access His throne of grace through prayer 24/7/365.

God will create that clean heart and right spirit in all who come to him with a contrite spirit in true repentance.

Father, thank you for the recalls of the Holy Spirit bring me back under the shelter of your wings of grace. In Jesus name, Amen

Life Support

"Cast your burden on the Lord, And He shall sustain you; He shall never permit the righteous to be moved." Psalm 55:22

With all of the life support systems available to keep dying and

"They confronted me in the day of my calamity, But the LORD was my support." Psalm 18:18

literally dead people alive there comes a time for many to make the decision of when to pull the plug and when to forbid artificial life support.

We should never lose sight of the fact that we are all on life support systems of some kind literally all the days of our life on this earth.

Our parents and family members support and us through the nurturing and care of infancy and childhood, and we should daily give thanks for them.

There comes a time of choosing what or who we will lean on to provide the security and significance we all need to live satisfying lives.

Many will lean on friendship and relationships with peers. Many will seek security in wealth and possessions. Food, Sex, alcohol, or drugs sometimes become the life support systems some on which some depend.

Others will depend on their own strengths, talents, and energies to support the basic inner need to feel good about themselves through self worth.

As important as some of these supports may be, they must never become our primary source for security and significance. God has provided faith in Jesus Christ as the original, totally reliable life support system that will never need to be unplugged.

The abundant life that Jesus came to bring us is the well spring from on high that will never run dry.

"In his kindness God called you to his eternal glory by means of Jesus Christ. After you have suffered a little while, he will restore, support, and strengthen you, and he will place you on a firm foundation."
1 Peter 5:10

Instead of just maintaining life, the life support that we receive through faith in Jesus Christ not only maintains, but it grows and strengthens our peace and security even when any of our other support systems fail.

Father, keep me on your life support of the Holy Spirit who is the guarantor of my forever life in Christ. In Jesus' name, Amen

Hunger and Thirst

"And Jesus said to them, "I am the bread of life. He who comes to Me shall never hunger, and he who believes in Me shall never thirst."
John 6:35 KJV

Satisfying these two basic drives physically is essential to sustain life on this planet. Satisfying these two basic drives philosophically is the way most people spend most of their waking hours.

"When you open your hand, you satisfy the hunger and thirst of every living thing."
Psalm 145:18: NLT

Whether it's hungering and thirsting for the approval of others, material or vocational success, health, pleasure, knowledge, or financial security – we all pursue in pursuit of significance.

The sad part is that we often miss out on satisfying these hungers because we overlook the spiritual importance of hunger and thirst. Our hunger and thirst for the righteousness of Christ would probably not show up on anyone's top ten list, and yet it should be the number one hunger and thirst of every believer.

When we understand that God's perfect plan and desire for our lives is all about us imitating His holiness and righteousness in every area of our lives, we will realize how radically we need to reprioritize our lives.

When we seek the kingdom of God and His righteousness we find our significance and security in the unconditional love of God that can never be taken away from us.

"What I'm trying to do here is to get you to relax, to not be so preoccupied with getting, so you can respond to God's giving. People who don't know God and the way he works fuss over these things, but you know both God and how he works. Steep your life in God-reality, God-initiative, God-provisions. Don't worry about missing out. You'll find all your everyday human concerns will be met."
Matthew 6:32-33 MSG

As we live our lives becoming as righteous and holy in our words and deeds in actuality as we became theologically the hour we first believed, we are going to find the true secret of the "bread of life" and "living water" that satisfies every thirst and hunger as the Lord delights in giving us the desires of our heart.

Father, keep me always hungering and thirsting for Your righteousness so that I can know true satisfaction.. In Jesus' name, Amen

137

Upgrades in Heaven
"[Born anew] into an inheritance which is beyond the reach of change and decay [imperishable], unsullied and unfading, reserved in heaven for you," 1 Peter 1:4 AMP.

How sad for those who think that this life is all there is, and have nothing to look forward to except the eternal torments of hell that they will finally believe in when they get there.

"Yes, I'm on my way! I'll be there soon! I'm bringing my payroll with me. I'll pay all people in full for their life's work." Revelation 22:12 MSG

How sweet it is to know that as we persevere through all of the trials and sorrows of life while being conformed into the image of Christ,we are being prepared to live with Him forever in the perfect bliss of heaven. It's almost enough to make us want to check out early, but we can't get there until we are fully conformed and so we wait in eager anticipation.

As good or as bad as this life has been, we all have upgrades to look forward to with great anticipation and delight. Whether physical, mental, relational, or spiritual, we all have some great upgrades to look forward to in heaven.

The idea of what upgrades those stored up treasures are going to provide is mind boggling. There can't be anything better than heaven itself and the absence of sin will make the absence of jealousy or envy of others over the different stages or privileges of heaven of no consequence.

The fact that salvation is a gift freely given and not a reward coupled with too many mentions of rewards to ignore should encourage us all to become more proactive in storing up those treasures in heaven by thanksliving for Christ here below.

" You do this because you are looking forward to the joys of heaven – as you have been ever since you first heard the truth of the Good News." Colossians 1:5 NLT

Thank you for upgrading me from sinner to saint here below. May there be enough of any good that I have done after all of the wood, hay, and stubble is burned away, that I will be upgraded to love and serve you even more in heaven. In Jesus' name, Amen

138

Happy Hour

"Happy are your men and happy are these your servants, who stand continually before you and hear your wisdom!" 2 Chronicles 9:7

How sad to think of "Happy Hour" as a time we can get half price drinks at the local bar or restaurant. No matter how **"I'm happy from the** hard one might try there is not enough booze in the **inside out, and from** world to truly drown away sorrows or problems.
the outside in, I'm
firmly formed. You The real "Happy Hour" should be that hour
canceled my ticket to of each day reserved for standing before God and:
hell— that's not my 1.Drowning the sorrows of our sins with the blood
destination! of Jesus through confessing with godly sorrow and
Psalm 16:9 MSG true repentance;2, Praying with praise in our hearts
and thanksgiving on our lips for Who God is and what He has done for us in Christ:3. Seeking God's wisdom by abiding, growing in, and obeying His Word.

Every other substitute for God we pursue is sooner or later going to turn out to be a trivial pursuit that will leave us spiritually bankrupt and empty handed when we reach that great "Happy Hour" where we see Jesus face to face and give an accounting for the stewardship of our lives.

The true happy hours of our lives should be those where we experience the blessings of abiding in Christ.

When our security is based on Whose we are, we will find the true happiness of peace that surpasses all understanding. We will be filled with Jesus' joy, the awareness of His love and the love of others. We will find our prayers being answered because we will start **" David also spoke of this** praying Christ centered instead of self- **when he described the** centered prayers. **happiness of those who**
are declared righteous
During our "Happy Hours" in Christ,we **without working for it:"** will experience more and more of the sacred **Romans 4:6 NLT** delights reserved for those who love and earnestly seek Him.

Father, help me to fill my days with happy hours in and with you.In Jesus" name, Amen

139

Why Settle for Less?

"With all my heart I want your blessings. Be merciful as you promised. I pondered the direction of my life, and I turned to follow your laws." Psalm 119:57-58 NIV

Before we make a rash judgment of those we see living apart from the express will and commandments of God, we need to remember the times we were doing the same thing, and pray for God's patience and forbearance for those presently living in sin that He extended us when we were struggling with some sin and disobedience issues of our own.

> " How joyful are those who fear the LORD and delight in obeying his commands"
> Psalm 112:1 NLT

What we really need to show concern about is not the sin, but the fact that it is keeping someone we know and love from settling for less than God's best for their lives.

When we rebell and insist on doing life with what we think is best for us instead of seeking God's best for our lives, we are going to miss out on so many of the blessings of obedience that God promises to those who obey.

Whether we miss the blessings of obedience promised in the beatitudes, obeying the Ten Commandments, or abiding in Christ; we are missing out on God's best for our lives. We need to understand that although God loves us unconditionally, many of his best blessings are conditional upon our obedience.

Instead of judging and condemning those who shutting themselves off from God's best by the way they are living their lives, we should keep on praying them towards true repentance and back into the circle of God's will and the best of His blessings.

Only God can change hearts and convict others of their need to repent and be restored. We need to keep on praying for those who have gone astray and take comfort in knowing that God is faithful and will restore those who are truly His.

> "God blesses those whose hearts are pure, for they will see God."
> Matthew 5:8 NLT

Father, help me to live and encourage others to live fruitful lives pleasing to you so that we can enjoy Your best in our lives. In Jesus' name, Amen.

Thank God for Crutches
"But blessed are those who trust in the LORD and have made the LORD their hope and confidence" Jeremiah 17:17 NLT

Dear friend, don't let this bad example influence you. Follow only what
"We depend on the LORD alone to save us. Only he can help us, protecting us like a shield."
Psalm 33:20 NLT
is good. Remember that those who do good prove that they are God's children, and those who do evil prove that they do not know God.

A lot of people have tried to put faith in God down over the centuries by calling religion a crutch, or a Lenin once said "an opiate for the people".

Having God as "our refuge and strength", and "very present help in time of trouble" is a crutch for which we can all be thankful.

As we live life experiencing the troubles we have been promised, how good it is to know that we do not have to go through them alone, and that we do have someone to lean on.

The One who made the physically lame to walk is also a crutch to help the emotionally or relationally lame walk in the valleys and tough times of life.

To know that God will never leave us or forsake us, that He is working all things for our good, and that He will supply His all sufficient grace for our every need helps us rejoice and walk worthy of our calling even when the walking gets tough.

At sometime or another, we are all going to need others to lean on. God is continually going to use us to be crutches for others who need someone to lean on as they go through spiritual, physical, emotional, financial, or relational problems.

"In his kindness God called you to his eternal glory by means of Jesus Christ. After you have suffered a little while, he will restore, support, and strengthen you, and he will place you on a firm foundation.
1 Peter 5:10 NLT

Whether it's listening, encouraging, feeding, consoling, or just loving,our high calling to love others as Christ loves us will often involve us being crutches to help others walk through pain, suffering, and sorrow.

Father, help me to be someone others can lean on when they need encouragement, comfort, and love. In Jesus' name, Amen

The Decisive Issue

"Not all people who sound religious are really godly. They may refer to me as 'Lord,' but they still won't enter the Kingdom of Heaven. The decisive issue is whether they obey my Father in heaven." Matthew 7:21 NLT

"I have decided to follow Jesus" is a very popular hymn in some churches, but it is dangerous theology. We cannot take credit for something we have done when the glory belongs to God for what He has done.

"But they delight in doing everything the LORD wants; day and night they think about his law."
Psalm 1:2 NLT

Scripture clearly teaches that no man can call Jesus Lord except by the power of the Holy Spirit. Our salvation is not of our doing but of God working faith in us through the Holy Spirit.

Jesus clearly defines obedience as the decisive issue of eternal life. When we say we believe in God but don't obey Him we are going to be trespassing our way through life no better than the devil who also believes in God.

The old question of: "if we were ever arrested for being a Christian would there be enough evidence to convict us" is a very convicting question for many.

As professing believers, we are all going stand before Christ to give an accounting of our stewardship of the lives we have been given. We should all be living to have some fruits of our obedience left over after all of the wood, hay, and stubble of our lives has been burned away.

Whether our disobedience is expressed in the idolatry of putting power, pleasure, approval, pride or possessions above our love of God, or failing to love and forgive others as God loves and forgives us our entrance into the kingdom of heaven may be at risk.

"And remember, it is a message to obey, not just to listen to. If you don't obey, you are only fooling yourself."
James 1:22 NLT

May we all grow in spiritual maturity to where faith and obedience become the defining characteristics of our lives well lived in Christ.

Father, by the power of the Holy Spirit, help me to be not only a believer, but an obeyer. In Jesus' name, Amen

Butchers Beware!
"Do not misuse the name of the LORD your God. The LORD will not let you go unpunished if you misuse his name. Exodus 20:7 NLT

Although we may have never butchered a steer or any other animal, we all at some time or another have a tendency to butcher something or some one.

"I will take up the cup of salvation, And call upon the name of the LORD." Psalm 116:13 NLT

We often hear people "butcher the king's English", or the reputation and good name of others.

The worst form of butchering is when it comes to butchering the name of the Lord.

In spite of the clear command of God we are all probably guilty of butchering the name of the Lord, often without even realizing it.

Misusing or butchering the name of the Lord goes way beyond the common misuse of venting our anger by using God's name to curse or swear.

Anytime we swear in the name of the Lord to validate our truthfulness we are misusing the name of the Lord.

When we practice hypocrisy while professing to be Christians, we are butchering the name of the Lord by calling ourselves by His name.

Using the Lord's name to pursue our own agendas is probably the most common misuse of all. We all too often hear of someone's idea or will being promoted as being the Lord's will or idea.

We never call upon the name of the Lord in vain when we call upon Him for salvation, to praise and worship Him, and to offer our lives as living sacrifices we will find the peace and joy of our salvation and experience the security of His love.

"Finally, dear brothers and sisters, we urge you in the name of the Lord Jesus to live in a way that pleases God, as we have taught you" 1 Thessalonians 4:1 NLT

When we live in the name of the Lord with a broken spirit and contrite heart we will always find forgiveness and restoration. Proper use of the name of the Lord should be a priority for every believer.

Father, help me to always use your name with the reverence and respect you deserve. In Jesus' name, Amen

143

Don't Let the World Dumb You Down
"But I, like a deaf man, hear not; and I am like a dumb man who opens not his mouth." Psalm 38:13 AMP

It is not hard to pin point the exact time it happened. When Eve succumbed to the temptation of the Devil in the Garden of Eden, instead of getting to become all knowing like God, she and Adam and all who would follow got "dumbed" down into sin.

> "Do you think I'm dumb enough to challenge God? Wouldn't that just be asking for trouble?"
> Job 37:20 MSG

The Old Testament is the history of generation after generation of people who got "dumbed down" into worshipping false idols and disobeying the God of their Covenants and God of Abraham, Isaac, and Jacob.

By the time Jesus Christ came into the World as the Messiah, the religious leaders were so "dumbed down" and wise in their own conceits they knew Him not. It seems to be happening again today.

How it must break God's heart to see the apple of His eye, the highest order of His creation that He made in His image getting so "dumbed down" that He is ignored, disobeyed, and so easily forgotten by so many.

Like the frog in the kettle, many have gotten so "dumbed down" by the worship of pleasure, power, and possessions we no longer sense outrage or shock at anything.

> "Human wisdom is so tinny, so impotent, next to the seeming absurdity of God. Human strength can't begin to compete with God's "weakness".
> I Corinthians 1:25 MSG

The Way of life continues to call out to all who will still listen. It's time for us all to "wise up" instead of continuing to get "dumbed down"!

Father, forgive me for falling into the traps of the world, my flesh, and the devil and create in me a clean heart and restore the joy of my salvation. In Jesus' name, Amen

Somethings Got a Hold on Me

"Then the LORD said to me, "Son of man, on the day I take away their stronghold—their joy and glory, their heart's desire, their dearest treasure" Ezekiel 24:25a NLT

"The LORD is my rock, my fortress, and my Savior ;my God is my rock, in whom I find protection.He is my shield, the strength of my salvation, and my stronghold. Psalm 18:2 NLT

This old song was never intended to be a hymn, but the truth that "somethings got a hold on me" is true of every child born of woman.

We are all born with the strongholds of sins of the world, our flesh, and the devil already rooted and starting to grow within us from the time we are born.

When our base sin nature takes hold of us we are controlled by anger, lust, pride, jealousy, envy and all of the natural instincts of the world. These are the strongholds that hold us captive and will keep us from ever knowing the true security and significance that comes only when God becomes our stronghold through faith in Jesus Christ.

When that "something that's got a hold on me" is the strength and power of the Holy Spirit coming to live within us, the strongholds of our flesh are overcome by the stronghold of faith that gives us a new birth and a whole new way of living.

When the Holy Spirit gets hold of us, our selfishness gives way to selflessness, and our joy and glory is in the Lord.   When we find our security and pride in being a redeemed child of God the Lord becomes our stronghold.

Our lives will bear witness as to who has hold of us. If we continue to live in bondage to the strongholds of sin we will continue to be controlled by sin.

"We use God's mighty weapons, not mere worldly weapons, to knock down the Devil's strongholds" 2 Corinthians 10:4 NLT

When the love of God takes hold of us we will be controlled by the Holy Spirit and exhibit the love, joy, peace, longsuffering, kindness, goodness, faithfulness, gentleness, and self-control that give evidence of Who has hold of us.

Father, may you always be my stronghold. In Jesus' name, Amen

Read 1 Timothy 6:19-32, 1 Corinthians 3:12-20
The Best Investment Portfolio
"Wherever your treasure is, there your heart and thoughts will also be."
Matthew 6:21 NLT

We usually think of stocks and bonds, 401's and material assets when we think of portfolios. Many depend on money managers or financial advisors to manage their portfolios to see that they grow and provide a good rate of return.

"Tell them to use their money to do good. They should be rich in good works and should give generously to those in need, always being ready to share with others whatever God has given them."
1 Timothy 6:18 NLT

We also have a portfolio of good deeds that consist of the time, talents and treasures we invest in discipling others and building up the kingdom of God.

We all have been given a life to live and resources to manage until the Lord returns. Those who manage well will be rewarded with more to manage, while those who invest in the trivial pursuits of pleasure, power, and possessions will miss out on the rewards in this life and the next promised to those who manage their portfolio of life well here on earth.

When we put God first in our wallets, we are told that we will not only have more than enough for our needs, but also an abundance with which to be generous on every occasion.

Wise planning based on who we are in Christ, where we are going because of our faith in Christ leads to wise living where we seek to please God in all that we do by doing the good deeds which he purposed us to do before we were even born.

"But there is going to come a time of testing at the judgment day to see what kind of work each builder has done. Everyone's work will be put through the fire to see whether or not it keeps its value"
1 Corinthians 3:13 NLT

It behooves us all to make the best investment of the time, talents, and treasures we have been given so that when our portfolio of good deeds is opened there will be plenty left after the wood, hay, and stubble is burned away.

Father, help me to manage well and be found faithful in every area of my life when I am called to give an accounting to You.. In Jesus' name, Amen

Whitewash

"You can't whitewash your sins and get by with it; you find mercy by admitting and leaving them." Proverbs 28:13 MSG

As individuals we have a tendency to whitewash our sins through denial, justification, ignoring, or rationalization. Eve started this practice by blaming the devil for her disobedience.

"Tell these whitewashers that their wall will soon fall down. A heavy rainstorm will undermine it; great hailstones and mighty winds will knock it down"
Ezekiel 13:11 NLT

Sin has become an unpopular subject in many pulpits and churches. We like to get puffed up instead of beat up.

We want all of the sweetness, beauty and grace of God's love and well we should. We should dwell on these things and live lives as positive Christians.

Through all this, we must never ignore the reality of sin and sinfulness in us, and in the world around us.

We must never forget that as much as God loves us, He hates sin even more. He takes sin very seriously and so should we.

Sin is just an unholy thought, unkind word or disobedient act away. Knowing that there is a roaring lion on the loose seeking whom he may devour should make us mindful of the need to put on the full armor of God daily.

"If we say that we have no sin, we deceive ourselves, and the truth is not in us."
1 John 1:8

Jesus Christ had to die for our sins. We need to be ever mindful of this and cleansed by His blood through confession and true repentance which is God's way of whitewashing us with the righteousness of Christ and making us as pure and white as snow.

Father, keep me ever mindful of the real and present danger of sin from within and without and give me the strength and power of the Holy Spirit to overcome the temptations that come my way. In Jesus' name, Amen

Right on the Money
"Remember this—a farmer who plants only a few seeds will get a small crop. But the one who plants generously will get a generous crop."
2 Corinthians 9:6 NLT

To be "right on the money" is to be correct, true, or "hit the nail on the head". When used in terms of our relationship with God it should be one of the guiding principles of life for every believer.

"Bring all the tithes into the storehouse so there will be enough food in my Temple. If you do," says the LORD Almighty, "I will open the windows of heaven for you. I will pour out a blessing so great you won't have enough room to take it in! Try it! Let me prove it to you!"
Malachi 3:11 NLT

When Jesus said that your treasure is where your heart is , He is telling us to get "right on the money".!

The rich young ruler went away very sad because he could not get "right on the money".

When we love money more than we love God we become very selfish and self centered instead of selfless and Christ centered. When the pursuit of riches becomes the burning passion of our lives, the pursuit of holiness takes the back seat and we will never be conformed into the image of Christ.

Abel was "right on the money" when He gave the first fruit sacrifice of his best. David was "right on the money" when he insisted on paying for the land instead of offering a sacrifice that cost him nothing. Judas was "wrong on the money". Ananias and Sapphira were 'wrong on the money" and struck dead instantly.

God's law of sewing and reaping is also the law of "getting right on the money." When we are generous with God, he has promised to be generous to us. We cannot out give God!

"No one can serve two masters. For you will hate one and love the other, or be devoted to one and despise the other. You cannot serve both God and money."
Matthew 6:24 NLT

The material blessings that flow to those whose hearts are right with God are blessings untainted by greed that allow us to be generous on every occasion to the praise of God and His glory.

Father, help me to stay "right on the money" with You. In Jesus' name, Amen

Monuments to Stupidity

"Therefore, their land will become desolate, a monument to their stupidity. All who pass by will be astonished and shake their heads in amazement at its utter desolation." Jeremiah 18:16 NLT

It is easy for us to look back with 20/20 hindsight and wonder how the Israelites could have been so slow to learn.

"Are you amazed and incredulous? Do you not believe it? Then go ahead and be blind if you must. You are stupid, but not from wine!"
Isaiah 29:9 NLT

God poured out every conceivable blessing to them, forgave, forgave, and forgave to no avail. They continued to wander deeper and deeper into the sin and idolatry that brought about their destruction and captivity.

Before we get filled with hypocritical glory about their stupidity, we had best look at some of the monuments to stupidity in our own lives.

How many times have we gone down the primrose path of putting other things over God? The worship of the idols of power, possessions, pleasure, accomplishment, and the worship of man continues to increase at warp speed.

We get conned and cheated by other people and wonder how we could have been so stupid. We pursue the glitter of what the world defines as success that leave a wake of bitterness and disappointment when these idols of gold turn to brass.

Our lives are given to us to be lived as trophies of God's grace and glory. We should be all about fulfilling the purposes for which God created us before we were ever born.

When our ignorance of God is taken away when we hear the Good News about Jesus, we dare not let our stupidity seal our fate of eternal destruction that awaits all who reject God's wonderful gift of salvation that is freely given to all who call upon the name of the Lord to be saved.

"Yes, a person is a fool to store up earthly wealth but not have a rich relationship with God."
Luke 12:21 NLT

Father, forgive me my monumental stupidity. In Jesus' name, Amen.

149

Assisted Living
"God is our refuge and strength, an ever-present help in trouble."
Psalm 46:1 NIV

Assisted living facilities have been one of the biggest growth

" Blessed is he whose help is the God of Jacob, whose hope is in the LORD his God, Psalm 146:5 NIV businesses for many years. As people live longer, and families become more mobile, the responsibility for having parents move in has just about disappeared, and moving into assisted living facilities has become the residency of choice for millions of seniors who are no longer able to keep up a house, prepare meals, and take care of

themselves.

We need to keep in mind that we do not have to get old to enjoy the blessings of assisted living. The very minute we receive Jesus Christ as Lord and Savior, the Holy Spirit moves in to assist us in living life to the fullest in Christ.

This assisted living resource costs us nothing, but cost the provider everything. Jesus Christ had to die in order to pay for all of the benefits we receive.

When we experience real assisted living that comes from abiding in Christ and Him abiding in us through the power of the Holy Spirit, we not only find strength for the journey of life, we receive incredible joy for the journey, and security and peace that surpasses all understanding.

"Let us then approach the throne of grace with confidence, so that we may receive mercy and find grace to help us in our time of need. Hebrews 4:16 NIV

Our indwelling assisted living provider is present and on call 24/7/365 to heal our diseases, guide us in all truth, pray for us, mend our broken hearts, and comfort us with God's love.

May God grant us all the peace and joy of assisted living in Christ all the days of our lives.

Father, keep me ever mindful that I am totally dependent upon the assisted living you so generously supply. In Jesus' name, Amen

Prevailing Prayer
"The eyes of the Lord watch over those who do right, and his ears are open to their prayers. But the Lord turns his face against those who do evil."
1 Peter 3:12 NLT

Prevailing or effective prayer is one of the greatest teachings in Scripture.

"Then the man said, "Let me go, for it is dawn." But Jacob panted, "I will not let you go unless you bless me." Genesis 32:26 NLT

The story of Jacob's wrestling with God and winning is one of the best examples of the importance of persistency in prayer.

It is not coincidental that Jesus taught the parable of the man waking his friend in the middle of the night and knocking until he opened the door right after giving us the Lord's prayer as a model prayer.

It is encouraging that he teaches us to keep on asking, seeking, and knocking. This is what prevailing prayer is all about.

God answers all our prayers.. He sometimes says "no", sometimes "yes", and sometimes "not now", but He always answers.

God knows our hearts and our motives, and He does not pay a whole lot of attention to selfish prayers, or prayers from an unrepentant heart.

Jesus has promised that God will answer our prayers that seek to Glorify God and are in harmony with God's good pleasure and will. The better we get to know Jesus, the more unselfish and Christ like our prayers will become, and the more prayers we will have answered.

"And so I tell you, keep on asking, and you will be given what you ask for. Keep on looking, and you will find. Keep on knocking, and the door will be opened" Luke 11:9 NLT

When we come to God's throne of grace cleansed by confession and repentance and in true submission to His good and gracious will, we can pray with great anticipation and godly confidence that God will do whatever we ask according to His good pleasure.

Father, thank you for all the prayers you have answered and are going to answer as I offer them to you in sincerity and faith. In Jesus' name, Amen.

Spiritual Bankruptcy

"For you know that God paid a ransom to save you from the empty life you inherited from your ancestors. And the ransom he paid was not mere gold or silver." 1 Peter 1:18 NLT

Bankruptcies and Foreclosures have been occurring at record numbers over the past several years of economic decline as people struggle with increased debt and decreased income.

"At the end of every seventh year you must cancel the debts of everyone who owes you money.
Deuteronomy 15:1 NLT

The bankruptcy law is designed to protect debtors from going to debtor's prison when they can't pay their bills, which was the law and custom for centuries.

The two most common types of bankruptcy are chapter 7, wherein all but exempted assets are liquidated and the proceeds distributed to creditors, or chapter 13 where the debts are restructured and a repayment plan is presented.

In either instance, the judge will appoint a trustee to see that the terms of the bankruptcy are fulfilled.

Practically every statistic used to measure the moral wealth of a nation indicate that moral and spiritual bankruptcy is increasing even more than financial.

What great comfort there is in knowing that God made provision for our spiritual bankruptcy by sending His Son to pay our sin debt in full, and sent the Holy Spirit as our trustee to help us live free of condemnation and slavery to sin.

"For if you live according to [the dictates of] the flesh, you will surely die. But if through the power of the [Holy] Spirit you are [habitually] putting to death (making extinct, deadening) the [evil] deeds prompted by the body, you shall [really and genuinely] live forever."
Romans 8:13 AMP

When we acknowledge, apologize for and renounce our sins at God's throne of grace, we can avoid the moral and spiritual bankruptcy of the soul and be sure that we have forever forgiveness and redemptive grace.

Father, thank you for rescuing me from spiritual bankruptcy and restoring my righteousness account through the blood of Jesus. In Jesus' name, Amen

Pick Your Poison

"Go and say to David, 'This is what the Lord says: I will give you three choices. Choose one of these punishments, and I will inflict it on you.'"
2 Samuel 24 NLT

God's gift of free choice always comes with free consequences. When someone chooses to reject God's wonderful gift of eternal life, they are also choosing to die in eternal torment.

"They do not see your punishment awaiting them. They sneer at all their enemies."
Psalm 10:5 NLT

The prodigal son thought He was choosing a life of luxury, fun and games in the big city and, to his great sorrow found that he had chosen, hunger, misery, and eating with the pigs.

Even blood bought, born again believers who have been set free from bondage to sin find themselves choosing and the inevitable consequences of sin without even realizing it until too late.

God does not allow us to choose the consequences as He allowed David. But we would do well to think about the consequence we are choosing before we choose to lose by sinning.

Broken homes, STS, guilt, shame, jail, unwanted pregnancies, addiction, dismissal from school, work, or even church are just a few of the poisons we are free to choose when we exercise our free will to sin.

Once we have been set free from the dominion of sin through faith in Jesus Christ, we can no longer use the excuse "I'm only human" as though we couldn't help choosing to sin. Jesus Christ died to set us free to say no to sin and yes to Him and His righteousness.

The next time temptation comes knocking we need to read the warning label of the poison that comes without succumbing to it.

"But because you are stubborn and refuse to turn from your sin, you are storing up terrible punishment for yourself. For a day of anger is coming, when God's righteous judgment will be revealed."
Romans 2:5 NLT

God has provided a means of escape from any temptation that may attack us. When we stand firm in the full armor of God, temptation will flee.

Father, bind satan that his poison not corrupt me. In Jesus' name, Amen

An Unwelcome Guest
"Judge not [neither pronouncing judgment nor subjecting to censure], and you will not be judged; do not condemn and pronounce guilty, and you will not be condemned and pronounced guilty; acquit and forgive and release (give up **resentment**, let it drop), and you will be acquitted and forgiven and released."Luke 6:36-38 AMP

A critical and judgmental spirit fueled by jealousy is an unwelcome guest that douses the flames of friendship in any relationship. The ill will of resentment is a real crippler.

"It is a sin to belittle one's neighbor; blessed are those who help the poor." Proverbs 14:21 NLT

Instead of finding fault and begrudging the success or popularity of another, we should be praising the Lord for their success and popularity instead of feeling threatened by it.

The religious leaders of Jesus' day were so blinded by resentment that they missed out on recognizing the Messiah when He walked among them. King Saul became so resentful of David's popularity that he sought to kill him.

As long as resentment toward anyone takes up residence in our heart, it will be a barrier that will stifle the growth and joy of any relationship.

When we are looking to find fault with someone, we can surely find it. When we use someone's real or imagined fault trying to make them seem worse in order for us to seem better, we are letting resentment reign and will be the worse because of it.

Friendship and ill will cannot co-exist. We should never allow resentment to find a home in our hearts and diminish our relationship with others.

"Let all bitterness and indignation and wrath (passion, rage, bad temper) and resentment (anger, animosity) and quarreling (brawling, clamor, contention) and slander (evil-speaking, abusive or blasphemous language) be banished from you, with all malice (spite, ill will, or baseness of any kind) Ephesians 4:30 AMP

If we find ourselves harboring any jealousy or resentment toward any one, we need to ask God to help us to release and bury it in His sea of forgetfulness.

Father, let no ill will towards anyone take root in my heart. In Jesus' name, Amen

Playing "Peek-a-boo" with God

"Can anyone hide in secret places so that I cannot see him?" declares the LORD. "Do not I fill heaven and earth?" declares the LORD."
Jeremiah 23, 24 NIV

"Where can I go from your Spirit? Where can I flee from your presence?"
Psalm 139:7 NIV

Playing 'peek-a-boo" with babies has been a time honored pastime for years. There usually comes a time when the child thinks that if they close their eyes, or cover their eyes with their hands, that we can't see them.

Unfortunately, we too often have the tendency to play "peek-a-boo" with God as though He doesn't see us when we choose to rebel against Him and go merrily on our way sinning up a storm as though he can't see us.

The truth is that we all stand naked to the core physically, spiritually, and emotionally before our all knowing, ever present heavenly Father. This is a sobering thought indeed.

How good it is to know that God does see and know us as we really are, and still loves us in spite of our moral meltdowns. When we receive Jesus Christ as our Savior we are covered by the righteousness of Christ.

God sees us justified, or just as if we had never sinnned. We are clothed in robes washed clean by the blood of Jesus and stand before God as one of His redeemed and beloved children.

"He doesn't play hide-and-seek with us. He's not remote; he's near. We live and move in him, can't get away from him!
Acts 17:27 MSG

When the Holy Spirit comes into our hearts and begins the process of holy transformation within us, the childish game of "peek-a-boo" should give way to the "see and do" of spiritual maturity as we become imitators of Christ in every area of our lives.

Father, strip me of all my cover ups as I seek to grow in the image of Christ. In Jesus' name, Amen

Don't Get Sin Burnt

"Can a man scoop fire into his lap without his clothes being burned?"
Proverbs 6:27 NIV

We have all probably suffered the pain of sun burn at some time or
another. With all the preventatives available more and more people are
getting sun burned less and less.

"Restore us, O God of hosts; Cause Your face to shine, And we shall be saved!"
Psalm 80:3

It's a shame that the same cannot be said
for sin burn. Although the full armor of God is
readily available to all believers, more and more
seem to be getting sin burned more and more.

It is a sad commentary that divorces are as
common among the saved as among the unsaved. There seem to be far too
many professing Christians in our jails and prisons and even more out of jail
but imprisoned by bondage to sins of every kind.

The pride and selfishness of our flesh and lusts of our heart produce
anger, envy, manipulation, strife, greed and other moral impurities that can
leave us burned up and burned out before we even realize it.

The heart burn that results from sin burn is tragic. Our hearts become
hardened and our consciences dulled as we give up Spirit control and let our
besetting sins lead us out of control and headed for the "big burn" of eternal
torment and separation from God.

Of all the miracle drugs on the
market today there is none to compare
with the wonderful healing and soothing
of God's forgiveness and restoration that
he offers to all who turn to Him with
godly sorrow for their sin in true
repentance.

The Son of Man will send out His angels, and they will gather out of His kingdom all things that offend, and those who practice lawlessness, and will cast them into the furnace of fire. There will be wailing and gnashing of teeth
Matthew 13:41,42

No matter how badly sin burned
we may have become, the all sufficient grace of God is more than adequate
to heal and restore.

Father, shelter me under your wings of grace that I might not get sin burnt.
In Jesus' name, Amen

156

How to Become a 10 Mina Christian

"Those who are wise will shine like the brightness of the heavens, and those who lead many to righteousness, like the stars for ever and ever." Daniel 12:3 NIV

Everyone who claims the name of Christ should seek to become a 10 Mina Christian.

> "How beautiful on the mountains are the feet of those who bring good news, who proclaim peace, who bring good tidings,who proclaim salvation, who say to Zion, "Your God reigns!"
> Isaiah 52.7 NIV

When we consider that we have a lifetime to do it, we should realize that there is absolutely no reason in the world for us not multiplying our faith in the lives of 10 others God places in our paths.

When we consider that we have been given the gift of eternal life,the greatest gift ever given, our gratitude should leave us no choice but to help others receive all of the peace and joy of this gift forever.

Becoming a 10 Mina Christian is about becoming an imitator of Christ through the process of Holy Transformation that begins the hour we first believe. The more we become like Christ the more powerful our witness and testimony will be.

We should ask the Lord daily to make us ever mindful of witnessing opportunities, and to give us the wisdom and discernment to make the most of them in the strength and power of the Holy Spirit.

Many seem to want to hoard their wonderful gift of salvation and not share it with anyone.

People who need the Lord are going to wander aimlessly lost in and out of the lives of many believers who have buried their faith in the darkness of doubt, fear of rejection, or self centered pursuits.

> "He said, 'That's what I mean: Risk your life and get more than you ever dreamed of. Play it safe and end up holding the bag."
> Luke 19:26 MSG

The gospel spread throughout the world on the backs of 10 Mina Christians who took their faith in Christ and obedience to the Great Commandment and Great Commission seriously.

Father, don't let me stand before you empty handed when I give an account of my mina of life. In Jesus: name, Amen

Our First Response

"The old sinful nature loves to do evil, which is just opposite from what the Holy Spirit wants. And the Spirit gives us desires that are opposite from what the sinful nature desires. These two forces are constantly fighting each other, and your choices are never free from this conflict." Galatians 5:17 NLT

Differences of opinion and relational conflicts are among the most common of the troubles Jesus said we would have in this world. The fact that we are co existing with the sinful nature of our flesh and with others with the same problem makes it important that we know how to respond to conflicts especially with brothers and sisters in Christ.

"Come now, let us reason together," says the LORD." Isaiah 1:18 NIV

Our first response can often limit the severity of the conflict and bring about a God pleasing resolution.

When we, as an intentional act of our will remember to respond in the *"love, joy, peace, patience, kindness, goodness, faithfulness,"* and *self control of the Spirit,* we will not be able to respond in the pride, anger, envy, ego, or jealousy of the flesh, and the disagreement will be minimized instead of escalated.

The healing effect this kind of response has on our hearts cannot be minimized. When we are bearing the fruit of the Spirit, we are going to receive the comfort and grace of the Spirit that will promote reconciliation and healing, and keep any bitterness or unforgiveness from taking root in our souls.

Resolving to remember to bear the fruit of the Spirit when responding to any marital conflict that might arise can go a long way towards nipping conflicts in the bud before they can escalate.

Even when we need to speak the truth in love, when we speak it graciously bearing the fruit of the Spirit, we will most often find others much more receptive to what we are saying, and much less prone to respond in the anger and pride of the flesh.

"Blessed are the peacemakers, for they will be called sons of God. Matthew 5:9 NIV"

Father, help me to make the fruit of your Spirit my first response when disagreements and conflicts arise. In Jesus' name, Amen

Not Knowing

"For ever since the world was created, people have seen the earth and sky. Through everything God made, they can clearly see his invisible qualities—his eternal power and divine nature. So they have no excuse for not knowing God." Romans 1:20 NLT

Not knowing can be a blessing or a curse, depending on what we don't know. There are probably a lot of things in all our lives that we would have been better off not knowing.

> "Ah, God, listen to my prayer, my cry—open your ears. Don't be callous; just look at these tears of mine. I'm a stranger here. I don't know my way"
> Psalm 39:12 MSG

I wish I had not known an elder was keeping a mistress for years, some of the sins of my children, and some of the betrayals of what I thought were friends.

Perhaps the worst kind of not knowing is not knowing that you don't know. When people get over their heads trying to use their heads, the results can be disastrous. When I was 7 I helped my dad by putting water in the crankcase of his new car.

The old adage about power corrupting really comes to bear when people get elected to an office and start thinking they are infallible and don't know what they don't know.

There is absolutely no excuse for a confessing Christian not knowing God and His explicit instructions for how we should live our lives. He not only taught it, but He came down to earth and lived among us to model it. All we need to do is learn what Jesus did and we will know what we should do as we try to be imitators of Christ in every area of our lives.

> "It wasn't long ago that you were doing all that stuff and not knowing any better. But you know better now, so make sure it's all gone for good: bad temper, irritability, meanness, profanity, dirty talk."
> Colossians 3:6 MSG

The biggest mistake any of us can make is to let those we love not know the true happiness and peace of knowing Jesus Christ as Savior and Lord.

Father, help me to know you better through your Word day by day, year by year, until I see you face to face. In Jesus' name, Amen

No Exceptions

""For it's God's Name I'm preaching— respond to the greatness of our God! The Rock: His works are perfect, and the way he works is fair and just; A God you can depend upon, no exceptions, a straight-arrow God."
Deuteronomy 32:1 MSG

Many good lawyers spend a great deal of their time looking for exceptions to any law at issue. Many look for exceptions to get out of jury duty, military service, curfews, or other restrictions.

"Don't excuse yourself by saying, "Look, we didn't know."For God understands all hearts, and he sees you. He who guards your soul knows you knew.He will repay all people as their actions deserve"
Proverbs 24:12 NLT

Murderers have been set free, damages awarded, and jail avoided by finding loop holes or exceptions.

The truth is that there are no exceptions for sin. God hates it, we all commit it, and to choose to live in willful disobedience to God's commandments is choosing to lose.

God's love and forgiveness is unconditional, but it is foolish to think we have God's exception for any willful and deliberate sin.

While "once saved always saved" is surely true, choosing to harden our heart and let unconfessed and unrepented sins take root in our soul brings up the question of whether we were ever truly saved.

By the blood of Jesus, God has excused every repented sin we have ever committed, and given us an exception to pass over the gate to hell and enter the pearly gates of heaven.

Be agreeable, be sympathetic, be loving, be compassionate, be humble. That goes for all of you, no exceptions. No retaliation.
1 Peter 3:8 MSG

It is up to us to harness the power of the Holy Spirit to renew our minds daily and make our election sure by living lives pleasing to God and fruitful in every good work. There are no exceptions to this.

Father, keep me out of the slippery slopes of denial and rationalization and help me to pursue the holiness you desire for all your children. In Jesus name, Amen.

God Doesn't Grade on the Curve

"For it is by grace you have been saved, through faith—and this is not from yourselves, it is the gift of God—" Ephesians2:8 NIV

A lot of people seem to believe that God grades on some sort of curve and that as long as our good out weighs our bad, we will go to heaven.

"I give all people their due rewards, according to what their actions deserve."
Jeremiah 17:10b NLT

Time after time, when people are asked why God will let them in to heaven they express hope in their righteousness. "I've lead a good life", "I belong to church", "I give to charities", etc are common answers.

The truth is that God doesn't grade at all. God Judges! He judges that we are saved or lost, going to heaven or hell, with no shading or in-betweens.

If we were able to meet God's standard of perfect righteousness, we wouldn't need a Savior. The old covenant of the law proved that no one could pass the test of perfect righteousness.

In his mercy, God came in the flesh of man to fulfill the righteous demands of the law on our behalf and impute this perfect righteousness of Christ to all who would call upon His name. We are judged righteous and saved by the blood of Jesus.

Eternal life is not a reward for what we do, but a gift of God's grace based on what Jesus Christ did for us on the cross. We did nothing to earn our salvation.

If this is true (the Bible clearly says that it is), what are the rewards we earn by our good grades in living lives pleasing to God?

"But on the judgment day, fire will reveal what kind of work each builder has done. The fire will show if a person's work has any value."
1 Corinthians 3:13 NLT

All of us who have been judged righteous by believing in Jesus Christ will find out when we stand before Christ to give an account of the lives we have lived at the great white throne of judgment of our works.

Father, help me to live a life fully pleasing to you to show my appreciation for your dying on the cross to earn eternal life for me.In Jesus' name, Amen

Our Three Amigos

We're speaking for Christ himself now: Become friends with God; he's already a friend with you." 2 Corinthians 5:20 MSG,

Who are your 3 best friends? If you are like me you probably missed 2 out of 3. I am happy and of to name my dear bride of 59 years one of the 3. I would have to include my children, so my 3 best is filled before I even get started.

" **The LORD is a friend to those who fear him. He teaches them his covenant."** **Psalm 25:14 NLT**

First of all we need to know that God is our friend. He created us for fellowship and friendship with Him. He loves us with an everlasting love, and is always working all things for our good and His glory.

He specifically named Abraham, Job and Daniel as His friends, and Scripture tells us that He is a friend to all who love Him.

What comfort and peace there is in knowing that we are friends with the all powerful, all knowing, ever present Creator and Ruler of the universe and everything and everyone in it. He is our refuge and strength.

When we received Jesus Christ as our Savior, He also became our friend and brother and invites us into this great family relationship where we can grow in a personal, blessing filled relationship with Him.

And then there is the Holy Spirit who sticks closer than a brother, who comes to live in us and through us, who guides us into all truth, and fills us with the goodness and grace of God. He has been given as a deposit and guarantee that the good work of sanctification that God began in us the hour we first believed will lead us safely home to heaven.

"Abraham believed God, and God counted him as righteous because of his faith."[g] He was even called the friend of God.[h] 24 So you see, we are shown to be right with God by what we do, not by faith alone." **James 2:23,24 NLT**

To know that we have two of these friends continually praying on our behalf for things we don't even know how to pray, and for giving us access to the very heart of God by faith is just too much for our finite minds to comprehend. Thanks be to all 3 for their true and lasting friendship.

May I never lose sight of or devalue the truth and importance of my "3 Amigos". In Jesus' name, Amen

162

Prayer Busters and Boosters
"God's there, listening for all who pray, for all who pray and mean it."
Psalm 145:18 MSG

Prayer is one of the greatest privileges and most effective powers God gives freely to every believer in Jesus Christ. It gives us access to God's throne of grace 24/7/365.

God not only gives us prayer power. He also gives guidelines for using it. He does not honor selfish or inappropriate requests. He desires a broken spirit and contrite heart. He doesn't appreciate cheating by praying with unconfessed sins. We are told to forgive and be reconciled. We should not approach God's throne of grace with a distracted or divided heart

"God said to Solomon, "Because your greatest desire is to help your people, and you did not ask for wealth, riches, fame, or even the death of your enemies or a long life, but rather you asked for wisdom and knowledge to properly govern my people—"
1 Chronicles 1:8 NLT

Many times we don't have the power simply because we don't pray. We must have faith that God hears and is willing and able to answer our prayers. We often give up and quit praying too soon.

The millions of restored prodigals, saved marriages, healings, and other great supplications prayed on behalf of others give convincing testimony to the boost we experience from the prayers of others.

"But when you ask, you must believe and not doubt, because the one who doubts is like a wave of the sea, blown and tossed by the wind. [7] That person should not expect to receive anything from the Lord."
James 1:6-7

The sooner we learn to identify and avoid the prayer busters, and harness the power of prayer boosters by asking for their prayers, the sooner we will experience the power of prayer at its best.

Mountain moving requires mountain moving prayers. Is there anything in your life hindering yours? Could you use a boost or boost someone by praying?

Father, forgive me all my vain repetitions and half hearted prayers. Help me to acknowledge, appreciate, apologize, ask, and get more and better answers. In Jesus' name, Amen

Judgmentability

"Judgment [neither pronouncing judgment nor subjecting to censure], and you will not be judged; do not condemn and pronounce guilty, and you will not be condemned and pronounced guilty; acquit and forgive and release (give up resentment, let it drop), and you will be acquitted and forgiven and released." Luke 6;37 AMP

Unless we are the only other perfect human being the world has ever known, we need to take it easy about depending on our good lives, moral conduct, or personal holiness getting us into heaven.

> **"Against you, you only, have I sinned and done what is evil in your sight; so you are right in your verdict and justified when you judge."I**
> **Psalm 51:4 NIV**

Judgmentability is serious attitude that can not only be harmful but even fatal in terms of where we will spend eternity.

It actually carries an implied lack of faith that Jesus took our death judgment to the cross when He died so that we would never have too. To believe that we could do anything to improve on Jesus' perfect life and perfect sacrifice for our sins is to have too high an opinion of ourselves and too low opinion of Jesus.

We need to avoid and mourn over our sins and the sins of others. We may need to speak the truth in love when a Christian brother or sister is being held captive to a besetting sin;

We can be fruit inspectors for ourselves and for others, but never judges. Instead of judging we need to focus our heart's attention and mind's affection on appreciating that our righteous judge has declared us "Not Guilty" by seeking to live faithful lives fruitful in every good work.

> **"[God's Judgment of Sin] You may think you can condemn such people, but you are just as bad, and you have no excuse! When you say they are wicked and should be punished, you are condemning yourself, for you who judge others do these very same things."**
> **Romans 2:1 NLT**

When we consider all of the grace, mercy, and forgiveness God has given us because of Jesus, we dare not consider judgmentability a becoming pastime or response.

Father, take away my critical and judgmental spirit, that I might be more like Jesus. In Jesus' name, Amen.

Homeless Christians
The one thing I ask of the Lord—the thing I seek most—is to live in the house of the Lord all the days of my life, delighting in the Lord's perfections and meditating in his Temple." Psalm 27:4 NLT

If declining church attendance statistics are true, there are a lot of homeless Christians wandering around and growing further and further away from their faith.

"Seek, inquire for, and require the Lord while He may be found [claiming Him by necessity and by right]; call upon Him while He is near." Isaiah 55:6 AMP

Too many children who have been brought up in the church leave the minute they get out on their own, often because they have not seen the blessings of authentic Christianity being modeled in the home.

And then there are the homeless Christians who keep shopping around for the "perfect" church, which does not exist. (Even if it did, it would cease being perfect when they joined).

Homeless Christians seek the Lord in the most amazing places. They look for him on the golf course, at stock car races, rock concerts, and various watering holes. A lot seem to believe in osmosis and that they can find a home with God by sleeping in Sunday mornings.,

Every Christian needs the security and support of a good body of believers where they will find God in the Word, the strength and encouragement of the Lord's Supper, and the accountability, love and support of other seekers.

"Let's see how inventive we can be in encouraging love and helping out, not avoiding worshiping together as some do but spurring each other on, especially as we see the big Day approaching." Hebrews 10:25 MSG"

Jesus Christ and His church is the tie that binds our hearts in Christian love. If our heart is not in His home, what does that say about the condition of our heart?

If we are not at home in an authentic, Bible believing, Christ centered church, we might consider moving to a new home, but never becoming homeless.

Father, thank you for giving me your bride where I can feel at home with you, and find the all sufficient grace for my every need. In Jesus' name, Amen

The Greener Grass
"He makes me lie down in [fresh, tender] green pastures; He leads me beside the still and restful waters." Psalm 23:2 AMP

Whether it's chasing rainbows or often looking at the greener grass in lives of others lives, occupations, or churches, we sometimes seem to be looking for something better others seem to have.

"Whoever governs fairly and well, who rules in the Fear-of-God, Is like first light at daybreak without a cloud in the sky, Like green grass carpeting earth, glistening under fresh rain."
2 Samuel 23:4 MSG

"Just look,at ____(he's) (she's) got it made"; "_____'s church really does things right";"I sure wish I had a job like _____ ; Lot's of pay, little work or worries", etc.

We have role models kids grow up wanting to be like, dreams we pursue, and expectations and adventures we look forward to with great anticipation and pleasure.

Most often we find that the grass that looked so much greener to us is just as hard to mow. That person who seemingly has it made, that church that seems so much better than ours,and what we thought would be a dream job turns out to be a nightmare.

Our role models turn out to have worse problems than ours, the things that we thought would make us happy leave us unfulfilled, and those big adventures turn out to be big misadventures.

When we discover the joy of blooming where we are planted by abiding in Christ and growing in our faith relationship with Him, we will find the greener grass of eternal life that He has already mowed for us beside the still waters of God's peace.

"This is why the fulfillment of God's promise depends entirely on trusting God and his way, and then simply embracing him and what he does."
Romans 4:16a MSG

When we keep our eyes on:that "*green hill far away, Without a city wall, Where the dear Lord was crucified, Who died to save us all, "*we will no longer be looking for greener grass, we will be enjoying what we have and who we have become as sons and daughters of the living Lord.

Father, help me to abide in the green pastures and still waters of Your peace. In Jesus name, Amen

Avoiding the Acrimony of Matrimony
"For I hate divorce!" says the Lord, the God of Israel. "To divorce your wife is to overwhelm her with cruelty," Malachi 2:16 NLT

I don't know of anyone who ever went into a marriage thinking about getting a divorce. Knowing that God hates it does not make it any easier.

"Enjoy the wife you married as a young man! Lovely as an angel, beautiful as a rose—"
Proverbs 5:23 MSG

God still hates all sin but we are still imperfect people living in an imperfect world.. That's why Jesus had to die for us.

The alarming increase in the divorce rate and cohabiting outside of marriage among Christians is something we should try to avoid at all costs.

The truth is that what God has joined together sometimes falls apart, and people grow apart and desert each other physically, spiritually, and emotionally. Sometimes the deceiver of our souls sends predatory tempters or temptresses to fill the vacuum. God still forgives, and He still can and will turn our worst into His best.

We need to be aware of and avoid at all costs perhaps the worst sin of any divorce: acrimony, or the harsh and biting sharpness of an unforgiving heart. This is often the most devastating consequence of any divorce.

"In prayer there is a connection between what God does and what you do. You can't get forgiveness from God, for instance, without also forgiving others. If you refuse to do your part, you cut yourself off from God's part."
Matthew 6:14 MSG

Unforgiveness hurts the unforgiver much more than the unforgiven. When it takes root in the heart, the actual and collateral damage can be devastating, especially to children and others affected by the divorce.

God has made us all to love and hurt deeply. Thank God, we can overcome our hurts by harnessing the supernatural power of the Holy Spirit to grant forgiveness we don't have the strength or desire to grant in our own flesh.

When God says He will not forgive us unless we forgive others, does this not make unforgiveness an unforgivable sin?

Father, give me the grace and strength I need to forgive. In Jesus' name, Amen.

How Do You Know Him?
"Now this is eternal life: that they may know you, the only true God, and Jesus Christ, whom you have sent" .John 17:3 NIV

Someone's name often comes up in a casual conversation, and

"Those who know your name will trust in you, for you, LORD, have never forsaken those who seek you."
Psalm 9:10 NIV

we ask how your know him or her. Other times, someone will ask if we know a particular person, and what we know about them.

As followers and modelers of Jesus we would hope that someone would have something good to say about us when our name comes up. Unfortunately most of us have our bad moments where our pride, anger, envy, ego, or lust takes control and we do not make the best of impressions on some people.

The saddest part of all is that one momentary moral melt down can wipe out years of great testimony and witness.

I personally enjoy sharing my joy in knowing someone with another friend of that same person. When old classmates, church members, horse friends, or former business associates names come up I am always glad to get updates and know more about them, especially if it's good.

All of this leads up to the big question "how do you know Jesus"?

When we first meet Him, we probably know Him as forgiver and Savior. As we get to know Him better by spending more time with Him in His Word and the fellowship of other believers, we will get to know Him as brother, friend, joy giver, peace giver, and the one who gets God to answer our prayers.

"But in your hearts set apart Christ as Lord. Always be prepared to give an answer to everyone who asks you to give the reason for the hope that you have. But do this with gentleness and respect,"
1 Peter 3:15

Jesus wants to be that "friend that sticks closer than a brother", confidant, supporter and encourager.

Father, let me live my life in the power of the Holy Spirit, that all might know how well I know and how much I love Jesus. In Jesus' name, Amen.

Whose Shoes?

"My dear friends, what I would really like you to do is try to put yourselves in my shoes to the same extent that I, when I was with you, put myself in yours" Galatians 4:12a. MSG

We have all probably tried to walk in our mom or dad's shoes during our childhood years. I can remember how clumsy I felt and how difficult it was.

"Stalwart walks in step with God; his path blazed by God, he's happy. If he stumbles, he's not down for long; God has a grip on his hand."
Psalm 37:23 MSG

When a pastor, boss, or other leader leaves, we often think of what big shoes it is going to take to fill the void left, if that leader was a good one.

One of the most important things about shoes is the fit. We can get blisters, bunions, and other problems from wearing ill fitting shoes. When we find ourselves in a job or task that we are not well fit for, we will find little joy and usually little success in the job.

We are all exhorted to wear the sandals of peace as part of the armor of life the Holy Spirit gives to help us overcome or escape the temptations of our flesh, the world, and the devil.

As imitators of Christ we are asked to fill the shoes of the greatest man who ever lived by loving others as He taught us. When we walk in the Spirit, we will avoid the pitfalls and consequences of walking in the flesh.

When we learn to quit walking in anger, ego, malice, pride, and self centered control of our flesh, and walk in the humility love, peace, joy, obedience and kindness of Jesus, we won't have to worry about getting any blisters or bunions.

" For shoes, put on the peace that comes from the Good News so that you will be fully prepared."
Ephesians 6:15 NLT

Father, You have left big shoes to fill by faith and obedience. Thank you for imparting your perfection so that I only have to be faithful and obedient, and never perfect. In Jesus'name, Amen

Hold That Line

"I pray to God—my life a prayer— and wait for what he'll say and do. My life's on the line before God, my Lord, waiting and watching till morning, waiting and watching till morning." Psalm 130:5 MSG

There are all sorts of lines in every area of life. We have boundary lines with regard to territory and conduct, defense lines to hold in football, fires, and battles, etc.

"A life frittered away disgusts God; he loves those who run straight for the finish line."

Proverbs 15:9 MSG

We hear that Wal Mart is holding the line on prices, Johnny Cash singing about "walking the line", And the morning line in sports betting.

Scripture speaks of a plumb line with which the Lord measures righteousness. It is a good thing that Jesus came to die for us and straighten the crooked lines we create walking through life in the flesh.

God sends us all life lines of answered prayers, favorable circumstances, protection, and a life line grace sufficient for our every need.

God has given us the Holy Spirit as a deposit and guarantee that all who truly believe in salvation by faith in Jesus alone through grace alone will reach the finish line leading to eternal life.

Jesus died to redeem, forgive our sins, and set us free from bondage to sin so that we would not even consider living in willful disobedience and sin if we are truly born again believers.

"For the Word that God speaks is alive and full of power [making it active, operative, energizing, and effective]; it is sharper than any two-edged sword, penetrating to the dividing line of the breath of life (soul) and [the immortal] spirit, and of joints and marrow [of the deepest parts of our nature], exposing and sifting and analyzing and judging the very thoughts and purposes of the heart

Hebrews 4:12 AMP

We hold onto the life line Jesus died to give us by submitting to His lordship in the power of the Holy Spirit Who God sent to make sure we reached the finish line. May we all always hold on tight.

Father, help me to hold on to the finish line that is beginning line of my forever life with you in heaven. In Jesus' name, Amen

Unlimited Salad Bar

"If you are filled with light, with no dark corners, then your whole life will be radiant, as though a floodlight were filling you with light."
Luke 11:36 NLT

"[Growing in grace] they shall still bring forth fruit in old age; they shall be full of sap [of spiritual vitality] and [rich in the] verdure [of trust, love, and contentment]."
Psalm 92:14 AMP

Unlimited salad bars became quite the rage in the late 60's and early 70's, and are still popular at some restaurants, especially Ruby Tuesday's.

God has given us all access to the greatest salad bar ever. It's the unlimited fruit salad bar prepared fresh daily by the Holy Spirit.

When St. Paul exhorted us to be filled with the Spirit, he was talking about an ongoing, continuous filling. The truth is, that these tents we are co inhabiting with our flesh leak a lot. The temptations and cares of the world, our flesh and the devil continually drain us.

Left to our own flesh, we are going to bear the anger, jealousy, lust, envy and pride of the flesh. It is only when we submit to the control of the Holy Spirit in our lives that He fills us with the fruit of *"Love, joy, peace, long-suffering, kindness, goodness, faith, and self control"*(Galatians 5:22), which we are all called to bear.

We can't always control our circumstances, but we can control how we respond. What a difference it can make when we respond with the fruit of the Spirit instead of the fruit of our sinful flesh.

"For the fruit (the effect, the product) of the Light or the Spirit [consists] in every form of kindly goodness, uprightness of heart, and trueness of life.
Ephesians 5;9 AMP

The fruit of the Spirit is an unlimited salad bar which we can visit as often as we like. When we empty our selves of the sinfulness of our flesh through contrition, confession, and repentance we will receive the renewing of our minds and God will produce the fruit of the Spirit for us to bear.

Father, help me to keep my cup filled to overflowing with the fruit of your Spirit so that I can bear it and share it with others. In Jesus' name, Amen

Majoring in Minors

"Wherefore, my beloved, as ye have always obeyed, not as in my presence only, but now much more in my absence, work out your own salvation with fear and trembling."Philippians 2:11

There are a lot of feelings hurt and stumblings caused by people, churches, and pastors, trying to impose their personal belief on others in spite of the fact that God neither upholds or forbids this particular belief or practice.

"The Spirit of the Lord GOD is upon me; because the LORD hath anointed me to preach good tidings unto the meek; he hath sent me to bind up the brokenhearted, to proclaim liberty to the captives, and the opening of the prison to them that are bound;"
Isaiah 61:1 KJV

Although Christian liberty should never be used as an excuse for sin, it is certainly a proper antidote against legalism and self righteousness.

The worship wars that continue to plague many churches are a good example of what can happen when we start trying to dictate what kind of music and what order of service we should have in our church.

Life is too short and we have too many real sins to worry about instead of majoring in minors that are neither commanded nor forbidden in Scripture.

What matters to God is the centrality of the Gospel that we are saved by grace alone, through faith alone, as taught by Scripture alone that Jesus Christ is our Savior.

"That's why Jesus lived and died and then lived again: so that he could be our Master across the entire range of life and death, and free us from the petty tyrannies of each other."
Romans 14:9 MSG

True Christian liberty calls us all to worship Him in spirit and in truth with a broken spirit and contrite heart and to work out our own salvation with fear and trembling.

Father, help keep me from becoming a Pharisee who concentrates more on minors than majors. In Jesus' name, Amen

Spiritual Sensitivity

"Make a clean break with all cutting, backbiting, profane talk. Be gentle with one another, sensitive. Forgive one another as quickly and thoroughly as God in Christ forgave you." Ephesians 4:31 MSG

"they who [diligently] seek for, inquire of and for Him, and require Him [as their greatest need]. May your hearts be quickened now and forever!"
Psalm 22:26b AMP

Being aware of the sensitivity of others is one of the best people skills one can ever develop. I am probably not the only one who has given unintended, needless offense, by ignoring the sensitivity of my wife, children, friends and others. The kidding can often be cutting, the sarcasm sour, and the criticisms hurtful.

Sometimes we need to be singing "be still my soul" to remind us to be listening for the leadings of the Holy Spirit. We sometimes get so caught up in business we miss holiness and divine appointments.

I still remember with sadness one Saturday morning when a lady new in town stopped by our church for information, and I was so engrossed in getting ready for a Promise Keeper's meeting I barely gave her the time of day. I thank God that she was not discouraged by me and became a member and dear sister in Christ.

Jesus was the most spiritually sensitive man who ever lived. He listened for the leadings of His Father, and always obeyed and followed them.

Better yet, redouble your efforts. Be energetic in your life of salvation, reverent and sensitive before God. That energy is God's energy, an energy deep within you, God himself willing and working at what will give him the most pleasure."
Philippians 2:12 b MSG

If we ask God to give us a more sensitive heart, He most certainly will, as this is in conformity to His will. When we look at and love every person the way Christ looks at and loves us we are going to be blessed to be able to encourage, comfort, and bless them.

. When we develop this same sensitivity to the presence and needs of those God sends our way, we will be well on our way to becoming imitators of Christ.

Father, help me to keep my spiritual ears and eyes and heart sensitive and obedient to your leadings. In Jesus' name, Amen

Collateral Damage

"Blind guides! You strain your water so you won't accidentally swallow a gnat, but you swallow a camel!"Matthew 23:24 NLT

Collateral damage is the term used to describe unintended damage incidental to the outcome of a mission. The casualties accidentally inflicted on friends instead of foes continues to be a problem in every war and battle

**"Then the Lord said to me, Out of the north the evil [which the prophets had foretold as the result of national sin] shall disclose itself and break forth upon all the inhabitants of the land."
Jeremiah 1;4 AMP**

Unintended damage done by many Christians and many churches often does more damage than all of their kingdom building efforts.

A list of possible side effects of any prescription drug warn of collateral damage that can often be worse than the cure

The collateral damage of telling people they weren't healed because of lack of faith has hurt and discouraged a lot of people.

Almost every conflict or disagreement among a body of believers often results in a lot of collateral damage. Legalistic lists and teachings of what you must do to earn your salvation bring back the collateral damage of the yoke of the law which Jesus died to fulfill.

We all are going to experience collateral damage as long as we live in a sin sick world. Whether it's being in the wrong place at the wrong time, the consequences of bad choices, or a manifestation of the evil in the world, the permissive will of God will often allow unintended damage incidental to His promise and declared intention to work all things for our good.

**"I suspect you would never intend this, but this is what happens. When you attempt to live by your own religious plans and projects, you are cut off from Christ, you fall out of grace",
Galatians 5:3-5 MSG**

We need to recognize, respond in the best way we know how, and, above all, never let collateral damage deal a fatal blow to our faith or our joy in the Lord.

Father, keep me ever mindful of the unintended damage done by sin and help me to avoid it. In Jesus' name, Amen

Summing it Up

"Summing it all up, friends, I'd say you'll do best by filling your minds and meditating on things true, noble, reputable, authentic, compelling, gracious-- the best, not the worst; the beautiful, not the ugly; things to praise, not things to curse." Philippians 4:8 Phillips NT

Of all the many wonderful books and chapters of Scripture, Philippians 4 has to be one of the most wonderful. Of all the good advice contained in the Bible, this is some of the best.

"That person is like a tree planted by streams of water, which yields its fruit in season and whose leaf does not wither— whatever they do prospers." Psalm 1:3 NIV

The devil's favorite strategy is to get us majoring in minors and dwelling on the ugly instead of the beautiful. If we are living in a glass that's half empty instead of half full, it's probably because we insist on being filled with the worries of the flesh instead of being filled with the fruit of the Spirit by rejoicing.

There seems to be a lot of half truths and spin garbage being forwarded around and passed on by people who do not even realize they may be bearing false witness; I have taken to replying with Philippian 4:8.

Scripture reminds us to be "wise as serpents and harmless as doves". We can be aware and concerned about a lot of problems, but we will be better served by turning these problems over to the sovereignty of our problem solver, and meditating on things *"true, noble, reputable, authentic, compelling, gracious--the best, not the worst; the beautiful, not the ugly; things to praise, not things to curse."*:

"Let your light so shine before men that they may see your moral excellence and your praiseworthy, noble, and good deeds and recognize and honor and praise and glorify your Father Who is in heaven." Matthew 5:16 AMP

The more we concentrate on controlling our thoughts and choosing just not to think where and what we shouldn't be thinking, the more fruit of the Spirit we will be bearing in our lives.

Father, help me to stay out of the worry and complaining zone, and in the joy zone you died to provide for me. In Jesus' name, Amen

Shopper's Guide for Spouses

"Drink waters out of your own cistern [of a pure marriage relationship], and fresh running waters out of your own well." Proverbs 5:15 AMP

Internet match making has become a big business and popular place to shop for a prospective mate. I personally know of some great marriages of people who have been brought together through e-harmony.I am sure that there have been others with sad results.

" God, not you, made marriage. His Spirit inhabits even the smallest details of marriage. And what does he want from marriage? Children of God, that's what. So guard the spirit of marriage within you. Don't cheat on your spouse."
Malachi 2:13b MSG

Cultures change but God's Word is still the gold standard for all who would enjoy the abundant blessings of doing life God's way.

God says we should leave, cleave and become one. He says we should not be yoked with unbelievers, and that marriage should be forever until death.

You don't have to be a rocket scientist to know where to fish if you want to land a prize catch. The best guide may be whether this prospective spouse is going build you up or pull you down.

Every serious shopper should consider whether this prospect would be a suitable mother or father for their children. .

The road to divorce court and broken homes is paved with the good intentions but disastrous results of disregarding God's marriage shopping instructions.

"But Jesus said, "Not everyone is mature enough to live a married life. It requires a certain aptitude and grace."
Matthew 19:11 MSG

God can help us all rise above dysfunctional family backgrounds, but it is not too likely if we haven't risen above our sinful nature and into God's covenant of grace through faith in Jesus Christ.

Father, help me to find what I need in a spouse to build me up and let me know the true joy having you as my marriage advisor. In Jesus name', Amen

The Bottom Line

"Cheerfully pleasing God is the main thing, and that's what we aim to do, regardless of our conditions. Sooner or later we'll all have to face God, regardless of our conditions. We will appear before Christ and take what's coming to us as a result of our actions, either good or bad."
2 Corinthians 5:8-9 MSG

"Your righteous testimonies are everlasting and Your decrees are binding to eternity; give me understanding and I shall live [give me discernment and comprehension and I shall not die]."
Psalm 119:144 AMP

The profit line is the bottom line of every business. Every area of life has a most important bottom line.

We eat and drink to survive...study to learn...work to succeed...practice to perfect or improve...exercise to stay fit and healthy...etc.

As we pursue all of these and other activities, we should always be aware of how whatever we do affects the bottom line.

When it comes to living we need to know that the bottom line of the finish line is determined by what we do about Jesus.

We can choose to lose by making momentary pleasures and pride and ego choices to reject Christ and do life our way controlled by our flesh, or to do life God's way by accepting Jesus Christ as Savior and Lord and submitting our lives to the God control of the Holy Spirit.

The misspent years of wandering aimlessly lost is a high price to pay for ignoring the bottom line.

The earlier we make eternal life our bottom line, the sooner we will start enjoying the abundant life that can only be found by having our minds transformed and spirits renewed by the power of he Holy Spirit.

"And He replied to him, You shall love the Lord your God with all your heart and with all your soul and with all your mind (intellect)This is the great (most important, principal) and first commandment."
Matthew 22:37,38 AMP

The main thing is that knowing that we are going to have eternal life in heaven through faith in Jesus Christ is the most important bottom line of life.

Father, keep me ever mindful of the only bottom line that really matters. In Jesus' name, Amen

Holy Consternation

"Then they went out [and] fled from the tomb, for trembling and bewilderment and consternation had seized them. And they said nothing about it to anyone, for they were held by alarm and fear. 'Mark 16;8 AMP

We constantly have some dismaying experiences that hinder and confuse us and test our faith. This consternation is especially tough when we see bad things happening to good people.

"The nations shall see [God's deliverance] and be ashamed of all their might [which cannot be compared to His]. They shall lay their hands upon their mouths in consternation; their ears shall be deaf."
Micah 7:16 AMP

With trials and tragedies rampant throughout the World even the strongest of faiths have to draw from the living waters of God's grace to rinse away the bitterness of sorrow and despair of holy consternation.

When we add all of the consequences to our own bad choices to the troubles of the world and satanic attacks of the devil, we sometimes seem to have more troubles than we can bear, and begin to doubt that even The One Who has promised to bear our burdens is really working all things for our good and His glory.

This is when we need to put on that sword of the Spirit and believe, trust and obey.

The best cure for holy consternation is holy rejoicing. When we do, God promises to calm our troubled spirits, and fill us with that peace that surpasses all understanding.

"And they recognized him as the man who usually sat [begging] for alms at the Beautiful Gate of the temple; and they were filled with wonder and amazement (bewilderment, consternation) over what had occurred to him.
Acts 3:10 AMP

When we receive God's supernatural grace to respond to troubles by rejoicing, and by bearing the fruit of the Spirit instead of the anger, and self centeredness of our flesh, we will be well on our way to experiencing the holy transformation God wants for all His children.

Father give me the wisdom and discernment I need to avoid the consternations of this life. In Jesus' name, Amen

Are you a Cleaver?

"That thou mayest love the LORD thy God, and that thou mayest obey his voice, and that thou mayest cleave unto him: for he is thy life, and the length of thy days" Deuteronomy 30:20a KJV:

The King James Version of the Bible is one of the few Bibles that contains this great old word that means: "*to adhere firmly and closely or loyally and unwaveringly*".

> ⁰Thou shalt fear the LORD thy God; him shalt thou serve, and to him shalt thou cleave, and swear by his name.
> Deuteronomy 10:20 KJV

We still hear the word a lot at weddings and in marriage counseling sessions for good reason. The commandment to cleave or stick with someone is the glue that bonds and holds together all lasting marriages.

The utter disregard for this commandment is probably the biggest single cause of the abysmally high and getting higher divorce rate in this country. Commitment or cleaving both seem to have become outdated and forgotten concepts in today's throw away world.

The "take this job and shove it" or "I'm out of here" response to often the slightest irritations have taken people out of jobs, marriages,and the pews of many churches.

The truth is that "cleavers" or committed Christians, spouses, employees, or friends are not only the best of the best, but also the most blessed of the blessed.

God loves and blesses "cleavers".because they are being faithful and obedient to their calling.

> "And He said to all, If any person wills to come after Me, let him deny himself [disown himself, forget, lose sight of himself and his own interests, refuse and give up himself] and take up his cross daily and follow Me [cleave steadfastly to Me, conform wholly to My example in living and, if need be, in dying also].
> Luke 9:23 AMP

Without cleaving faith, there will be no growing into the fullness of Christ, and we will most likely be left withering on the vine living unfruitful lives and missing out on so many of the great plans God has for us.

:*Father, help me to be a loyal, unwavering cleaver. In Jesus' name,*

What Kind of Wall Are You?

"Pile your troubles on God's shoulders— he'll carry your load, he'll help you out. He'll never let good people topple into ruin"
Psalm 55:22a MSG

Just as every building has two types of walls, every human is living in a house with the same two walls. A load

"The LORD is my strength and shield.I trust him with all my heart"
Psalm 28:7a NLT

bearing wall carries the weight above it, while a curtain wall affords no structural support.

Many people are wandering aimlessly lost as curtain walls with nothing to support or encourage them.

When we build our marriages, families, careers, and relationships on the load bearing wall of God's love, we are going to build a life that will live forever.

As long as we insist on being our own load bearing wall, the weight of the world and the temptations of our flesh are going to continually bring our world tumbling down under the weight of living in a sin sick world and dying and spending eternity suffering the torments of hell.

When Jesus Christ is our cornerstone and the Holy Spirit our load bearer, we can face all of the problems of today and tomorrow knowing that we have God as our ever present help in time of trouble and His all sufficient grace to see us through the trials of life.

"But the firm foundation of (laid by) God stands, sure and unshaken, bearing this seal (inscription): The Lord knows those who are His, and, Let everyone who names [himself by] the name of the Lord give up all iniquity and stand aloof from it."
2 Timothy 2:19 AMP

When we feel overcome trying to bear the weight of the world on our shoulders, we need to turn these weights over to the one God has given to bear these weights for us.

Father, thank you for being the load bearing wall of my life and giving me the support I need to overcome the trials and temptations of the world. In Jesus' name, Amen

180

Beast of Burden

"Give your burdens to the Lord, and he will take care of you. He will not permit the godly to slip and fall." Psalm 55:22 NLT

In God's wonderful plan of creation, he created donkeys, mules, camels, elephants, horses, etc., to be load bearers. That is why some are also known as beasts of burdens.

"Blessed be the Lord, Who bears our burdens and carries us day by day, even the God Who is our salvation! Selah [pause, and calmly think of that]!"
Psalm 68:19 AMP

He never intended that we would be beasts of burdens, and yet that is what many of us have become. We all too often bear the spiritual burdens, of bitterness, guilt, shame, unforgiveness, pride, anger, envy, hatred, malice, and lust. These by products of our fallen nature are all burdens we were never created to bear.

If all this is true why do we choose to lose by trying to bear these burdens that pull us down instead of lift us up? The truth may well lie in the fact that the deceiver of our souls keeps us into bondage to them because we do not fully accept or believe the truth that Jesus Christ gave us victory over sin and death, and that we are no longer beasts of burdens.

"Are you tired? Worn out? Burned out on religion? Come to me. Get away with me and you'll recover your life. I'll show you how to take a real rest. Walk with me and work with me— watch how I do it. Learn the unforced rhythms of grace. I won't lay anything heavy or ill-fitting on you. Keep company with me and you'll learn to live freely and lightly."
Matthew 11:28-30 MSG

Jesus came to live and die to become our burden bearer. We need to recognize this truth and take advantage of His generous offer to: *"come unto me all who are heavy laden"* and to dump our burdens at the cross.

Jesus wants to bear our burdens so that we can bear the fruit of the Spirit. When we replace the burdens of sin with the "*love, joy, peace, forbearance, kindness, goodness, faithfulness, gentleness and self-control we will have* more and more of the peace and joy of the burden free life Jesus died to give us.

Father help me to lay down my burdens daily into your sea of forgetfulness. In Jesus' name Amen

Is Your Grace Being Multiplied?

"May grace (God's favor) and peace (which is [a]perfect well-being, all necessary good, all spiritual prosperity, and[b]freedom from fears and agitating passions and moral conflicts) be multiplied to you in [the full, personal, [c]precise, and correct] knowledge of God and of Jesus our Lord 2 Peter 1:2 AMP.

Of all the great books and chapters of the Bible chapter 1 of 2nd Peter may well deserve to be one of the top ten favorite chapters of every believer. To understand and put into practice these verses will assure the grace of God being multiplied in any life.

As wonderful the grace of God for salvation, there is so much more grace that He wants to multiply within the hearts of all His children.

"For as these qualities are yours and increasingly abound in you, they will keep [you] from being idle or unfruitful unto the [full personal] knowledge of our Lord Jesus Christ (the Messiah, the Anointed One)".
2 Peter 1:8 AMP

Faith is not our get out of jail card to be cashed in when we die. Faith is our living hope in the exceeding riches of God's grace as we seek to become more like Jesus by exercising it daily.

As we "employ every effort in [d]exercising your faith to develop virtue (excellence, resolution, Christian energy), and in [exercising] virtue [develop] knowledge (intelligence)," (2 Peter 1:5b AMP), we are going to find God's grace being multiplied in every area of our lives giving us the abundant life He came to give us.

Faith in Jesus Christ is a living faith in a living Lord. Every living thing has to be "nourished to flourish".

We must exercise our spiritual muscles through developing knowledge, self-control, patience, endurance, godliness, brotherly affection, and Christian love.

"Because of this, brethren, be all the more solicitous and eager to make sure (to ratify, to strengthen, to make steadfast) your calling and election; for if you do this, you will never stumble or fall.
2 Peter 1:10 AMP

May we all treasure and earnestly seek the abundant grace of God by exercising the disciplines of our Christian faith.

Father, help me to become more "graceable". In Jesus' name, Amen

Living Up to Our Potential

"For I know the plans I have for you," says the Lord. "They are plans for good and not for disaster, to give you a future and a hope." Jeremiah 29:11 NLT

When it comes to living up to our potential, we need to be living

"He holds success in store for the upright, he is a shield to those whose walk is blameless," Proverbs 2:7 NIV

down our past. Before we became born again believers we were doomed to living down in the bondage of sin with no hope of earning anything except its wages.

When Jesus Christ died on the cross to set us free from death and bondage to sin, He also started a process of helping us to live up to our full potential as sons and daughters of the living God, and brothers and sisters of the living Lord.

The Holy Spirit came to live in us in order to help us "live it up!" He has been given as a deposit and guarantee that we live up to the very likeness of Christ Himself by becoming more like Him day by day, year by year, until we are glorified with Him in heaven.

Jesus set the bar high for living up to God's standards in every area of our lives. We will never achieve perfection in this life, but we can seek to live up to our full potential by the daily renewal of our minds and surrendering to the Lordship of Jesus Christ.

"And I ask him that with both feet planted firmly on love, you'll be able to take in with all followers of Jesus the extravagant dimensions of Christ's love. Reach out and experience the breadth! Test its length! Plumb the depths! Rise to the heights! Live full lives, full in the fullness of God. Ephesians 3:13-15

When we are living up to our potential we will be trading our sorrows for abiding in the joy of the Lord. We will be living those fully pleasing lives, fruitful in every good work, which God planned for us before we were ever born.

There will always be the unholy trifecta of the world, our flesh, and the devil fighting to keep us from living up to our full potential. We need to wear the full armor of God and pray for supernatural strength, wisdom, and discernment that we realize our full potential.

Father, convict me of and help me repent of the sins that are keeping me from living up to my potential in Christ. In Jesus' name, Amen.

Church Competition
"You're blessed when you can show people how to cooperate instead of compete or fight. That's when you discover who you really are, and your place in God's family." Matthew 5:9 MSG

The disciples seem to have been competing with each other for Jesus' favor. Even a mother got involved and asked that her sons get top billing.

"BEHOLD, HOW good and how pleasant it is for brethren to dwell together in unity!" Psalm 133:1 AMP

Jesus response was a good reminder to us that being the greatest meant being the greatest servant of all.

When competition trumps cooperation within a body of believers, a denomination, or among the many bodies of believers in any given city, the cause of Christ gets side tracked by divisions and personal agendas that give pleasure to the devil instead of the One we seek to serve.

When pride and ego take control and individuals start competing for control instead of cooperating, people are actually more interested in building up their own little kingdoms instead of the Kingdom of God.

Church polity on a denominational level finds groups trying to take control to further their agenda rather than cooperate and find a better means for fulfilling the church's mission to seek and save the lost.

In spite of everyone's agreement that the number one goal is winning the presidency for their party, the presidential primary campaigns often get so competitive that the winner has to overcome more damage caused by his own party than he will suffer from his opponent in the presidential election.

In many communities doctrinal differences and tradition take precedence over agreeing on the centrality of the Gospel and unifying and cooperating to do things together to better feed and care for the needy and seek and save the lost.

"She said, "Grant that one of these two sons of mine may sit at your right and the other at your left in your kingdom." Matthew 20:21b NLT

We should all be more mindful of how to become great in God's eyes by cooperating instead of competing with other brothers and sisters in Christ.

Father help me to be a building block of cooperation instead of a stumbling block of competition in building your Kingdom. In Jesus' name, Amen.

High Risk Christianity
"Don't be bluffed into silence by the threats of bullies. There's nothing they can do to your soul, your core being. Save your fear for God, who holds your entire life—body and soul—in his hands." Matthew 10:28 MSG

"In the day when I cried out, You answered me, *And* made me bold *with* strength in my soul"

Psalm 138:3 NKJV

The growing persecution of Christians around the world should be cause for great sadness. The cost of discipleship keeps going up in this country as secular and satanic humanists have succeeded in undermining our Christian beliefs and practices in almost every area of life in this country.

Crime and punishment have become games lawyers. judges, and legislatures play. Who would have ever dreamed that crooks, thieves, homosexuals, terrorists and atheists would ever seem to have more protection under the law than Christians?

Thank God we are yet not put to the test of "standing up for Jesus" as In many areas of the world where Christians are massacred, jailed, beaten, or robbed with no defense except the protective grace of God.

When we look at not having the boldness or passion to witness or spread the Gospel for fear of risking rejection or ridicule, how shallow has our faith become?

Before we risk our future and well being on the approval of people and love of the world, we would all do well to remember Jesus came to lose it all to eliminate the risk of losing our eternal salvation.

"[For that matter], why do I live [dangerously as I do, running such risks that I am] in peril every hour?"

1 Corinthians 15:30 AMP

While our Christian Faith can often have us facing high risk situations in our on-going battles of life, we can take real comfort and find real courage in knowing that our ultimate reward far outweighs any risk.

Father, give me the strength, grace, and power to "count it all joy" when my faith is challenged and tested by my high risk Christianity. In Jesus' name, Amen

185

Our Declaration of Independence

"Oh, thank God—he's so good! His love never runs out. All of you set free by God, tell the world! Tell how he freed you from oppression,"
Psalm 107:1-2 MSG

The Fourth of July is always a happy reminder that our country declared its freedom from rule by England. The Emancipation proclamation reminds us that all of the slaves were set free in this country.

> "I will say to the prisoners, 'Come out in freedom,and to those in darkness, 'Come into the light.They will be my sheep, grazing in green pastures and on hills that were previously bare"
> Isaiah 49:9 NLT

As important as these events were, everyone of us should have our own happy reminder of when we were declared free from sin, death, and the devil.

All of us should remember and celebrate the hour we first believed, and, perhaps more importantly, the hour we declared our Independence from sin and became disciples by surrendering to the Lordship of Jesus Christ.

When we look back upon being held captive by sin and hostage to the guilt and shame we had to bear, we are filled with thanksgiving and praise to the burden bearer of our sins, who took them with Him to the cross when He died so that we would never have to pay the death penalty the law required.

"Free at last" has had special meaning for the founding fathers of our country and leaders of the civil rights movement. It should give us all cause to shout it out with joy when we think of all of the sins we have been freed from, and for all love, peace, and joy we have been freed to enjoy.

> "We know that our old sinful selves were crucified with Christ so that sin might lose its power in our lives. We are no longer slaves to sin.'
> Romans 6:6 NLT

Like many of the slaves after the Civil War, we have been set free and don't even know it. We still need to declare that we are no longer dependent upon and slaves to our addictions, anger, lust, envy and pride, and start living like the Savior whose name we claim.

Father, keep me ever mindful of the price You paid for our freedom and continue to give me the strength and power live in it. In Jesus' name, Amen

Peaceable Release

"Then Abraham's spirit was released, and he died at a good (ample, full) old age, an old man, satisfied and satiated, and was gathered to his people." Genesis 25:8 AMP

Some churches give members a peaceable release when they move, transfer out, or ask to be removed from membership. Some churches give pastors peaceable releases when they leave to accept another call.

"My eyes are ever on the LORD, for only he will release my feet from the snare"
Psalm 25:15 NIV

Some spouses give each other peaceable releases when they divorce and leave with no ill feelings towards each other.

There is coming a time when we all are going to need a peaceable release from this life into the eternal joy of life in heaven.

We can only get this peaceable release by making peace with God through receiving Jesus Christ as our Savior before we die.

The contrast between the mocker and the thief who received Jesus on the Cross points out the difference between dying saved and unsaved. How sad it is to go to a funeral of a friend or loved one who has died without a peaceable release from bondage and death to sin.

The salvation of the thief on the cross gives the encouragement we all need that it is never too late for anyone to get a peaceable release. This is why we should never stop praying that the Lord remove the scales of blindness from those we know are wandering aimlessly lost towards the eternal torments of hell.

"To open their eyes that they may turn from darkness to light and from the power of Satan to God, so that they may thus receive forgiveness and release from their sins and a place and portion among those who are consecrated and purified by faith in Me."
Acts 16:18 AMP

The reality that the angel of death can come anytime without any warning should keep us praying and witnessing intently for those we love.

This matter of getting a peaceable release is a very serious matter. May we all make sure that we have it, and pray fervently for those who don't.

Father, thank you for sending Jesus to die to give me that peaceable release to avoid the torments of hell. In Jesus' name, Amen.

187

The One Thing Needed

"Yes, everything else is worthless when compared with the infinite value of knowing Christ Jesus my Lord. For his sake I have discarded everything else, counting it all as garbage, so that I could gain Christ. "Philippians 3:8 NLT

In this fast track roller coaster life in the 21st century, it is easy to get so distracted doing that we forget all about being.

"Nothing will hurt or destroy in all my holy mountain,for as the waters fill the sea,so the earth will be filled with people who know the LORD."
Isaiah 9:ll NLT

There's a living to earn, chores to be done, and so many of our own needs and the needs of others to be met that it's easy to get overwhelmed or distracted.

When we learn to quit majoring in minors that may be the majors of the moment, and major on the main thing, we are going to begin enjoying the abundant life Jesus died to give us in all its fullness.

The one thing needed, simply put, is to "know Jesus"! We may know him as a casual friend, as our forgiver, and even as Savior, but do we really know Him as Lord and Savior and best friend?

When we really get to know Jesus, we will get to know what He did so we can know what we should do as imitators of Christ.

When we really get to know Jesus by abiding in Him through His Word we are going to experience the wonderful blessings of His friendship and His joy, more God pleasing answered prayers prayed to His glory and not our own, and a heightened awareness of Jesus living in and through us by the power of the Holy Spirit.,

"But Martha [overly occupied and too busy] was distracted with much serving; and she came up to Him and said, Lord, is it nothing to You that my sister has left me to serve alone? Tell her then to help me [to lend a hand and do her part along with me]!
Luke 10:40 AMP

Now is the time to get rid of the trivial pursuits and concentrate on the one thing needed!

Father, help me to make knowing You the number one desire of my heart and priority of my life. In Jesus name, Amen

How Good Do We Have to Be?

"You, therefore, must be perfect [growing into complete maturity of godliness in mind and character, having reached the proper height of virtue and integrity], as your heavenly Father is perfect." Matthew 5:48 AMP

There seems to be a wide divergence of opinions on how good we have to be to get to heaven. When asked what they would answer if God should ask why He should let you into heaven, a lot of life long Christians seem to think their church membership, good conduct ,or absence of major sins will make them good enough to get in.

"If his good deeds had made him acceptable to God, he would have had something to boast about. But that was not God's way."
Romans 4:2 NLT

Some churches teach that if you participate in all the sacraments or good works of the Church you will be good enough to get in.

Works righteousness is a slippery slope that is going to take anyone who actually thinks they can be good enough to get to heaven down to the wrong destination.

How sweet it is to know that we don't have to pin our hope for heaven on how good we have been, but rather on our faith in how good Jesus Christ was in dying as the perfect, unblemished sacfrice for our sins.

The only caveat to knowing that we are going to heaven on the goodness of Christ is that this is not a license go sin, but a freedom to fill God's plans for fulfilling His purposes through us as we are free to live lives fully pleasing to Him and fruitful in the good works that glorify, honor, and please Him.

"I thank my God at all times for you because of the grace (the favor and spiritual blessing) of God which was bestowed on you in Christ Jesus,"
1 Corinthians 1:4 AMP

"When our perceived goodness gets derailed by our sins in thought, word, deed, omission, and commission, how sweet it is to know that Jesus was more than good enough so that we don't have to be.

Father, thank you that I do not have to depend on my flawed goodness to get to heaven. In Jesus' name, Amen

Richer Than We Realize
"Riches and honor are with me, enduring wealth and righteousness (uprightness in every area and relation, and right standing with God)" Proverbs 8:18 AMP

We may not always realize it, but as true believers in Jesus Christ, we are some of the richest people in all the world. When we receive the favor and spiritual blessings of God by faith, we become instant millionaires in the manifold grace of God.

"You satisfy me more than the richest feast. I will praise you with songs of joy." Psalm 63:5 NLT

Along with that precious gift of eternal life, we receive a heavenly bank account with our name in the book of life and a passbook with automatic overdraft protection from a treasury that will never refuse our requests due to insufficient funds.

We have grace accounts for encouragement, strength, peace, joy, and security that is beyond anything the FDIC can cover.

When we remember the riches of God's grace that are ours in Jesus Christ, we have absolutely no excuse for living like paupers or refusing to share these riches with others.

These riches are from a well of living water that never runs dry primed by the Holy Spirit pumping them out in a supply that will never be exhausted.

When Jesus Christ promised grace sufficient for our every need He promised the abundance of wisdom, faith, strength, and repentance we need to overcome any obstacle that might threaten to separate us from His love.

"I thank my God at all times for you because of the grace (the favor and spiritual blessing) of God which was bestowed on you in Christ Jesus," 1 Corinthians 1:4 AMP

We should not only glory in the Cross of Christ for our salvation but also in the riches of His marvelous favor and grace for living Spirit enriched lives to the praise of His Glory.

Father, keep me ever mindful of the great riches I have in You. In Jesus' name, Amen

The Sin of Insincerity

"But the wisdom that comes from heaven is first of all pure. It is also peace loving, gentle at all times, and willing to yield to others. It is full of mercy and good deeds. It shows no partiality and is always sincere." James 3:17 NLT

"Who may worship in your sanctuary, LORD?Who may enter your presence on your holy hill?Those who lead blameless lives and do what is right, speaking the truth from sincere hearts.
Psalm 15:1,2 NLT

Whoever warned that *"the road to hell is paved with good intentions"*might well have added *"insincerity"* to the warning. Of all the vices within the church and out, the sin of insincerity looms large.

In this age of relative truth, we are told that we can believe anything we want as long as we are sincere. The deceiver of our souls has us all sincerely wrong in rationalizing our decisions and conduct as we willfully and knowingly disregard the clear teachings of Scripture in many areas of life.

The Church of our Lord and Savior, Jesus Christ continues to get polluted with the hypocrisy and insincerity of leaders and members from around the world on a daily basis.

Where is the sincerity of our faith when we continually disobey God? Where is the sincerity of faith when preachers tell people what they want to hear instead of what God wants them to hear?

The most important responsibility of any parent is to model the sincerity of their faith so that their children will catch it and follow in their footsteps. How sad that children see insincerity instead of a real and personal faith being lived out by their parents.

"The purpose of my instruction is that all the Christians there would be filled with love that comes from a pure heart, a clear conscience, and sincere faith."
1 Timothy 1:5 NLT

The only cure for insincerity is sincerely saying what we mean and meaning what we say, and depending upon God's Word instead of our sincerity in growing in our beliefs and living them out.

Father, forgive me for all my insincerity in failing to live my life as a true believer should. Help me to do better by the power of the Holy Spirit. In Jesus'name, Amen

191

The Abundant Life

"The thief does not come except to steal, and to kill, and to destroy. I have come that they may have life, and that they may have it more abundantly."
John 10:10 KJV

When it comes to defining the abundant life, our first thoughts seem to identify with material abundance.

"You feed them from the abundance of your own house, letting them drink from your rivers of delight"
Psalm 36:8 NLT

Jesus did not come to give us material prosperity. The truth is that material prosperity too often replaces many people's need for God.

This key verse of Scripture plainly warns about the devil or wolf seeking to devour, and tells about our Good Shepherd who has come to protect and preserve His sheep with the abundance of His grace.

Jesus came to give us the abundance of forgiveness, comfort, encouragement, joy, and the peace that surpasses all understanding.

These are all divine abundances that the world cannot give although the deceiver of our souls and the world offer counterfeits that promise much but can never really deliver the abundance of the soul we all long for.

Our God is not a stingy God. God lavishes guilt free pleasures that far exceed any of the cheap imitations of the world. He is *"able to to do exceedingly abundantly above all that we ask or think, according to the power that works in us." (Ephesians 3:20)*

This is power we can all access by faith through prayer, confession, and repentance and by growing in our knowledge of God's Word and letting God control our lives by the daily renewal of our minds.

Thus there will be richly and abundantly provided for you entry into the eternal kingdom of our Lord and Savior Jesus Christ.
2 Peter 1:11 AMP

May God forbid that any of us go wandering aimlessly lost outside of the sheep fold of our abundant life in Christ.

Father, keep me ever mindful of the abundant life You died to give me, and let me pursue it with the faith and obedience you desire. In Jesus' name, Amen

192

Living Faith

[Faith without Good Deeds Is Dead] What good is it, dear brothers and sisters, if you say you have faith but don't show it by your actions? Can that kind of faith save anyone? James 2:13 NLT

Although many consider it a precept rather than an organism, faith is

"For Sheol (the place of the dead) cannot confess and reach out the hand to You, death cannot praise and rejoice in You; they who go down to the pit cannot hope for Your faithfulness [to Your promises; their probation is at an end, their destiny is sealed].
Isaiah 38:18 AMP

a living thing created to grow to maturity like all living things.

Faith receives nourishment and grows through feeding on the Word of God, prayer, the encouragement and support of other believers, and cultivation by the Holy Spirit.

Like any plant or animal, it withers and dies if cut off from the source of nourishment'

How sad that so many who were wandering aimlessly lost were redeemed and became dead to sin and alive in Christ only to die and go back to bondage to sin.

A faith not lived is not living, but dead. Faith cannot flourish and grow without bearing fruit or giving other evidence that it is alive and well in the heart of any professing believer.

We must daily put on the full armor of God and keep it sharp through daily confession and repentance. As long as our faith is alive and being nourished, we have God's promise that we will escape or overcome by His grace.

"Do we then by [this] faith make the Law of no effect, overthrow it or make it a dead letter? Certainly not! On the contrary, we confirm and establish and uphold the Law."
Romans 3:31 AMP

When we stop feeding our faith it will start bleeding. It can weaken and die from lack of nourishment. We must never let sin and death return by using our free will to disobey and return to the bondage from which we have been redeemed.

We are told to continually make a sober assessment of ourselves. We all might do well to consider how well we are living our living faith by loving and serving others.

Father, help me to live my faith in every area of my life. In Jesus' name, Amen.

Giving In

"Give in to God, come to terms with him and everything will turn out just fine. Let him tell you what to do; take his words to heart. Come back to God Almighty and he'll rebuild your life." Job 22:21a MSG

Of all the paradoxes of life, giving in may well be near the top of everyone's list, whether we realize it or not.

"My son, if sinful men entice you, do not give in to them."
Proverbs 1:10 NIV

We don't seem to have much of a problem giving in to sin. This is part of our inherited nature. Everyone has temptations that we give in to often and easily.

The weaknesses of our flesh are not all the same. We often get filled with hypocritical glory when we hear the preacher condemning sins we don't give in to because it makes us feel that we are at least not as bad as those who give in to that sin that doesn't tempt us.

Before we get so filled with the self righteousness of a pharisee we need to be mourning over our own sin "give in's" and asking the Lord's help in overcoming and repenting of them.

Giving in to Christ and His righteousness is not only hard, it's impossible except by the supernatural power of the Holy Spirit. To give in to God involves giving up the pride, anger, envy, greed, and lust of the flesh and giving in to the long suffering, patience, kindness, joy, love, and self control of the Spirit.

When we consider the benefits of giving in to God, it is hard to understand why anyone would insist on holding out. There is absolutely no fleshly or wordly pleasure to compare with the pleasure of His joy and friendship when we abide in Him through abiding in His Word.

"Do not let sin control the way you live; do not give in to sinful desires."
Romans 6:12 NLT

Best of all, when we give in to God's call on our life, we are promised that we will enter in to that mansion of eternal joy that Jesus has gone to prepare for us in heaven.

Father, help me to quit giving in to sin and to give in to You and Your will in every area of my life today. In Jesus' name, Amen

194

A Living Sacrament

"I beseech you therefore, brethren, by the mercies of God, that ye present your bodies a living sacrifice, holy, acceptable unto God, which is your reasonable service." Romans 12:1 KJV

Different churches have different sacraments including some instituted by Christ and some instituted by the early organized church as outward signs of inward spiritual grace. Baptism and the Lords Supper are the two of the most universally observed sacred acts. Some denominations observe footwashing, Penance, Marriage, Holy Orders, and Anointing the sick as Sacramental means of grace along with the preaching of the Word.

> "This is a sacred day before our Lord. Don't be dejected and sad, for the joy of the Lord is your strength!"
> Nehemiah 8:10b NLT

We should all seek to be living sacrifices to the praise of God's glory for the great thing He has done in dying on the cross so that we will live forever.

When we start the day by renewing our minds through prayer and growing in God's Word we will be cushioned by the all sufficient grace of God.

When we dump all of our sin into God's sea of forgetfulness through daily confession and repentance we will experience our burdens and spirits lifted.

Bearing the fruit of love, patience, joy, peace, gentleness and self control is a great way to display outward signs of inward spiritual grace.

When we get to know Jesus well enough to know what He did, we will be able to make our lives a sacred act of imitating Christ in every area of our lives and want to reflect His love and proclaim His saving grace to others.

> "You realize, don't you, that you are the temple of God, and God himself is present in you? No one will get by with vandalizing God's temple, you can be sure of that. God's temple is sacred—and you, remember, are the temple."
> 1 Corinthians 3:17 MSG

God moved His dwelling place from the temple of a building into the temple of our hearts by the indwelling presence of the Holy Spirit living within us. All we have to do is move our faith from our head to our hearts and our lives can indeed be a sacrament .

Father, help me to reflect your grace working within me by letting it shine through me to others.In Jesus' name, Amen

Principles of Accounting

"And it will be accounted as righteousness (conformity to God's will in word, thought, and action) for us if we are watchful to do all this commandment before the Lord our God, as He has commanded us" Deuteronomy 6:24 AMP

Accounting and accountability have been with us in some form or another since the beginning of time. Adam and Eve were held accountable for their disobedience and there has been hell to pay ever since.

"Therefore if you have not been faithful in the [case of] unrighteous mammon (deceitful riches, money, possessions), who will entrust to you the true riches"
Proverbs 16:11 AMP

The frequent references to counting people and treasures, and the parable of the talents and stewards indicate that accounting was in play centuries ago.

Recognized accounting practices allow monetary value to be *assigned to "non-monetary assets that cannot be seen, touched or physically measured, which are created through time and/or effort and that are identifiable as a separate asset"(definition from Wikipedia).*

Scripture indicates that intangible assets may well be the most valuable and important assets of all in God's economy.

God's treasures are available to all through faith in Jesus Christ. He debits Jesus' perfect righteousness to our righteousness account giving us a substantial net worth in God's eyes.

In God's economy,many people who seem to have nothing have everything, and many people who seem to have everything have nothing.

it is not a mistake to store up some treasures in heaven by seeking to show our love and appreciation for what He has done for us by obeying and seeking to live fruitful lives fully pleasing to Him.

"Now an eager contention arose among them [as to] which of them was considered and reputed to be the greatest"
Luke 22:24 AMP

May we always remember that our real Net Worth is not based on what we have but in Who we have in our heart.

Father thank You for debiting the righteousness of Christ to wipe out my sin liability account. In Jesus' name, Amen

Through Whose Eyes?

And Jesus went on with His disciples to the villages of Caesarea Philippi; and on the way He asked His disciples, Who do people say that I am?" Mark 8:27 AMP

We have probably all often heard that beauty is in the eye of the beholder. We sometimes wonder what he or she sees in him or her when we learn of a romance, engagement, or marriage.

> Don't lose your grip on Love and Loyalty. Tie them around your neck; carve their initials on your heart. Earn a reputation for living well in God's eyes and the eyes of the people."
> Proverbs 3;3 MSG

It is interesting to get opinions of people, events, places, and things through different eyes.

All one has to do is go read the reviews of any product or book on Amazon, and you will wonder if everyone is talking about the same product or book.

One of the most challenging and sobering task every Christian has been given is to be salt and light and ambassadors for Christ in our neighborhoods, schools. Jobs, churches and community at large.

A lot of reputations depend on who you ask. Some of the people we view as some of the best in the world are viewed as jerks by others.

How sad that so many people have left so many churches because of the hypocrisy they have viewed or perceived among many who claim to be followers of Jesus Christ.

Author Steve Brown raised the question of who we are when no one's looking. This is a question we should all be asking ourselves daily and be striving to giving an honest, God pleasing answer.

> "Having eyes, do you not see [with them], and having ears, do you not hear and perceive and understand the sense of what is said? And do you not remember?"
> Mark 8:18 AMP

How great to know that God views us as children and co heirs with Christ and does not look upon or remember our sins, but upon Jesus dying on the cross to give all who believe a favorable view.

Father, help what You see become what others see in me by helping me to become more like Christ. In Jesus' name, Amen

Getting Hell Scared Out
"But I will show you whom you should fear: Fear him who after the killing of the body, has power to throw you into hell. Yes, I tell you, fear him." Luke 12:5 NIV

"The wicked bought a one-way ticket to hell."
Psalm 9:17 MSG

Doing away with the fear of Hell has been one of the biggest deterrents to saving faith the world has ever known. Hell has become a joke and laughing matter in much of the world at large and the cause of Christ and salvation of millions of souls has been lost in the process.

As the secular society we live in continues to deny the existence of sin and the everlasting torments of hell, more and more people are enticed into living the world's way instead of God's way, and our moral meltdown continues.

The best response I have ever heard to an atheist who said he didn't believe in hell was; "you will when you get there".

It is a sad fact that cigarette sales are booming throughout the world in spite of the proven fact that they kill. The Bible says that the rich man's plea for Lazarus to warn his brothers to stay out of hell would not do any good.

The truth is that no one can avoid the torments of hell until they come to the realization that they are sinners who need a Savior.

God will not be mocked. The ever increasing natural disasters around the world continue to display the unlimited power of our almighty God.

We can be sure that God is going to do whatever it takes to see that every knee will bow and every tongue confess Jesus Christ as Lord.

"In hell and in torment, he looked up and saw Abraham in the distance and Lazarus in his lap."
Luke 16:23 MSG

In the mean time we all need to pray that God will bring revival and scare the hell out of all before they go there by bringing them under the protection of His grace by bringing them to faith through sorrow for their sins and true repentance.

Father, give us the courage and strength to speak the truth in love about the reality and pitfall of hell. In Jesus' name, Amen

Added Value Options

"Be joyful. Grow to maturity. Encourage each other. Live in harmony and peace. Then the God of love and peace will be with you." 2 Corinthians 11b NLT

"The liberal person shall be enriched, and he who waters shall himself be watered."
Proverbs 11:26 MSG

Whether its driving through McDonald's, buying a car, or banking, we hear about added value options. For just a little bit more, we are promised a whole lot more of something.

When we take a few minutes to think about all those who have added value to our lives, we will be amazed at how many people the Lord has used and continues to use to guide, inspire, and encourage us in His ongoing character development plan for our lives.

No matter how old we are, we can all remember that special teacher, coach, scoutmaster, who added value to our lives by making us feel special.

If we have saving faith, it most likely because our parents or a close friend have added this value by modeling Christ's love in our lives.

Whether faith, confidence, correction, or encouragement we can all use a boost from time to time.

By the grace of God, and in intentional obedience to His will, we can all add value into the lives of others by coming along side to help them become all that God would have them be.

"Therefore encourage (admonish, exhort) one another and edify (strengthen and build up) one another, just as you are doing."
1 Thessaloinians 5:11 AMP

There are several excellent organized mentoring programs we can join, or we can work with the young or old in our church, nursing homes, neighborhoods, prisons or workplaces.

The treasures in heaven have nothing to do with money. They are the people the Lord has graciously lead us to invest our lives in in order to add value to theirs that we may see them with us in heaven.

Father help me to add value to someone's life this day. In Jesus' name, Amen.

The Big Sell Out

"Thus they exchanged Him Who was their Glory for the image of an ox that eats grass [they traded their Honor for the image of a calf]! Psalm 106:20 AMP

"One day Jacob was cooking a stew. Esau came in from the field, starved. Esau said to Jacob, "Give me some of that red stew—I'm starved!" Genesis 25:20 MSG

Jacob may have been the greatest salesman who ever lived. Getting Esau to sell his birth rite for a bowl of soup was one of the biggest sales ever made.

Before we get too hard on Esau, we had best think about what the deceiver of our souls has gotten us to sell out for.

Millions have sold out for the promise of sinful sex. Others have sold out for the quick fix of drugs or alcohol. Many sell out for popularity or ego.

We all have sold out to sin one way or another many times, and have had a hard time keeping the change Jesus sent the Holy Spirit to give us the hour we bought into our eternal birth right by believing in Him.

The Holy Spirit will fill our consciences with sin remorse when we sell out to the world, our flesh or the devil. At this point we can choose to confess and repent and have our righteousness account credited, or we can willfully choose to buy back into the domination of sin from which we have been set free by the blood of Jesus.

"For what can a man give as an exchange (a compensation, a ransom, in return) for his [blessed] life [in the eternal kingdom of God]?" Mark 8:37 AMP

The longer we keep the sin we sold out to, the harder it is to get our righteousness account back in good standing. The longer we persist in a sin, the harder our hearts and consciences become.

We can all praise and thank God that He will do whatever it takes to help us when we come back to Him with a broken spirit and contrite heart.

Wouldn't we all better living in the light of God's love and abundance instead of selling out to the temptations that come our way?

Father, help me to quit selling out to _____. In Jesus' name, Amen

Stepping out of Bounds .

"Since a man's days are all determined, and the number of his months is wholly in Your control, and he cannot pass the bounds of his allotted time" Job 14:5 AMP

Stepping out of bounds can be a game changing mistake in any sport. Touchdowns have been called back, baskets not counted, and goals not scored all because someone stepped out of bounds.

"'Judgment Day! Fate has caught up with you. The scepter outsized and pretentious, pride bursting all bounds, Violence strutting, brandishing the evil scepter. But there's nothing to them, and nothing will be left of them." Ezekiel 7:10 a MSG

When we step out of the bounds of law, we can expect to be fined, imprisoned, or both.

God knows us better than we know ourselves. He knows left under the control of our sin natures we are going to stay outside the boundaries He has set for all of us.

Whoever has the idea that God is a kill joy God just waiting to zap us when we step out of bounds did not get this from God but from the deceiver of our souls or one of his many messengers disguised as preachers, teachers, or friends.

God wants to bless us, not us or make us miserable. God knows our every weakness, and knows that we need boundaries in order to live the abundant lives for which He created us.

God set the boundaries in the commandments that no one kept. He then came to earth as man to keep them for all who would call upon His name. He left the commandments as a mirror, guide and curb, and then moved them from the altar to the conscience of our hearts.

"We aren't making outrageous claims here. We're sticking to the limits of what God has set for us. But there can be no question that those limits reach to and include you." 2 Corinthians 10:13a MSG

God also sent the Holy Spirit to give us the strength and power to live within the bounds of His will for how we should live.

We should always remember that God has set no boundaries when it comes to loving and serving Him and others.

Father, help me to live within the bounds of Your will, that I might experience the abundant life you died to give. In Jesus' name, Amen

Home Invasions

"The worst of my fears has come true,what I've dreaded most has happened.My repose is shattered, my peace destroyed. No rest for me, ever—death has invaded life." Job 3:26 MSG

Although there are no exact statistics available because of the many variants, some insurance companies claim that 1 out of every 5 homes will experience a home invasion or burglary in any given year;

"A vast army of locusts has invaded my land,a terrible army too numerous to count.Its teeth are like lions' teeth,its fangs like those of a lioness"
Joel 1:6 NLT

As alarming as this fact of life in today's sin sick society may be, there is another type of home invasion that is much more wide spread, and probably a lot more damaging.

The invasion of our homes and hearts with locusts of lust, doubt, and discontent is ongoing and insidious. Many TV's, computers, radios, and x-box games are attacking our core values and faith with subtle and not so subtle enticements that can eventually take root and damage our souls and rob us of the abundant life God wants for all His children.

The roaring lion who comes like a thief in the night is alive and well and has appropriated the latest high tech weapons to attack our faith.

I am warning you ahead of time, dear friends. Be on guard so that you will not be carried away by the errors of these wicked people and lose your own secure footing
2 Peter 3:17 NLT

Eternal vigilance is the price we must pay for the eternal security Jesus Christ died on the cross to give us. We need to be careful to identify and avoid the home invasions that can rob us of our peace and joy and our identity in Christ.

Father, bless our homes and keep your holy angels on guard to protect us from the thief who would come invade our souls. In Jesus' name, Amen.

Sugar Free Diets
"The decrees of the LORD are firm, and all of them are righteous. They are more precious than gold, than much pure gold; they are sweeter than honey, than honey from the honeycomb" Psalm 19:9b,10 NIV

The diet cola wars have been leading the charge in sugar free diets for almost 50 years to assist in losing weight, saving teeth, and for diabetic blood sugar control.

"All his days also he eats in darkness [cheerlessly, with no sweetness and light in them], and much sorrow and sickness and wrath are his."
Ecclesiastics 5:17 AMP

Many nutrition experts point out the toxic qualities of sugar as another reason for going sugar free.

There is one area of life where sugar free is a real problem. Living life without the sweetness of the Gospel of Jesus Christ is fatal.

There are no substitutes for the sugar of God's grace that sweetens our lives with peace, joy, purpose, and meaning. This sugar actually frees us from bondage to sin and death and fuels the abundant life God wants to give us.

When we go on a grace free diet by absenting ourselves from the grace of corporate worship, prayer, and daily study of God's Word, we leave room for the temptations of the world, our flesh, and the devil to fill us instead of the Holy Spirit.

"And walk in love, [esteeming and delighting in one another] as Christ loved us and gave Himself up for us, a [a]slain offering and sacrifice to God [for you, so that it became] a sweet fragrance."
Ephesians 5:2: AMP

Without the sweetness of God's grace we experience bitterness of the soul which robs us of our joy and peace that surpasses all understanding.

There are many substitutes for sugar, but man has not been able to produce a substitute for grace. The grace substitutes of man invariably leave a bad taste that can only be overcome by going back to the real thing that God promises to supply sufficient for our every need.

Father, in your mercy, let me never go on a sugar free diet for my soul. In Jesus' name, Amen.

Never Say Never

"Satisfied desire is sweet to a person; therefore it is hateful and exceedingly offensive to [self-confident] fools to give up evil [upon which they have set their hearts]." Proverbs 13:19 AMP

We have all heard exhortation after exhortation to "never give up". While this is very inspiring and appropriate in a lot of situations, there are exceptions we all need to avoid.

> " a time to search and a time to give up, a time to keep and a time to throw away"
> Ecclesiastes 3:6 NIV

Pride born stubbornness can prevent us giving up false beliefs and ideas, and continue to lead us down to the pit. Until we give up self centeredness and embrace Christ centeredness, we are never going to experience the abundant life Jesus came to give us all.

Every one of us, no matter how holy probably still have some sins that we can't seem to give up. Whether it's gossiping, lusting, envying, anger, or greed, some besetting sins are hard if not impossible to give up except by the supernatural power of the Holy Spirit living within us.

As a Christian optimist who truly believes that God works all things for our good and His glory, I have pursued almost every perceived opportunity for growth or success until something told me to stop.

While it is true that we should never give up when the game is still going on, or when impatience, fear, or doubt is motivating us, we need to be ever mindful of the necessity to have the wisdom and spiritual discernment to know when to fold.

Most of the disappointments of my life have come from not giving up when God's Word, friends, or circumstances have sent out stop signs that I have ignored.

If God had not given up His Son, none of us would have anything to look forward to other than the torments of hell.

> "If you cling to your life, you will lose it; but if you give up your life for me, you will find it."
> Matthew 10:39 NLT

In view of what's been given up for our salvation, may we never give up our faith in the one who died so that we would never have to.

Father, give me the wisdom to know and the strength to do the giving up I need to do. In Jesus' name, Amen

Is God's Reputation Safe with Us?
"God's reputation is twenty-four-carat gold, with a lifetime guarantee. The decisions of God are accurate down to the nth degree." Psalm 19:7 b MSG

Before we breathe a sigh of relief and thankfulness that God's reputation does not depend on us and our constant moral and spiritual meltdowns, we had better give this question more thought.

"Give thanks to God. Call out his name. Ask him anything! Shout to the nations, tell them what he's done, spread the news of his great reputation!" Isaiah 12:4 MSG

God's reputation may well depend on us to some people and in some situations as we do life under the banner of His love and importance in our lives.

When we go through life as joyless, judgmental, and legalistic professing Christians, we are hurting God's reputation.

When we pick up the paper and read about the moral meltdowns of pastors, and divisions and quarrels within churches and denominations, we should mourn that God's reputation is being besmirched.

God's reputation has always taken a big hit from the hypocrites and hypocritical glory prevalent among too many churches and Christians.

When we consider how God staked His reputation on Job's love and faithfulness in spite of anything short of death the devil could throw at Him, we get some idea of the glory and power of God.

"When God made his promise to Abraham, he backed it to the hilt, putting his own reputation on the line." Hebrews 6:13a MSG

God sacrificed His reputation as a perfect, sinless man to take our sins to the Cross and die so that we would never die.

We need to be thankful that Jesus' reputation Is more than good enough to get us to heaven. We need to be so thankful that we live a life that reflects God's great reputation to others.

Father,May I live a fruitful life obedient and fully pleasing to You so that Your reputation will be safe with me. In Jesus' name, Amen.

Seeing Clearly on a Cloudy Day

"I also pray that your mind might see more clearly. Then you will know the hope God has chosen you to receive. You will know that the things God's people will receive are rich and glorious." Ephesians 1:18 NIV

Our hindsight vision is usually much better than our foresight. We all have difficulty seeing clearly sometimes, especially when going through difficult circumstances.

"—be sure now to keep your distance!—and you'll see clearly the route to take."
Joshua 3:1b MSG

We often wonder what we did wrong to deserve a misfortune. We often don't know what to do or not to do in certain situations.

Keeping our eyes on the problem solver instead of the problem is a good place to start. It is amazing how taking time to be holy by praising and praying to God improves our vision..

When we rejoice and receive the peace of God that surpasses all understanding our fears and worries diminish and our faith and strength increase.

We should always remember that God wants us to pray for wisdom. We should be ever mindful that God is working all things for our good and His glory

If never hurts to judge ourselves to see if there is any wrong doing on our part causing the problem, and do whatever is necessary to correct our conduct or thinking.

"[For my determined purpose is] that I may know Him [that I may progressively become more deeply and intimately acquainted with Him, perceiving and recognizing and understanding the wonders of His Person more strongly and more clearly],
Philippians 3:10 AMP

When our minds are stayed on Him, we will find ourselves responding to problems with the longsuffering, patience, kindness, gentleness, love and self control that the Holy Spirit will produce within us.

We can all see a lot more clearly with faith sight!

Father, help me see more clearly through the wisdom, knowledge and discernment of Your Word. In Jesus' name, Amen

Bad Credit No Problem

"For I know the plans I have for you," says the Lord. "They are plans for good and not for disaster, to give you a future and a hope." Jeremiah 29:11 NLT

"But suppose a sinful person turns away from all of the sins he has committed. And he keeps all my rules. He does what is fair and right. Then you can be sure he will live. He will not die"
Ezekiel 18:21 NRIV

One of the most wonderful things about God is that He is more interested in our future than in our past. Bad credit is not a problem with Him.

When we come to God with a broken spirit and contrite heart He forgives and forgets. He will remember our sins no more. Jesus paid our sin debt in full when He died on the cross. Our righteousness account will always be current in God's eyes when we apologize, repent and ask God's forgiveness.

Anyone who has gotten out of financial bondage and set free from debt `has been set free from spiritual bondage to sin. It's like having the weight of the world lifted from our souls.

The new Chris Tomlin verses written for the "Amazing Grace" movie sums it up well:*"My chains are gone, I've been set free, My God, my Savior has ransomed me, And like a flood His mercy reigns, unending love, Amazing Grace"*

In view of this wonderful freedom, why oh why do we return to sin like a dog returns to its vomit? Why oh why do we let ourselves get back into financial bondage?

When God chose to give us free will he also gave us the freedom to make bad choices. Ever since Adam and Eve chose to disobey, God's children have chosen to worship idols instead of God, and we continue to do the same.

"and he having begun to take account, there was brought near to him one debtor of a myriad of talents,"
Matthew 18:24 YLT

Thank God our good credit with God is not dependent upon our righteousness, but upon the righteousness of Jesus Christ whose blood cleanses and takes away all our sins.

Father, help me to keep my righteousness account current through daily confession, repentance, and obedience. In Jesus' name, Amen

The Power of Purpose
"[We pray] that you may be invigorated and strengthened with all power according to the might of His glory, [to exercise] every kind of endurance and patience (perseverance and forbearance) with joy" Colossians 1:11 AMP

Strength and power and the ability to use it comes from God. The pooling of power for a common goal is also a gift God has given us.

"You hold strength and power in the palm of your hand to build up and strengthen all."
1 Chronicles 29:13 MSG

Whether on the little league or big league sports field, the battlefield of war, or life when people unite for a common purpose, good things happen.

I have been blessed to be part of the pooling power that has funded many church projects and other purposes. In the secular world, I was blessed to experience the pleasure of being part of many exciting endeavors that became successful through pooling the power of purpose.

When teams play together as a team, churches pray together as a body, and people work together towards a common goal the accomplishments of the whole are generally much greater than could be realized by any individual effort.

When any team or organization loses unity of purpose, the power is often diffused into disagreements, divisions, and lose lose situations for everyone involved. Teams lose, businesses go broke, and churches split.

"So let's not allow ourselves to get fatigued doing good. At the right time we will harvest a good crop if we don't give up, or quit. Right now, therefore, every time we get the chance, let us work for the benefit of all, starting with the people closest to us in the community of faith."
Galatians 6:9 MSG

The power of purpose for doing life is the key to living a God pleasing life. We must wilfully , deliberately, and intentionally commit to obeying God and submitting to the Lordship of Jesus Christ and the power of the Holy Spirit.

Father give me Your power of purpose in every area of my life. In Jesus' name, Amen

Reciprocity

"Do not be deceived and deluded and misled; God will not allow Himself to be sneered at (scorned, disdained, or mocked by mere pretensions or professions, or by His precepts being set aside.) [He inevitably deludes himself who attempts to delude God.] For whatever a man sows, that and that only is what he will reap." Galations 6:7 AMP

Of all the universal laws of life, reciprocity is one of the truest.

"What shall I render to the Lord for all His benefits toward me? [How can I repay Him for all His bountiful dealings?]" Psalm 116:13 AMP

Whether we call it "reaping what you sow","doing to others as we would have them do unto us", or "what goes around comes around" –the principle of reciprocity is alive and well in every culture.

Scripture teaches that generosity begets generosity, anger begets anger, goodness and mercy beget goodness and mercy.and that forgiveness promotes forgiveness.

Mutual respect and understanding are sorely needed in Christ's church. If only half of the time spent criticizing other denominations was spent on sharing the Good News with others, we'd all have fewer unfilled seats in our churches.

When someone invites us to dinner, we try to reciprocate by inviting them. When someone does us a favor, we are anxious to reciprocate.

A right relationship with God through faith in Jesus Christ involves a lot of reciprocity. We can reciprocate His love by loving Him through thanksgiving, praise, worship, loving and serving others, and obedience.

As we do this, God reciprocates by granting us the desires of our hearts and filling us with the joy of our salvation and the all surpassing security and peace that only He can provide.

Jesus did not come to make our lives miserable and burdensome. He came to give us a life of abundance which we can all discover and enjoy by abiding in Him through His Word, and reciprocating His love.

Gentleness (meekness, humility), self-control (self-restraint, continence). Against such things there is no law [that can bring a charge] Galatians 5:23 AMP

It is good to know that just as we can never out give God, we will never be able to out reciprocate Him.

Father, help me to reciprocate your love to You and to others. In Jesus' name, Amen.

Wellness

"It is well with the man who deals generously and lends, who conducts his affairs with justice."Psalm 112:5 AMP

Wellness is probably the biggest business in the world today. Health care, fitness centers, drugs, books and medications promoting wellness abound.

> " I bless GOD every chance I get; my lungs expand with his praise. I live and breathe GOD; if things aren't going well, hear this and be happy:"
> Psalm 34:1,2 MSG

Good spiritual health is the well spring of real wellness. When we are well with God, the living waters of peace, joy, and security flow in and wash away the deterioration of mind, body, and spirit in the sin sick world and flesh in which we live.

It is well with our soul when we allow the Holy Spirit to replace our anger, envy, pride, jealousy, lust, and ego with His love, patience, kindness, gentleness and self control. It is well with our soul when we respond to trials and temptations by leaning on the Lord instead of alcohol, drugs, or other addictions.

It is well with our soul when we learn to rejoice in our circumstances and receive that all surpassing peace and prosperity that only God can give.

Horatio Spafford's writing of the hymn that exemplifies wellness at its best tells it all.

> "·That's why we live with such good cheer. You won't see us drooping our heads or dragging our feet! Cramped conditions here don't get us down. They only remind us of the spacious living conditions ahead. It's what we trust in but don't yet see that keeps us going."
> 2 Corinthians 5:8,9 MSG

He lost his son and fortune in a Chicago fire in 1871, He planned a trip to Europe with his wife and 4 daughters in 1873. He sent them on ahead after being delayed, and all 4 daughters were lost in a collision at sea. As he sailed to join his wife and passed near the site where the collision occurred, he penned the words to the great testimony to the wellness we all should strive to find: "It is Well With my Soul".

Father keep me ever mindful that any circumstance or heartbreak or disappointment I might have to endure in this life is nothing compared to the joy that awaits me and my believing loved ones in heaven. In Jesus' name, Amen.

Whose Got Your Back?

"Deeply respect God, your God. Serve and worship him exclusively. Back up your promises with his name only. Don't fool around with other gods, the gods of your neighbors, because God, your God, who is alive among you is a jealous God." Deuteronomy 6:13 MSG

'[*Tested in the Furnace of Affliction*] "And now listen to this, family of Jacob, you who are called by the name Israel: Who got you started in the loins of Judah, you who use God's name to back up your promises and pray to the God of Israel? Isaiah 48:1 MSG

This old fighter pilot lingo has become more and more popular in many areas of life. Military, police, and firemen are very conscious of having a buddy or back up.

We all yearn for friends who we know have our back and can be depended upon to come to our aid anytime.

It is utterly amazing that so many who yearn for the security of a friend who has their back have never discovered the greatest backer upper of all.

Jesus Christ came to let us turn our backs on sin and death. When we receive His wonderful gift of eternal life by accepting His invitation to believe on Him as a conscious act of our free will, Jesus comes not only to back us up, but to give us the abundant life that can only be experienced through personal friendship with Him.

When Jesus comes into our heart, He brings the power and presence of the Holy Spirit to back up our every weakness when we call upon His name.

"[He has also appropriated and acknowledged us as His by] putting His seal upon us and giving us His [Holy] Spirit in our hearts as the security deposit and guarantee [of the fulfillment of His promise]." 2 Corinthians 1:29 AMP

Sooner or later, friends, wealth, fame, or other things we hold dear are going to disappoint and leave us without a back up.

Judgment day is coming at a day and time certain for all of us. How foolish to reject the backup God sent to die in our place so that we would never have to.

Father, thank you for having my back so that I can look forward to the eternal bliss of heaven. In Jesus' name, Amen

211

Read Luke 6, Psalm 103

Graceless Faith

"God is all mercy and grace— not quick to anger, is rich in love.God is good to one and all; everything he does is with grace" Psalm 145:8,9 MSG

If faith without works is dead, how dead is faith without grace? In view of the riches of God's grace that we've received at Christ's expense, how can we not be gracious to others?

When we think of all of the forgiveness we have received and are going to need in the future how can we not forgive others?

"The Lord is merciful and gracious, slow to anger and plenteous in mercy and loving-kindness.9He will not always chide or be contending, neither will He keep His anger forever or hold a grudge."10He has not dealt with us after our sins nor rewarded us according to our iniquities."
Psalm 103:8-10 NIV

As a parent and grandparent I have had reason to be concerned about some questionable conduct.

It has personally been downright painful from a self centered perspective, but my real concern is that they may disqualify themselves from God's best reserved for those who are obedient

Just as God's grace allows Him to love us not because of our sin and disobedience but in spite of it, we need to extend this same grace to others. even to those who don't deserve it.

This whole concept of being gracious and affirming is not part of our inherited nature. It is so contrary to our pride and anger sin nature that we are only going to be able to do it by the supernatural power of the Holy Spirit producing the fruits of righteousness for us to bear.

"and -- if ye love those loving you, what grace have ye? for also the sinful love those loving them; 33and if ye do good to those doing good to you, what grace have ye? for also the sinful do the same;"
Luke 6:33,34 YLT

The risks of our graciousness being taken advantage of and misunderstood are great, but the rewards are even greater. A life lived without grace is never going to be the abundant life God wants for us.

Father, let my overflowing cup of grace flow through me to others that you might be glorified. In Jesus' name, Amen

212

The Great Exchange

"But to as many as did receive and welcome Him, He gave the authority (power, privilege, right) to become the children of God, that is, to those who believe in (adhere to, trust in, and rely on) His name" John 1:12 AMP

When Jesus exchanged His life for ours on the cross at Calvary, this is only the first of many great exchanges God makes in the lives of all who believe that Jesus Christ is their Savior.

Thus they exchanged Him Who was their Glory for the image of an ox that eats grass [they traded their Honor for the image of a calf]!"

Psalm 106:20 AMP

God not only exchanged bondage to sin and death for freedom and joy. He sent the Holy Spirit to change our thoughts, heart, conduct and attitudes as we grow in God's grace through the ongoing process of Holy transformation and the daily renewing of our minds.

We are free from the performance trap of the law. Jesus lived the perfect life and became the perfect sacrifice for our sins. When Jesus comes into our hearts in the power of the Holy Spirit He changes our "have to's" to "want to's". Instead of having to do anything, we want to do everything to praise God for sending His Son to die for us.

We exchange seeking to earn our salvation (which is our free gift of God's grace) to seeking to show our appreciation to God for what he has done for us by living obedient lives fully pleasing to Him.

"He wants not only us but everyone saved, you know, everyone to get to know the truth we've learned: that there's one God and only one, and one Priest-Mediator between God and us—Jesus, who offered himself in exchange for everyone held captive by sin, to set them all free"

1 Timothy 2:3 MSG

When our hearts are changed our mindset changes from "having to" to "getting to". We no longer look at going to church, giving to the Lord, or serving others as burdensome duties, but as high privileges.

Father, give me the right atttitudes of "wanting to " and "getting to" as I seek to live a life pleasing to you. In Jesus' name, Amen

213

Rise Above It

"I have told you these things, so that in Me you may have [perfect] peace and confidence. In the world you have tribulation and trials and distress and frustration; but be of good cheer [take courage; be confident, certain, undaunted]! For I have overcome the world. [I have deprived it of power to harm you and have conquered it for you.]John 16, 32,33 AMP

Relational, physical, emotional, vocational, and spiritual problems are awaiting us all in this world.

"He delivers me from my enemies.You also lift me up above those who rise against me; You have delivered me from the violent man." Psalm 18:48 NKJV

These troubles can sink us into misery fear and despair if we don't learn to rise above them.

The blessed assurance for every believer is that because Jesus has overcome sin, death, and the devil on our behalf, we can also overcome by God's grace and in the strength and power of the Holy Spirit.

We need not only know that we can rise above our troubles, but how to do it.

The attitude with which we respond to trouble often determines the severity and duration of the trouble. We can choose to respond by sinking to depths of pain and despair or by letting God help us rise above our problems by rejoicing.

The concept of rejoicing in our troubles is contrary to human nature and not easy to grasp. It is nevertheless true. When we rejoice and praise the Lord in our distress, we supernaturally receive that peace that surpasses all understanding that is God's gift of grace in helping us rise above our problems.

"Rejoice in the Lord always [delight, gladden yourselves in Him]; again I say, Rejoice!" Philippians 4:3 AMP

When we raise our sights above the problem and look up to our problem solver, We are going to receive the all sufficient grace we need to help us endure or overcome any problem. Do you need to rise and shine above any problem today?

Father, thank you for helping me to rise above my problems by the supernatural strength and power of the Holy Spirit. In Jesus name, Amen

The Turning Point

"Not everyone who says to me, 'Lord, Lord,' will enter the kingdom of heaven, but only the one who does the will of my Father who is in heaven." Matthew 7:21 NIV

We all have experienced and will experience some turning points of life. It may be illness, winning a lottery, leaving home, graduation, A career or relationship decision, confirmation, marriage, divorce, loss of a loved one or other tragedy, or good fortune.

'Disciples so often get into trouble; still, God is there every time." Psalm 34:19 MSG

Spiritually, the hour we were initiated into the family of God through Baptism and/or profession of faith is the biggest turning point we will ever experience. We are set free from the curse of original sin and receive the free gift of eternal life through our faith in Jesus Christ.

This turning point also initiates the arrival of the Holy Spirit into our hearts and souls. He comes to take up residency to guide us into all truth and conform us into the likeness of Christ through the ongoing process of renewing our minds through holy transformation.

We receive all of the Holy Spirit there is the hour we first believe, but we still have free will to choose to live self centered lives controlled by our flesh, or Christ centered lives controlled by the Holy Spirit who has come to indwell us with His presence.

Many draw a blank when asked when they experienced the turning point of becoming a disciple of Jesus Christ and started to make a conscious effort and ask for the supernatural power of the Holy Spirit to live like one.

All of the other turning points of life pale in comparision to the turning point of making Jesus Christ not only our Savior, but our Lord

"Therefore, I urge you, brothers and sisters, in view of God's mercy, to offer your bodies as a living sacrifice, holy and pleasing to God—this is your true and proper worship..
Romans 12:1 NIV

If you haven't done so,you can make today a real turning point in your life by surrendering to the Lordship of Jesus Christ in the power of the Holy Spirit.

Father, remind me to renew and honor the conscious commitment I made to You and Your :Lordship. In Jesus' name, Amen

Raising the Bar
"Stop deceiving yourselves. If you think you are wise by this
world's standards, you need to become a fool to be truly wise.1 Corinthians
3:18 NLT

We live in a record breaking age. The truth is, everyone has been

BLESSED (HAPPY, fortunate, to be envied) are the undefiled (the upright, truly sincere, and blameless) in the way [of th e revealed will of God], who walk (order their conduct and conversation) in the law of the Lord (the whole of God's revealed will). Psalm 119:1,2 AMP

living in a record breaking age since the beginning of time. Speed records, strength records, and performance records of every kind keep getting broken and new ones set as civilization marches onward, but not upward.

Unfortunately man's pursuit of knowledge and technological know how has lowered the bar for faith and living a God centered life and replacing it with faith in man and his abilities.

Biology, sociology, and greed have trumped theology and the moral boundary bar continues to be lowered as what God has called sin and forbidden are now called "alternative life styles" are now condoned and promoted.

"So then, brethren, we are debtors, but not to the flesh [we are not obligated to our carnal nature], to live [a life ruled by thestandards set up by the dictates] of the flesh. Romans 8:17 AMP"

The people of Christ's church must shoulder much of the blame for the moral meltdown which has lowered the bar of morality to near bottom.Hypocrisy, Idolatry, and moral failures of priests, pastors, and other leaders have seriously impeded the cause of Christ and His righteousness.

Raising the bar on what thoughts we allow into our hearts is a good place to start. The garbage we allow in through the television and internet we watch, the songs we should stop. Becoming more like Christ day by day is the bar we should be continually raising.

Father, as you raised the bar in giving us freedom from death and bondage to sin, give us the strength to raise the bar in our personal conduct to live in this freedom. In Jesus' name, Amen.

216

Dead Letter Office

"For the Lord God is a Sun and Shield; the Lord bestows [present] grace and favor and [future] glory (honor, splendor, and heavenly bliss)! No good thing will He withhold from those who walk uprightly." Psalm 89:11 AMP

The US government established a dead letter office jn 1825. There were over 60 million undeliverable letters mailed in 2006.

"One thing have I asked of the Lord, that will I seek, inquire for, and [insistently] require: that I may dwell in the house of the Lord [in His presence] all the days of my life,
Pslam 27:4a AMP

It is staggering to think of the many billion undelivered and undeliverable blessings that are in the Lord's dead blessing Office.

There are several pitfalls we need to avoid if we are going to enjoy the abundance of God's blessings..

First of all, we need to be blessable, by being obedient. God reserves His best for those who give Him their best by obeying Him in every area of life. Moses, and David, were   men after God's own heart because they always obeyed.

Secondly, we need to receive our blessings. God has blessing delivery offices at hundreds of locations in every city. God's blessing offices are called churches, and He has one that is just right for you. .   Thirdly, we need to ask for blessings and remember that God sometimes delivers theme through people. (Remember *"ask and it will be given to you?)*

Perhaps the biggest cause of most undelivered blessings, is that God cannot find anyone to deliver them. There is a lot of the street crossing pharisee in all of us who avoid opportunities to be a blessing by passing right on by someone in need.

"Up to this time you have not asked a [single] thing in My Name [as presenting all that I AM]; but now ask and keep on asking and you will receive, so that your joy (gladness, delight) may be full and complete."
John16:24 AMP

When our book of life is opened and we are called to give an account of what we did with the lives we have been given, we had better pray that we don't see the blessings we missed and left in God's dead blessing file.

Father, help me to keep from missing any undeliverable blessings. In Jesus' name, Amen

Dare to Compare?
"We do not dare to classify or compare ourselves with some who commend themselves."2 Corinthians 10:12 NIV

We often seem to enjoy seeing someone with problems that make ours seem pale by comparison. Sometimes I have been overcome with

"Then I will not be ashamed when I compare my life with your commands." Psalm 119:6 NLT

shame over complaining about my problems when I see someone with twice as bad problems.

Unfortunately many of us have a hypocritical glory streak that we use to minimize our sinfulness by comparing our sins to those of others.

We should be so glad that we do not have to depend on how good we have been in order to inherit eternal life, knowing that:"*all have sinned and fallen short of the glory of God",*

Before we insist on validating our goodness by comparing it to others, we had best dare to compare our goodness with the perfect goodness of Jesus Christ. This will help us understand how far short we really fall from the perfect righteousness God requires.

This will also remind us quickly of how badly we need a Savior and how thankful we are to God that He sees Christ's righteousness instead of ours .

Getting saved and receiving the righteousness of Christ in God's sight is easy. All we have to do is confess, repent, and receive the wonderful gift when Jesus knocks on the door of our hearts and offers it to us by the power of the Holy Spirit.

"Pay careful attention to your own work, for then you will get the satisfaction of a job well done, and you won't need to compare yourself to anyone else." Galatians 6:4 NLT

Becoming as righteous in our living and loving in actuality as we became in spirituality is the hard part, but God has promised the supernatural power of the Holy Spirit to help us become more like Christ every day. When people start seeing Jesus in us we are being transformed. This is the comparison that matters. *Father help me to become more like Jesus every day of my life. In Jesus' name, Amen.*

Just a Little Bit More

'Why is everyone hungry for more? "More, more," they say. "More, more." I have God's more-than-enough" Psalm 4:6 MSG

I doubt if there is any phrase more common to man "just a little bit more". Everyone at some time or another wants or feels they need "just a little bit more."

> "Why is everyone hungry for more? "More, more," they say. More, more." I have God's more-than-enough,More joy in one ordinary day
> Psalm 4:6,7 MSG

When the greedy are asked how much is enough, they always want "just a little bit more." The alcohol, drug, sex or porn addict only wants "a little bit more."

Our misguided search for significance and contentment often deceives us into believing we would be happy if we only had better looks, a nicer car, or more popularity.

The one thing we can all use a whole lot more of is a growing relationship with Jesus Christ. The less self centered and more Christ centered we become, the more becoming to God we will be.

As we get "just a little bit more" of Jesus by walking and talking with Him and growing in His Word day by day, the abundant life that can only be found by abiding in Him, will be ours to enjoy now and forever.

> "Here's what I want you to do: Buy your gold from me, gold that's been through the refiner's fire. Then you'll be rich. Buy your clothes from me, clothes designed in Heaven. You've gone around half-naked long enough. And buy medicine for your eyes from me so you can see, really see.
> Revelation 3:18 MSG

Instead of wanting to get "just little bit more", we will want to give more love, blessings, and encouragement to others from our over flowing cup of blessings.

As we give "just a little bit more" praise, adoration, worship, and service to God, the all surpassing peace and godly contentment that the world cannot give will be ours to enjoy and to pass on to others.

This is a truth worth knowing and appropriating into our everyday walk of faith.

Father, let me hunger for a whole lot more of your holiness and righteousness as I seek to lead a fruitful life, fully pleasing to you. In Jesus' name, Amen.

Peddling Insecurities
"for the Lord is your security.He will keep your foot from being caught in a trap." Proverbs 3:26 NLT

It takes a lot of spiritual wisdom and discernment to navigate the muddy waters of life in today's world. I continue to get bombarded with cheap shots at political leaders, denominations, and other issues that often seem to be being passed on repeatedly by well meaning people who have no idea that they are actually peddling insecurities.

"Return to the stronghold [of security and prosperity], you prisoners of hope; even today do I declare that I will restore double your former prosperity to you.
Zechariah 9:9-12 AMP

We are all targets of armies of great marketing companies and advertising agencies that are finding peddling insecurities about our hair,eye makeup, popularity, and being perceived as "cool" among our peers.

The deceiver of our souls is a master at peddling insecurity about the reality of our salvation, God's perfect plan for our lives, whether His Word is really true.

The worry and depression our insecurities cause can rob us of our joy, and make us mentally and even physically ill. We can get down on our country and its leaders, our spouses, our friends, and about everything else that makes life worth living.

One of the absolute best gifts of God's grace is the security of His love. Only when we have this only true and lasting security and the joy of our salvation are we ever going to enjoy the truly abundant Jesus died to give us.

"For whoever is bent on saving his [temporal] life [his comfort and security here] shall lose it [eternal life]; and whoever loses his life [his comfort and security here] for My sake shall find it [life everlasting]."
Matthew 16:25 AMP

When the guy with the pitchfork comes trying to peddle the insecurities that rob us of our peace and joy just remember who is on our side and provides us with all of the security we will ever need.

Father help me to quit buying into the insecurities of the world.In Jesus' name, Amen

Well Remembered

"He will not be moved forever; the [uncompromisingly] righteous (the upright, in right standing with God) shall be in everlasting remembrance." Psalm 112:6 AMP

There is an interesting aspect to being remembered. A lot of people are well remembered, but not remembered well.

"Such people will not be overcome by evil.Those who are righteous will be long remembered." Psalm 112:6 NLT

Osama Bin Laden, Judas, Adolph Hitler, Benedict Arnold, and a lot of bad people are well remembered for all the wrong reasons.

Living as imperfect people in an imperfect world, even the best of us may not be remembered well by some we have offended or conflicted with along the road of life we have travelled. I personally mourn over some of the unintentional hurt I have caused others.

How sad but true many outstanding good people will be well remembered for one fault or mistake and not remembered well for all of the great accomplishments and good things they have done.

The tarnished reputations of Richard Nixon, Anthony Weiner, many well known preachers and priests and a host of other famous and not so famous people will not allow them to be well remembered.

"Dear friend, don't let this bad example influence you. Follow only what is good. Remember that those who do good prove that they are God's children, and those who do evil prove that they do not know God" 3 John 1:11 NLT

Although God remembers our sins no more when we confess and repent, the deceiver of our souls is never going to forget or let us forget them. He is always ready to remind us how rotten we really are.

As much as we should live a life that would like to be remembered well for our love of God and of others, the main thing to remember is to be remembered well by God. He has written our name in the book of life and will always remember that we are one of His own dear children because of our faith in Jesus Christ.

Father, may I never forget whose I am and the price that was paid to make me one of your redeemed children. In Jesus name, Amen

Outside the Loop

"So speak encouraging words to one another. Build up hope so you'll all be together in this, no one left out, no one left behind. I know you're already doing this; just keep on doing it." ! Thessalonians 5:9b MSG

We often find ourselves the last to know about a problem within our church, workplace, or even at home because we are left outside the loop of information.

For what they were not told, they will see, and what they have not heard, they will understand
Isaiah 52:15b MSG

Many church conflicts on a local or denominational level rage with most members not having any idea of what's going on because they are outside the loop. This is not always a bad thing. There may be some things going on that will only discourage or drive us away.

Workplace politics and intrigue often leave some outside the loop. Teen agers are especially good at keeping parents outside the loop of their activities and viewpoints.

There are millions of people wandering outside the loop of God's blessings through either neglect, choice, or never having heard or understood the Good News.

We should be constantly looking for those among our neighbors, friends, and co workers who are outside the loop of God's grace and tell them about the love of Jesus and what a difference it has made in our life.

"Work at getting along with each other and with God. Otherwise you'll never get so much as a glimpse of God. Make sure no one gets left out of God's generosity."
Hebrews 12:10 MSG

May there be no unbroken circles in heaven because some we love have been left out of the loop.

Father,help me to stay in the loop of your love, grace, and mercy, by staying connected through staying in Your Word, Your church, and prayer. In Jesus' name, Amen.

222

Hopes of Glory

"The merchants will say, 'The pleasure you longed for has left you. All your riches and glory have disappeared forever.'" Revelation 18:13,NIV

We all have hopes of "accomplishing something that secures praise or renown from someone." Whether it be athletics, vocational, recreational, financial, relational, or spiritual, we all like to have something to make us feel good about ourselves.

Lord, may glory be given to you, not to us. You are loving and faithful.
Psalm 115:1 NIV

As we pursue praise, power, status, and all of the attributes of worldly glory we often make compromises that cause more shame than gain, and ruin than riches.

The hallowed ground of Christ's church too often becomes the devil's play ground for glory seekers. When pastors and people alike become too full of themselves and their glory, they leave little room for the fruit of the Holy Spirit to be produced.

God too often gets misquoted as saying that He told someone that we need a new building, parking lot, or church bus.

From the pulpit to the choir loft to the elder's deliberations, God's glory gets stiff armed when personal egos and self glory get in the way of glorifying God.

As true believers, we have all the self glory we should ever seek. When "Christ in you" is our hope of glory and we become dead to sin and alive in Christ, seeking God's glory and His righteousness will be the number one priority of our lives.

This is in keeping with my own eager desire and persistent expectation and hope, that I shall not disgrace myself nor be put to shame in anything; but that with the utmost freedom of speech and unfailing courage, now as always heretofore, Christ (the Messiah) will be magnified and get glory and praise in this body of mine and be boldly exalted in my person, whether through (by) life or through (by) death.
Philippians 1:20 AMP

Father, keep me ever mindful of whose glory I should seek. In Jesus name, Amen

Sibling Rivalry

"For wherever there is jealousy (envy) and contention (rivalry and selfish ambition), there will also be confusion (unrest, disharmony, rebellion) and all sorts of evil and vile practices" James 3:16

When we think of sibling rivalry, we generally think of the common conflicts between brothers and sisters as they grow up together.

**"Esau said to his father,
"Do you have only one
blessing, my father?
Bless me too, my father!"
Then Esau wept aloud."
Genesis 27:38 NIV**

Sometimes it is caused by parental favor, birth order, or pesonaltiy. If we were blessed to grow up with brothers or sisters, we can readily identify with sibling rivalary.

Esau and Jacob, and Joseph and his brothers, are a couple of scriptural examples of extreme sibling rivalry.

While age and maturity resolve most sibling rivalries, the deceiver of our souls uses sibling rivalry as one of his best weapons of choice in trying to bring down Christ's Church and His mission.

When brothers and sisters in Christ start competing against each other in trying to be the greatest in the local kingdom of believers sibling rivalry takes on an entirely different meaning and perspective..

When the devil can get a body of believers quarrelling among themselves and pulling the body apart instead of dwelling and pulling together in the bond of peace and unity of spirit and purpose, a church becomes a place that Jesus is ashamed to call His own.

Sibling rivaly can and should be a beautiful thing to behold when brothers and sisters in Christ start seeking to out love, out give, and out serve one another.

There is nothing sweeter than being united by faith and filling a God equipped role within a body of believers as they come together for a common cause and purpose in glorifying God and building up His kingdom. Love and humility will outrival selfish ambition and pride any time.

**"leave your gift there in
front of the altar. First go
and be reconciled to
them; then come and offer
your gift.
Matthew 5:24 NIV**

Father, help me to outgrow my sibling rivalry with my brothers and sisters in Christ as I did with my blood brothers and sisters. In Jesus' name, Amen

Inflammation of the Soul

"For he will rescue you from every trap and protect you from deadly disease"
Psalm 91:3 MSG

Inflammation is the cause of almost all diseases. When any part of our body gets irritated or inflamed, we have a physical problem.

"The Lord will smite you with consumption, with fever and inflammation, fiery heat, sword and drought, blasting and mildew; they shall pursue you until you perish."
Deuteronomy 28:22 AMP

It might well be true that inflammation is the cause of most all people problems. When relationships become irritated or inflamed we have a problem.

Sin is the biggest source of inflammation known to man. It entered with the fall of man in the garden and brought the curses of disease and death into God's perfect world.

Every medical treatment is based on reducing or eliminating inflammation or repairing damage caused by inflammation.

God has provided the cure for our spiritual inflammation by coming to live on earth as a man, live the perfect life to fulfill the law and then die on the cross to pay the penalty for our sin and break the curse of sin for all who would believe.

How refreshing to know that paradise has been restored for us
In our forever life in heaven, and that God has provided the perfect analgesic to provide relief from our frequent inflammations of sin that linger on through the battles of life on this earth.

Tylenol, Advil, Aleve, Motrin, aspirin or any of the other anti inflammatory drugs or anti biotics are nothing compared to God's ultimate anti-inflammatory called grace.

"And thus He fulfilled what was spoken by the prophet Isaiah, He Himself took [in order to carry away] our weaknesses and infirmities and bore away our diseases."
Matthew 8:17 AMP

God's grace will cure the inflammation of pride, anger, envy, lust, selfishness, ego, and leave you free to bear the longsuffering, patience, kindness, love, joy,and self control of the Spirit and restore your spiritual health to a fullness of peace and joy and the security of God's love that surpasses all understanding.

Father, may your all sufficient grace cure the inflammation of my soul as I confess and repent. In Jesus' name, Amen

225

Two Kinds of People

"At that time the Spirit of the Lord will come powerfully upon you, and you will prophesy with them. You will be changed into a different person." 1 Samuel 10:6 NLT

There are all kinds of people inhabiting planet earth, and God loves them all. The fact that out of the billions of people no two DNA's are alike proves that people are different.

"Solid food is for those who are mature, who have trained themselves to recognize the difference between right and wrong and then do what is right." Hebews 5;14

Characteristics are a different story. Scripture reminds us that there is no sin that is not common to man. We characterize by physical appearance, talents, abilities, personality traits, performance and conduct.

Two extremes at each end of the personality or character scale are the difference makers and trouble makers.

Trouble makers are often fault finders, gossipers, whiners and complainers who look for problems and shortcomings in others and are most often the cause or part of the problem.

Nehemiah is a great example of a great difference maker. He made a difference in the lives of many by rebuilding the wall of Jerusalem, (the city of God), in spite of all the efforts of trouble makers..

Difference makers are always looking for solutions and ways to build up instead of tear down.

Although a lot of good can come through trouble makers like Joseph's brothers and Pharoah's wife because God can use evil and evil intentions for His good, Scripture warns us to "mark well those who cause divisions" among us and to avoid the trouble makers.

Now they are here, and they are the ones who are creating divisions among you. They live by natural instinct because they do not have God's Spirit living in them. Jude 1:19 NLT

Has Jesus, the greatest difference maker who ever lived, inspired you to become a difference maker by loving and serving others?

Father, help me to guard my thoughts, my heart, my tongue and my conduct in order to be a difference maker. In Jesus' name, Amen

Default Christianity

"I know you inside and out, and find little to my liking. You're not cold, you're not hot--far better to be either cold or hot!" Rev 3:15

Default has been widely used to describe the horrific mortgage foreclosures triggered by failing to make or defaulting in payments. Default has become popular in computer programing lingo to specify the automatic setting made by the computer in absence of a choice made by the computer operator.

"GOD-of-the-Angel-Armies, Israel's God, has this to say to you: "'Clean up your act--the way you live, the things you do--so I can make my home with you in this place.
Jeremiah 7:3 MSG

We read of sports games and other competitions being won by default when a team didn't show up,or was disqualified for some reason.

There also seem to be many defaulting Christians who don't show up, or get disqualified by deliberate sinning until their hearts are hardened and they don't even care.

In the 80/20 dynamics of most churches, too many positions are filled by default among the 20% faithful few because there are no other choices. The defaults in tithing would be enough to feed all the hungry in the world if the churches' Christians would discover the blessings and joy of tithing.

We have over half of couples getting married ending up defaulting on their vows and commitments. We are all far too guilty at some time or another or defaulting on our commitment to become disciples of Jesus Christ and living to please Him instead of our flesh.

When we quit defaulting on living Christ centered lives bearing the fruit of the Spirit instead of choosing selfish self centered lives bearing the pride, anger, envy, jealousy, selfishness of our egocentric flesh, we will find the real happiness and peace that only a life well lived in Christ can provide.

"They profess to know God, but in works they deny Him, being abominable, disobedient, and disqualified for every good work.
Titus 1:16

Father, thank you for allowing me to default back to your grace and forgiveness through apology, sorrow, and repentance. In Jesus' name, Amen

Mind's Attention and Heart's Affection

"You will keep him in perfect peace, Whose mind is stayed on You,
Because he trusts in You." Isaiah 26:2-4 NLT

There is no better advice for doing life in these troubling times than to keep our mind's attention and heart's affection on the one who is in total control.

"My mouth shall speak the praise of the Lord; and let all flesh bless (affectionately and gratefully praise) His holy name forever and ever"
Psalm 145:21 AMP

When we worry about the world and all its problems we have forgotten that God has already made provision for all these so that we don't have to try to carry the weight of the world on our shoulders.

The deceiver of our souls is going to push every one of our "hot buttons" to to distract our attention away from God's will, calling, and purposes for your lives and divert it to obeying the selfish and unholy desires of the flesh.

As we grow in our knowledge of the Lord, our tender attachment or affection is going to grow into a full blown relationship of abiding love. We will waste and less time and energy on our worldly worries and frustrations, and experience more and more of the security of God's love and promises.

We have the promise that nothing can ever separate us from God's love that is ours through our faith in Jesus. We can also be assured that God is not only in control or our lives as individuals and as a body of believers, and in the prosperity of our country, but also working all things for the good of those who love Him.

"My dear friends, this is now the second time I've written to you, both letters reminders to hold your minds in a state of undistracted attention. Keep in mind what the holy prophets said, and the command of our Master and Savior that was passed on by your apostles"
2 Peter 3:1 MSG"

When we keep our mind's attention and heart's affection focused on these facts nothing will be able to keep us from fulfilling the purposes for which we were created.

Father, help me keep my mind's attention and heart's affection on you,the Lord and lover of my soul. In Jesus' name, Amen

228

Coming to Our Selves

"And when he came to himself, he said, How many hired servants of my father's have bread enough and to spare, and I perish with hunger! I will arise and go to my father, and will say unto him, Father, I have sinned against heaven, and before thee," Luke 15:17,18 NLT

The parable of the Prodigal Son should be a reminder to us all to admit that we have a problem when we are beset by a sin or temptation.

"Your wickedness will punish you; your backsliding will rebuke you. Consider then and realize how evil and bitter it is for you when you forsake the LORD your God and have no awe of me," declares the Lord, the LORD Almighty." Jeremiah 2:19 NIV

My understanding of alcohol, drug, and any other addiction is until we come to our senses and where admit that we have a problem we will never arrive at a cure.

First of all, we must come to our senses and under conviction that we are sinners who need a Savior and allow Jesus into our hearts. If we say we have no sin, we deceive ourselves, and will continue to wander lost separated from God and the joy of our salvation.

As soon as we become aware of a sin, we need to recognize, mourn over, confess and repent in order to receive God's forgiveness and in many cases the forgiveness of others.

Sometimes the power of our sin is so strong we wallow in it and hold on to it until the pain of consequences over powers the pleasure of the sin and we are ready to deal with the problem.

If we have ever been truly saved, we can be sure that God can and will forgive and rescue us from any sin bondage we may have fallen into. He can and does often turn our worst into His best and cause us to love and serve Him even more.

The millions of testimonies of restored lives testify to the fact that God is faithful and that He does answer our prayers for our loved ones who have "come unto themselves."

"and that they will come to their senses and escape from the trap of the devil, who has taken them captive to do his will." 2 Timothy 2:26 NIV

The question we should all be asking is whether we have truly "come to our selves " and became disciples of Jesus living like disciples of Jesus.

Father, thank you that I am able to come to you for the forgiveness, love, grace, and mercy I need anytime I come in true faith and repentance. In Jesus' name, Amen.

229

The Oxenized Church

"The one who plants and the one who waters work together with the same purpose. And both will be rewarded for their own hard work." 1 Corinthians 3:8 NLT

"For because of Him the whole body (the church, in all its various parts), closely joined and firmly knit together by the joints and ligaments with which it is supplied, when each part [with power adapted to its need] is working properly [in all its functions], grows to full maturity, building itself up in love."
Ephesians 4:16 AMP

I would like to propose another saying to introduce the mission statement for a great church growth principle I call the "oxenized" church.

The "oxenized" church operates on the truth that a church that pulls together stays together.

When we think of a span of 16 oxen yoked together to pull the heavy loads we can readily see how a body of 50, 75, 100, 1000, believers pulling together under the yoke of Jesus Christ will not only stay together, but will continue to grow and build up the kingdom of God.

When an "oxenized" body of believers start pulling together, there is no limit to what God can do through them. When time, talents, and resources are pooled Christ's church starts swimming with a vitality and unity of Spirit and purpose that will see names added to God's book of life, back door exits closed, buildings built, and God's people living more and more like God's people.

I have also been saddened to suffer or see the consequences of seeing what happens when the great deceiver gets Christian brothers and sisters arguing and pulling a church apart.

"Then make me truly happy by agreeing wholeheartedly with each other, loving one another, and working togethe r with one mind and purpose."
Philippians 2:2 NLT

The "oxenized" church realizes that God has gifted a body of believers with everything needed to grow and prosper His kingdom on earth, and encourages everyone to discover their giftings and use them for the common good.

Father, help me to always be ready and willing to pull my share of Your kingdom building load. In Jesus name, Amen.

Pillow to Lean On

"I have told you these things, so that in me you may have peace. In this world you will have trouble. But take heart! I have overcome the world." John 16:22

NLT

How good it is to know that Jesus overcame sin and death on the cross for us. When we receive Jesus Christ as our Savior, we receive His pillow of grace sufficient for all our needs in this world and the next.

"Trust in the LORD with all your heart and lean not on your own understanding;" Proverbs 3:5 NIV

As we move from being saved to being sanctified through the life long process of being made over into the image of Christ, we are going to need that pillow of grace to lean on every step of the way as we persevere through the battles of life.

Although the war has been won, and we know we are winners, the mortally wounded but not yet defeated roaring lion is still seeking to devour us through deception, trickery, bribery, or whatever means to get us to follow our flesh and ways of the world that lead to destruction.

When temptations come, as they often seem to do on even a daily basis, God's pillow of grace becomes a set of armor guaranteed to help us overcome or escape any temptation that comes our way if we will just put it on.

The deceiver of our soul's sole purpose is to get us to do as Job's wife told him to do: "curse God and die."

God's pillow of grace comforts us with the assurance that nothing can separate us from the Love of God that is ours in Christ Jesus, and that because He lives we can face every trial with the peace and security of knowing that we will live forever in the "sweet by and by".

"But he said to me, "My grace is sufficient for you, for my power is made perfect in weakness." 2 Corinthians 12:9a NIV

In the meantime God's pillow of grace will make it possible for us to rejoice in our trials and tribulations and give us that peace that surpasses all understanding as we endure and persevere knowing that God is working all things for our good and His glory.

Father, thank you for my pillow of grace which comforts me through all of the issues of life. In Jesus' name, Amen

231

Suspicious Conduct

"And do not bring sorrow to God's Holy Spirit by the way you live. Remember, he has identified you as his own,guaranteeing that you will be saved on the day of redemption." Ephesians 4:30 NLT

Although we are told not to judge anyone but ourselves, we do need to be concerned about the suspicious conduct of all of us who claim the name of Christian.

"There are six things the LORD hates, seven that are detestable to him: haughty eyes, a lying tongue,   hands that shed innocent blood, a heart that devises wicked schemes, feet that are quick to rush into evil, a false witness who pours out lies and a person who stirs up conflict in the community." Proverbs 6:6-19

All of the pious claims and professions of faith in the world don't mean much if our walk does not back up our talk.

Some of the "jot and tittles" of conduct are nothing but legalistic shenanigans that often distract us from recognizing real sin.

It is part of our old sin nature to validate how good we are by pointing out how bad are others.

What we really need to do is consider how good Christ was, and continually mourn the fact that we continue to fall so short of His goodness.

Suspicious conduct that might cause us or anyone observing us to doubt the sincerity of our faith can generally be found when we continually and repeatedly bear the pride, anger, envy, lust, and greed of the flesh.

Conversely, we can validate the sincerity of our faith and give evidence of our holy transformation by bearing the patience, love, joy, peace, kindness, gentleness, and self-control of the Spirit as we live our lives above suspicion.

"When you follow the desires of your sinful nature, the results are very clear: sexual immorality, impurity, lustful pleasures, idolatry, sorcery, hostility, quarreling, jealousy, outbursts of anger, selfish ambition, dissension, division, envy, drunkenness, wild parties, and other sins like these. Let me tell you again, as I have before, that anyone living that sort of life will not inherit the Kingdom of God" Galatians 6:19-21 NLT

Father, help me to guard my thoughts, my heart, my tongue, and my conduct so that I can live above suspicion and reproach. In Jesus' name, Amen

Are You Going to be DOA?

"A man who wanders from the way of understanding will rest in the assembly of the dead." Proverbs 21:16 NKJV

Newspaper accounts of accidents frequently mention victims being DOA or dead on arrival at hospitals. As sad as this is, I would suggest to you that it is even sadder to think of the millions of people who are going to be found DOA at heaven's gate.

"For the Lord knows and is fully acquainted with the way of the righteous, but the way of the ungodly [those living outside God's will] shall perish (end in ruin and come to nought).
Psalm 1:6 AMP

Unless we are all born again through faith in Jesus Christ, we are already dead in trespasses and sin spiritually and are doomed to the torments of hell when we die physically. Without saving faith, we are going to be DOA when we die, and miss out on all of the perfect bliss and joy of eternal life in heaven.

As the signs of the end times continue to mount, the fact that the Lord is about to reach His required number of saved souls before destroying the world and coming again in glory, we all need to play close attention to the state of our souls and the souls of the ones we love.

Our God is a pro choice God in that He never forces Himself on anyone, and gives us all free will to accept or reject Him.

Today's culture that is being shaped more and more by the world, our flesh, and the devil continues to erode our faith and the existence of hell. As the fear of God has gone, so has our morality and moral compass.

More and more people are destined to become DOA as the deceiver of our souls makes what God calls abomination and sin so appealing and righteousness seem so "uncool".

"And anyone whose name was not found recorded in the Book of Life was thrown into the lake of fire."
Revelation 20:15 AMP

Before you let someone you love find out how real and how "uncool" hell is do everything in your power to witness and pray for saving faith for them so that they won't be DOA.

Father, help me to be your witness to help save others from being DOA. In Jesus' name, Amen

When God Answer Is No

"For the Lord God is our sun and our shield. He gives us grace and glory. The Lord will withhold no good thing from those who do what is right." Psalm 84:11 NLT

"I prayed to the LORD, and he answered me. He freed me from all my fears." Psalm 34:4 NLT

With the 20/20 perfect vision of hindsight we can all probably think of times God answered "no" or "not now" to our prayer.

We can be sure that God does hear and answer all our prayers. We need to understand that a lot of what we consider His favorable responses are conditional upon timing, the sincerity of our faith, the unselfishness of the prayer, and our obedient conduct.

The older we get the easier it will become to accept and praise God's "no" because we will see the more and more averted disasters we have been spared because He said no.

It may have been a no to a temporal healing, marriage, job, promotion, failed business deal, or lottery winning, but God's working all things for our good and His glory often involves His saying "no" or "not now" to some of our prayers.

The apostle Paul prayed and prayed that God would remove his thorn in the flesh before he realized that the Lord was protecting him from becoming too puffed up with pride.

The next time you feel that God has said no, try to discern whether He has said "not now", or whether you have prayed with an unclean heart or selfish motive. If His "no" is really a "no" learn to rejoice and be glad that "Father knows best."

Jesus prayed that God would deliver Him from His suffering and death on the cross in the total peace and submission to God's good and gracious will. We can all rejoice in knowing that because God said "no", all who say "yes" to Jesus have been redeemed by perhaps God's greatest "no".

He went on a little farther and bowed with his face to the ground, praying, "My Father! If it is possible, let this cup of suffering be taken away from me. Yet I want your will to be done, not mine. Matthew 26:39 NLT

Father, I believe that you do hear and answer my prayers and that You do work all things for good. Help my unbelief. In Jesus' name, Amen

234

The Biggest Political Party

"So get rid of all evil behavior. Be done with all deceit, hypocrisy, jealousy, and all unkind speech."1 Peter 2:1 AMP

"Let not mercy and kindness [shutting out all hatred and selfishness] and truth [shutting out all deliberate hypocrisy or falsehood] forsake you; bind them about your neck, write them upon the tablet of your heart.
Proverbs 3:3 AMP

When we think of political affiliations, we generally think of Republican, Democratic, Independent, and more and more often, Tea Party. If the truth were known, I would suggest to you that there is a much larger and more popular party made of many of all of the above parties.

This party is all inclusive, does not discriminate sexual orientation, religious denomination, age, or gender. It is a champion of all the special interests, self seeking, self promoting agendas and pork barrel politics.

We people of every profession and persuasion coming together under the umbrella of THE HYPOCRATIC PARTY!

This is the party that preaches equality, social justice, freedom and the good of the country, but defines it with a "me first" mentality that makes a mockery of common good and has turned politics from a high calling of service to a low class "on the take" profession.

The spin masters and "rhetoriticians" of The Hypocratic Party have succeeded beyond belief in convincing millions that black is white, truth is relative, that we don't need God, that we can borrow our way into prosperity and that Americans are free. Hypocrats practice legendary dirty tricks and then bemoan the dirty trick of others.

The hypocratic party can trace all the way back to Jesus day, when he reserved his severest condemnation for the hypocrites in the church who talked the talk but didn't walk the walk.   .

'through the hypocrisy and pretensions of liars whose consciences are seared (cauterized),"
I Timothy 4:2 AMP

We are losing, if not already lost God's favor as a nation by letting the Hypocrats take over and mock or ignore God's providence and our dependence upon it. May God have mercy on us all.

Father, forgive me for all of my hypocritical glory and for going with the Hypocrats who support my selfish interests. In Jesus' name, Amen.

Read Philippians 3, Hosea 6

Getting Over and Getting On

"For whatever is born of God overcomes the world. And this is the victory that has overcome the world—our faith." 1 John 5:4 NKJV

Life is often like a steeple chase with hurdle after hurdle to get over to win the race.

Among the most common and painful getting over experiences involve broken romances, marriages, homes, and other relationships. It is extremely important to remember not to let unforgiveness or a victim mentality take root. This only compounds the problem and makes the getting over and on much more difficult if not impossible.

"Oh, that we might know the Lord! Let us press on to know him.He will respond to us as surely as the arrival of dawn or the coming of rains in early spring." Hosea 6:3 NLT

We all are going to have financial, health, vocational, and even spiritual issues to get over and on with as we do life in today's world.

Taking time to compare how much worse what we have to get over could be is a good way to trigger that "rejoice" button that promises the peace that surpasses all understanding no matter what our circumstances.

The Bible is full of people who had a lot of getting over to do. Joseph had set back after set back to get over and get on with.

The disciples had to get over the fact that they were not going to be big shots in a new earthly kingdom but rather have to suffer and endure.

The apostle Paul had to get over His past as a persecuter and hater of Christians, and move on and then get over being persecuted, beaten,and jailed;

"[Pressing toward the Goal] I don't mean to say that I have already achieved these things or that I have already reached perfection. But I press on to possess that perfection for which Christ Jesus first possessed me. Philippians 3:12 NLT

How liberating it is when we can take our hurts and failures to the cross and get over them with the help of the all sufficient grace and power of the Holy Spirt.

One of my favorite country and western singers, Hank Snow, had the perfect recipe for getting over. It's called "Moving On!"

Father, thank you for not giving me more to get over than your all sufficient grace will let me bear. In Jesus' name, Amen

Reach Out and Touch Someone

"Suddenly, a hand touched me, which made me tremble on my knees and on the palms of my hands. And he said to me, "O Daniel, man greatly beloved, understand the words that I speak to you, and stand upright, for I have now been sent to you." While he was speaking this word to me, I stood trembling." Daniel 10:10-11 NKJV

There is Scripture rich evidence of the healing power of Jesus' touch. The blind, lame, afflicted in every way, and even the dead were healed by the Master's touch.

"Then one of the seraphim flew to me with a burning coal he had taken from the altar with a pair of tongs. 7 He touched my lips with it and said, "See, this coal has touched your lips. Now your guilt is removed, and your sins are forgiven."
Isaiah 6:6 NLT

As believers we are all called to live lives "fully pleasing to God and fruitful in every good work" as evidence that we have been spiritually healed by the Master's touch.

As disciples of Jesus Christ, we are all called to touch others with His love by responding to them with *love, joy, peace, patience, kindness, goodness, faithfulness, gentleness, and self-control.*

One of the most enjoyable and inspiring features at any wake or funeral is when people gather and share how the deceased touched their lives.

"Then the proconsul believed (became a Christian) when he saw what had occurred, for he was astonished and deeply touched at the teaching concerning the Lord and from Him."
Acts 13:12 AMP

We should be ever mindful that funerals are going to bring a lot of people into a church or gathering of believers that may have never or would never again ordinarily darken the door of a church or assembly of believers.   What an opportunity this is to touch them with the living love of the Lord leading to the salvation of their souls.

It is good for all of us to make a sober assessment of our lives and how we are living them to touch others with the love of Christ. What will mourners say about how you touched their lives? What can you do to leave good memories of God's loving touch through you?

Father, as you have touched me with your love and given me the joy of your salvation, help me to touch others. In Jesus' name, Amen

237

Breaking Up is Hard to Do

"But if wicked people turn away from all their sins and begin to obey my decrees and do what is just and right, they will surely live and not die. Ezekiel 18:20-22

Whether it's fights, gangs, wild parties, bad habits, or abusive relationships, it is often easier to start them than to break them up.

The on going saga of abused wives continuing to suffer continual abuse because they are afraid or don't know how to break up the relationship appears to be more widespread than anyone ever imagined.

The ever increasing divorce rate would seem to indicate that it is too easy to break up marriages and families. A lot of people choosing to live together outside of marriage point to the frequency and expense of divorces as justification for living in sin.

"Break in, God, and break up this fight; if you love me at all, get me out of here. I'm no good to you dead, am I? I can't sing in your choir if I'm buried in some tomb!"
Psalm 6:4 MSG

Breaking up the destructive dependency of addictions has proven a near impossible task. The success rates for many drug or substance abuse programs remain so low while the percentage of addicts remains so high.

The truth of the matter is that rampant sin captures and holds on tight to the lives it claims and overcomes. Even Christians who have been set free theologically from bondage to sin have a hard time breaking up old sinful habits and lifestyles and continue to fall into temptations of every description being thrown at us daily by the world, our flesh, and the devil.

"And someone asked Him, Lord, will only a few be saved (rescued, delivered from the penalties of the last judgment, and made partakers of the salvation by Christ)? And He said to them,"
Luke 13.23 AMP

Jesus never promised that life would be easy. He told us that in this world we would have troubles. But we must never forget that He has promised to provide a means of escape to break free from the chains that bind us.

The sooner we realize that we need the supernatural strength and power to free us from what is poisoning our souls and keeping us in bondage, the easier breaking up will become.

Father, help me to break up and away from the harmful relationships and sins that are holding me back from being all that You have created and called me to be. In Jesus' name, Amen

Chasing Someday

"You won't spend the rest of your lives chasing your own desires, but you will be anxious to do the will of God." 1 Peter 4:2 NLT

My reporter grandson's review of a CD album with this catchy title got me thinking "How True"! "Chasing Someday" so aptly describes the way a lot of people are spending their lives.

"Take your stand with God's loyal community and live, or chase after phantoms of evil and die."
Proverbs 11:19 MSG

"Someday my prince will come", I will have a nice house, a nice car, a nice figure, a good job. etc. ad infinitum.

Whether it's chasing fame, fortune, or significance, we need to be aware that all that glitters is not gold, and that we had better be careful of what we are chasing and hope that we don't catch it.

We have been put on this earth to chase holiness and the fear of the Lord in preparation for that "someday" that is to come and that will last forever.

I doubt if anyone in their right mind is seriously chasing a lifetime of torment in hell, yet they blatantly reject the call to the only thing that can keep them from getting there and keep on wandering aimlessly lost living self centered lives chasing the somedays that the world, our flesh, and the devil would have us believe are what life is all about.

There is absolutely nothing wrong with seeking to acquire most all of the things we are chasing, as long as we don't let them acquire us.

"But seek first the kingdom of God and His righteousness, and all these things shall be added to you."
Matthew 6:33 NLT

When we seek first the kingdom of God and His righteousness, we are going to find the incredible peace and joy that only a love relationship with God through a personal relationship with His Son can bring us. This will lead us to chasing the someday of a life of perfect bliss in heaven as the only race worth running.

Lord, deliver me from the wild goose chases that lead to the everlasting someday in Hell. In Jesus' name, Amen

Read 2 Peter 2, Proverbs 3

Running the Gauntlet

"Be generous to the poor—you'll never go hungry; shut your eyes to their needs, and run a gauntlet of curses" Proverbs 28:17 MSG

The pre medieval practice of punishing offenders by having them run between two rows of soldiers flailing away with whips seems to have been a preferred method of maintaining discipline and order.

> "My son, do not despise or shrink from the chastening of the Lord [His correction by punishment or by subjection to suffering or trial]; neither be weary of or impatient about or loathe or abhor His reproof,"
> Proverbs 3:11 AMP

Many can identify in principle as they find themselves running the gauntlet of punishment for or because of the sins of the world, the flesh, or the devil.

The enemy of our souls is constantly throwing pain and misery our way to try to destroy our faith and to get us to curse God and die.

The lover of our souls (who never wastes a hurt) is often forced to resort to the same sort of punishment to discipline and correct us as He conforms us into the image of Christ.

Running the gauntlet is not a pleasant experience and one that we should seek to avoid by avoiding the causes which are most often choosing to live the way of the world instead of the way of the Cross.

Guilt and shame, imprisonment, divorce, disease, loss of job, loss of friends, addiction, etc., are just some of the gauntlets we can expect to run when we choose to live to lose.

When we submit to the Lordship of Jesus Christ, He will chisel away at us until the pride, anger, envy, lust, jealousy and sins of the flesh are replaced by the long suffering, patience, kindness, love, and self control of the Spirit living within and producing this fruit for us to bear.

When we sense we are running a gauntlet, we need to do some self judging and sober assessment to determine the cause, and ask the Lord to give us the strength and power to remove the cause through godly sorrow, confession, and repentance.

> "then the Lord knows how to deliver the godly out of temptations and to reserve the unjust under punishment for the day of judgment,"
> Proverbs 2:9

Father, give me fewer gauntlets to run and more peace to enjoy as I seek to live my life to the praise of Your glory. In Jesus' name, Amen

The Scars Remain

"He heals the brokenhearted and binds up their wounds [curing their pains and their sorrows] .Psalm 147:3 AMP

Most of us are carrying scars from injuries or operations, many of which we have had since childhood. I have a 75 year old scar on the inside base of my thumb I got from a piece of broken glass.

"My wounds fester and stink because of my foolish sins."
Psalm 38:5 NLT

I see the scar running up the middle of my belly from my AAA surgery a few years back every time I shower. Scars are visible reminders that remain long after the wound has healed.

These physical scars are no longer painful, which is more than we can say about the scars of sin that remain long after the sin if not forever. These emotional scars are just one of the many self inflicted consequences of the bad choices we make when we sin.

Although we are forever given the moment we confess and repent some of the scars of the pain and heartbreak we have caused others and ourselves will linger on and on. Even the blood of Jesus, which washes away all of the shame and guilt of our sin and provides the healing power of God's grace will not remove some of the scars.

The best thing we can do when the scars of our sins come to mind is to remember our Lord's beatitude in which He taught *"blessed are those who mourn, for they will be comforted"*

We do need to mourn and be forever sorry for our sins. We do need the comfort of knowing that our sins have been forgiven and forgotten by God, and always remember to thank and praise God for His grace in forgiving and forgetting them even when we can't.

We also need to pray that the Lord will take away the bitterness of an unforgiving spirit which can cause those we have sinned against to have wounds that never scar over and heal.

"He personally carried our sins in his body on the cross so that we can be dead to sin and live for what is right. By his wounds you are healed."
1 Peter 2:24 NLT

Father let my physical and emotional scars continually remind me of your healing power for both. In Jesus' name, Amen

241

Enthusiasm

"Work with enthusiasm, as though you were working for the Lord rather than for people" Ephesians 6:7 NLT

The Lord is continually searching for believers who are excited about their faith. Christ not only built His Church by performing miracles, but also by the enthusiasm of the disciples and early Christians.

"If you do not serve the LORD your God with joy and enthusiasm for the abundant benefits you have received, 48 you will serve your enemies whom the LORD will send against you."
Deuteronomy 28:47 NLT

Among the many characteristics of a growing church, I can say without fear of contradiction that enthusiastic Christians fill the pews at that church.

I like to define a great church as one "you can't wait to get to and hate to leave on Sunday mornings." Although I haven't done any church shopping, I have been blessed to attend a lot of different churches of different denominations over my lifetime.

Enthusiasm is contagious and you can see it being lived out by the way members love one another, welcome and receive strangers, and exude the joy of the Lord instead of the gloom of the gloomy.

Although there is certainly nothing wrong with raising hands and shouting for joy in the Lord, it is important to remember to raise our hearts in passion and adoration through intentional worship and concentration on Who we are worshipping and Why we are worshipping.

An enthusiastic Christian will also have a great hunger and passion for growing in the Word. As good as excitement and feelings are, they are not going to suffice or last if they are not continually nourished by the strength and power manifested in God's Word.

"I know all the things you do, that you are neither hot nor cold. I wish that you were one or the other!"
Revelation 3:15 NLT

Enthusiasm turns our "have to's" into "want to's", and fills us with the all surpassing peace and joy of our salvation as we get truly excited about what God has done for us through our faith in Jesus.

Father, help me to be a cheerleader through becoming a more enthusiastic Christian as I walk closer to You In Jesus' name.

242

When Papa's Happy…

"For God is working in you, giving you the desire and the power to do what pleases him." Philippians 2:13 NLT

There's a popular saying around a lot of households to the effect that "when mama's happy everyone's happy". It is a recognition of the love and desire to please our mothers.

"We have happy memories of the godly, but the name of a wicked person rots away"
Proverbs 10:7 NLT

It might be a good idea to appropriate this recognition into the way we live our lives by recognizing that when God's happy, everyone's happy, especially us.

When our love and appreciation for God's love for us gives us the love and desire to please Him, we become usable vessels of God's love and grace to others.

If we want to know what makes God happy, all we have to do is turn our eyes upon Jesus, God's beloved Son in whom He was well pleased. Jesus lived love and obedience not only to live the perfect life and become the perfect sacrifice for our sins, but also to model how we should live a life of love and obedience as we are conformed into His image.

To know that we are unconditionally loved, forever forgiven, and Important to God should fill us with the security, peace, and joy of our salvation that defines true happiness.

An old Sunday School song says, ":when you're happy and you know it, clap your hands". We should not only clap our hands, but seek to please God in every area of our lives every day of our lives that we may know the joy of hearing Jesus say "well done thou good and faithful servant" when we stand before Him and give an accounting of our lives at the great white throne of judgment for believers.

"The Great White Throne pf Judgment] Then I saw a great white throne and Him who sat on it, from whose face the earth and the heaven fled away. And there was found no place for them."
Rev 20:11 NKJV

When we live each day intentionally seeking to make God happy, we are going to experience joy like we have never experienced before.

Father, by Your grace, and in Your strength and power help me to live a God pleasing life. In Jesus' name, Amen.

243

How's That Working for You?
"There is a way which seems right to a man and appears straight before him, but at the end of it is the way of death."Proverbs 14:11-13

Dr. Phil's classic question he addresses to his dysfunctional patients is one we should all appropriate for personal and spiritual application in our lives and the lives of others.

Trust in the LORD with all your heart, And lean not on your own understanding; Proverbs 3:4-6

When people are dealing with the consequences of their addictions or immoral conduct, this question often serves as to making positive changes in their lives.

When people are wandering aimlessly lost doing life with no purpose and without that "peace that surpasses all understanding", this question can help convict them of their need for a future and a hope through faith in Jesus Christ.

As Proverbs 26:11 so vividly states: "*As a dog returns to his vomit, so a fool returns to his folly.* The truth of the matter is that we are born in bondage to sin and there is only one way out! We need to quit and repent after we have confessed.

Even as we born again believers traverse the hills and valleys of life we are going to hit distractions and detours that will beg this question for us so that we can get back on the highway to heaven.

We need to know that God is going to do whatever it takes to bring us back to His sheepfold when we stray. Our loving father chastens as needed, and hopefully we will quit living the way and doing the things that are not working according to His good pleasure and purposes.

"Live in harmony with one another; do not be haughty (snobbish, high-minded, exclusive), but readily adjust yourself to [people, things] and give yourselves to humble tasks. Never overestimate yourself or be wise in your own conceits" Romans 12:16 AMP

He is always ready to do for us what He did for David and for others. He will create in us a clean heart, renew a right spirit. and restore the joy of His salvation to all who turn to Him in true faith and repentance.

Lord, help my relationship with You through faith in Jesus continue to work the wonder of your love, grace and mercy for me. In Jesus' name, Amen

Beware of "Bragimony"

"Since we believe human testimony, surely we can believe the greater testimony that comes from God. And God has testified about his Son" John 5:9 NLT

We are all called to be ready to give an account for the hope that is within us, and many denominations emphasize having a testimony of how and when we got saved, and what the results have been.

'God's Message: "Don't let the wise brag of their wisdom. Don't let heroes brag of their exploits. Don't let the rich brag of their riches. If you brag, brag of this and this only: That you understand and know me. I'm God, and I act in loyal love" Jeremiah 9:23a MSG

There are many people in heaven and going there every day as a result of the Holy Spirit speaking to their hearts through the testimony of a believer. Studies show that this is still an effective means of building Christ's Church.

We must be careful never to rob God of His glory for the great thing He has done for us. A dear former pastor of mine rightly points out: "And for me that's the test of a good testimony - Is God the hero or is somebody else? If God isn't the hero then it isn't a very good testimony."

Decision theology often tends to turn the testimony into what I have done instead of what God has done.

We can all get carried away from time to time in our passion and joy in the Lord and what He has done for us and forget to give Him the glory.

The worst "bragimony" of all is from people who brag about being Christians and don't live like Christians. The stench of hypocrisy which Jesus smelled in the Scribes and Pharisees remains one of the most offensive odors coming out of many churches and professing Christian homes and kept many from coming in.

"Should I desire to boast, I shall not be a witless **brag**gart, for I shall be speaking the truth. But I abstain [from it] so that no one may form a higher estimate of me than [is justified by] what he sees in me or hears from me." 2 Corinthians 12:5 AMP

Father help me to make you the hero of any testimony I may have the opportunity to share. In Jesus' name, Amen

Losing God's Favor

May grace (God's favor) and peace (which is perfect well-being, all necessary good, all spiritual prosperity, and freedom from fears and agitating passions and moral conflicts) be multiplied to you in [the full, personal, precise, and correct] knowledge of God and of Jesus our Lord." 2 Peter 1:2 AMP

Although God's love is unconditional, His favor can certainly be lost. When we shut ourselves off from the flow of God's favor by ignoring His Word, forsaking the assembling of our selves with other believers, praying half heartedly if at all, and failing to love Him and others, we cannot expect the prosperity of the soul God wants for all His Children.

For the Lord God is our sun and our shield.He gives us grace and glory.The Lord will withhold no good thing from those who do what is right.
Psalm 84:11 NLT

To lose the favor of God is a terrible loss. When we insist on living life our way instead of God's way we are telling God that we no longer need Him and are setting ourselves up for a big fall from grace.

God loves us too much to allow us to live as ones who have not been set free to live lives fully pleasing to Him. He is going to do whatever it takes to bring us back into the green pastures of a life well lived according to His plans and purposes instead of our own self centered, sin centered, wayward life controlled by our flesh rather than His Spirit.

We can all thank God that the Holy Spirit was given not only for us to receive the life giving love of Jesus Christ as Savior, but also as a deposit and guarantee that the good work begun in us would continue to grow us into the fullness of Christ all our lives.

"Look after each other so that none of you fails to receive the grace of God. Watch out that no poisonous root of bitterness grows up to trouble you, corrupting many."
Hebrews 12:15 NLT

Whenever we willfully and continually ignore the warnings of conscience and God's Word we are going to pay the price of losing God's favor and the joy of His salvation until we ask for and receive the forgiveness and power we need to live in the freedom from bondage to sin Christ died to give us.

Father, may I never lose or abuse the favor of Your grace. In Jesus' strong name, Amen.

Poisoned Water

"Jesus stood and shouted to the crowds, "Anyone who is thirsty may come to me! Anyone who believes in me may come and drink! For the Scriptures declare, 'Rivers of living water will flow from his heart.': John 37b,38 NLT

Some of us still remember the old cowboy and Indian movies and the Skull and Crossbones "poison" signs at the watering holes.

"The Fear-of-God is a spring of living water so you won't go off drinking from poisoned wells."
Proverbs 14:27 MSG

In spite of all the warnings, the poisoned water of pornography is rampant throughout the world, and has millions of even Christian drinkers spending billions of dollars annually to satisfy a seemingly insatiable thirst that pollutes our faith, our witness, and our relationship with God and with others.

People have been calling TV the vast wasteland for years now, and just when you think it can't get any worse, it does. It has poisoned family values, sexual orientation, and continues to lower the standards and impeded the spiritual growth of all who drink enough of it.

The poison of gossip and bearing false witness fan the flames of disunity and strife. Unforgiveness is probably going to keep more professing Christians out of heaven than any other poison.

Scripture has over 500 references to water, mostly related to its essential life sustaining qualities. Jesus promised thirst proof living water to the woman at the well. Baptism illustrates the cleansing water that washes all our sins away. Revelation promises us water from the river of life flowing right down Main Street in Heaven.

. Jesus bids us all come and drink of the living water the Holy Spirit provides on a daily basis to all those who thirst.

"The Spirit and the bride say, "Come." Let anyone who hears this say, "Come." Let anyone who is thirsty come. Let anyone who desires drink freely from the water of life"
Revelation 22:17 NLT

When we learn to call on the strength and power of the Holy Spirit to help us avoid the poisoned waters of temptation all around us, we can all look forward to drinking the sweet and pure living water in heaven forever.

Father help me to avoid the poisoned watering holes of life. In Jesus' name, Amen

247

Harder and Harder

"Let's not pretend this is easier than it really is. If you want to live a morally pure life, here's what you have to do: You have to blind your right eye the moment you catch it in a lustful leer. You have to choose to live one-eyed or else be dumped on a moral trash pile. " Matthew 5:29 MSG

"You have been very hard on us, making us drink wine that sent us reeling."
Psalm 60:3 NLT

As the moral values and prevailing standards of today's culture continue to decline, it becomes easier and easier to sin, and harder and harder to pursue holiness and righteousness without which no one will enter the kingdom of God.

As more and more fall into the sink holes of "relative truth", "if it feels good do it", "everyone's doing it', "God wants me to be happy", etc. there seem to be fewer and fewer left living under and proclaiming God's Covenant of Grace.

In too many instances the Christian majority has become the Christian minority to be ridiculed and looked down upon.

We should be sad, but not surprised or shocked by this. There is nothing new under the sun, and down through history God's people seem to fall into idolatry and sin to the point that God gets fed up and lets the consequences destroy, before He brings revival and restoration.

The truth is that we were never promised that living our lives as the redeemed children of God would ever be easy. But we have been promised that God would give us the strength and power we need to live in the freedom from bondage to sin he died to give us even when it is hard to do.

"It is easier for heaven and earth to disappear than for the smallest point of God's law to be overturned."
Luke 16:23b NLT

As things get worse we need to be on guard that the deceiver of our souls not pull us under in the riptides of sin all around us. The more we keep our eyes upon Jesus, "*the author and perfecter of our faith*" the Lord will turn the tables and make it easier and easier for us to live in the security of His sheepfold, and harder and harder to stray.

Father, thank you for removing the guilt and burden of my sins, and making it easier to live in the freedom You give to obey you.In Jesus' name, Amen

Armor All for the Soul

"No temptation has overtaken you except such as is common to man; but God is faithful, who will not allow you to be tempted beyond what you are able, but with the temptation will also make the way of escape, that you may be able to bear it."1 Corinthians 10:12

Armor All is one of the most successful products ever offered to protect and beautify car dashboards and interior trim. God has an "armor for all" that will beautify and protect our souls from the temptations of the world, our flesh, and the devil.

"Then I will rejoice in the LORD. I will be glad because he rescues me."
Psalm 35:9 NLT

God knows that in our own strength we are no match for the power of our flesh and the devil to tempt us beyond what we are able to withstand.

No matter how full of the Holy Spirit we are, the truth is that we are still cracked pots who leak a lot and need to always wear the full armor of God to protect us from the continual attacks that keep coming.

God assures us that there are no temptations given that are not common to man, and that with the temptation He will provide the means to escape, withstand, or defeat them.

When we are armed with the righteousness of Christ, the peace of the gospel, faith, the joy of our salvation, and the power of God's Word we will be able to stand firm not in our strength but in the supernatural strength and power of the Holy Spirit living within us.

"Put on God's whole armor [the armor of a heavy-armed soldier which God supplies], that you may be able successfully to stand up against [all] the strategies and the deceits of the devil.
Ephesians 6:10 AMP

This armor comes in a refillable container in our soul housed in our earthly bodies. Our abundant life depends on keeping it in good repair by frequent visits to the prayer throne, and house of worship.

How empowering it is to be able to tell temptation to "take a hike" and see it flee when we stand fully armed.

Father, thank you for giving me a powerful means of defense when temptations come knocking at the door of my heart. . In Jesus' name, Amen

September 6   Read 1 Thessalonians 5:8-10, Deuteronomy 15:8-11
The Triggers of Life
"That triggered a response from one of the guests: "How fortunate the one who gets to eat dinner in God's kingdom!" Luke 14:15 MSG

We all come with more buttons than the average computer keyboard and they are getting continually pushed as we do life today.

"Give freely and spontaneously. Don't have a stingy heart. The way you handle matters like this triggers God, your God's, blessing in everything you do, all your work and ventures."
Deuteronomy 15:10 MSG

We are all wired with sin buttons triggered by anger, pride, envy, lust, hatred, fear, depression, greed, selfishness, and many other negative aspects of life.

On a more positive note, God's love triggers our patience, kindness, joy, generosity, hope, forgiveness, love and self control buttons that help us be conformed into the image of Christ.

According to the Maslow's *hierarchy of needs theory*, we have physiological, safety, love and belonging, esteem, self actualization, and self transcendence needs that must be met if we are to be successful and complete. All of these needs are standard on our keyboard of life, and we need to understand how to push these buttons and to realize when others are trying to push them.

We all need to seek wisdom and spiritual strength and discernment in order to respond to our needs triggers in the right way and at the right time. Sometimes the difference between success and failure is determined by knowing the difference between needs and wants.

We especially need to know where our "stop", "go",and flee" buttons are located and be ready to use them.

Learning to push God's armor buttons will assure that we can live with all the satisfaction we will ever need. God's "peace that surpasses all understanding" is the pot of gold awaiting all who push the right buttons.

" God didn't set us up for an angry rejection but for salvation by our Master, Jesus Christ. He died for us, a death that triggered life"
1 Thessalonians 5:9 MSG

Father, help me trigger my love buttons more and sin buttons less That I might know the real peace and joy that only a life well lived in and through you can afford. In Jesus' name, Amen

You Can Take it With You

"For the Son of Man is going to come in the glory (majesty, splendor) of His Father with His angels, and then He will render account and reward every man in accordance with what he has done.' Matthew 16:27 AMP

Although we may never have our hearse pulling a u-haul trailer with all of our earthly treasures it's important to know

"And he believed in the LORD, and He accounted it to him for righteousness."
Genesis 15:6

that there are a couple of things we can take with us when we leave this veil of tears and enter into the kingdom of eternal glory.

First and foremost, we can take Jesus as our passover lamb and our faith in Him as the passport for our souls. He is not only the truth and the life now and forever, but He is the only Way to heaven.

When we grow in grace to the point where Jesus abides in and lives in and through us we can enter the great city of God looking forward to the great welcome that awaits us from those who have gone before.

We can also take our personal righteousness account to which all of the plans, purposes, and pleasures of God have been credited. We should always remember that although God has amnesia as far as our confessed and repented sins are concerned, He is not going to forget the love we have shown to Him and to others as we have followed and obeyed Jesus during our life on earth.

All of the good things we have done are on deposit in our 100% insured and assured account and we will be taking the receipts in the pocketbook of our soul when we are transported to glory.

"Not that I seek or am eager for [your] gift, but I do seek and am eager for the fruit which increases to your credit [the harvest of blessing that is accumulating to your account]."
Philippians 4:17 AMP

If we want to enjoy the all surpassing joy that will be ours when we hear the Lord say: "Well done thou good and faithful servant", we had better be living like one while there is still time.

Father, may I never lose my passport to glory and may I make daily deposits to my righteousness account by the supernatural strength and power of the Holy Spirit. In Jesus' name, Amen

Stand by Your Man

"Let your love, God, shape my life with salvation, exactly as you promised; Then I'll be able to stand up to mockery because I trusted your Word. Don't ever deprive me of truth, not ever— your commandments are what I depend on." Psalm 119:41a MSG

This old country and western classic has been as high as #1 on the 100 all time country hits list and still enjoys world wide play and popularity.

"Stand up for me among the people you meet and the Son of Man will stand up for you before all God's angels. But if you pretend you don't know me, do you think I'll defend you before God's angels?
Luke 12:8-9 MSG

The title makes a great anthem we should all be carrying in our hearts as we think about "Our Man", and "Our Lord" – Jesus Christ.

Even the last verse of the song is worth singing as a reminder of what we should be doing: *"Stand by your man, And tell the world you love him, keep giving all the love you can."*

The one who has stood up and died for us so that we would never have to, and Who has sent the Holy Spirit to stand by us through thick and thin and all the struggles of life is certainly worthy of standing up for.

As Jesus Christ and His Church are under attack more and more from secular humanists and false religions the reality of suffering persecution because of our faith becomes more real every day.

There is even hate crime legislation that can imprison those who speak God's Word condemning homosexuality, even though our liberal interpretation of free speech allows venom against Christians to be protected.

"No one can serve two masters; for either he will hate the one and love the other, or he will stand by and be devoted to the one and despise and be against the other. You cannot serve God and mammon (deceitful riches, money, possessions, or whatever is trusted in)."
Matthew 6:24 AMP

We should "stand by our "Man", not only out of gratitude for what He has done for us, or because it is simply the right thing to do. We should "stand by our Man" because He promises to stand up for us when we do!

Father, help me to be a stand up Christian in the power and strength of the Holy Spirit. In Jesus' name, Amen

Bitter or Better?

"Each heart knows its own bitterness, and no one else can fully share its joy."Proverbs 14:10 NLT

Free choice can be a terrible burden sometimes, especially when we consider that our sinful nature will not allow us to make wise choices much

"Then I realized that my heart was bitter, and I was all torn up inside."
Psalm 73:21 NLT

of the time. When we are living outside of the sustaining grace of God, chances are we are going to choose to lose instead of to gain.

The troubles that Jesus warned us about are all around us and although we cannot control circumstances we can control how we will respond.

We do not have a mean or sadistic God who sends pain, suffering and disappointment to harm us. Our God never wastes a hurt, and in working all things for our good and His glory sends exactly what we need to help conform us into the image of Christ.

This free will we have been given will often mislead us into choosing to become bitter instead of better.

The lives of the great heroes of the faith in Scripture are great examples of choosing to rejoice in all situations that we might know that perfect peace that surpasses all our human understanding.

When we take hold of the fact that nothing can separate us from God's love that is ours through faith in Jesus, we have every reason to "count it all joy" and seek to become better instead of bitter.

"But if you have bitter jealousy (envy) and contention (rivalry, selfish ambition) in your hearts, do not pride yourselves on it and thus be in defiance of and false to the Truth."
James 3:14 NLT

When we let our problems overwhelm us and give us a victim mentality we are inviting the roots of bitterness to take root in our hearts and crowd out the all sufficient grace that God promises to provide by the power of the Holy Spirit.

We will never know the fullness of Jesus' joy that He promises all who abide in Him when we allow our thoughts and hearts to dwell in the darkness of bitterness and despair.

Father may I seek to become better instead of bitter in every area of my life by the supernatural power of the Holy Spirit. In Jesus' name, Amen

253

September 10 Read Luke 8:24-26, 2 Samuel 22

Beware of the Riptides

"But me he caught—reached all the way from sky to sea; he pulled me out of that ocean of hate, that enemy chaos, the void in which I was drowning," Psalm 18:16 MSG

Anyone familiar with Daytona Beach, Florida, and any number of other beach areas know that riptides come in and sweep a few unsuspecting souls to death every year.

"He reached down from heaven and rescued me; he drew me out of deep waters"
2 Samuel 22:17 NLT

Although lifeguards stand watch, alarms are sounded, and all sorts of warnings posted, riptides continue to take their toll.

As bad and dangerous as these are, we all face the dangers of riptides every day of our lives, and we don't even have to go to the beach.

We can hardly pick up a newspaper or watch the news without learning of someone who has gotten caught up in the riptide of sin and caused great harm and even death to themselves and to others.

How great it is to know that "greater is He that is in you thanhe that is in the world", and that God provides us a non sinkable life vest to protect us from the riptides of temptation and sin that we face on a daily basis.

This life vest is our breast plate of righteousness, sandals of peace, helmet of salvation, sword of the spirit, and shield of faith. This full armor of God is so heavy and strong that even riptides can't even budge It.

"**The disciples went and woke him up, shouting, "Master, Master, we're going to drown!" When Jesus woke up, he rebuked the wind and the raging waves. Suddenly the storm stopped and all was calm. 25 Then he asked them, "Where is your faith?"**
Luke 8:24 NLT

The next time you feel yourself being tempted to give in, shout out to the Lord in prayer and He will provide a means of escape.

When we put on our full armor life jacket daily we will find ourselves getting blind sided and swept away less, and standing taller and stronger in God's strength and power more.

Father, in your mercy, and by the strength and power of the Holy Spirit living within me, protect me from the riptides of sin. In Jesus' name, Amen.

Overlooking

"From high in the skies God looks around, he sees all Adam's brood. From where he sits he overlooks all us earth-dwellers. He has shaped each person in turn; now he watches everything we do." Psalm 33:13 MSG

We are all *overlookers* or *overlookees* from time to time. This can be a really good or a really bad condition.

It is wonderful that God has forgiven, overlooked and forgotten our confessed and repented sins. It is wonderful that He overlooks what we actually are in the flesh and sees us as He has made us to be in Christ.

> "Overlook an offense and bond a friendship; fasten on to a slight and—good-bye, friend!
> Proverbs 17:9 MSG

It is a blessing when people overlook and forgive our sins and offenses.

About the only bad thing about being an overlookee is when we seem to have gotten overlooked when the promotions are passed out, when we see others so much more intelligent, strong, athletic, or better looking.

God calls upon all who claim the name of Jesus to be overlookers in forgiving others. He calls us to overlook the momentary troubles and struggles of life by looking over the problem and up to the Problem Solver.

The real key to finding the joy of overlooking is to look up to what we have to look forward to, and the joy that is set before us in Christ. The result of this rejoicing is that we are always going to receive that peace that surpasses all understanding.

God is never going to look over or ignore the cries of one of His true children. He is our very present help in time of trouble and has promised that He will never leave us or forsake us.

We claim these great promises along with believing that He is working all things for our good.

> "Lift up your eyes to the heavens, and look upon the earth beneath;"
> Isaiah 51:6

Although we may get overlooked by fame, fortune, and other people, we can be sure that God never overlooks us, and that nothing can ever separate us from His love that is ours through faith in Jesus Christ.

Father, thank you for never overlooking anything about me except my sins. In Jesus' name, Amen

The Secret of Happiness

"All has been heard; the end of the matter is: Fear God [revere and worship Him, knowing that He is] and keep His commandments, for this is the whole of man [the full, original purpose of his creation, the object of God's providence, the root of character, the foundation of all happiness, the adjustment to all inharmonious circumstances and conditions under the sun] and the whole [duty] for every man." Ecclesiastes 12:13 AMP

The pursuit of happiness is one of the biggest preoccupations of life. When we hear "I would be happy if...", "I just want my children to be happy", "God wants me to be happy", or many other common comments, we are merely echoing the heart cry of a vast majority of people.

"Make me walk along the path of your commands, for that is where my happiness is found"
Psalm 119:35

We often base our pursuits of happiness on the flawed basic premise that leaves God out of the equation. When we use possessions, popularity, and the pleasures of the world, the flesh and the devil to define happiness we are missing the point.

We need to begin our pursuit of happiness by understanding and acknowledging that God has not called any of us to be happy, but to be Holy, and that there can never be any real *"well being, contentment, or joy"* without pursuing the Holiness of God.

True happiness is not a product of our flesh. True happiness is a product of our faith and the degree that we experience true happiness is directly proportional to the degree we pursue holiness.

"May he, as a result, make your hearts strong, blameless, and holy as you stand before God our Father when our Lord Jesus comes again with all his holy people. Amen."
1 Thessalonians 3:13 NLT

Our God is not a kill joy. He loves to give good gifts to His children. He did not come to earth and live a life of perfect holiness and righteousness to rob us of our happiness and joy, but to make it complete by giving us guidelines for living the abundant life He died to give us.

May we always remember that there is not true happiness to be found outside of a close personal relationship with Jesus Christ.

Father, keep me ever mindful that pursuing holiness offers my best hope of finding happiness. In Jesus' name, Amen

256

Unconditional Love is for Sinners, Not for Sin

"And all these blessings shall come upon you and overtake you, because you obey the voice of the LORD your God" ' Deuteronomy 28:1b MSG

The wonderful truth that God loves us unconditionally, will not only forgive but also forget any and all confessed and repented sins is one of the true sacred delights of amazing grace.

> "So, my dear friends, listen carefully; those who embrace these my ways are most blessed. Mark a life of discipline and live wisely; don't squander your precious life."
> Proverbs 8:31 MSG

In relishing this wonderful truth we sometimes tend to forget that our Holy and Righteous God hates sin and that He doesn't' love us because of our sins, but in spite of them.

Knowing the price Christ paid for our forgiveness and for our freedom from bondage to sin should make us all take sin seriously and never use God's amazing grace as a license to keep on sinning.

When we are struggling in the flesh with our own sins or concerned about another's, we should keep in mind that sin is not only an insult to God, but that it robs us of many of the blessings and joy that God wants for all who call Him Savior and Lord.

As we appreciate God's unconditional love, we should also appreciate and seek His conditional blessings reserved for those who obey.

When we break God's heart and the hearts of others when we willfully disobey God in the way we live our lives, we are also cutting our self off from many of God's best blessings which are promised to those who obey God.

The beatitudes illustrate just a few of God's conditional blessings promised to the meek, the humble, to those who mourn over their sins, hunger and thirst for righteousness, are merciful ,who stand up for their faith, and peacemakers.

> "But He said, Blessed (happy and [a]to be envied) rather are those who hear the Word of God and obey and practice it!"
> Luke 11:28 AMP

Lord, thank you for helping me understand how to enjoy the blessings reserved for those who trust and obey. In Jesus' name, Amen.

Non Profit Christians
"Let those who favor my righteous cause and have pleasure in my uprightness shout for joy and be glad and say continually, Let the Lord be magnified, Who takes pleasure in the prosperity of His servant" Psalm 35:27 AMP

"Who is the Almighty, that we should serve Him? And what profit do we have if we pray to Him"
Job 21:15 AMP

Profits are the grease that make the wheels turn in our capitalistic society. Our country has been built and blessed by a profit oriented society, and we see the same thing happening in China, India and many other nations.

Although many non profit organizations make great and admirable accomplishments, even these are made possible by contributions from the profits of individuals and companies.

The Christian faith is a very profit oriented religion. The parable of the talents seems to indicate that God expects a return on the investment He has made in giving us a new life in Christ. We were put on this earth for His profit and purposes, not ours!

The main differences between profit and non profit Christians is obedience. James 2:14 asks: *"What does it profit, my brethren, if someone says he has faith but does not have works? Can faith save him?"*

Those who find obedience burdensome are forgetting that Jesus said: *"For My yoke is wholesome (useful, good-- not harsh, hard, sharp, or pressing, but comfortable, gracious, and pleasant), and My burden is light and easy to be borne."* Matthew 11:39 AMP.

May grace (God's favor) and peace (which is perfect well-being, all necessary good, all spiritual prosperity, and freedom from fears and agitating passions and moral conflicts) be multiplied to you in [the full, personal, precise, and correct] knowledge of God and of Jesus our Lord.
2 Peter 1:2 AMP

Jesus came to give us the abundant life in the fullness of His joy and has shown us the profitable way to live as His disciples.

Father, may I never be found living like a non profit Christian. In Jesus'name, Amen.

258

Cost Accounting

" MY SON, be attentive to my Wisdom [godly Wisdom learned by actual and costly experience], and incline your ear to my understanding [of what is becoming and prudent for you]," Proverbs 5:1 AMP

In business, government, or private life understanding true costs Is essential for lasting real prosperity.

"For the ransom of a life is too costly, and [the price one can pay] can never suffice-"
Psalm 49:8 AMP

I have seen many businesses come and go because the owners did not know how to determine true cost. You may buy something for a dollar and sell it for two, but you may have lost a dollar in the process because your overhead and other costs have totaled three dollars.

We see state, local, and federal governments going bankrupt because of entitlements and benefits given years ago without understanding the long term costs and effects.

The pursuit of the "good life" as promoted in all the slick marketing ads and promotion has allowed instant gratification to imprison millions in bondage to debt because they failed to take into account the interest and other real costs of buying things or borrowing money they could not afford or ever pay back.

A lot of people are suffering the consequences of failing to count the cost of their sins. Whether its failed health, broken homes, shattered dreams, or a life behind bars, most all will realize only too late that the sin is never worth the cost.

God counted the cost of coming to earth to be reviled, humiliated, mocked, tortured, and crucified in order to pay our sin debt in full. How sad that so many appreciate what He did so little that they continue to fall back into the bondage from which they have been set free without counting the cost to God, themselves, and to others.

"But don't begin until you count the cost. For who would begin construction of a building without first calculating the cost to see if there is enough money to finish it?"
Luke 14:28 NLT

Father help me to consider the cost to you, myself, and to those I love when I am tempted to sin and realize it's never worth the cost. In Jesus' name, Amen.;

Detour
"Good men and women travel right into life; sin's detours take you straight to hell." Proverbs 12:28 MSG

Unexpected detours are the norm rather than the exception in doing life today. We never know what any given day can hold, but we can be sure that many days will bring forth challenges that dictate a change of plans..

> "I watch my step, avoiding the ditches and ruts of evil so I can spend all my time keeping your Word. I never make detours from the route you laid out; you gave me such good directions. Your words are so choice, so tasty; I prefer them to the best home cooking"
> **Psalm 119:97 MSG**

Whether it's getting involved in a fender bender on the way to work, an emergency appendectomy, or some other totally unexpected circumstance, these temporary road blocks often force us to alter our immediate plans or routines.

Divorce, death of a loved one, financial set backs, lingering consequences of bad choices or insisting on doing life our way instead of God's way create obstacles that we must find a way to get around or through and the grace to survive.

The prodigal son is a great illustration of the detour from the highway of holiness through the primrose path of pleasure and decadence that eventually leads to hopelessness, pain, and misery.

It is troubling that such a vast majority of youth being raised in even Christian homes are taking detours from their faith and imitating the prodigal son of the Bible instead of the living Lord who came that they might have the truly abundant life that only a personal relationship with Him can provide.

God has not only plans to bless us and not harm us, but He is constantly working all things for our good. May we always seek to cooperate with His plan to make us more like Jesus and avoid the roadblocks of temptation that cause us to detour down dead end roads.

> "You may be asking why I changed my plan. Do you think I make my plans carelessly? Do you think I am like people of the world who say "Yes" when they really mean "No"?
> **2 Corinthians 1:17 NLT**

Father, may your grace sustain me and keep me headed in your direction as I encounter the detours of life. In Jesus' name, Amen

The Fly in the Ointment

"Dead flies in perfume make it stink, And a little foolishness decomposes much wisdom" Ecclesiastes 10:1 (MSG)

In spite of the great advances in medicine and pharmacology. the warnings of possible side effects on about every prescription written continue to remind us of "flies in the ointment" that may make the treatment worse than what the doctor is trying to cure.

"How can an ordinary person pretend to be guiltless? Why, even the moon has its flaws, even the stars aren't perfect in God's eyes"
Job 25:1 MSG

Law suits and safety are rampant over unexpected flaws or "flies in the ointment" in medicines, automobiles, foods and products of every description.

From a character or performance standpoint most everyone has some known or unknown flaw that causes all kinds of health, wealth, relational, or vocational problems.

From God's perspective we are all born with a fly in the ointment that makes it impossible to lead the fully pleasing lives for which we were created. Original sin will produce compost instead fruit if not dealt with.

Even after the sin problem is dealt with by confessing our sin and receiving Jesus Christ as our Savior and Lord, the foolishness of the world, our flesh, and the devil will continue to beckon us and bring out flaws that will continually plague us and decompose our witness if not recognized and dealt with by confession and true repentance and our Spirit given strength and power to overcome.

"But now you are free from the power of sin and have become slaves of God. Now you do those things that lead to holiness and result in eternal life."
Romans 6:22 NLT

Doubt, fear, lust, anger, envy, and pride are the most common flies in the ointment that will often show up especially when we fail to put on and keep on the full armor of God that He has provided to protect us from these flaws.

We all need to seek the soothing and "fly free" ointment of God's grace when the old nature tries to take over. His grace is always only a prayer of sincere confession and repentance away.

Father, thank you for the grace, mercy, and strength you have provided to forgive me and protect me from the devastating effects of the flies of sin in my ointment of life.. In Jesus' name, Amen

261

It Runs In the Family

"And I will establish My covenant between Me and you and your descendants after you throughout their generations for an everlasting, solemn pledge, to be a God to you and to your posterity after you." Genesis 17:6-8

Almost every new patient information or hospital admittance form asks for the cause of death or illnesses or diseases of your parents, grandparents and siblings in order to see if any inherited diseases "run in the family".

> **"And this is my covenant with them," says the LORD. "My Spirit will not leave them, and neither will these words I have given you. They will be on your lips and on the lips of your children and your children's children forever. I, the LORD, have spoken!"**
> **Isaiah 59:21 NLT**

We all can identify physical characteristics, personality traits, and special talents and aptitudes that "run in our family".

My particular church denomination seems to have a large number of families where becoming pastors has "run in the family".

God's covenant blessings have been made to "run in the family" of all generations.

When it comes to understanding and dealing with our original sin problem we need to begin by realizing that it "runs in the family" of every child born of woman as a result of Eve's disobedience to God in the Garden of Eden.

Scripture makes it very clear in 1 John 8 that: *"If we say we have no sin, we deceive ourselves and the truth is not in us."*

The alarming decline in church attendance and morals should give us all concern that God is running out of families pass on the covenant blessings He promises to all who call upon His name, *and to their children.*

> **"I'm sending you off to present my offer of sins forgiven, and a place in the family, inviting them into the company of those who begin real living by believing in me.'**
> **Acts 26:18 MSG**

As family values decline to all time lows Christian faith and virtue are no longer to be found "running in the family." May God have mercy upon all who have shut off or been shut off from God's covenant grace "running in the family."

Father, may faith in Jesus Christ and all the blessings thereof always be found running in my family. In Jesus' name, Amen

Am I A "Good" Christian?
"Meanwhile, God's firm foundation is as firm as ever, these sentences engraved on the stones: God knows who belongs to him. spurn evil, all you who name God as God." Timothy 2:19 MSG

There are as many definitions of a Christian as the minds of man and doctrines of different denominations can think of. Dictionaries vary. One says it *is "one who professes belief in the teachings of Jesus Christ".*

> **" And so the Lord says, "These people say they are mine. They honor me with their lips, but their hearts are far from me. And their worship of me is nothing but man-made rules learned by rote"**
> **Isaiah 29:13 NLT**

We often have the tendency to describe someone who attends church regularly or someone who does good works as a "Good" Christian.

Jesus said that only God was Good. He also said that many would prophesy in His name who were not Christians. Scripture reminds us that even demons believe in God. We are told that all our own righteousness is as "filthy rags".

As good as it is to have knowledge of God and all that He has done for us in our heads we are not Christians until we have the faith in Jesus in our hearts.

We all need to constantly strive to have our obedience to Jesus match what we say we believe.

How do we view grace? It is an empowerment to live as a Christian or a license to keep on living in bondage to the sins of our flesh, the world, and the devil?

How much fruit of the Spirit (*"love, joy (gladness), peace, patience (an even temper, forbearance), kindness, goodness (benevolence), faithfulness," and self control) are we bearing in our daily lives?*

As Christians we can never rest on our laurels but need to continually press forward in the life long process of becoming like Christ, while being ever thankful that we have His righteousness to rest on while ours is being perfected.

> **"Why do you call me good?" Jesus asked. "Only God is truly good."**
> **Luke 10:18 NLT**

Father give me a broken spirit and contrite and obedient heart that I may ever be known as a Christian by You. In Jesus' name, Amen

263

Over Our Heads

""But who are we to tell God how to run his affairs? He's dealing with matters that are way over our heads." Job 21:22 MSG

If we say we have never gotten over our head in some area of our life, we are probably in denial.

> "There's a way that looks harmless enough; look again—it leads straight to hell."

The millions of home foreclosures and bankruptcies throughout the country are a sobering reminder of what happens when we get over our head financially.

One of the most frustrating and stressful lives we can lead is working at a job that is over our heads ability, interest, and talent wise.

Many have gotten over their heads in running with the wrong crowd and getting into all kinds of trouble.

The Scribes and Pharisees of Jesus day, and unfortunately many pastors and churches today get over their heads in worshipping legalism and traditions instead of the living Lord.

We sometimes get over our head when we become self righteous and judgmental of those who are apparently not as Holy as we.

Our biggest problems of all come from trying to get over our "Head of Life" by living self centered instead of Christ centered lives. When we try to take control of our lives, instead of submitting to the Lordship of Jesus Christ, we are going to get so far over our heads that only the chastening love of God is ever going to bring us back to where we need to be if we are ever to be conformed into the image of Christ.

> "So you also are complete through your union with Christ, who is the head over every ruler and authority." Colossians 2:10 NLT

Before we go over the head of The One who loves us with an everlasting love and truly wants only good for us by disobeying Him, we had better get under the yoke of His love, grace and mercy so that we can enjoy all of the benefits that come only from putting Him and His will for our lives ahead of everything.

Father, keep me head over heels in love with you. In Jesus' name, Amen

Whatever it Takes

"That [Spirit] is the guarantee of our inheritance [the first fruits, the pledge and foretaste, the down payment on our heritage], in anticipation of its full redemption and our acquiring [complete] possession of it--to the praise of His glory." Ephesians 1:12 AMP

Those who are truly saved and who are truly God's elect can find great comfort and peace in knowing that nothing can ever separate them from God's love.

"For whom the Lord loves He corrects, even as a father corrects the son in whom he delights." Proverbs 3:12 AMP

They can also be assured that God is going to do whatever it takes to bring them back into the sheepfold and continue to mold them into the image of Christ.

If it took humiliation and denial for Peter, a thorn in the flesh for Paul, eating with the pigs for the prodigal, kidnapping and slavery for Joseph, and dying martyrs deaths for the apostles, what makes us think that God is not going to do whatever it takes to bring us back to the rock of our salvation when we stumble and fall in our walk?

The parable of the seed falling on different types of ground, and the teaching that many who prophesy and claim Jesus with their lips will not enter the kingdom of heaven indicates that not all who say Lord, Lord are true believers. Obedience Is still the best evidence of faith.

Sometimes it takes terrible consequences to bring one of God's own back into the sheepfold of faith and obedience. Many have gone to jail, become addicted, lost families, fortunes and friends before they were able to come to God with the broken spirit and contrite heart needed to make Jesus the Lord of their life.

"Therefore, since the promise of entering his rest still stands, let us be careful that none of you be found to have fallen short of it.2 For we also have had the good news proclaimed to us, just as they did; but the message they heard was of no value to them, because they did not share the faith of those who obeyed.[a]" Hebrews 4:1 NIV

How comforting to know that God can and will do whatever it takes to turn our worst into His best.

Father give me your strength and power to live so close to You that You never have to resort to such drastic measures to keep me in your sheepfold. In Jesus' name, Amen

Read Ephesians 4, Isaiah 57:14-21

Do You Need to be Refurbished?

"but those who hope in the LORD will renew their strength. They will soar on wings like eagles; they will run and not grow weary, they will walk and not be faint." Isaiah 40:31 NIV

"I live in a high and holy place, but also with him who is contrite and lowly in spirit, to revive the spirit of the lowly and to revive the heart of the contrite."
Isaiah 57:15b NIV

Renovating or renewing defective products is a multi billion dollar business. You can buy refurbished computers, cameras, tv's, cell phones, and hundreds of other products often at a fraction of the original price.

Like it or not, we are all defective products that need to be refurbished by our Creator before we can become "good as new".

Whether we call it "refurbished", "saved", or "born again". we must all confess and repent of the defective sinful nature we inherited as a result of the sin of Adam and Eve in the garden of Eden.

Even after we have been set free from condemnation and death through faith in Jesus Christ and His death on the cross for our salvation; the forces of evil continue to tempt, distract, and destroy the joy of our salvation. We too often stumble and succumb to the temptations of the world, our flesh, and the wiles of the devil.

We are not only "refurbished" in the one time renewal of our salvation by faith, we must have this faith continually refurbished as we experience the holy transformation taking place within us as we are gradually being transformed into the likeness of Christ.

The stories of the prodigal son and the heroes of the faith remind us that we can never fall away too far or fall too short of the glory of God to have our faith refurbished when we come back to the Father with a broken spirit and contrite heart.

"You were taught, with regard to your former way of life, to put off your old self, which is being corrupted by its deceitful desires; to be made new in the attitude of your minds;"
Ephesians 4:22 NIV

Father, in your mercy and by your grace refurbish me and keep me "good as new" through daily confession and repentance.

Use but don't Abuse!

" Are you tired? Worn out? Burned out on religion? Come to me. Get away with me and you'll recover your life. I'll show you how to take a real rest. Walk with me and work with me—watch how I do it. Learn the unforced rhythms of grace. I won't lay anything heavy or ill-fitting on you. Keep company with me and you'll learn to live freely and lightly." Matthew 11:28 MSG

"For the Lord God is a Sun and Shield; the Lord bestows [present] grace and favor and [future] glory (honor, splendor, and heavenly bliss)! No good thing will He withhold from those who walk uprightly."
Psalm 84:10-12

The grace of God is the greatest and most precious gift we could ever receive. It is grace that saved us and gave us eternal life. It is grace that is supplied daily sufficient for our every need.

How wonderful to enjoy living unconditionally loved, forever forgiven, guilt free, bondage free lives that are possible only by the grace of God. .

The transforming grace of God that renews our minds and gives us the strength we need to lead lives pleasing to God is the birth right of every born again believer. It frees us to become imitators of Christ and live like children of the living God.

How sad it is to have this inexhaustible resource and not use it by accessing it through daily confession and repentance, abiding in Christ through His Word, and the encouragement and support of others through fellowship with other believers.

It is even sadder to abuse this most wonderful gift by continuing to live in bondage to sin either because we think we can get away with it because of God's grace, by failing to recognize that we can no longer play the "I'm only human" card, or by living only to please ourselves.

"Sin is no longer your master, for you no longer live under the requirements of the law. Instead, you live under the freedom of God's grace."
Romans 6:14 NLT

Jesus Christ died to set us free from being "only human" and being in bondage to our human selfish sin nature. He has set us free to grow into the fullness of Christ by walking in the freedom to imitate, serve and obey Him.

Father, may I always enjoy and appreciate but never abuse your grace. In Jesus' name. Amen

Don't Forget Your Password

"Knowing the correct password—saying 'Master, Master,' for instance—isn't going to get you anywhere with me. What is required is serious obedience—doing what my Father wills." Matthew 7:21a MSG

The more we use the internet, the more we use passwords.

Thankfully, most have a provision to email you a new temporary password when we forget.

"I will offer to You the sacrifice of thanksgiving and will call on the name of the Lord."
Psalm 116:17 AMP

When we consider the possibility of identity theft if our password should fall into the wrong hands, we should be happy that our internet banks, merchants, and service providers require passports.

We have another password far more important. This one is a matter of life or death. It might well determine whether we spend eternity in heaven or hell.

If God should ask you why He should allow you to pass over from this life into the eternal joy of heaven, what is your password?

"Good person", "good parent", "church member","generous giver",

"loving spouse", and so many of the character and conduct attributes are all very good things and some may be well remembered and be rewarded when we get to heaven, but they will not get us there.

If getting to heaven was based on what we do or how good we were, none of us would make it for *"all have sinned and fallen short of the righteousness of God".*

We can only get to heaven by knowing and believing the Good News that *""For God loved the world so much that he gave his one and only Son, so that everyone who believes in him will not perish but have eternal life."* The password that we must never forget is "Blood of Jesus"

"Therefore, brethren, since we have full freedom and confidence to enter into the [Holy of] Holies [by the power and virtue] in the blood of Jesus"
Hebrews 10:19 AMP

Father let me never forget Whose I am, where I am going, and how I am going to get there. In Jesus' name, Amen.

268

Underdog

"You're here to defend the defenseless, to make sure that underdogs get a fair break;" Psalm 82:3 MSG

In sports, many love to root for and experience great joy when the underdog wins.

> "[The Lord] raises the poor out of the dust and lifts the needy from the ash heap and the dung hill,"
> Psalm 113:7 AMP

Scripture is filled with stories about underdogs coming out on top under the mighty hand of God. Moses, Joseph, David, and all the apostles were underdogs.

Jesus came into the culture of the day as an underdog. Whoever would have thought that the Lord of Lords, King of Kings, and Savior of the World, would be born in a lowly stable. Scripture mentions people wondering if "anything good could come out of Nazereth."

Although Psalm 82 is a condemnation of judges, this particular verse might well describe the bottom line of Jesus' coming to make sure that all underdogs get a fair break in the eyes of God.

When it comes to having sinless perfection, we are all born underdogs under the curse of sin and would have no defense against dominion by and condemnation of our sins were it not for Jesus becoming an underdog for us.

That Jesus would humble himself in obedience to God and die a criminal's death on the cross so that we could live forever is still the greatest story ever told and most important fact we should always remember.

> "And being found in appearance as a man, he humbled himself by becoming obedient to death—
> even death on a cross!"
> Philippians 2:8 NIV

It doesn't matter how high anyone flies, what greatness they achieve, how much money they have, or any other worldly success. All are going to need a Savior when they go under to the grave.

Jesus was and is the champion of the underdogs. He has come to assure that all who call upon His name will become "top dogs" as children of God and heirs to all the riches of the kingdom of God.

Father, thank you for coming to rescue a sinner like me from the torments of hell. In Jesus' name, Amen

What Price?

"I have swept away your sins like a cloud. I have scattered your offenses like the morning mist. Oh, return to me, for I have paid the price to set you free." Isaiah 44:21-23

You rulers make decisions based on bribes; you priests teach God's laws only for a price; Malachi 3:11 NLT

There are literally thousands of lobbyists trying to figure out at what price they can get a politician's help. Before sexual harassment; came on the books and so severely punished, the price of promotion or of a job all too often carried another kind of price.

Accounts and "numbers crunchers" spend a lot of time compiling cost vs. benefit studies. If we would count the cost vs. the benefit of our sins, we would find them not worth committing.

The government and many people and businesses spend a whole lot more to get a whole lot less than the price paid.

When it comes to fame and fortune the price some pay is too much and get too little.

The old Levitical law put a price on about every transgression, and today's courts do about the same.

The Bible talks about the "pearl of great price". Judas set a price of 30 pieces of silver to betray Jesus. We too often betray Him for far far less by denying and willfully disobeying Him.

The rich young ruler was doomed for eternity because he was unwilling to pay the price Jesus asked.

The truth is that almost everything carries a price. Punishment, incarceration, poor health, failure, success, popularity, and significance all come at a price.

When it comes to eternal life, Jesus paid the ultimate price to earn it for us, and we dare not sell Him out by selling out to the world, our flesh, or the devil.

"We, of course, have plenty of wisdom to pass on to you once you get your feet on firm spiritual ground, but it's not popular wisdom, the fashionable wisdom of high-priced experts that will be out-of-date in a year or so." 1 Corinthians 2:6 MSG

Father, thank you for the priceless gift of eternal life You have given me through Jesus. May I always live like I treasure it as the greatest gift I have ever been given. In Jesus' name, Amen

Can You Stomach It?

My stomach aches and burns with pain. Sharp pangs of anguish are upon me, like those of a woman in labor .I grow faint when I hear what God is planning;I am too afraid to look. Isaiah 21:2-4 MSG

"They spoke out against God and Moses: "Why did you drag us out of Egypt to die in this god forsaken country? No decent food; no water—we can't stomach this stuff any longer."
Numbers 21:4b MSG

We have all had foods, medicines, or liquids that we couldn't stomach. Vomiting or taking a tums usually solves the problem.

Being able to stomach the trials and temptations of life is not that simple. We all are going to have hard to stomach financial, marital, relational, and spiritual problems as long as we live.

Loss of job, loss on investments, unexpected illnesses, repairs, and especially loss of value of our homes are all hard to stomach.

As much as we love our spouses, we are all going to find some hard to stomach faults we need to learn to live with. Suffering from abuse, unfaithfulness, or desertion are problems many are called upon to stomach.

In our family relationships, at work, play, neighborhoods, and churches, we are going to find people and actions that are hard to stomach, and others may find the same things in us.

"I see what you've done, your hard, hard work, your refusal to quit. I know you can't stomach evil, that you weed out apostolic pretenders. I know your persistence, your courage in my cause, that you never wear out."
Revelation 2:2,3 MSG

Spiritually, we often have the problem of stomaching bad things happening to good people, apparently unanswered prayers, lack of faith,and our own sinfulness.

We often lack the guts to stomach standing up for what we believe or fighting the good fights.

The good news is that God has given us all the greatest antacid for stomach upset we will ever need. It's called GRACE! How sweet it is to have God's all sufficient supply to ease the discomfort of any upset stomach.

Father help me to stomach troubles with your grace. In Jesus' name, Amen.

A Cultural Perspective

" Abram fell facedown, and God said to him, "As for me, this is my covenant with you: You will be the father of many nations"Genesis 17:3,4   NIV

The apparently ever increasing and never ending conflict between Christians and Muslims should be a concern and sadness for us all.

"But when all is said and done, God's Temple on the mountain, Firmly fixed, will dominate all mountains, towering above surrounding hills. People will stream to it and many nations set out for it, Saying, "Come, let's climb God's mountain. Let's go to the Temple of Jacob's God."
Micah 4:1 MSG

Understanding the roots may help us better understand what we are seeing, and perhaps a better way to deal with it.

If we look back at all the wars and atrocities committed by Israelites and Christians especially during the inquisition and disputes between catholics and protestants.we will find that it was as bad if not worse than what some Muslims are doing today.

As we have forgotten to preach and teach both Law and Gospel, many have become very grace oriented in permissiveness, judgment, and lack of fear of God to the point that we have to wonder how long before God spits us out as He did the Laodoceans.

It is a sad commentary that divorce rates, alcohol addiction, and many other symptoms of moral meltdown seem more prevalent among Christians than among Muslims

I have more questions than answers, but know that people of all faiths need to cut out the hate mongering and rhetoric and pray for God's wisdom in taking a humble approach in dealing with this problem.

"I know you inside and out, and find little to my liking. You're not cold, you're not hot—far better to be either cold or hot! You're stale. You're stagnant. You make me want to vomit. You brag, 'I'm rich, I've got it made, I need nothing from anyone,' oblivious that in fact you're a pitiful, blind beggar, threadbare and homeless."
Revelation 3:15 MSG

Father, give us all the worldly and spiritual wisdom and discernment we need to seek your solution to the divisions among us. In Jesus' name, Amen

The Crisis of Belief

"Therefore put on God's complete armor, that you may be able to resist and stand your ground on the evil day [of danger], and, having done all [the crisis demands], to stand [firmly in your place]." Ephesians 6:12-14

Dr. Henry Blackaby and Claude King's classic "Experiencing God – Knowing and Doing the Will of God"* has been an eye opener and life changer for hundreds of thousands of Christians around the world.

"But Moses protested to God, "Who am I to appear before Pharaoh? Who am I to lead the people of Israel out of Egypt?"
Exodus 3:11 NLT

It forewarns us that we can expect to experience a crisis of belief every time God purposes to do a God-sized task that only He can do through us. We think about our own limitations instead of God's almighty power.

We sometimes suffer "buyer's remorse","getting cold feet", or "what was I thinking?" as a crisis of belief grips us after we have bought that new car or house, gotten engaged, or made an unwise decision.
These are not God-sized encounters, but just normal occurrences in living as imperfect people in an imperfect world.

When God calls us through prayer, His Word, Church, or other circumstances to do something that will be impossible without Him, we must be ready to step out in faith in the strength and power the Holy Spirit provides.

We need spiritual wisdom and discernment to know that God is speaking, and not some well meaning leader promoting their own agenda, or the deceiver of our souls trying to mislead us.

"And He said to them, Why are you timid and afraid, O you of little faith? Then He got up and rebuked the winds and the sea, and there was a great and wonderful calm ([m]a perfect peaceableness")
Matthew 8:25 AMP

We also need to know that God is never going to call us to do anything contrary to His Word and that He promises to hear and answer our prayers that are in with His will.

Father, give me spiritual discernment to know, the faith to obey, and the courage and supernatural strength I need for you to accomplish God sized purposes through me. In Jesus name,Amen ..

(*Experiencing God-Knowing and Doing the Will of God" available from Lifeway Press, Nashville TN)

Just Say No

"Sweep your lives clean of your evildoings so I don't have to look at them any longer. Say no to wrong. Learn to do good. Work for justice. Help the down-and-out. Stand up for the homeless. Go to bat for the defenseless."
Isaiah 1:13 MSG

"Therefore, put on every piece of God's armor so you will be able to resist the enemy in the time of evil. Then after the battle you will still be standing firm. Ephesians 6:13

Have you noticed how easy it is to say no to things you don't like? I don't have a bit of trouble saying no to brussell sprouts, liver, or chicken gizzards.

When the preacher mentions sins we don't have a problem saying no to, we start getting that rush of hypocritical glory that makes us think we are not so bad after all. When he starts talking about sins that we can't say no to, we get uncomfortable and think he is "meddling".

The truth is that none of us were born with the desire or capacity to say no to sin. It's the curse we were born with and there's only one known cure. The blood of Jesus not only washes away all our confessed sins, but sets us free to say no to the temptations of our flesh, the world and the devil.

So many who are or were hooked on drugs, alcohol, or any other sin will often remark; "I never thought it could happen to me". Young people especially often have a feeling of invincibility that makes them disregard the age old reminders that if you "play with fire, your going to get burned". "if you lie down with dog, you will get up with fleas", etc.

"For the grace of God has appeared that offers salvation to all people. It teaches us to say "No" to ungodliness and worldly passions, and to live self-controlled, upright and godly lives in this present age" Titus 3:11.12 NIV

Our all knowing Savior realized our every weakness, and sent the Holy Spirit to live within us and give us the strength and power to say no to the sins we have not been able to repent of on our own.

This supernatural power is only a prayer of surrender and repentance away. When we say "Yes" to inviting Jesus to come into our hearts as not only Savior, but also Lord, we will find it a lot easier to say "No" to sin.

Father, You are my only shield and defense against the temptations of sin that come my way daily. Give me Your strength to say "No", when I am not able to resist in my own strength. In Jesus' name, Amen

274

No Laughing Matter

"Stay alert! Watch out for your great enemy, the devil. He prowls around like a roaring lion, looking for someone to devour.'1 Peter 5:8 NLT

The deceiver of our souls and ruler of the World of darkness has done a wonderful job of brainwashing. The fear of God and evil has been replaced by mocking, making fun of, and refusing to believe that there is such a being as the devil and forces of evil out to destroy us.

"God looked and saw evil looming on the horizon— so much evil and no sign of Justice.He couldn't believe what he saw: not a soul around to correct this awful situation.So he did it himself, took on the work of Salvation,fueled by his own Righteousness."
Isaiah 59:19+ MSG

We wink at sin, and smile as we say "the devil made me do it" and fall deeper and deeper into bondage to sin and being controlled by our flesh, the world the devil rules (remember what he offered Christ in the temptation), and the "roaring lion" himself.

It is so bad that we blindly want to blame God for the misfortunes we suffer as consequences of our own sinful acts, or as a result of the satanic oppression brought into the world when Adam and Eve gave up their authority in the world when they succumbed to the temptation of the devil in the garden.

The pitiful plea of the rich man trying to get someone to go warn his brothers about the torments of hell should warn us all that hell is real and no laughing matter.

The only cure for the curse of our sin nature, the world, and the devil is the blood of Jesus. .

When we consider that He loved us so much that He died on the cross to save us from the torments of hell, how can we not believe that He loves us?

"Therefore put on the full armor of God, so that when the day of evil comes, you may be able to stand your ground, and after you have done everything, to stand."
Ephesians 6:13 NIV

Having our faith destroyed is no laughing matter. We must flee temptation and put on the full armor of God daily.

Father, forgive me for laughing at the devil and not taking his power as seriously as I should. In Jesus' name. Amen

Truth or Consequences

"But to as many as did receive and welcome Him, He gave the authority (power, privilege, right) to become the children of God, that is, to those who believe in (adhere to, trust in, and rely on) His name--John 1:12 AMP

There are bad consequences for not telling the truth and even worse consequences for not believing the Truth.

"Walk straight, act right, tell the truth."
Psalm 15:2 MSG

When someone lies under oath, they can go to jail for perjury. When someone lies they can be sued for slander, fired, or any number of other bad consequences. . When someone gets a reputation for not telling the truth, their credibility is gone.

Refusing to believe the truth causes all kinds of problems for now and forever. When we refuse to believe that Jesus is the Way, the Truth and the Life, we forfeit all rights to all the wonderful blessings He promises to those who will believe the truth that He was who He said He was, and came to do what He said He would so.

When we refuse to believe God's truth as revealed in the Bible, we are left to wander aimlessly lost in a sin sick world with no bright hope for tomorrow. We will live out our lives in bondage to the curse of sin, and end up suffering the eternal torment of separation from God in Hell.

When we do not believe that God answers prayers, we can be sure that ours will go unanswered. When we do not believe that God sent Jesus to give us a future and a hope, we are not going get one.

If we do not believe that God loves us, and wants His very best for us we are never going to enjoy the abundant life He promises to all who believe.

How sad it is that we will believe the devil, dope peddlers, con men, unbelieving friends, and the current TV trash and movies, and not believe our pastors, or Christian parents or friends who love us and want us to experience the blessings of eternal life in this world and the next.

"So watch your step, friends. Make sure there's no evil unbelief lying around that will trip you up and throw you off course, diverting you from the living God."
Hebrews 3:12 a MSG

Before we consider not telling the truth or not believing the truth may we consider of the consequences of a bad decision.

Father, thank You for helping me to avoid the consequences of not telling or believing the truth. In Jesus'name, Amen

276

Rewards of Servanthood

"Behold, I am coming soon, and I shall bring My wages and rewards with Me, to repay and render to each one just what his own actions and his own work merit." Revelation 22:12 AMP

Every born again believer is going to have a personal inspection by Jesus at the great white throne judgment.

"But I said, "I have labored to no purpose; I have spent my strength in vain and for nothing. Yet what is due me is in the LORD's hand, and my reward is with my God."
Isaiah 49:4 NLT

We will give an account of what we did with the lives we have been given. All of the trivial pursuits and self indulgence will be burned away, and hopefully we will all have some good works remaining for which we will hear our Lord's "well done".

We cannot earn our salvation which is a gift of God's grace, but If we are truly saved and truly love God we can earn His "well done" and receive the servant's rewards promised for obedience and servanthood.

We all have the choice of getting to heaven as carnal Christians with as little effort as possible, or as faithful servants who will hear "good job" from the One who did the great job of dying on the Cross to get us there.

The way we manage our time, talents, and treasures in accomplishing God's purposes in this life will determine whether we will pass inspection with Jesus and whether we will have His reward for servant hood.

How gracious is our God to forgive and remember our sins no more, while remembering all of the kindness and love we show Him and others while living in this world May we all have many good things for Him to remember us by when we meet Him face to face.

"If the work survives the fire, that builder will receive a reward."
1 Corinthians 3:14 NLT

Father, let me live in the joy of my salvation and faithful obedience toYou. In Jesus' name, Amen

Read Colossians 3, John 14

Heaven is for Real!

""No eye has seen, no ear has heard,and no mind has imagined what God has prepared for those who love him. But it was to us that God revealed these things by his Spirit. For his Spirit searches out everything and shows us God's deep secrets" 1 Corinthians 2 9b,10 NLT

People use the first verse of the above Scripture to discourage learning more about heaven. They fail to include verse 10 that says God has revealed a lot about heaven by His Spirit. The Bible reveals a lot more about heaven than most people realize.

> **"And if I go and prepare a place for you, I will come back and take you to be with me that you also may be where I am."**
> **John 14:3 NIV**

The devil doesn't want us knowing about the joys of heaven because it strengthens us and encourages others. As long as he can have people believing that heaven is going to be boring with nothing to do except sitting around in choir robes and singing hymns all day he robs us of our passion to go there.

The foretaste of glory we all received the hour we first believed will take on new meaning and give us even more joy as we learn more about heaven. It will be a great comfort when we grieve for loved ones, and a great source of encouragement for us as we prepare to go there.

We all need to believe and know for sure: 1. Our souls will go into the presence of Jesus in a temporary heaven the hour we leave our bodies. 2, When Jesus Christ returns. this present earth will be replaced by a new sinless paradise where we will receive our new resurrection bodies and live forever with our loved ones with no more sickness, sadness, sorrow, suffering, or sin.

> **"Since you have been raised to new life with Christ, set your sights on the realities of heaven, where Christ sits in the place of honor at God's right hand."**
> **Colossians 3:1 NLT**

I praise the Lord for Randy Alcorn (epm.org) for inspiring him to write "Heaven". This is probably the most biblically accurate teaching on heaven ever done, and I heartily recommend the book, the dvd and the small group Bible study offered.

I urge you to take advantage of this means of learning more about the reality of heaven, and what you have to look forward to there.

Father, thank you for Your Word through which I can know that I have eternal life with you and a new home in heaven. In Jesus' name, Amen

GIGO

Blessed is the one who does not walk in step with the wicked or stand in the way that sinners take or sit in the company of mockers," Psalm 1:1 NIV

"Maintain justice and do what is right, for my salvation is close at hand and my righteousness will soon be revealed. Blessed is the one who does this—"
Isaiah 56:1-2a NIV

The computer age brought it into everyday life, and today's instant communication gives it extra meaning and importance. "Garbage in garbage out" is a biblically sound scriptural doctrine that we often ignore to our sorrow.

Like the frog in the kettle which died as the water gradually got hotter and we allow our hearts and minds to become so saturated with TV and internet trash that our consciences become dulled to where sin no longer shocks us.

We sit around and laugh at TV sitcoms that promote homosexuality, adultery, and pre marital sex as though they were perfectly acceptable practices in a liberated life style that promises pleasure and ends up causing so much pain.

It becomes too easy to forget that God is not mocked, and that there will be a price to pay all who join the choir of mockers who are paving their road to hell with moral garbage.

We think that we should be able to relax our guard in the privacy of our homes, or in church; but the truth is that eternal vigilance and wearing the full armor of God every waking hour is our only sure defense against the garbage temptations the deceiver of our souls uses to bring us down.

"Finally, brothers and sisters, whatever is true, whatever is noble, whatever is right, whatever is pure, whatever is lovely, whatever is admirable— if anything is excellent or praiseworthy—think about such things."
Phillipians 4:9 NIV

Only when we purpose in our hearts as an intentional act of our will that we will let no unwholesome word thought or deed take root and grow in our heart wll we be able to avoid the GIGO syndrome.

Father, my spirit is willing, but my flesh is weak. Help me guard my heart with the breastplate of righteousness, shield of faith and sword of the Spirit You have given me to withstand the temptations that come my way. In Jesus' name, Amen

Willingness Counts
. "If you say you're going to do something, do it. Keep the vow you willingly vowed to God, your God. You promised it, so do it." Deuteronomy 23:21

In addition to teaching faith, hope and love, Scripture teaches a lot about the importance of willingness. God provided a substitute sacrifice for Isaac because Abraham willingly obeyed God.

The rich young ruler would not have had to give all he had to follow Jesus if he had been willing.

"And Solomon, my son, learn to know the God of your ancestors intimately. Worship and serve him with your whole heart and a willing mind. For the Lord sees every heart and knows every plan and thought. If you seek him, you will find him. But if you forsake him, he will reject you forever"
1 Chronicles 28:9 NLT

God forces nothing on anyone. He wants our hearts and minds to be willing whether working, giving, or learning. We should always keep in mind that God is always looking for undivided and willing hearts that are committed to loving and serving Him.

When we value any person, plan, passion, or possession above God we are proving that we are unwilling to make God number one in our lives. Luke 14:32 in the Message sums it up very well: "*Simply put, if you're not willing to take what is dearest to you, whether plans or people, and kiss it good-bye, you can't be my disciple,*"

No one has ever suggested that willing obedience is always easy.

We have the willingness of the Holy Spirit living within us but the weakness of our flesh is constantly causing us to fall when tempted. This is why we are warned to "*watch and pray*".

"But I didn't want to do anything without your consent. I wanted you to help because you were willing, not because you were forced"

There is something about being willing to obey that satisfies God to the extent that we can minimize a lot of the consequences of our unwillingness that most always follows sin and disobedience.

Father, give me the blessing of a willing heart as I seek to grow into the fullness of Your Son. In Jesus' name, Amen

Whose Fan Club?

"For where two or three gather together as my followers, I am there among them."Matthew 18:20 NLT

"But may all who search for you be filled with joy and gladness in you.May those who love your salvation repeatedly shout, "The LORD is great!"
Psalm 40:16 NLT

Thousands upon thousands of fan clubs with millions upon millions of members joined together to share a common interest in a person, building, groups, idea, or item are an integral part of life.

Fan club members fill stadiums and concert halls where their Heroes Perform. Las Vegas, Orlando, and other major convention and exhibition centers large and small host fan club conventions of most every description on a regular basis.

People have developed lasting friendships, and sometimes met their spouses as a result of being in a particular fan club. There is nothing wrong with spending your leisure time and extra resources in enjoying a shared interest in a fan club, but this should never take precedence over your membership in the greatest fan club of all time – Christ's church.

If the members of Jesus' fan club had the same passion and dedication displayed among many of the members of a lot of different fan clubs, this world would be better place, and Christ's Church would be growing instead of declining.

If you will study the benefits people get from their secular fan clubs, you can see that Jesus offers all of these and more to His fans.

Through followers of Jesus like yourselves gathered in churches, this extraordinary plan of God is becoming known and talked about even among the angels!
Ephesians 3:8 MSG

No other club offers the benefit of the presence of the object of our interest and affection at every meeting and eternal life that will last long after the passions and time spent in most fan clubs will be burned when it comes to give an accounting of the life we have been given.

May we all give our best to fulfilling the purposes for which we were called when we became members of the "Jesus Fan Club!"

"Father help me recruit more members to your fan club so that they might enjoy the benefits you offer to all who join in faith. In Jesus' name, Amen

Hardball

"For the Israelites walked forty years in the wilderness till all who were men of war who came out of Egypt perished, because they did not hearken to the voice of the Lord; to them the Lord swore that He would not let them see the land which the Lord swore to their fathers to give us, a land flowing with milk and honey. Joshua 5:6 AMP

Great is his faithfulness; his mercies begin afresh each morning.
Lamentations 3:23 NLT

When it comes to *"forceful, uncompromising methods to gain an end"* we don't have to look too far to see hardball being played all around us in politics, business, and even the church.

Constantine played hardball in decreeing that everyone would become a Christian. The leaders of the Spanish Inquisition decreed death for any heretics or unbelievers.

A study of the Old Testament will reveal that God played hardball throughout the Old Testament to those who chased after false Gods or the evils of the flesh. Things got so bad that He destroyed the world by flood to give His creation a second chance.

How blessed we are that God quit playing hard ball with us by pouring out His wrath on His Son to die on the cross so that we would never have to die.

Although He will often severely chasten us when we play hardball with him, God never forcefully imposes His will on anyone.

In the New Covenant of Grace, God has covered all who truly believe with the righteousness of Christ. He has forgiven all our sins, and remembers them no more.

"The Word became flesh and made his dwelling among us. We have seen his glory, the glory of the one and only Son, who came from the Father, full of grace and truth'
John 1:14

We must come to Christ of our own free will. Although God would have all to be saved, many play hardball with God by rejecting Him and suffering the consequences of eternal damnation.

God leaves hardball to the world, our flesh, and the devil, He is full of love, grace, and mercy, which he renews daily to those who come to him in true faith and repentance.

Father, thank you for pouring Your wrath out on the cross instead of on me. In Jesus' name, Amen

Redefining Christianity

"Do not judge others, and you will not be judged. Do not condemn others, or it will all come back against you. Forgive others, and you will be forgiven. Luke 6:37 NLT

We often hear what Christians must do or must believe in order to be a Christian. We are told that we cannot be a Christian and a democrat, liberal, or pro life. Some believe that we must be dipped instead of sprinkled, or have the gift of tongues.

" The one thing I ask of the Lord—the thing I seek most—is to live in the house of the Lord all the days of my life,delighting in the Lord's perfections and meditating in his Temple" Psalm 27:4 NIV

Passions run high among many Christians on some of these issues, and they cannot understand why others do not believe and understand as they do .   There is sometimes a little self righteous gloating lurking under the surface often accompanied by the assumption that someone who doesn't agree does not believe the Bible.

Through all of the defining and redefining of Christianity, the fact that we are saved by grace alone through faith alone sometimes gets thrown out with the bath waters because of where we stand on a particular issue or agenda.

We need to understand that our Salvation is based on our belief in what Jesus Christ did on the cross for us, and is not dependent upon our conduct but upon His living a perfect life and becoming the perfect sacrifice for our sins.

'Let me ask you this one question: Did you receive the Holy Spirit by obeying the law of Moses? Of course not! You received the Spirit because you believed the message you heard about Christ." Galatians 3:1 NLT

If we are going to disqualify any one's Christianity by their belief or stand on anything other than the centrality of the Gospel, we had better make sure that there are no issues that God is not pleased with in our own lives that might be worse in God's sight.

We should all be thankful that we have His perfection to cover our imperfections for now and forever.

Father, as I seek to live out your perfect plan in my imperfect life, Give me the spiritual wisdom and discernment I need to live as one of your children in every area of my life. In Jesus' name, Amen

Working Out Instead of Walking Off
"Bear with each other and forgive one another if any of you has a grievance against someone. Forgive as the Lord forgave you" Colossians 3:12 NIV

Every human endeavor is subject to differences of opinion, conflicts, and misunderstandings from time to time. We and everyone else are imperfect people living in an imperfect world.

"Don't be obsessed with getting more material things. Be relaxed with what you have. Since God assured us, "I'll never let you down, never walk off and leave you,"
Hebrews 13:5 MSG

The soaring divorce rate among Christians and non Christians alike give stark testimony to the fact that many are choosing to walk out instead of work out misunderstandings.

Ever since the devil gained a toe hold in Christ's church from the very beginning many have walked out because they have refused to work out their differences. Many churches in most every city and the thousands of denominations now in existence have come about primarily because people chose to walk out instead of work out differences.

There is a pride streak in most of us that makes us prefer being right to being reconciled. Pride somehow makes it very difficult to take our share of the blame, and to rise above other"s failure to do the same.

The realization of where we would all be today if God had let us walk out instead of work out our spiritual problems should encourage us all to try to work it out in every situation. Worse still, where would we be if God had walked out on us the many times he could and probably should have.

Jesus Christ came to reconcile us to God, and we should always seek to be reconciled with those he has commanded us to love. We need to learn how to forgive and forget from The One who has not only forgiven us, but forgotten every sin we have every committed.

"But now he has reconciled you by Christ's physical body through death to present you holy in his sight, without blemish and free from accusation— "
Colossians 1:22 NIV

Father, give me the supernatural power of the Holy Spirit to work out instead of walk out whenever possible. In Jesus' name. Amen

The Big Melt Down

"The great city split into three parts, and the cities of the nations collapsed. God remembered Babylon the Great and gave her the cup filled with the wine of the fury of his wrath." Revelation 16:19 NIV

Melt down became a popular term for describing collapses and failures of every kind after being widely used to describe the nuclear melt down disaster at Chernobyl, Russia.

"this sin will become for you like a high wall, cracked and bulging, that collapses suddenly, in an instant"
Isaiah 30:13 NIV

As a nation and world, we have experienced melt downs in the stock market, international relations, and morality.

As individuals, we are sometimes called upon to endure financial, emotional, relational, and physical melt downs. Sometimes we forget to wear our armor and experience severe sin melt downs.

Sin and death had a big melt down when Jesus Christ died on the cross to free us from the bondage and condemnation of sin.

We must all experience the big melt down of our hearts when the Holy Spirit convicts us of our sinfulness and need for a Savior! We must be born again!

It is only when Jesus melts us down that He can mold us up into His image as His brothers and sisters through the ongoing process of Holy Transformation.

No matter how bad the melt downs we experience or read about we need to always remember that the worst is yet to be and be prepared for it. It truly is a matter of life or death forever.

There's coming a day when every knee will bow and every tongue will wish they had confessed that Jesus Christ is Lord.

Since everything here today might well be gone tomorrow, do you see how essential it is to live a holy life? Daily expect the Day of God, eager for its arrival. The galaxies will burn up and the elements melt down that day— but we'll hardly notice. We'll be looking the other way, ready for the promised new heavens and the promised new earth, all landscaped with righteousness.
2 Peter 3:11 MSG

Father, may I ever be found faithful and ready when you bring the big melt down to this sin sick world. In Jesus' name, Amen

285

True Colors
"Here's another way to put it: You're here to be light, bringing out the God-colors in the world. God is not a secret to be kept. We're going public with this, as public as a city on a hill." Matthew 5:14 MSG

Joseph was not the only one with a coat of many colors. The virgin queens of the harem were said to wear robes of many colors. If the truth were known, we all change colors more than the spots on a leopard over the course of our lives.

"All who are victorious will be clothed in white. I will never erase their names from the Book of Life, but I will announce before my Father and his angels that they are mine."
Revelation 3:4-6

There is a popular personality test that classifies whether you are compassionate blue, responsible gold, spontaneous orange, or conceptual green.

A hit song describes true colors as being beautiful like a rainbow.

Colors have often been used to describe character traits. We have heard of red blooded courage, green with envy, blue with sadness, yellow bellied coward, scarlet sin. and white as pure.

Many of our colors are on display outwardly for the world and acquaintances to see. Some are true, and some are as phoney as a three dollar bill. Some of our true colors don't come out until we are tested by fame, fortune, or adversity.

We need to keep in mind that white is the true color that really matters. We need to have our sin stains washed white as snow by the blood of Jesus.

" Consider it a sheer gift, friends, when tests and challenges come at you from all sides. You know that under pressure, your faith-life is forced into the open and shows its true colors. So don't try to get out of anything prematurely. Let it do its work so you become mature and well-developed, not deficient in any way."
James 1:1-3 MSG

Whether this is our true color will be revealed on that last day when we are gathered around the throne with the white robe of righteousness fashioned for us on the cross of Calvary.

May we all seek the true color of a right relationship with God through faith in Jesus Christ.

Father, thank you for washing me as white as snow through your wonderful baptismal grace. In Jesus' name, Amen

Intentional Christianity

"So here's what I want you to do, God helping you: Take your everyday, ordinary life—your sleeping, eating, going-to-work, and walking-around life—and place it before God as an offering. Embracing what God does for you is the best thing you can do for him" Romans 12:1 MSG

If you were asked to describe your Christianity, what would your answer be? Carnal? Professing? Fanatical? Nominal? Lukewarm? Salad Bar? Phony? Hypocritical? Good?

> "And all your [spiritual] children shall be disciples [taught by the Lord and obedient to His will], and great shall be the peace and undisturbed composure of your children."
> Isaiah 54:13 AMP

It seems that we are all asking and answering the wrong questions when it comes to defining Christianity. Many most commonly define it by membership in a church. Most can tell you when they were confirmed, baptized, or made a profession of faith but cannot tell you when they became a disciple. Sadly, many do not even know what this means

The question I have today is: When did you become an intentional Christian a/k/a disciple?

When we receive God's *saving grace*, we also receive the Holy Spirit to give us the *sanctifying* grace and power to become disciples, or intentional Christians. The extent to which we intentionally and purposefully take advantage of this supernatural power to surrender our lives to the Lordship of Jesus Christ determines whether we are true disciples.

When Holy Transformation takes place and we experience the renewing of our minds on a daily basis, we will be conformed into the image of Christ and become more like Him day by day, month by month, year by year, until we behold Him face to face in heaven. We will have become intentional Christians!

> Don't copy the behavior and customs of this world, but let God transform you into a new person by changing the way you think. Then you will learn to know God's will for you, which is good and pleasing and perfect."
> Romans 12:2 NLT

Father, help me to be ever focused, purposeful, and intentional in being your disciple. In Jesus' name, Amen

287

What's In Your Wallet?
"Guard your heart above all else, for it determines the course of your life."
Proverbs 4:12 NLT

**"The precepts of the LORD are right, giving joy to the heart."
Psalm 19:8 NLT**

If you think you would be amazed to see what people carry in their purses or wallets think how much more amazed you would be to find what they are carrying in the wallet of their heart.

Many are carrying shame, guilt, anger, and bitterness from their past. . Some are carrying concerns and pressures of pressing problems. Others are carrying hopes and dreams for the future.

Scripture often refers to stubbornness, hardness, weakness, grieving, deceitfulness, troubled, and blindness as evils that take root in and corrupt our hearts.

The Bible also encourages us to keep love, purity, integrity, strength, righteousness, cleanliness, peace, understanding, generosity, and joy in the treasury of our heart.

We need to be ever mindful that: *""The human heart is the most deceitful of all things, and desperately wicked. Jeremiah 17:9a NLT*

When we are saved, we have our hearts changed by the only one who can change them. We also have the Holy Spirit as a deposit and guarantee of the fulfillment of His promise to give us eternal life.

**"A good person produces good things from the treasury of a good heart, and an evil person produces evil things from the treasury of an evil heart. What you say flows from what is in your heart"
Luke 6:45 NLT**

We need to submit to the Lordship of Jesus Christ and carry the strength and power of the Holy Spirit in the wallet of our heart to help us guard our thoughts, words, and conduct.

We need to check the wallet of our heart daily so that the daily cleansing and renewing of our minds and hearts will make us children after God's own heart.

Father, help me to guard my heart by the power of the Holy Spirit You have sent to live within me. In Jesus' name, Amen.

Bearing by Baring

'Who shall separate us from the love of Christ? Shall tribulation, or distress, or persecution, or famine, or nakedness, or peril, or sword?' Romans 8:35

Whether taking off all your clothes or trying to get rid of your biggest burdens, baring all is hard to do for most people.

"At that moment their eyes were opened, and they suddenly felt shame at their nakedness. So they sewed fig leaves together to cover themselves."
Genesis 3:7 NLT

We often have issues we would rather forget, and are often ashamed to bare them so that others can help us bear them. Even Adam and Eve hid from God and were ashamed for Him to see their nakedness.

Among the many wonderful promises we have through faith in Jesus Christ is His promise to help us bear our burdens. Whether it is burden and shame over a sin, financial, physical, or relational problems,"*He will all our burdens bear*" when we take them to Him in prayer.

Pride is often our biggest problem in admitting we have a burden too big for us to bear. Whether it is in recognizing that we are sinners who need a Savior, or that we have let the world, our flesh, or the devil take control of us, almost everyone hates to admit they were or did wrong, and will turn their problem "every which way but loose" before baring them to The One who has promised to lighten the burden of shame, guilt, and consequences of our sins.

Adam and Eve not only invented the shame and embarrassment of nakedness, they also invented the blame game that is usually our first line of defense when we get ambushed by sin. .

When we sin in the weakness of our flesh we need to know that when we bare all at God's throne of grace in true sorrow and repentance, He will supply His all sufficient grace to help us bear and overcome our shame and guilt.

"Nothing in all creation is hidden from God. Everything is naked and exposed before his eyes, and he is the one to whom we are accountable."
Hebrews 4:13 NLT

Father, let me never be afraid, ashamed, or too proud to bare my every weakness and receive the grace I need to bear through and overcome them. In Jesus' name, Amen

October 16

Someone to Watch Over Me

"Because if I do not go away, the Comforter (Counselor, Helper, Advocate, Intercessor, Strengthener, Standby) will not come to you [into close fellowship with you]; but if I go away, I will send Him to you [to be in close fellowship with you]."John 16:7 AMP

" The LORD will watch over your coming and going both now and forevermore." Psalm 121:8 NIV

Self reliance is good, but there are times when we all need others to cover our backs and help us in times of weakness, trouble, sorrow and success. Jesus knew this about His disciples and about us. This is why He sent the Holy Spirit to live within the hearts of all believers.

To have someone watching over us with our best interests at heart is one of God's greatest gifts of love to His children. He knows our every weakness just as He knew Peter's and Paul's.

How comforting it is to know that in addition to God's holy angels, we have the Holy Spirit guaranteeing our safe arrival into heaven and giving us the supernatural power from on high to live like Christians here below.

We have someone to strengthen us when we are weak, encourage us when we are discouraged, and to guide us into all truth. He is always praying for us for things we don't even know we need.

The Holy Spirit is at His best when we are at our worst. He is committed to watching over us and doing whatever it takes to conform us into the likeness of Christ.

He will sear our consciences when we sin and renew our minds when we confess and repent. He will give us the strength to stand and the wisdom to flee temptation.

The Holy Spirit will often delegate others to help watch over us. He gives us friends to encourage and hold us accountable. He gives us a church and pastor to channel His grace through worship, communion, and fellowship.

When you believed, you were marked in him with a seal, the promised Holy Spirit, who is a deposit guaranteeing our inheritance until the redemption of those who are God's possession—to the praise of his glory. Ephesians 1:13b, 14 NIV

When we surrender self reliance to reliance on the Holy Spirit we will experience the joy of having someone watch over us to the fullest.

Father, thank you for sending the Holy Spirit to live within me to make your strength perfect in my weakness. In Jesus' name, Amen

290

Does Your Bucket "Got A Hole in it"?

"My people have committed a compound sin: they've walked out on me, the fountain of fresh flowing waters, and then dug cisterns— cisterns that leak, cisterns that are no better than sieves."Jeremiah 2:11 MSG

"I feel hollow inside. My life leaks away, groan by groan; my years fade out in sighs. My troubles have worn me out, turned my bones to powder."

Psalm 31:6 MSG

The old Hank Williams hit about being broke is a good reminder that sometimes our spiritual well runs dry. The truth is that although we are filled with the Holy Spirit the instant we are born again, the temptations of the world, our flesh, and the devil are constantly piercing holes in our souls that causes our "living water" to leak.

The fact that St. Paul tells us to "be filled" with the Holy Spirit, knowing that we were filled indicates that we need continual filling to make sure that our cup continues to be filled in spite of these leaks.

Confession and repentance are God's means of repairing our soul leaks. Putting on the full armor of God daily is the means of being filled daily through prayer and abiding in Christ through His Word.

When we starve the Holy Spirit by not praying or feeding on God's Word, we create a vacuum in our soul that is too often filled with our self centered desires of the flesh that stunts our spiritual growth and keeps us from becoming and doing all for which we were called to do and be in Christ.

If we do not allow ourselves be be filled with the *"love, joy, peace, forbearance, kindness, goodness, faithfulness, gentleness and self-control"* of the Spirit, we are certainly not going to bear this fruit in our every day lives..

And I know that nothing good lives in me, that is, in my sinful nature.[d] I want to do what is right, but I can't. 19 I want to do what is good, but I don't. I don't want to do what is wrong, but I do it anyway. 20 But if I do what I don't want to do, I am not really the one doing wrong; it is sin living in me that does it

Romans 7:13 NLT

Father help me to plug the leaks in my soul by daily confession, repentance, and abiding in You through Your Word. In Jesus' name, Amen

Yes or No

"Keep watch and pray, so that you will not give in to temptation. For the spirit is willing, but the body is weak! Matthew 26:41 NLT

If we were to reduce living life down to the basics, we would find that

"That you may exercise proper discrimination and discretion and your lips may guard and keep knowledge and the wise answer [to temptation]" Proverbs 5:2 AMP

how we use our yes and no responses is the key to our living life well.

As imperfect people living in an imperfect world, we are tempted, tried, and forced to make yes and no choices on a daily basis.

Once we are born again we are no longer under bondage to or the condemnation of sin or the wrath of God's law. Sin can have no more dominion over us if we choose to surrender to the Lordship of Jesus Christ and say "yes" to the law God has written in our hearts, and "no" to the temptations to violate God's guidelines for living the abundant life in Christ He died to provide for us.

Our excuses for saying "yes" to the world, the flesh, and the devil were buried with Jesus at the cross of Calvary. Along with the grace to save us, God gives us the grace to say "no" to the temptations that come our way and has promised to provide a means of escape from them.

When we revert to living self centered lives instead of Christ centered lives filled with the Holy Spirit Who came to live within us the hour we first believed, we are going to go back to saying "no" to God and "yes" to the sinful temptations the world and the devil throw our way.

When we abide in Christ, wear the full armor of God, and ask for the grace and power of the Holy Spirit to guard our thoughts, our heart, our tongue, and our conduct, we will begin to experience the incredible joy that God wants and Jesus promises to all who say "yes" to Him.

"For no temptation (no trial regarded as enticing to sin), [no matter how it comes or where it leads] has overtaken you and laid hold on you that is not common to man [that is, no temptation or trial has come to you that is beyond human resistance and that is not adjusted and adapted and belonging to human experience, and such as man can bear]." 1 Corinthians 10:12 AMP

"Yes Lord, Yes Lord! Keep me ever mindful that I have your power to say no to sin and yes to You. In Jesus' name. Amen

292

Praying Successfully

"In prayer there is a connection between what God does and what you do. You can't get forgiveness from God, for instance, without also forgiving others. If you refuse to do your part, you cut yourself off from God's part." Matthew 6:13-15. MSG

When it comes to getting more and better answered prayers, we should always be praying prayers we believe He will answer because they are prayed in accordance with His will and instructions. Even more importantly, we should know how to pray more successfully.

Scripture teaches: *"the fervent prayers of a righteous man availeth much"*. Are we praying intently and without any unconfessed or unrepented sin?

We are also told to: *"pray without ceasing"*. We need to persist in praying.

God was pleased when Solomon asked for wisdom, and James tells us to ask for and receive it. He also reminds us to pray with confidence and without doubt.

Are we praying in accordance with God's will? The more we abide in Christ and His Word, the better we will know His will and purposes, and the more confidence we can have in His promise to answer our prayers.

Scripture refers to some prayers as "mindless babbling". Even the Lord's Prayer can become a vain repetition if we don't pray it reverently. We need to realize that it is a formula for how to pray with Adoration, Confession, Thanksgiving, and Supplication (ACTS)

"When you pray, don't babble on and on as people of other religions do" Matthew 6:7 NLT

Knowing that God does hear and answer hope, and also pause to ponder what we may be doing or not doing to short circuit our prayers .

Father, help me to appreciate your wonderful gift of access through prayer, and give me the wisdom to use it wisely. In Jesus' name, Amen

Living for the Joy of the Lord

"The Message that points to Christ on the Cross seems like sheer silliness to those hell bent on destruction, but for those on the way of salvation it makes perfect sense." 1 Corinthians 1:18 MSG

Then you beg the LORD for help in times of trouble!   Do you really expect him to answer? After all the evil you have done, he won't even look at you!"
Micah 3:4 NLT

As we peruse the news in papers, internet, or media it seems that there are a whole of people living life aimlessly lost in bondage to sin and separated from God.

Any time we choose to reject or willfully disobey God, we are going to experience painful consequences in this world, and eternal torment in the next.

The truth is that we are all born doomed because of our inherited sin nature. It was only when God came down and lived the perfect life to become the perfect sacrifice for our sins so that we could quit living in bondage to sin.

When we receive God's wonderful gift of eternal life through faith in Jesus Christ, we begin living a life of purpose and reason. We begin living to carry out God's purposes for our life in appreciation for the wonderful gift of salvation He earned for us.

We will find ourselves no longer taking pleasure in doing evil. We will find ourselves finding meaning and purpose in doing good. *"Our chains are gone, and we've been set free"* to be all that we can be by the power of the Holy Spirit when we surrender control of our lives to the Lordship of Jesus Christ, and seek to become more like Him.

"Since they didn't bother to acknowledge God, God quit bothering them and let them run loose. And then all hell broke loose: rampant evil, grabbing and grasping, vicious backstabbing."
Romans 1:28 MSG

As we start living "just for the joy of it", we are going to find that all surpassing peace as we learn to rejoice and thank God through every circumstance of life.

Father help me to live a life serving and pleasing you just for the joy of it!. In Jesus' name, Amen

0
0
0

Putting More Time on the Clock

"Quiet now! Reverent silence before me, God, the Master! Time's up. My Judgment Day is near: The Holy Day is all set, the invited guests made holy. On the Holy Day, God's Judgment Day, Zephaniah 1:7 MSG

Any one watching football or basketball games has become well aware of game time being extended by "putting more time on the clock" for any number of reasons.

"I will ᵃadd to your life fifteen years and deliver you and this city [Jerusalem] out of the hand of the king of Assyria; and I will defend this city for My own sake and for My servant David's sake."
2 Kings 20:9 AMP

The story of Hezekiah, Lazarus, and the many biblical characters being raised from the dead indicate that even though God has our days numbered, He can and sometimes will add more time to the days of our lives according to His good purposes and pleasure.

Prayers for God to spare the lives of our loved ones are probably the most often prayed prayers of all. Sometimes these prayers turn into prayers to give our friends and loved ones a peaceable release as we see them suffering through the extra time on the clock provided by the artificial life extending practices of today's medicine and technology.

God has put extra time on the clock so that many unbelievers will be alive long enough to become saved.

As believers, one of the greatest gifts of our salvation is the blessed assurance that we have Jesus' victory over death and the grave and the promise for an even better life to come in heaven. We should never worry about death like ones who have no hope.

"For God saved us and called us to live a holy life. He did this, not because we deserved it, but because that was his plan from before the beginning of time—to show us his grace through Christ Jesus.
2 Timothy 1:9 NLT

When God is pleased to answer our prayers to put more "time on the clock" for our lives, we should be praying daily for how to use the extra time in fulfilling his purposes. That's what all time is really about.

Father, help me to use all the time you graciously give me in this life to be about those things for which you created me. In Jesus' name, Amen

Something We All Need to Know

"Be gentle and forbearing with one another and, if one has a difference (a grievance or complaint) against another, readily pardoning each other; even as the Lord has [freely] forgiven you, so must you also [forgive]"
Colossians 3:12-14 AMP

Whenever our spouses, children, family or friends disappoint us, (as they are sure to do) we need to consider how often and how badly we all disappoint God, and pray for the grace to respond with the grace with which he responds when we disappoint Him.

"Who is a God like You, Who forgives iniquity and passes over the transgression of the remnant of His heritage? He retains not His anger forever, because He delights in mercy and loving-kindness."
Micah 7:18 AMP

God loves us unconditionally, but certainly not because of our sins and mistakes. He loves us in spite of them, and is committed to doing whatever it takes to help us rise above them and pursue the perfection of Christ as we grow in our faith, knowledge, and love of God.

We are all fellow pilgrims traveling through a humanistic, hedonistic, sin sick world with a sin nature that is prone to wander and be less than God and others expect us to be from time to time.

We need to know that we are never going to be able to change some of these problems, and learn to accept and live with them by God's grace, the comfort of His love and faith in His power to effect needed changes.

It's all about hating the sin but loving the sinner in spite of their sins. We can speak the truth in love, pray for them in love, and when necessary discipline or separate from them in love, but we must remember to love others in spite of their problems.

"Do you think anyone is going to be able to drive a wedge between us and Christ's love for us? There is no way! Not trouble, not hard times, not hatred, not hunger, not homelessness, not bullying threats, not backstabbing, not even the worst sins listed in Scripture:"
Romans 8:38 MSG

Father, thank you for your unconditional love freely given to me. Let me freely pass it on to others. In Jesus' name, Amen

Extreme Takeovers

"No temptation has overtaken you except what is common to mankind. And God is faithful; he will not let you be tempted beyond what you can bear. But when you are tempted, he will also provide a way out so that you can endure it." 1 Corinthians 10:12-14 NIV

There is still a roaring lion roaming around seeking whom he may devour. When the arrows of rebellion, anger, pride, envy, lust, addiction, or unforgiveness take over, there is often hell to pay. Sin always produces consequences.

"But for you who fear my name, the Sun of Righteousness will rise with healing in his wings.And you will go free, leaping with joy like calves let out to pasture. Malachi 4:2 NLT

Prisons are filled with victims of extreme takeovers where they have given in to their baser instincts and committed crimes of passion leading to confinement.

Besetting sins can even take over in the hearts of professing Christians, as Scripture's warnings and exhortations to put on the full armor of God go unheeded.

When we see these bad things happening to good and bad people, we can take consolation in knowing that God is still in control, and that where sin abounds, His grace abounds even more.

The apostle Paul is a perfect example of the other side of "extreme takeovers". When God took over this murderer and persecutor of Christians, Paul became perhaps the greatest advocate for the Christian Faith this world has ever known.

The Lord continues to demonstrate that He is mighty to save by doing extreme takeovers in the lives of many wretches where His love, grace, mercy, and peace produce the patience, kindness, love, joy, peace, and self control of His Spirit living within us.

"Therefore put on the full armor of God, so that when the day of evil comes, you may be able to stand your ground, and after you have done everything, to stand." Ephesians 6:13 NIV

No matter how extreme the takeover, we all need the extreme makeover by the transforming power of the Holy Spirit if we are to become and accomplish all that God created us for before we were ever born.

Father help me to avoid the takeover of any besetting sin, and help me to cooperate with the takeover of the Holy Spirit in controlling my life. In Jesus' name, Amen

297

Rise Above It

"ARISE [from the depression and prostration in which circumstances have kept you--rise to a new life]! Shine (be radiant with the glory of the Lord), for your light has come, and the glory of the Lord has risen upon you!." Isaiah 60:1 AMP)

Of all of the gifts given to us by our gracious God, the supernatural power to rise above our sins, tragedies, mistakes, and circumstances is certainly one of the greatest gifts of all.

"And [your] life shall be clearer than the noonday and rise above it; though there be darkness, it shall be as the morning"
Job 11:17 AMP

When we think we have problems, we need to go back to the book of Job and remind ourselves how much worse our problems could be and how great and powerful is our God.

Are you laid low by bitterness and unforgiveness? Are you being defeated by besetting sins or other failures? Are you sinking into despair by financial, relational, physical, or spiritual problems? Instead of being shocked and surprised, be comforted in knowing that troubles are to be expected but that help is on the way.

It is good to remember that there is no temptation or problem given that is not common to man. It is even better to remember that where sin abounds, God's grace abounds even more, and His power is more than sufficient to help us to rise above any problems when we confess, repent, and acknowledge that we do not have the strength to rise on our own.

The supernatural resurrection power that raised Christ from the dead is the same supernatural power that is ours to claim by faith to help us rise above anything that the deceiver of our souls, the world, or our flesh may send to bring us down.

Our Lord tells us *"arise, take your bed and walk"*, and to rejoice in our troubles. Rejoicing is the channel for receiving that "peace that surpasses all understanding" and the power to arise with healing above anything that we may face living life in a sin sick world.

"But you, beloved, build yourselves up [founded] on your most holy faith [[d]make progress, rise like an edifice higher and higher], praying in the Holy Spirit;'"
Jude 1:20 AMP

Father, let the rising of the sun be a daily reminder that the rising of the Son means that I too will rise. In Jesus' strong name, Amen

Are You a "Yes" Man?

"The eyes of the LORD search the whole earth in order to strengthen those whose hearts are fully committed to him" 2 Chronicles 16:9a NLT

For better or for worse, leaders of every description seem to seek out yes men to serve on their boards and committees.

> "Then I heard the voice of the Lord saying, "Whom shall I send? And who will go for us?" And I said, "Here am I. Send me!" Isaiah 6:8 NIV

While they promote unity and support for carrying out the leaders job or agenda, yes men do not always protect or hold the leader accountable from and for their mistakes and weaknesses.

While it takes a very secure leader to welcome an independent thinker into their midst, and one negative person can often cause a lot of dissent and problems, all leaders (and especially pastors) should be open to receiving input and suggestions from others instead of seeking a bunch of "rubber stamps" .

God is the only one to whom we should always be "Yes Men", because He is all powerful, all knowing, and has never made a mistake.(You can never argue or disagree with perfection). God is the only one to whom we should ever extend total obedience.

Scripture is full of the consequences of those who said no to God. Jonah got swallowed up by a big fish. Moses never got to enter the promised land. The rich young ruler missed out. Adam and Eve got us all into a lot of trouble by disobeying God.

God is holding on to many wonderful gifts of salvation waiting for some one to deliver them to their loved ones, friends, neighbors, and others throughout the world.

He has miracles going begging because He has no one to deliver them because His children are not saying yes to His "knudges". May God forbid that none of us miss out on the blessings of doing all for which He created us, because we are not God's "Yes" Children.

> "Where is your faith?" he asked his disciples. In fear and amazement they asked one another, "Who is this? He commands even the winds and the water, and they obey him."

Father, by the power of the Holy Spirit may I always be counted among your "Yes Men". In Jesus' name, Amen

The World's Biggest Little Word

"When people do not accept divine guidance, they run wild. But whoever obeys the law is joyful. Proverbs 29:17-19

If we are ever asked to list the ten most important words in any language, we should always include the little two letter word "no".(and it's cousins "don't","stop",and "beware")

"So obey the commands of the LORD your God by walking in his ways and fearing him."
Deuteronomy 8:6 NLT

"No" is the most important word we can ever teach our children. It can keep them safe in the yard, away from the hot stove, dangerous electrical outlets, and from misbehaving in public.

Any child that is allowed to grow up without obeying the word "no" Is most likely going to grow up spoiled rotten and rebellious if they survive failing to heed the warning "no" imparts in dangerous situations.

If you think failing to obey the "no" of a parent, spouse, boss, military superior, or policeman can have serious consequences, think of how much more serious and lasting the consequences of failing to heed God's "no's".

God tells us no other Gods before Him, to say "no" to sin and the temptations of the world, the flesh, and the devil. While the world tends to view God's "no" as a straight jacket and pleasure quencher, the truth is that God's "no's" are guidelines for glory and boundaries that keep the blessings of our abundant life in Christ flowing.

The original sin that we are all born with and begins to show up early in children is most often the rebellious spirit that encourages us to ignore "no's". We want to be in control and we don't want anyone telling us what to do, and especially what not to do.

Do not be misled: "Bad company corrupts good character." Come back to your senses as you ought, and stop sinning; for there are some who are ignorant of God—I say this to your shame."
I Corinthians 15:30 NLT

When we respond to God's wonderful free gift of eternal life with a "no" of our own, we are going to bear the severest consequences of all.

Father, by the power of the Holy Spirit, give me the strength to hear and obey your "no's", and to realize that they are for our good and your glory. In Jesus' name, Amen

The Total Package

"The Spirit of the LORD is upon me, for he has anointed me to bring Good News to the poor. He has sent me to proclaim that captives will be released, that the blind will see, that the oppressed will be set free, and that the time of the LORD's favor has come" Luke 4:18 NLT

The grace of God is like a diamond of many facets, all reflecting the light of His wonderful love and power at work in our lives.

> "But let all who take refuge in you rejoice; let them sing joyful praises forever. Spread your protection over them,that all who love your name may be filled with joy."
> **Psalm 5:11 NLT**

God's wonderful grace not only saves us, it keeps us under the shelter of His manifold graces that guard, protect, and bless us with the all sufficient grace we need for living our abundant new life in Christ.

God's sanctifying grace begins transforming and conforming us into the image of Christ the hour we first believe until the day we see Jesus face to face in heaven. The Holy Spirit has been given as our deposit that none of us who are truly saved will ever be lost.

God's prospering grace blesses the work of our hands and our hearts as he provides for all of our material, emotional, spiritual, and relational needs.

When we see the tragedies, heartbreak, and suffering around us and among our friends, after expressing our sorrow, we should remember that any of these things could have befallen us were it not for the grace of God. As bad as things are, we always need to keep in mind that they could be a whole lot worse if not for the protective grace of God.

God's liberating grace not only frees us from the guilt and condemnation of sin, but also frees us to extend grace to others

> "Out of his fullness we have all received grace in place of grace already given."
> **John 1:16 NIV**

Whether in prayer, worship, getting to know God better through His Word, partaking of the sacraments, or abiding, God will provide the total package of His graces to all those who earnestly seek Him.

Father, keep me totally sheltered under the wings of your grace and let your goodness and mercy follow me all the days of my life. In Jesus' name. Amen

Everybody's Got a Story

" So we, numerous as we are, are one body in Christ (the Messiah) and individually we are parts one of another [mutually dependent on one another]." Romans 12:5 AMP

In our ongoing kaleidoscope of life we see patterns, stories, and experiences of every description. The Bible is full of life stories. We learn a lot from the varied assortment of talents, interests, successes and failures, preoccupations, characteristics, and experiences of Biblical characters.

"I will praise You, for I am fearfully and wonderfully made; Marvelous are Your works, And that my soul knows very well."
Psalm 139:14

We can also learn a lot from people the Lord puts across our path as we journey through life.

We can learn from their mistakes and try to avoid them, and from discovering the keys to their success and trying to appropriate them into our own recipe for success.

The scientific fact that every single person has a totally unique DNA confirms the fact that we are all custom made by God and different from anyone else.

The more time we spend listening and learning from and about the lives of others, the more we can appreciate our own.

When we learn of heartbreaks and tragedies, we can not only minister by comforting them but also appreciate that we have been spared of so many of these by the grace of God.

When we learn of good fortunes and accomplishments we can minister by multiplying their joy in sharing it.

The bottom line is that the Lord surrounds us with a lot of wonderful life stories to enjoy.

All these [gifts, achievements, abilities] are inspired and brought to pass by one and the same [Holy] Spirit, Who apportions to each person individually [exactly] as He chooses.
1 Corinthians 12:10-12

We can start by thinking and talking less about ourselves and our stories, and listening to, enjoying, and learning from the life stories of others. Listening and showing an interest in the lives of others is the glue that builds friendships that last.

Father, help me to take time to listen and learn from others. In Jesus' name, Amen

Contradictions

"My thoughts are nothing like your thoughts," says the Lord. "And my ways are far beyond anything you could imagine" Isaiah 55:8 NLT

To understand that some of God's higher ways are not always going to make sense to us is to understand how great is our God.

> "There is a way that appears to be right, but in the end it leads to death."
> Proverbs 14:12 NIV

The idea that we should love our enemies and bless those who persecute us makes no sense from a human perspective. To understand that the more we give the more we will have is totally foreign to the world's view.

The whole idea that we should "count it all joy" when troubles come and rejoice when bad things happen tests the limits of our faith and understanding.

We need to begin by asking ourselves whether we really believe that God is Sovereign, that He really does work all things for our good, and that he truly loves us and wants His best for us.

When we can accept these truths by faith, we are going to find that God's apparent contradictions are really God's recipe for making us better instead of bitter as we struggle through the troubles of this world He said we would experience.

> "For our light, momentary affliction (this slight distress of the passing hour) is ever more and more abundantly preparing and producing and achieving for us an everlasting weight of glory [beyond all measure, excessively surpassing all comparisons and all calculations, a vast and transcendent glory and blessedness never to cease!"
> 2 Corinthians 4:17 AMP

The idea that our Holy and Perfect God could love wretches like us leads us into perhaps the most amazing contradiction of all. That He would love us enough to come live through all the troubles this world has to offer and die in order that we might live forever is the greatest contradiction of all. This is why it's called Amazing Grace.

Father, give me the faith and power and strength of your Spirit to accept and believe Your truths that are higher than my understanding. In Jesus' name, Amen

Read Mark 2:25-53, Psalm 119:98-106,

How to Live Life Well

"You shall have charge over my house, and all my people shall be governed according to your word [with reverence, submission, and obedience]. Only in matters of the throne will I be greater than you are.Genesis 41:40 AMP

Psalm 119 is not only the longest, but may well be the most insightful in teaching the benefits of living according to God's

"Thy word *is* a lamp unto my feet, and a light unto my path." Psalm 119:105 KJV

Word.

When we live according to God's Word, we can stay on the path of purity. (Psalm 119:9). We can be revived and stimulated\ (v25). When weary and overcome by sorrow, we can be strengthened "according to Your Word." (v28)

God can turn our eyes away from worthless things and preserve our life in Him :"according to Your Word" (v37). God can and will do good to us when we ask "according to Your Word". (v65) God can and will renew and quicken us "according to Your Word" (v107)

God will answer our prayer; "Direct my footsteps "according to Your Word"; let no sin rule over me" (v132).Jesus will:"Plead my cause and redeem me; revive me and give me life "according to Your Word".(v153)

We can receive understanding (discernment and comprehension) "according to \Word" (of assurance and promise) (v168) We will receive deliverance "according to Your Word". (v170).

"And now, Lord, You are releasing Your servant to depart (leave this world) in peace, according to Your word." Mark 2:29 AMP

We can only do life well "according in Your Word", by knowing God's Word. It is a treasury of promises that deliver the abundant life Jesus promises all who seek.

The great recipes for living life well are available to all who will exercise the spiritual discipline of growing in the knowledge of God's Word.

Father,help me to better live my life "according in Your Word", by abiding in Your Word. In Jesus'name, Amen

'

304

Receptivity

""If any of you are embarrassed over me and the way I'm **leading** you when you get around your fickle and unfocused friends, know that you'll be an even greater embarrassment to the Son of Man when he arrives in all the splendor of God, his Father, with an army of the holy angels." Mark 8:38 MSG

Receptivity to faith based experiences and leadings will add an exciting dimension to our life in Christ, and is a great antidote for boredom and depression.

"For I give you good doctrine [what is to be received]; do not forsake my teaching."
Proverbs 4:2 AMP

Politicians, manufacturers, businesses, and other organizations spend millions on marketing research trying to determine our receptivity to their products, platforms, and agendas.

Jesus Christ was the greatest teacher of receptivity the world has ever known. When we are receptive to the Good News He came to bring us, we begin a new life as a redeemed child of God.

As we become receptive to the leadings of the Holy Spirit in our life we find ourselves receiving God's all sufficient and abundantly exceeding grace in every area where we are obedient.

We are promised wisdom if we will pray for it. Along with the wisdom comes spiritual discernment with which we can be even more receptive to learning and living the will of God in our everyday life.

As we become more sensitive and receptive to the Holy Spirit's leadings we will become less receptive to the selfish and sinful demands of our flesh and find ourselves becoming more and more like Jesus as we are transformed by the renewing of our minds.

"But as many as received him, to them gave he power to become the sons of God, even to them that believe on his name:
John 1:4 KJV

This is God's plan and will for every believer and we should cooperate by being receptive to the leadings of the Holy Spirit as we pray, worship, fellowship and grow in God's Word,

Father, give me a willing and discerning spirit that will make me receptive to Your leadings in my life. In Jesus' name,Amen

Are You Being Sifted

"For the Word that God speaks is alive and full of power [making it active, operative, energizing, and effective]; it is sharper than any two-edged sword, penetrating to the dividing line of the breath of life (soul) and [the immortal] spirit, and of joints and marrow [of the deepest parts of our nature], exposing and sifting and analyzing and judging the very thoughts and purposes of the heart." Hebrews 4:12 AMP

"After the Lord has washed away the [moral] filth of the daughters of Zion [pride, vanity, haughtiness] and has purged the bloodstains of Jerusalem from the midst of it by the spirit and blast of judgment and by the spirit and blast of burning and sifting."
Isaiah 4:4 AMP

God is working all things for our good in conforming us into the image of Christ. This often requires a lot of sifting. We are sometimes sifted physically, relationally, financially, or spiritually as part of God's purification process.

Most people will testify that their faith grows the most when they need God the most in times of sifting. As we experience His strength helping us overcome our weakness we are drawn closer to Him and learn to trust Him more.

God sieves us with any number of tools in order to get the job done. Sometimes our conscience sifts out our sins even before we commit them.

When our conscience convicts, we need to confess and repent as soon as possible. When others speak the truth in love to us we need to listen and respond accordingly. When circumstances cause us to wonder, we need to seek the "Wonder Worker".

The Word of God is the greatest sieve of all. It separates truth from fiction much like wheat is separated from chaff. As we sift our thoughts, words, and deeds through the Word, we will find our strength increasing and our heart being purified,

When we are being sifted by troubles, we should count it all joy in knowing that God is working through them to achieve His purpose for us. He always has our best interests at heart.

"because the Lord disciplines the one he loves, and he chastens everyone he accepts as his son."
Hebrews 4:12 NIV

Father, help me to rejoice in whatever sifting you deem necessary to make me more like Jesus. In Jesus' name, Amen

Terrifying Turbulence
"Then he got in the boat, his disciples with him. The next thing they knew, they were in a severe storm. Waves were crashing into the boat—and he was sound asleep! They roused him, pleading, "Master, save us! We're going down!" Matthew 8:23

"Do you know how God controls the storm and causes the lightning to flash from his clouds?" Job 37:15 NLT

Anyone who has done much flying is well aware of turbulence. We regularly read about people being injured when their plane encounted air turbulence.

In spite of advanced technology and flying around suspected turbulence. planes still hit rough air that can send them into free fall and bouncing like a paddle ball on a string.

I once had a flight with some 100-passengers that had ir to fly through a hurricane off Bermuda on a transoceanic flight where over half the people left their breakfasts in the air sick bags and even one of the pilots got air sick. I well remember saying good bye to this world and all I held dear here, and hello to God on a brutal flight from Cincinatti to Asheville one night.

The Delta overnight flight from LA to Atlanta is sometimes referred to as the salvation express because many often had hell scared out of them and they made their peace with God flying the unfriendly skies.

The sense of impending disaster and realizing that there is absolutely nothing we can do about it except pray during flight turbulence is a good illustration of what happens when we experience the turbulences of life.

"For you have not come [as did the Israelites in the wilderness] to a [material] mountain that can be touched, [a mountain] that is ablaze with fire, and to gloom and darkness and a raging storm" Hebrews 12:18 AMP

What comfort, peace, and joy there is in knowing that the pilot of our souls has a perfect record of seeing us safely through when we put our faith and trust in Him. "Jesus, Savior Pilot Me" is a good hymn to always remember.

Father, help me to keep my seat belt fastened on You and Your promises as I experience turbulence in my life. In Jesus' name, Amen

The Ripple Effect
"But the wicked are like the tossing sea, which cannot rest, whose waves cast up mire and mud." Isaiah 57:20 NIV

"⁴The Lord on high is mightier and more glorious than the noise of many waters, yes, than the mighty breakers and waves of the sea" Psalm 93:4 AMP

A small pebble thrown into the water or the wake of a giant ship both have something in common. They create a ripple effect that makes waves upon the surrounding water.

We need to be aware that we are making ripples in the lives of others on a daily basis.

The ripple of gossip can start a tidal wave of trouble. The ripple of anger, pride, lust, or envy can shipwreck friendships and create conflicts in every area of life.

We are amazed when we look at the ripple effect Jesus and His disciples had on the world.

The ripple effect of reflecting the love, grace, joy and peace we have in Christ should result in waves of love and kindness that will spread living water into the lives of others.

As sure as it only takes a spark to get a fire going, it often only takes a ripple of witness by word or example to get faith, renewal or restoration going in the life of someone the Lord puts in our path.

Unfortunately our sins produce ripple effects that make us stumbling blocks listead of building blocks.

It is a law of life that we reap what we sew. When we send out ripples of kindness and generosity we will find waves of the same returning to us.

"Be kind and compassionate to one another, forgiving each other, just as in Christ God forgave you." Ephesians 4:32 NIV

May we all be ripples of God's grace spread freely on our river of life.

Father, let my ripples be created by the fruit of righteousness of the Holy Spirit living in and working through me for Your glory. In Jesus' name, Amen

The River of Delights
"You feed them from the abundance of your own house ,letting them drink from your river of delights." Psalm 36:8 NLT

There is no better place to be than under the shelter of God's wing of grace where we find not only protection but the abundance of grace more than sufficient for our every need.

"O GOD, You are my God, earnestly will I seek You; my inner self thirsts for You, my flesh longs and is faint for You, in a dry and weary land where no water is".
Psalm 63:1 AMP

God's river of delights is an inexhaustible source for all who will come and drink through coming to Jesus Christ and receiving the water of eternal life by believing that He died on the Cross for our sins.

As we learn to swim instead of just wade in this river by being conformed into the image of Christ by the renewing of our minds, we discover and enjoy more and more of the sacred delights of a life well lived under the banner of God's love.

God's house is a good place to go to receive sacred delights from God's river of grace that flows through the Word taught, sacraments partaken of, praise and worship offered, and encouragement received from fellowship with other believers.

The more we abide in Christ by abiding in His Word, the deeper our river of delights becomes. As our relationship grows from Jesus being our Savior to being the Lord of our life we are promised the sacred delight of His friendship, His joy, and more answered prayers.

"Whoever believes in me, as Scripture has said, rivers of living water will flow from within them."
John 7:38 NIV

How good it is to know that when we have Jesus as our "all in all" we will have all we will ever need to draw from God's river of delights forever, and that nothing will ever separate us from His love.

Father, help me to discover more and more of the sacred delights you have in store for all who delight in You. In Jesus' name, Amen

309

80 /20 Christianity
"fulfill my joy by being like-minded, having the same love, being of one accord, of one mind." Philippians 2:2 NKJV

"Behold, how good and how pleasant it is For brethren to dwell together in unity! Psalm 133:4 NKJV

The Pareto principle (also known as the 80-20 rule) states that 80% of the output come from 20% of the input. Although we do not find this in the Bible, it teaches an important law of life that can be used to improve an individual, business, church or home.

In many businesses 80% of the business is generated by 20% of the sales force, 80% of the profits are produced by 20% of the products.

The 80/20 rule is a key element in many time management Improvement programs. The idea is to put more time where you are most productive and less time in other areas where you are wasting or not utilizing your time profitably..

We have 20% of the population in the world with 80% of the wealth controlled by 20% of the people and 80% of health benefits going to 20%, etc.

It is a generally accepted fact in most churches that 80% of the total offerings come from 20% of the members. It is also all too often true that 80% of the ministry in most churches is done by 20% of the members.

This being true, we all need to do some serious self examination and determine what I need to do in order to become a 20 if we find ourselves as part of 80.

As we concentrate on allocating more of our time, talents, and resources where they will do the most good we can, with God's help, and by the power of the best and most productive efforts

" know your deeds, that you are neither cold nor hot. I wish you were either one or the other!" Revelation 3:14 NIV

become a "20" based on the skills and talents we have been given.

Father help me to become a better disciple in every area of my life. In Jesus' name, Amen

Wasting God's Time

"You were bought with a price [purchased with a preciousness and paid for, made His own]. So then, honor God and bring glory to Him in your body." 1 Corinthians 6:19 AMP

"Teach us to number our days, that we may gain a heart of wisdom." Psalm 90:12 AMP

We need to understand what it means to have been bought for a price and that our life is no longer ours but Christ's Who lives in us. We need to realize that when we waste our time, we are actually wasting God's time.

All of the trivial pursuits we waste God's time on are going to be burned like the wood, hay and stubble they are, and leave little to earn the Lord's "well done, thou good and faifhful servant."

Of all the physical, mental and spiritual time we waste each day means that we have that much less time to do the good works God created us to do before we were ever born and to become the imitators of Christ we are being conformed to become.

At its worst, we can waste so much of our time pursuing the pleasures and possessions of this world that we will end up living wasted lives with no really worthwhile thing to show for them.

Worry may well be the biggest waster of God's time in the lives of most believers. In spite of the fact that God tells us not to worry about any thing but rejoice in everything, our lack of faith kicks in and the blessed assurance that Jesus died to give us gets left out.

"God is love. When we take up permanent residence in a life of love, we live in God and God lives in us. This way, love has the run of the house, becomes at home and mature in us, so that we're free of worry on Judgment Day— "1 John 4:17 MSG

The perfect love that casts out all fear is the perfect love that is working all things for the good of those who love God and who are being made more like Jesus through every circumstance that comes our way.

If we would turn the time we are prone to worry into time praising and seeking to live the fruitful lives fully pleasing to God that He wants for us there will be no limit to what God can and will do through us as we live like followers of Jesus.

Lord help me to worry less about my problems and spend the time counting my joy in being a blood bought son or daughter of the living Lord. In Jesus' name, Amen

311

Here Comes the Judge

"For the Son of Man will come with his angels in the glory of his Father and will judge all people according to their deeds." Matthew 16:27 NLT

We are going to experience being judged by many people as we journey through life. We will be judged in different ways by different people. Appearance, ability, personality, honesty, and conduct are just a few of the attributes on which others judge us.

"The Lord judges the people; judge me, O Lord, and do me justice according to my righteousness [my rightness, justice, and right standing with You] and according to the integrity that is in me."

Although we should all seek to be give a good witness and impression as ambassadors of Christ, these judgments pale in comparison to The judgment of God for salvation, and the judgment of believers by Jesus when He returns as our righteous judge

Jesus did not come to condemn us. He came to save us. We condemn ourselves by rejecting His wonderful gift of salvation for which He died in order to save all who would believe.

Although condemnation was not His mission, He will judge the stewardship of the lives we have been given as part of His purpose in coming to earth to show us how to be good stewards and live lives fully pleasing to God.

Because of Christ's righteousness God judged us righteous when we put on the righteousness of Christ by faith. We will stand before Jesus and be judged by the fruit of this righteousness as evidenced by our good works.

"You take over. I'm about to die, my life an offering on God's altar. This is the only race worth running. I've run hard right to the finish, believed all the way. All that's left now is the shouting—God's applause! Depend on it, he's an honest judge. He'll do right not only by me, but by everyone eager for his coming.
2 Timothy 4:5-7

When it comes to judging our fruits of righteousness, we need to be continually judging ourselves and do whatever might be necessary to assure that we have some good works to set before King Jesus when we stand before Him at the resurrection of the just.

Father, let me be a channel of your love living a life of obedience to your Great Commandment and Great Commission. In Jesus' name, Amen

312

We Can Only Imagine

"No one's ever seen or heard anything like this, Never so much as imagined anything quite like it— What God has arranged for those who love him.But you've seen and heard it because God by his Spirit has brought it all out into the open before you." 1 Corinthians 2:9.10 MSG

The erroneous idea that we are going to be floating around in the clouds singing hymns all day seems to be one of the most popular concepts of heaven. It doesn't sound too appealing to a lot of people.This is exactly why the devil planted this thought

"You get a hint at the diversity of resurrection glory by looking at the diversity of bodies not only on earth but in the skies—sun, moon, stars—all these varieties of beauty and brightness. And we're only looking at pre-esurrection"seeds"—who can imagine what the resurrection "plants" will be like!"
1 Corinthians 15:39 MSG

While we cannot fully comprehend what's going to happen when we die there is a lot of scriptural teaching that we will go into the presence of Jesus when we die where we will await the resurrection with new bodies on a new earth when Jesus returns.   Randy Alcorn has done an outstanding job of researching what the Bible teaches about heaven, and gives all who will study Randy's Bible study (available from Lifeway.com or epm.com.)

A better idea of what heaven is going to be like might well be imagining what this present world would be like without the curse and presence of sin.

We should get excited about being reunited with our loved ones in new pain free, decay free, sin free resurrection bodies on a new sin free, pain free, decay free world where we will work, worship, live and play in love and peace with God and others forever.

" Since you have been raised to new life with Christ, set your sights on the realities of heaven, where Christ sits in the place of honor at God's right hand.
Colossian 3:1 NLT

These are indeed high expectations that we can only imagine in our present condition, but Scripture teaches that we have all this and more to look forward to when Jesus returns and takes us to our eternal home.

Father, help me to keep my eye on the prize full of excitement and joy in imagining all that I have to look forward to in my eternal home with You. In Jesus' name, Amen

Full of Potential

"Therefore let anyone who thinks he stands [who feels sure that he has a steadfast mind and is standing firm], take heed lest he fall [into sin]."
1 Corinthians 10:12 AMP

"For the enemy has pursued and persecuted my soul, he has crushed my life down to the ground; he has made me to dwell in dark places as those who have been long dead.
Psalm 143:3 AMP

We often speak and think about potentials. Whether talking about the possibilities of hurricanes or a given sports team or a gifted child we often hear about them being full of potential.

..No matter how long we have been saved and how strong our faith the battle raging within between our flesh and our spirit which coexist in the same body will continue until the day we die.

Peter was deeply hurt and insulted when the Lord predicted that He would deny him. We find ourselves shocked when we see others falling into sins that we think could never happen to us.

The truth is that although all us who have received Jesus Christ as our Savior have been set free from domination by our sin nature, the roaring lion keeps seeking to destroy us by every possible temptation.

This is why we received the full armor of God and must wear it always. When we begin thinking we are able to withstand the ongoing temptations of the world, our flesh, and the devil in our own strength we are setting ourselves up to fall.

Jails, divorce courts, and prisons of the soul are full of the remorse, guilt, and shame of those who boasted that it could never happen to them.

'Stay alert! Watch out for your great enemy, the devil. He prowls around like a roaring lion, looking for someone to devour.
1 Peter 5:8 NLT

We all need to be ever mindful that we are full of potential to sin at any given time on any given day and daily seek protection under the shelter of God's wings that this potential never become a reality.

Father, help me to wear the armor you have given me at all times that I might not realize my potential to sin. In Jesus' name, Amen

Putting off Self

"Do not lie to each other, since you have taken off your old **self** with its practices and have put on the new **self**, which is being renewed in knowledge in the image of its Creator.Colossians 3:9:10 NIV

When we become disciples of Jesus we find ourselves dying to self and becoming alive in Christ. As the Holy Spirit performs the ongoing work of holy transformation, we experience a fundamental change into doing life God's way instead of our selfish way.

> "Your testimonies are wonderful [far exceeding anything conceived by man]; therefore my [penitent] self keeps them [hearing, receiving, loving, and obeying them]."
> Psalm119:129 NIV

When we turn our self-sufficiency into God-sufficiency we find it more than adequate for our every need.

As God continues to work on and in us, we find our self-confidence being replaced by God confidence which makes us believe that we can do all things through Christ Who strengthens us, and that God really is working all things for our good.

When we put off self-interest for God-interest we find our focus on God and others instead of on ourselves.

. As our self-promotion turns into God promotion we discover the special joy of leading others to Christ. Our self-justification based on basing our right standing with God on our performance is turned into faith justification when we believe we are justified by God's grace and Jesus' death on the cross not our works.

Putting off self-seeking for God seeking takes us into the wonderful world of rewards God promises to those who seek Him.

> "You were taught, with regard to your former way of life, to put off your old self, which is being corrupted by its deceitful desires;to be made new in the attitude of your minds;"
> Ephesians 4:22.23 NIV

We need to make a regular sober assessment of what part of self we are holding onto that need to be put off so that we can cooperate with the Holy Spirit's work of conforming us into the image of Christ.

Father, Help me to live life selflessly instead of selfishly that I might grow into the fullness of Christ. In Jesus' name, Amen

315

Spiritual Enemy #1

"Do you see a man wise in his own eyes and conceit? There is more hope for a [self-confident] fool than for him." Proverbs 26:12 AMP

"Who may worship in your sanctuary, Lord?Who may enter your presence on your holy hill?"
Psalm 15;1 NLT

The wonderful gift of God's presence signified by the rending of the veil in the temple the hour Christ died is a theological truth that many believers fail to experience personally because the veils of self keep us from enjoying the wonders of practicing the presence of God in our every day lives.

There are more self lives running amuck in than we have fingers to count. Self-righteousness, self-pity, self-confidence, self-sufficiency, self-admiration, self-love, self-promotion, self-justification, self-seeking are just a few of the many deal breakers that keep us from fully submitting to the Lordship of Jesus Christ and experiencing God's reign in the temple of our souls.

We were created to glorify and enjoy God. He created us for His pleasure and for divine fellowship and communion with Him through a close and personal relationship with Jesus.

As long as we remain under the self-seeking control of our old sin nature, we will never experience the abundant life in all its fullness that comes only by selling out to self and buying into the incredible power and promises of God control.

The more we abide in Christ through His Word, the more of His presence we will enjoy in our lives. We will enjoy His friendship, and joy as we become more like Him by getting to know Him better and serving Him more as we live under the control of the Holy Spirit instead of our flesh.

"God removes the veil and there they are—face-to-face! They suddenly recognize that God is a living, personal presence, not a piece of chiseled stone."
1 Corinthians 3:16 MSG

Only when we quit sleeping with the enemy can we awaken to the incredible joy of living with God's presence actually as well as theologically.

Father,keep me ever mindful of being my own worst enemy, and help me to die to self so that I can fully live in Christ. In Jesus' name, Amen

316

Are We Possessed?

"So it is with the one who continues to lay up and hoard possessions for himself and is not rich [in his relation] to God [this is how he fares]."
Luke 12:21 AMP

Better is the little that the [uncompromisingly] righteous have than the abundance [of possessions] of many who are wrong and wicked.
Psalm 37:16 AMP

The pursuit of possessions instead of God continues to be one of the biggest problems in the lives of most believers. When our possessions possess us it is impossible to give God the undivided attention and worship He deserves.

When we pursue the prosperity of possessions, we are going to experience the poverty of our souls. Our God is a jealous God, and He will not tolerate idolatry of any kind.

We are sometimes like the rich young ruler who could not bear the thought of giving up His riches in order to experience the abundant life Christ came to give us.

God has no problems with material prosperity. He blessed many of the heroes of the faith with great wealth. He gifts many of us with an abundance of material possessions and the wherewithal to acquire more. The problem comes when we love our material prosperity more than we love God and spend our lives acquiring and pursuing possessions instead of seeking the kingdom of God and His righteousness.

When we concern ourselves more about our self worth than about our God worth we are going to find that we end up with less of either. God makes it very clear that we cannot serve both God and money.

God often tests whether we are possessed by testing our willingness to give up any or all of our possessions for His

"No one can serve two masters; for either he will hate the one and love the other, or he will stand by and be devoted to the one and despise and be against the other. You cannot serve God and mammon (deceitful riches, money, possessions, or whatever is trusted in)"
Matthew 6:24 AMP

purposes. When we are generous and willing to give on all occasions as we have been blessed to do we will never give God cause to wonder Who possesses us.

Father, may I never sacrifice my soul on the altar of possessions by letting them possess me. In Jesus' name, Amen

Troubling Trips
"We all arrive at your doorstep sooner or later, loaded with guilt, Our sins too much for us— but you get rid of them once and for all." Psalm 65:2 MSG

Planes, trains, ships, and automobiles are filled with people taking trips of every description in every direction.

"Yes, what joy for those whose record the Lord has cleared of guilt, whose lives are lived in complete honesty!"
Psalm 32:2 NLT

Of all the trips we take there are none to compare with our guilt trips. As imperfect people living in an imperfect world we are all at times standing in line awaiting our next visit to the guilt factory.

Whether triggered by lust, anger, pride, envy, or ego, we are barraged by temptations of thoughts, words, and deeds that are often going to produce shame and guilt.

Once we start travelling through life with shame and guilt, the burden often gets so heavy we need a travelling companion to help carry the load.   Alcohol, drugs, and other temporary fixes eventually increase the burden and make our guilt trip worse.

We need to know that the cross of Jesus Christ is the only place to go with our guilt and shame. When we realize that we are sinners who need a Savior and take our guilt and shame to the cross with godly sorrow and true repentance, our burden will be lifted.

"But if we [really] are living and walking in the Light, as He [Himself] is in the Light, we have [true, unbroken] fellowship with one another, and the blood of Jesus Christ His Son cleanses (removes) us from all sin and guilt [keeps us cleansed from sin in all its forms and manifestations].
1 John 1:8 AMP

Once we are set free from the condemnation of our sin that produced our guilt, we become free to pursue a guilt free new life in Christ filled with the love, joy, peace, faithfulness, gentleness, and self control produced by the Holy Spirit who comes to live in us.

God's forgiveness is a sea of forgetfulness deep enough to drown all our guilt and remember our sins no more when we take them to the cross.

Father, thank you for cancelling my guilt by dying on the cross for my sins. In Jesus' name, Amen.

Doing Whatever We Want

"Then you'll be able to live out your days free to pursue what God wants instead of being tyrannized by what you want." 1 Peter 4.1 MSG

How many times have you heard someone say they still have a lot of things they want to enjoy before they're ready to become a Christian, as though God were a kill joy?

"So what do we do? Keep on sinning so God can keep on forgiving? I should hope not! "
Romans 6:1 MSG

When we become truly born again believers, something amazing happens. We become free to do whatever we want! We are set free from the dominion of sin, and can actually choose to live in the love, joy, and peace of the Lord.

The bottom line is that once we experience the new birth, we should experience an attitude adjustment that replaces old wants and desires with new desires and wants centered on loving and pleasing God instead of ourselves and our old selfish desires.

The pleasures of the world lose their glitter as we experience the pleasures of God's grace and Jesus' joy. The shameful things we used to enjoy are no longer enjoyable as we discover the all surpassing peace and joy of our new life in Christ.

We find ourselves mourning with Godly sorrow over the old things we used to do and and rejoicing in the freedom we have to do the things God wants us to do and being the disciples He has called us to be.

'The world and all its wanting, wanting, wanting is on the way out—but whoever does what God wants is set for eternity."
1 John 2:5 MSG

The more we abide in Christ by abiding in His Word, the more we discover that God is never a joy killer, but a joy giver. He will open the portals of real pleasure that will make us forget wanting to do the things we used to want to do by giving us so many better and more satisfying things to want to do.

Father, thank you for adjusting my wanter and letting me find my joy in wanting to do the things that please you. In Jesus' name, Amen

Taking God Seriously

"But he's already made it plain how to live, what to do, what God is looking for in men and women. It's quite simple: Do what is fair and just to your neighbor, be compassionate and loyal in your love, and don't take yourself too seriously— take God seriously. Micah 6:8 MSG

If we were to make a list of things we take seriously , based on the amount of time and energy we spend on them, where would God appear on our list?

God is serious business, take him seriously; he's put the earth in place and it's not moving. So let Heaven rejoice, let Earth be jubilant, and pass the word among the nations, "God reigns!"
1 Chronicles 16:30 MSG

On any given day we find ourselves so pre occupied with seemingly more important matters that we barely give God a passing thought.

When we are living life from a self centered perspective our needs and wants and problems are paramount and are the primary focus of our serious attention.

We often seem to spend so much time living up to our image and expectations that we fail to take God and His Word and expectations seriously and miss out on experiencing God's best in and for our lives.

"But remember, dear friends, that the apostles of our Master, Jesus Christ, told us this would happen: "In the last days there will be people who don't take these things seriously anymor e
Jude 1:17 MSG

It is only when we die to self and become alive in Christ through being born again that we can really begin to take God and His will for our lives seriously.

If our lives do not reflect serious obedience to God and His commands, we are not taking God seriously enough.

Father, help me to get more serious and focused about loving and obeying You by loving and serving others. In Jesus' name, Amen.

Are We Insulting God?

For it is by grace you have been saved, through faith—and this is not from yourselves, it is the gift of God— not by works, so that no one can boast. For we are God's handiwork, created in Christ Jesus to do good works, which God prepared in advance for us to do." Ephesians 2:8,9 NIV

There appears to be a devilish thought in the heart of too many believers that makes them think that Jesus' death on the cross was not sufficient for our salvation, and that we must still do something to earn it.

"You foolish Galatians! Who has bewitched you? Before your very eyes Jesus Christ was clearly portrayed as crucified. Galatians 3:1 NIV

We were created for good works purposed for us before we were ever born. These were planned for us to do after we are saved by grace alone through faith alone. God is always working all things for our good so that we can be more like Jesus and accomplish the purposes for which we were created.

We need to understand that these good works are not the reason for our salvation but the evidence of it. When we stand before Christ to give an account of what we did with the new life in Him we were given, the good works that remain after all of the trivial pursuits of our lives are burned away will earn our Lord's "well done" and become our heavenly treasures.

We should never diminish the amazing grace of God in coming to live the perfect life and dying as the perfect sacrifice for our sins so that we would never have to by thinking that this was not enough, and that we must add something to it in order to be saved.

The truth is that because we have been saved by the blood of Jesus, we should respond by living to please Him by being imitators of Him and doing all that we can do to love and serve Him in joyful obedience to His will.

"He then brought them out and asked, "Sirs, what must I do to be saved?" Acts 16:30 NIV

We were created to live our lives as living sacrifices of praise to God for His wonderful gift of eternal life. We should never insult God's great gift by thinking we must do anything to earn it.

Father,thank You for loving me enough to send your son to die for me. Help me to love You more.. In Jesus' name, Amen.

What's in Your Tank

"THEREFORE, SINCE these [great] promises are ours, beloved, let us cleanse ourselves from everything that contaminates and **defiles** body and spirit, and bring [our] consecration to completeness in the [reverential] fear of God.2 Corinthians 7:1 AMP

> He has put a new song in my mouth—
> Praise to our God;
> Many will
> see *it* and
> fear, And will trust
> in the LORD".
> Psalm 40:3 NKJV

The cars we drive, planes we fly, and lawn mowers we ride all have internal combustion engines where fuel is stored in a tank and turned into energy when burned in the engine.

The lives we live are similar in that we burn energy with every breath we take or step we walk. In addition to our physical energy, there is also a spiritual energy source in the heart of every person that has its own fuel source.

Unfortunately the fuel for our spiritual energy has been corrupted by sin and we run on a tankful of pride, anger, ego, envy, lust, jealousy, greed, which fuels our spiritual energy in the wrong direction.

The only known cure for this corruption is spiritual death. We must become dead to sin and alive in Christ as born again believers.

When we receive Jesus Christ as Savior and Lord, we also receive a new power source that fuels our energy with love, joy, peace, gentleness, patience, kindness and self control.

When we fill our spiritual tank through confession, repentance, and feeding on God's Word we find our minds being renewed and our hearts being conformed more and more like Christ.

This is the way God works all things for our good as we surrender self control to God control and allow the Holy Spirit free reign to continue the on going process of holy transformation.

> "It's not what goes into your body that defiles you; you are defiled by what comes from your heart."
> Mark 7:15 NLT

When God fills our tank to overflowing with His love, grace, and mercy we will have no room for the old fuel of the flesh to have any control or dominion over us.

Father, help me to keep my tank full of your power today that I would be and do all that you created me to be and do. In Jesus' name, Amen

God's Sandpaper

"And I am convinced and sure of this very thing, that He Who began a good work in you will continue until the day of Jesus Christ [right up to the time of His return], developing [that good work] and perfecting and bringing it to full completion in you."Philippians 1:5-7 AMP

Sandpaper as an abrasive to smooth, remove, improve, or prepare surfaces has been around since at least the 13th Century. It comes in many degrees of coarseness and with many different backings.

> "(You shall remember all the way which the LORD your God has (C)led you in the wilderness these forty years, that He might humble you, (D)testing you, to know what was in your heart, whether you would keep His commandments or not."
> Deuteronomy 8:2 NASB

The Holy Spirit brings an abundant supply of God's sandpaper to accomplish the same purposes as we are being conformed into the image of Christ.

He sometimes uses sandpaper people to get under our skin with their abrasive personalities to improve our longsuffering and patience. .

The Holy Spirit will use whatever degree of coarseness it takes to smooth out our rough edges, remove the worst of our sin stains, or prepare us to be equipped for the purposes for which God created us.

Anytime we experience the grinding of God's sandpaper in our health, wealth, jobs, or relationships , we need to make a sober asssessment as to whether we are being punished or pruned.

If we are being punished, godly sorrow and true repentance will stop the grinding. If we ar being pruned, we need to rejoice in our grinding and be confident that God is at work performing the holy transformation that will see us safely home.

> "Beloved, do not be surprised at the fiery ordeal among you, which comes upon you for your testing, as though some strange thing were happening to you;"
> 1 Peter 4:12

Father, help me to avoid as much of your sanding as possible by helping me to guard my thoughts, my heart, my tongue and my conduct. In Jesus' name, Amen

The Real Wild Card

"If your enemies are hungry, feed them. If they are thirsty, give them something to drink. In doing this, you will heap burning coals of shame on their heads."Romans 12:20 NLT

Playing the race card has long been a favorite ploy of politicians, people, lawyers, and social advocates to blame, shame, or otherwise try to win or confuse an argument by bringing up accusations of racial prejudice.

> **"You will heap burning coals of shame on their heads,and the Lord will reward you."**
> **Proverbs 25:21-23**

It seems that almost anytime you disagree with any agenda promoting certain causes or philosophies, you are a racist.

While many of the accusations and suspicions may be well founded, the blanket accusations and frequent playing of the race card
serve mostly to stir up more division and disharmony than they cure.

There is another card that will trump the race card most every time. It's called the grace card.

As themed in "The Grace Card" a very outstanding 2011 movie the grace card states: "*I promise to pray for you every day, ask your forgiveness grant you the same, and be your friend....always*"

When we appropriate this tool for reflecting God's love to others in obedience to the Great Commandment we will find it helpful in rebuilding relationships and healing deep wounds.

The "coals of fire" will melt the anger of bitterness or unforgiveness and clear the way for true reconciliation.

The grace card should be a welcome addition to the full armor of God arsenal of every believer.

> **"Then the name of our Lord Jesus will be honored because of the way you live, and you will be honored along with him. This is all made possible because of the grace of our God and Lord, Jesus Christ."**
> **2 Thessalonians 1:12 NLT**

Is there someone you need to send a grace card today?

Father, keep me ever mindful that all of the grace I have needed and received should be freely extended to others. In Jesus' name, Amen.

Self Judgment is Good for the Soul
"For if we would judge ourselves, we would not be judged" 1 Corinthians 11:30 NKJV

We all seem to be so good at judging the sins of others, but are often woefully lacking when it comes to judging our own.

" I'm the only God there is. Who compares with me? Speak up. See if you measure up. "
Isaiah 44:6 MSG

God gave us all a great 10 point standard to measure our sins. Although obeying the Ten Commandments cannot save us; they are still in effect as a reminder of how we fail to meaure up to God's standards of holiness and righteousness.

They remind us of how desperately we need and blessed we are to have Jesus as our Savior. They are also a wonderful guide to show us how to live an abundant life fully pleasing to God.

Scrpture tells us that we are to make a sober assessment of ourselves..Paul documents the sickness and even death amonth the Corinthians because they did not judge themselves and stop the sinning.

We can deceive ourselves and others, but we can never deceive our all knowing, ever present, and ever loving and forgiving God. How wonderful it is to know that he knows us better than we know ourselves, and continues to love us not because of our sins, but inspite of them.

Jesus Christ did not come into the world to judge us, but to save us. He died to pay our sin debt in full, and the Holy Spirit came to live within us and to write God's law into our hearts. He also gives us a conscience to help us judge ourselves the supernatural power we need to escape the temptations of sin.

"All Scripture is God-breathed and is useful for teaching, rebuking, correcting and training in righteousness, 17 so that the servant of God[a] may be thoroughly equipped for every good work."
2 Timothy 3:16

When we apologize, truly repent, and put on the full armor of God and renew our minds daily with the power of God's Word. we will find ourselves with less to apologize for and fewer sin consequences to bear.

Father, help me to judge and convict myself of my sins and turn away from them in true repentance. In Jesus' name, Amen.

All the More Reason

"She was forgiven many, many sins, and so she is very, very grateful. If the forgiveness is minimal, the gratitude is minimal." Luke 7:47 MSG

Thanksgiving is a great day to celebrate the blessings of family.

We can and should give thanks for all of our material blessings and

"as far as the east is from the west, so far has he removed our transgressions from us."

Psalm 103:4 NIV

realize that they come from the providential grace of God. We should never take good health for granted and never fail to thank God for this.

Of all the blessings for which we should be rejoicing always, there is none greater than the peace that comes from knowing that God has accepted our apologies for our sins and remembers them no more.

As imperfect people living in an imperfect world, we all fall short of the glory of God and will always need to confess and receive forgiveness.

We will never be able to apologize our guilt and shame away. We need to thank it away!

When we take St. Paul's advice to rejoice and thank Him for everything we will be able to thank our guilt and shame away by thanking God for His forgiveness and rejoicing in Him. When we do this, the Holy Spirit will restore our inner peace and security.

Even though the war has been won by Jesus' death and resurrection, the battle with our flesh, the world and the devil continues. We don't always win.

"Always be full of joy in the Lord. I say it again—rejoice!"

Philippians 4:4 NLT

We all, like St. Paul, struggle with the fact that the good we would do we do not, and the evil that we would not do we do.

When the deceiver of our souls brings up our past sins to try to discourage us we need to turn this into an opportunity to thank and praise God even more for His goodness and mercy in forgiving us.

Father, thank you for sending Jesus to die on the cross for my sins so that I can thank my guilt and shame away. In Jesus' name, Amen

Obeying What We Believe

"Your word is a lamp to guide my feet and a light for my path."
Psalm 119:5 NLT

"Good friend, follow your father's good advice; don't wander off from your mother's teachings"
Proverbs 6:20 MSG

Among the millions of professing Bible believers around the world many of us would often fail the belief test of obedience. Many denominations have watered down their statement of faith from believing that the Bible is the Word of God to that it "contains" the Word of God.

The wonderful freedom from bondage to sin we received when we received Jesus as our Savior did not include the freedom to pick and choose what commands and principles we could choose to obey or ignore.

Many immature, ignorant, and unregenerate hearts let denial, a rationalization,I and the error prone conscience of man overrule the clear commands and teachings of Scripture.

When we hear of and see professing Christians cohabitating apart from marriage, homosexuality accepted and promoted, abortion ok'd in the name of freedom of choice, and hypocritical glory exceeding the righteousness of the Scribes and Pharisees we must wonder what has happened to faith in Jesus Christ and His Kingdom on Earth.

When we think that God wants us to be happy means that we can disregard his clear teachings and example of how we should live our lives we are falling into the trap of the great deceiver who makes the apple trick on Eve look like child's play.

"All Scripture is inspired by God and is useful to teach us what is true and to make us realize what is wrong in our lives. It corrects us when we are wrong and teaches us to do what is right."
2 Timothy 3:16 NLT

The truth is that God wants us to be happy by becoming Holy, by living within the boundaries He set to assure our happiness. When we miss out on the blessings that only obedience to His Word and commands provide, we are going to miss out on the true peace and joy of our salvation.

Father, help me to not only know your Word, but to believe and obey it by the power of Your Spirit. In Jesus' name, Amen

327

Squeezing the Chocolates

"Examine me, God, from head to foot, order your battery of tests. Make sure I'm fit inside and out." Psalm 26:1 MSG

Growing up in poorer times, a box of candy was a rare treat at our house. Finding a nut was even rarer. My brothers and sisters and I found the nuts by squeezing the chocolate to see what was inside. I still remember opening boxes with nothing except white crèmes or jellies showing out of squeezed pieces.

I'm happy from the inside out, and from the outside in, I'm firmly formed. You canceled my ticket to hell— that's not my destination!
Psalm 16:9 MSG

We sometimes find God squeezing our comfort zones looking for some kernels of obedience, faith, courage, or passion.

Too often He finds only the soft crème or jelly and has to put us on His "spit out list" because we are too lukewarm.

The Good News for believers is that if we have found the pearl of great price a/k/a eternal life through faith in Jesus Christ, we can be comforted when bad things happen because we know that God can turn our worst into His best as He works even the bad for our good as he transforms us into the image of Christ.

The squeezing that Peter and all of the apostles endured resulted in a rock like boldness that overcame the jelly of their fears, and gave them the strength and power to establish Christ's Church throughout the known world.

"I know you inside and out, and find little to my liking. You're not cold, you're not hot—far better to be either cold or hot! You're stale."
Revelation 3:15a MSG

May God's "squeezings" always make us better instead of bitter, and always remember that whether in chocolates or our hearts, it's what's inside that counts,.

Father, may my life I lay before you on judgment day be filled with the "good stuff" according to your good will. In Jesus name, Amen.

Heaven Insurance
"And I will make them and the places round about My hill a blessing, and I will cause the showers to come down in their season; there shall be showers of blessing [of good **insure**d by God's favor]." Ezekiel 34:25-27

Insurance is a trillion dollar business.   You can insure against practically anything. You can buy insurance to pay off if someone makes a hole in one at a hole in one golf contest.

> "And I will make them and the places round about My hill a blessing, and I will cause the showers to come down in their season; there shall be showers of blessing [of good insured by God's favor]."
> Ezekiel 34:26 AMP

You can buy insurance against rain wiping out a planned event.

Life insurance is probably the biggest insurance business of all.

Heaven insurance is the best life insurance available in all the world. It is guaranteed by the Creator and Owner of the universe who came down from heaven and paid our one time lump sum premium by dying on the cross insuring that all policy holders will live forever.

Since this policy cost the beneficiary nothing it is sometimes taken too lightly and valued too little. When there is no evidence to support that our insurer is present and producing the fruit of the Spirit for us to bear in our lives, there should be cause for concern as to whether we actually are policy holders.

Heaven insurance is not also an umbrella to cover us with God's all sufficient grace as we go through the fires of life.

It continually appreciates in value as we show our appreciation for it by seeking to live fruitful lives fully pleasing to God in submission to His will and under the control of the Holy Spirit, who is our co-insuror and guarantor that our policy will remain in force and we receive all of the blessings and benefits our heaven insurance provides.

> "It is God who enables us, along with you, to stand firm for Christ. He has commissioned us, [22] and he has identified us as his own by placing the Holy Spirit in our hearts as the first installment that guarantees everything he has promised us."
> 2 Corinthians 1:21 NLT

Father, thank you for my heaven insurance which I received by faith the hour I first believed and accepted Jesus as my Savor.In Jesus' name, Amen

Manifold Pressure

"God can pour on the blessings in astonishing ways so that you're ready for anything and everything, more than just ready to do what needs to be done."2 Corinthians 9:8 MSG

In science and mechanics manifold pressure is about increasing horsepower and fuel utilization by supplying more air oxygen to the combustion chamber.

O LORD, how manifold are Your works! In wisdom You have made them all. The earth is full of Your possessions"
Psalm 104:24

In life manifold pressure is about the many varied and seemingly ever increasing problems of living our lives as fallen people in a fallen world. The pressures are many, some small, and some too big for us to handle in our own strength.

There are manifold pressures in families, marriages, finances, health, and relationships. As we experience these many and varied pressures, it is good to know that God's grace is more abundant and varied than all of our problems.

For those who believe help is often just a prayer away. For those who discover the secret of rejoicing amidst, through, and in spite of all the .manifold pressures of life God is always there to supply His all sufficient grace to meet our every need. There is not only the strengthening grace to persevere and overcome, but also the all surpassing peace of God which transcends our understanding and momentary concerns.

Some engine makers add a supercharger to supply more oxygen to the combustion chamber. For our manifold pressures, God has supplied us a "Spirit charger" to supply the grace we need when we need it most.

"And my God will liberally supply (⬚fill to the full) your every need according to His riches in glory in Christ Jesus"
Philippians 4:19 AMP

When we experience the Holy transformation that comes when we turn our lives over to the God control of the Spirit from the self control of our flesh we are going to experience that daily renewal, peace, and joy that only our "Spirit charger" can provide.

Father, thank you for keeping me super charged in Jesus. In Jesus' name, Amen

Suicide Watch

"Call heaven and earth to witness this day against you that I have set before you life and death, the blessings and the curses; therefore choose life, that you and your descendants may live." Deuteronomy 30:18-20 AMP

It's depressing but true. We live in a suicidal world. The poor deluded suicide bombers who think they are going to get their reward in heaven for blowing up non believers are just a tiny blip on the radar compared to the millions of people around the world, many who we know and love, who are committing spiritual suicide.

Whoever believes in him is not condemned, but whoever does not believe stands condemned already because they have not believed in the name of God's one and only Son
John 3:18 NIV

All who do not believe in hell will believe in it sooner or later. What a rude awakening it will be for anyone who find themselves doomed to the forever life of torment in hell.

As the vast majority of the world's people commit spiritual suicide by rejecting God's ways and embracing the world's, we can only give witness to God's truth, and pray that those who are spiritually suicidal will die to sin so that they can become alive in Christ before it's too late.

God wants all men to be saved by coming into a right relationship through faith in Jesus Christ. He wanted this enough to come live, suffer, and die so that all who believed would not have to suffer the eternal torments of hell.

God did not create us as robots. He gave us all the freedom to accept or reject His wonderful gift of eternal life in the eternal bliss of heaven.

"Then the rich man said, 'Please, Father Abraham, at least send him to my father's home. 28 For I have five brothers, and I want him to warn them so they don't end up in this place of torment."
Luke 16:2,28 NLT

Father, help me to put all my unsaved loved ones on a suicide watch list and pray fervently that they will receive your wonderful gift of salvation before it is too late. In Jesus name, Amen

331

The Acid Test

"But your iniquities have made a separation between you and your God, and your sins have hidden His face from you, so that He will not hear."
Isaiah 59:1-3 AMP

Acids are wicked chemicals. They can burn a hole in metal, concrete, or our skin. I am convinced that part of my breathing problems are from inhaling too much muriatic acid in maintaining my 350,000 gallon swimming pool years ago.

"He does not punish us for all our sins: he does not deal harshly with us, as we deserve."
Psalm 103:10 NLT

Sin has a lot of the characteristics of acids. It can burn a hole in our hearts, and totally corrode our character.

The acid of sexually transmitted sins can ravage our bodies and lead to slow painful deaths both physical and spiritual. The acid of unforgiveness can kill relationships and actually kill us physically and spiritually.

Anger, envy, jealousy, and strife are all inherited acids that can harm us and those we love.

Nitric acid is used to separate gold from impurities. This is where the term acid test originated. The deceiver of our souls often uses sin acids to separate us from our creation purpose of pleasing our God.

The Holy Spirit cannot function in a cess pool and cannot carry out His task of Holy Transformation in us as long as we insist on willfully sinning and living flesh controlled lives.

Our repentance can separate the acid of our sins as far as the east is from the west. His grace is more powerful than any acid, and is promised in amounts sufficient for all our needs.

"Oh, what joy for those whose disobedience is forgiven, whose sins are put out of sight. Yes, what joy for those whose record the Lord has cleared of sin"
Romans 4:7,8 NLT

Jesus Christ was and is our real acid test. He died on the cross to separate us from all the impurities of our sins and make us pure and holy in God's sight.

Father, thank you for dying on the cross so that I could pass the acid test by faith. In Jesus' name, Amen

Unholy Meditation

" And who of you by worrying and being anxious can add one unit of measure (cubit) to his stature or to the span of his life? "
Matthew 6:26-28 (AMP)

A lot of people seem to have a hard time understanding what the word meditate means, much less how to do it. Rick Warren gave the best insight I have ever heard when he said: *"If you know how to worry, you know how to meditate."*

> "Let the words of my mouth and the meditation of my heart Be pleasing to you, ,O LORD, my rock and my Redeemer."
> Psalm 19:13-14 NLT

We are all very good at spending a lot of time and energy *intently focusing* on everything except the most important thing.

Although our Lord clearly commanded us not to worry, we can't seem to help our selves from falling in to this sin of unholy meditation.

We have all forfeited a lot of peace and suffered a lot of needless pain worrying over so many things that never ever even happened.

How much better to meditate or focus our attention on our problem solver instead of our problems.

When we focus our mind's attention and heart's affection on the greatness and goodness of our God, we will find that our hearts will be filled with that all surpassing peace and confidence in knowing that God's grace is more than sufficient to deal with our concerns.

> "Don't fret or worry. Instead of worrying, pray. Let petitions and praises shape your worries into prayers, letting God know your concerns. Before you know it, a sense of God's wholeness, everything coming together for good, will come and settle you down. It's wonderful what happens when Christ displaces worry at the center of your life."
> Philippians 4:5-7 MSG

When we meditate on God's great goodness, love, and mercy, and our over flowing cup of blessings he showers upon us, we will be better able to pour our love, goodness, and mercy out on others.

Father, help me to to spend more time appreciating and less time worrying and complaining. In Jesus' name, Amen

What Are We Good At?

"That means we will not compare ourselves with each other as if one of us were better and another worse. We have far more interesting things to do with our lives. Each of us is an original." Galatian 5:26 MSG

The older I get the more amazed I become at the amazing talents and abilities of so many people. When we look around and see or read about

Doom to you who think you're so smart, who hold such a high opinion of yourselves! All you're good at is drinking—champion boozers who collect trophies from drinking bouts"
Isaiah 5:21 MSG

the accomplishments and talents of others, we are often humbled to realize that ours just don't compare with theirs.

This often causes the seed of jealousy to take root and cause us to begrudge others their talents and abilities.

It helps us rationalize and minimize the severity of our own sins when we are all perhaps a little too good at comparing ourselves with others who are much better at sinning in some areas. It salves our conscience when we can find worse sinners than we.

There are a lot of things that I am really good at that I wish I weren't. I am good at worrying, self centeredness, criticizing, complaining, wasting time, over eating, over talking, and having a little self righteous joy in gloating over some of the failures and mistakes of others.

If we want to compare ourselves with others, it would be a good idea to compare ourselves with Jesus. This will certainly leave no room for any of us to boast about what we are good at, but rather in that only Jesus was good enough to live the perfect life and die to make us good enough in God's sight to be

"Don't compare yourself with others. Each of you must take responsibility for doing the creative best you can with your own life."
Galatians 6:4b MSG

redeemed and crowned as children and heirs of the kingdom of God.

Father, by the power of the Holy Spirit, help me to get better at loving and serving you and others. In Jesus' name, Amen

What Can I Offer the LORD ?

"To love him with all your heart, with all your understanding and with all your strength, and to love your neighbor as yourself is more important than all burnt offerings and sacrifices."Mark 12:33 NIV

Jesus Christ not only died on the cross as the complete pefect sacrifice offering for our sins, He died to give us a new life free to offer God our sacrifices of praise.

"You take no delight in sacrifices or offerings. Now that you have made me listen, I finally understand —you don't require burnt offerings or sin offerings."
Psalm 40:6 NLT

When we think of the great thing God has done for us in Christ, how can we help but rejoice? And when we rejoice, we make God's joy so complete that He gives us that all surpassing peace and joy even in the worst of circumstances.

We no longer have to offer animals, we get to offer ourselves as living sacrifices in appreciation for what Christ has done.

We offer living sacrifices of praise everytime we worship either privately or as a church. When we offer our time, our talents, or our treasures to reflect God's goodness to us, we are going to experience more of the abundant life He came to give us.

As we begin each day asking Lord to let us be a conduit of His love to others we will find our joy being multiplied as we bless others with the love we have been given.

"Patient endurance is what you need now, so that you will continue to do God's will. Then you will receive all that he has promised."
Hebrews 12:36 NLT

Scripture makes it very clear that God doesn't care about the burnt offerings of animals. What He really wants is our heart.

Father, help me to offer my life as a living sacrifice to the praise of Your glory. In Jesus' name, Amen

Sin Offerings
"If we deliberately keep on sinning after we have received the knowledge of the truth, no sacrifice for sins is left," Hebrews 10:26 NIV

The Old Testament law was full of detailed instructions for sin offerings of every kind, almost as though every sin had a price. Our new covenant of grace that is ours through faith in Jesus Christ promises forgiveness and right standing with God for every sin when we confess and repent.

> "Sacrifice and offering You do not desire, nor have You delight in them; You have given me the capacity to hear and obey [Your law, a more valuable service than] burnt offerings and sin offerings [which] You do not require.
> Psalm 40:5-6 AMP

God makes it clear that He is no longer interested burnt offering sacrifices for sin; but is always pleased with sacrifices of praise and thanksgiving for what He has done and who He has made us to be in Christ.

Unfortunately we too often make sin offerings not for forgiveness or atonement but as willful disobedience and rebellion offerings of our sin nature that continues to try to control us.

Jesus Christ's death on the cross was the price He paid for every one of our sins. We should be grateful for what He has done for us that we live lives fully pleasing to Him and in freedom from the power of sin He died to give us.

When we keep on sinning after we have been set free from the domination and bondage to sin we are in effect making a sin offering to please our flesh and the devil who delights in them.

> " Well then, should we keep on sinning so that God can show us more and more of his wonderful grace?
> Romans 6:1 NLT

We should be mourning over our past sins rather than offering more up as though Jesus' sacrifice on the cross was in vain.

The sooner we learn to rejoice and make praise offerings instead of sin offerings, the sooner we will discover the abundant life Jesus died to give us in all its fullness.

Father, help me to avoid making sin offerings to my flesh and the devil by helping me to escape or resist temptations. In Jesus' name, Amen

Getting Dumbed Down

"Beware of false prophets, which come to you in sheep's clothing, but inwardly they are ravening wolves."Matthew 7:13 KJV

The need for Spiritual wisdom and discernment continues to grow as the tendency to dumb us down by advertisers, politicians, activists, bureaucrats, preachers and religious leaders seems to be growing all the time.

> ""If you're so smart, give us a lesson in how to address God. We're in the dark and can't figure it out. Do you think I'm dumb enough to challenge God?"
> Job 37:19 MSG

The instant communication via internet and TV is part of the problem. On any given day we will receive many spams or forwarded e-mails bearing false witness against others, or offers too good to be true. The fact that Nigerian scam artists are able to bilk millions of supposedly intelligent people offers proof that many have already been dumbed down beyond all reason.

Too many people underestimate our intelligence and presume to know what we will or will not understand. Many spin lies and half truths designed to mislead and misinform anyone dumb enough to believe them.

Unfortunately we have a lot of sincere but mistaken blind guides trying to dumb us down with their own biased opinions and agendas purportedly offered as God's will.

The best way to keep from getting "dumbed down" is to "listen up " to and know God's truths by abiding in His Word." If we don't know what we stand for, we can fall for anything. God's Word promises wisdom and discernment if we pray for it.

> "you are like a dumb carpenter who built a house but skipped the foundation."
> Luke 6:48 MSG

May we all be on guard against being "dumbed down"

Father, now that You have lifted me up in the joy of your salvation,help me be aware of and resist the efforts of the world, my flesh, and the devil to "dumb me down". In Jesus' name, Amen

The Only Safe Investment

" Relax your grip on your money and abandon your gold-plated luxury. God Almighty will be your treasure, more wealth than you can imagine." Job 22:20 MSG

With all the upside down mortgages and fore closures, stock market volatility, bank failures, etc many are beginning to wonder if there is any such thing as a safe investment.

"The generous will prosper; those who refresh others will themselves be refreshed."
Proverbs 22:25 NLT

Scripture makes it very clear that there is a place where we can put our treasures we cannot keep in a place where we can never lose them.

The guarantee of our less than 3 star rated government, pales in comparision to the guarantee of our Almighty, All Knowing, Ever Present, and Ever Faithful God who says: "Test me in this," says the LORD Almighty, "and see if I will not throw open the floodgates of heaven and pour out so much blessing that there will not be room enough to store it." (Malachi 3:9) We will find out whether this guarantee applies to the present or our future, lives or both only by taking God up on His challenge to test Him.

Many might wonder what use we will have for treasures in heaven, when it is going to be a perfect place where everything will be provided. We might think about this as we try understanding the judgement of all believers who will stand before Jesus and give and account of the lives we have been given at the resurrection of the just. (1 Cor 3:9-12)

We will go to heaven "as one barely escaping the fire, or as one who will hear our Lord say: "Well done thou good and faithful servant" when the treasures we have stored up in heaven remain after all the trivial pursuits of our lives is burned away. This should make us want to store up as much treasure while we still can by investing our time, talents, and material resources in God honoring Kingdom building purposes.

"For where your treasure is, there will your heart be also.
Matthew 6;21 MSG

Father there is no real security apart from You. Thank you for the safety of my soul and ownership of my heart and fpr all the possessions with which You have trusted me. In Jesus' name, Amen

Too Easily Pleased

"And it's trouble ahead if you're satisfied with yourself. Your self will not satisfy you for long. And it's trouble ahead if you think life's all fun and games. There's suffering to be met, and you're going to meet it

The wonderful free gift of eternal life that we receive through faith in Jesus Christ is undoubtedly the greatest gift we have ever been given. We should never stop rejoicing and living in the joy of our salvation.

> **Because you have satisfied me, God, I promise to do everything you say. I beg you from the bottom of my heart: smile, be gracious to me just as you promised.**
> **Psalm 119:57 MSG**

Accepting this wonderful gift and putting it in the wallet of our mind as an admission ticket to heaven when we die seems to be too prevalent among many professing Christians.

The sad truth is that we may be too easily pleased with our salvation. "I've been saved: - I don't need to go to church - I don't need to study the Bible – I don't need to obey – I don't need to give - I don't need to seek the kingdom of God and His righteousness" are some of the thoughts the deceiver of our souls plants to diminish our faith and our witness.

When we accept our receiving Christ as an end in itself we are too easily pleased, and will miss out on the abundant life Christ came to give us all in this world and the next. Accepting Christ is the beginning of a great new life in Him with a living faith that needs to grow until we are conformed into the image of Christ before we go to be with Him forever.

When we are too easily pleased, we are going to be among those mentioned in 1 Corinthians 3:15 as "one only escaping through the flames", instead of one hearing "well done, thou good and faithful servant" who will have the treasures stored up by a life well lived as disciples of Jesus.

> **"But for right now, friends, I'm completely frustrated by your unspiritual dealings with each other and with God. You're acting like infants in relation to Christ,"**
> **1 Corinthians 3:1 MSG**

Father, by the power of the Holy Spirit living within me, let me never be too easily pleased by accepting less than God's best that only comes through abiding. In Jesus' name, Amen.

Absent Minded Professors
"For this world's wisdom is foolishness (absurdity and stupidity) with God, for it is written, He lays hold of the wise in their [own] craftiness;"1 Corinthians 3:19

"For the scepter of wickedness shall not rest upon the land of the [uncompromisingly] righteous, lest the righteous (God's people) stretch forth their hands to iniquity and apostasy."
Psalm 125:3 AMP

The more learned in science and technology we become the more absent God seems to become in the minds of our college professors throughout the world.

How sad it is that the colleges and schools established to teach and proclaim God's truths seem now determined to replace God's truth with the false relative truth of man.

Unsuspecting parents pay to send children who have been brought up in the nurture and admonition of the Lord spiritually seduced into apostasy (renunciation of faith) by professors with God absent minds who worship man's intellect and knowledge instead of the Lord God Almighty.

Latest studies indicate that over 75% of children from even Christian homes will leave their churches on or before their second year of college. Many leave much sooner under the influence of absent minded teachers and schools where God has been kicked out.

We need to continually pray that God will open the eyes of our spiritually blind professors, and help us to do a better job of equipping our children with th full armor of God so that they will be able to stand against those who would rob them of their faith.

"Let no one deceive or beguile you in any way, for that day will not come except the [a]apostasy comes first [unless the predicted great [b]falling away of those who have professed to be Christians has come],"
2 Thessalonians 2:3a AMP

Father, in your mercy, help us do everything possible that we and our houses pass on the faith of our fathers to our children and children's children. In Jesus' name, Amen

For Better or For Worse

Husbands, go all out in your love for your wives, exactly as Christ did for the church—a love marked by giving, not getting. Christ's love makes the church whole. His words evoke her beauty." Ephesians 5:25 MSG

"Therefore keep a watch upon your spirit [that it may be controlled by My Spirit], that you deal not treacherously and faithlessly [with your marriage mate]."
Malachi 2:16b AMP

Although no one goes into marriage expecting the worst it seems that too many cannot handle the worst when it happens in their marriage.

The devil uses divorces to encourage others to live in sin outside of marriage in order to avoid it.

Becoming poorer instead of richer financially seems to be one of the big deal breakers in many marriages today. It's hard to live on love alone when arguments over money or the lack thereof move in.

Marriage needs to be approached as being a giving relationship Instead of a taking. God is the ultimate giver who loved us so much He gave us His only begotten Son.

When we give ourselves to each other unselfishly instead of selfishly taking from one another we will find that our joy is multiplied and our problems are minimized.

Perhaps the worst in any marriage break up is the hurt inflicted on any children who are often caught in the middle of a lot of strife and blame gaming and left with reservations about entering into any marriage commitment of their own in later years.

Just as when we are crucified with Christ our life is not our own, when we become one in marriage our lives are no longer our own, but we become new creatures united in our love for Christ and for each other. This is the real tie that binds, and the glue that will stick through those worst circumstances when they come.

"Jesus' disciples objected, "If those are the terms of marriage, we're stuck. Why get married?"
Matthew 19:10 MSG

For those who may have experienced a failed marriage, take comfort in knowing that as much as God hates divorce, He loves us more than divorce, and can and will use our worst for His good in conforming us into the image of Christ if we trust and obey Him.

Father, thank you for a marriage anchored in you and your love. In Jesus' name, Amen

Thorns of the Flesh

"Thorns and snares are in the way of the obstinate and willful; he who guards himself will be far from them." Proverbs 22:4-6 AMP

The Apostle Paul spoke of his thorn in the flesh with which satan constantly distracted him and tried to impede and destroy his ministry

"My people have planted wheat but are harvesting thorns. They have worn themselves out, but it has done them no good."
Jeremiah 12:13 NLT

. Although the exact malady Is unknown, it was believed to be a severe and painful physical Problem which persisted in spite of Paul's fervent prayers for healing.

The thorns that grow and try to choke out the seed of faith we received are the distractions that keep us from hearing, learning, and growing in the Word of God.

Tragic accidents, loss of loved ones, illnesses, financial reverses, and a host of other problems are some of the many circumstances that can be real thorns in the flesh.

Falling in love with the world and its ways choke our faith and leave weeds of guilt, shame, and eternally fatal consequences. We all know some who started well and had their walk of faith choked before it could take root and grow.

Strong believers will sometimes sit in church and let problems and worries distract. Some will be paying more attention to what people are wearing or where we are going for dinner after church than feasting on the faith building nourishment of the Word that is being preached.

"He also that received seed among the thorns is he that heareth the word; and the care of this world, and the deceitfulness of riches, choke the word, and he becometh unfruitful.
Matthew 13:22 KJV

God deserves and our growth into the fullness of Christ requires our undivided attention when we come to partake of the grace that is being imparted in the preaching and teaching of His Word.

We would all do well to pour out the weed killer of repentance where needed, and apply the healing balm of Gilead by rejoicing through all of God's other growth pills disguised as thorns.

Father, thank you for your thorns that humble and keep us full of dependence on you and less full of ourselves. In Jesus' name, Amen

Are You Narrow Minded?

"Enter through the narrow gate. For wide is the gate and broad is the road that leads to destruction,and many enter through it.But small is the gate and narrow the road that leads to life, and only a few find it. Matthew 7:13,14 NIV

Contrary to conventional wisdom being narrow minded is one of the greatest virtues of practicing Christians. Although the world goes ballistic when we speak of Jesus as the only way whereby we may be saved, or that alternative life styles are sin ifestyles, if we are going to obey the Bible we say we believe, we have no choice but to be narrow minded.

"Who may ascend the hill of the LORD ? Who may stand in his holy place? "
Psalm 24:3 NIV

Being narrow minded has nothing to do with being self righteous or judgmental. We Need to always remember there is non righteous other than Jesus Christ, and that God has reserved the right to judge and does not require our help.

We need to limit our judging to judging ourselves and praying for the Lord's forgiveness and strength to overcome our shortcomings.

Once we are born again through faith in Jesus Christ we are set free from domination and bondage to sin, and are at last able to pursue holiness without which we will never be like Jesus.

When we narrow our minds to leading fruitful lives fully pleasing to God and concentrate on bearing the longsuffering, patience, kindness, gentleness, love, faithfulnes and self control the Holy Spirit is producing within us, we are going to find the joy of our salvation and the gates to the abundant life Christ came to model for us and died to give opening wider and wider.

"Make" every effort to enter through the narrow door, because many, I tell you, will try to enter and will not be able to."
Luke 13;24 NIV

Father, in your mercy and by the power of the Holy Spirit, help me to be so narrow minded that I never fall into faith traps constantly being sprung on me. In Jesus' name, Amen

Forcing Love

"Or do you show contempt for the riches of his kindness, tolerance and patience, not realizing that God's kindness leads you toward repentance? " Romans 2:4 NIV

As strange as it may seem and even harder to understand, God does not force His will upon us. We don't have to do anything, But when God's love comes down and the Holy Spirit takes up residence In our hearts we find

"Delight yourself in the LORD and he will give you the desires of your heart." Psalm 37:4 NIV

ourselves wanting to do everything to honor God In all that we are, say, and do.

So many people seem to reject God's call to salvation because of what they would have to quit doing or what they would have to give up.

As Holy transformation begins taking place by the renewing of our minds, we find that we want to give up the things that we know are displeasing to God, and find pleasure in doing the things that please Him.

We can never earn or merit God's saving grace, but we can and will find ourselves wanting to respond to it with praise and thanksliving for what He has done for us.

As the desires of our hearts change during the ongoing process of being conformed Into the image of Christ we find God supplying these desires that allow us to honor and glorify Him.

"As a result, they do not live the rest of their earthly lives for evil human desires, but rather for the will of God." 1 Peter 4:2 NIV

God has placed in the hearts of all to know and love Him, but He will never force His Love, grace, and mercy on anyone. He gives us all the choice of not having to receive His love, but when we do He will turn our 'haves" into Wants and lead us beside the still waters of His Peace.

Father, Help me to keep wanting only what you want as I seek to lead a life Fully pleasing to you. In Jesus' name, Amen

The Pursuit of Pleasure

"That you may walk (live and conduct yourselves) in a manner worthy of the Lord, fully pleasing to Him and desiring to please Him in all things, bearing fruit in every good work and steadily growing and increasing in and by the knowledge of God [with fuller, deeper, and clearer insight, acquaintance, and recognition].Colossians 1:9 AMP

King Solomon was reportedly the wisest man who ever lived. Because he asked for wisdom, God was so pleased He also granted power and riches which the King did not handle well.

"because I do not seek or consult My own will [I have no desire to do what is pleasing to Myself, My own aim, My own purpose] but only the will and pleasure of the Father Who sent Me."
John 5:10b MSG

When he decided to pursue pleasure in enjoying the so called "good things in life" he had all of the resources needed to do anything he wanted to do whenever he wanted to do it and found nothing but meaningless vanity instead of happiness. The experience left him hating life.

We do not need the wisdom of Solomon to excessively pursue pleasure and suffer the consequences instead of the pleasure. There is nothing wrong with enjoying the pleasures of life which God has given us all to enjoy. It's when we pursue pleasure more than the kingdom of God and His righteousness that we will end up feeling remorseful and unfulfilled.

When we pursue the pleasure of pleasing God, we are going to face the end of this life with a lot more peace and joy, and have a lot more left for which we will receive the Lord's "well done" when the trivial pursuits of the pleasures of life are burned away.

Although wisdom is much more desirable than ignorance, we need to understand that wisdom and knowledge alone will never make us happy or let us escape the feeling of a meaningless life

"But as I looked at everything I had worked so hard to accomplish, it was all so meaningless—like chasing the wind. There was nothing really worthwhile anywhere."
Ecclesiastes 2:10 NLT

Jesus Christ came to show us the way to all the true pleasures of the abundant life He came to provide for us by His death on the cross. When the Holy Spirit gives us the spiritual wisdom and discernment to realize this truth, we will never be left feeling that our lives are vain or meaningless.

Father, teach me to seek my pleasure by seeking to be all that you have created me to be in Christ. In Jesus' name, Amen

Great Expectations

"For I know the plans I have for you," says the LORD. "They are plans for good and not for disaster, to give you a future and a hope."
Jeremiah 29:11 NLT

Our lives are often full of great expectations for and of ourselves and others. Our self worth is mainly determined by how well we live up to our expectations for ourselves.

> "Look at those who are honest and good, for a wonderful future awaits those who love peace."
> Psalm 37:36 NLT

We have great expectations for our marriages, our children, our careers. We plan vacations, trips, and visits in joyful anticipation.

We greet new pastors with great expectations. We buy beauty and health products with great expectations.

People buy billions of lottery tickets every day with great expectations.

When we or any other person does not live up to our expectations we are disappointed and perplexed. When we do not live up to someone elses expectations it diminishes their opinion of us.

We need to understand that as imperfect people living in an imperfect world we are going to be disappointed in our expectations of ourselves and others and move on. We will find that the way we respond to the disappointing expectations of others will often determine how others respond when we fail to meet their expectations.

Our forever life in heaven with no more sorrow, sickness, or sin is the one great expectation we can bank on. We can even store up treasures there by showing our appreciation here by living fruitful lives fully pleasing to the one who died to make sure that this great expectation will be met for everyone who believes.

> "As it is written, Behold I am laying in Zion a Stone that will make men stumble, a Rock that will make them fall; but he who believes in Him [who adheres to, trusts in, and relies on Him] shall not be put to shame nor be disappointed in his expectations."
> Romans 9:33 AMP

When we keep our eyes on this prize that has already been won for us we can be comforted through the unmet expectations of this world by knowing that the best is yet to be.

Father thank you for the hope that fills me with great expectations of my perfect life in your perfect heaven awaits me and all who trust in Your Son. In Jesus' name, Amen

Sitting on Top of the World
"Remember then from what heights you have fallen. Repent (change the inner man to meet God's will) and do the works you did previously [when first you knew the Lord], or else I will visit you and remove your lampstand from its place, unless you change your mind and repent." Revelation 2:5 AMP

Although this world is covered with a veil of tears caused by the curse of sin, there is still a lot of goodness, beauty, and a lot of mountain top experiences to enjoy.

"Your world will be washed in sunshine, every shadow dispersed by dayspring.Full of hope, you'll relax, confident again;" Job 11:17 MSG

There are moments in the lives of all of us when we feel that we are truly sitting on top of the world. It may be that new job or promotion, , marriage, or birth of a child. It may be winning an athletic contest, healing, or getting our dream car or dream home.

These are just a few examples of relational, material, physical, and spiritual blessings that fill our hearts with a great sense of well being and joy.

When we abide in Christ we experience sacred delight of answered prayers, friendship with Jesus and Jesus' joy that lift our spirit to new heights.

All of these are but a slight foretaste of what we have to look forward to in the new earth we are going to live on in our new resurrected bodies when Christ returns.

Instead of just glimpses, we will experience the fullness of living in a sin free world where there will be no more sorrow, pain or suffering. We will discover that what we thought doesn't get any better is much much better than anything we have ever experienced or dreamed of in this life.

When we get laid low by the difficulties encountered in living in an imperfect world with imperfect people and as an imperfect person,we need to look back to when we were sitting on top of the world and move onward filled with the blessed assurance that none of our difficulties will last forever and that there is a better world to come.

", you're sitting on top of the world—at least God's world—and we're right there, sitting alongside you!" 1 Corinthians 4:7b MSG

Father thank you for my mountain top experiences and my confidence that they are just a small sample of the joys awaiting me in heaven. In Jesus' name, Amen.

Read 1 Corinthians 3:18-23, Psalm 119:65-72

How Stupid Can We Get?

"I turned away from God, but then I was sorry. I kicked myself for my stupidity! I was thoroughly ashamed of all I did in my younger days." Jeremiah 31:19 MSG

Moron jokes used to be the rage years ago. We all seem to take little hypocritical delight in the stupidity of others which make us feel not so guilty about our own dumb mistakes.

'Their hearts are dull and stupid, but I delight in your law." Psalm 119:70 NLT

Some of the most brilliant people in the world do dumb things. God continually warns about the foolishness of man.

I have melted a watch trying to charge the battery but heating it in a microwave, driven a 10 ft horse van underneath a 9 foot underpass, and run out of gas in some 15 states. I can laugh about it now, but is was not funny at the time.

Regret Street is paved with the bricks of our stupidity. We sometimes have flash backs of godly sorrow that make us wonder how we could ever have been so dumb in making some of the decisions we have made financially, relationally, and spiritually.

How good it is to know that we have a Heavenly Father who forgives our stupidity. Even though we receive forgiveness and cleansing, the consequences of our stupidity can hurt ourselves and others for a lifetime. We must depend on the strength and power of the Holy Spirit for the all sufficient grace we need to rejoice and persevere through these consequences .

"Don't fool yourself. Don't think that you can be wise merely by being up-to-date with the times. Be God's fool—that's the path to true wisdom. What the world calls smart, God calls stupid. It's written in Scripture," 1 Corinthians 3:18 MSG

. The real sadness is that awaiting all who reject God's wonderful offer of eternal life with Him in heaven, and who are going to wake up to the torments of hell wondering how they could have been so stupid.

Father,give me the wisdom and spiritual discernment I need to avoid the folly of stupidity. In Jesus' name, Amen

When Our Comfort Zones Get Squeezed

"For whoever is bent on saving his [temporal] life [his comfort and security here] shall lose it [eternal life]; and whoever loses his life [his comfort and security here] for My sake shall find it [life everlasting]."Matthew 16:25 AMP

We all live well within the boundaries of a risk free comfort zone where we are secure and free of anxiety and stress. When we venture into new territories we often find our comfort zones getting squeezed..

"But they that wait upon the LORD shall renew their strength; they shall mount up with wings as eagles; they shall run, and not be weary; and they shall walk, and not faint."
Isaiah 40:33 KJV

Our comfort zones get squeezed every time we encounter relational, physical, financial or spiritual problems. The "no gain without pain" philosophy certainly holds true as we try to break through the barriers that fence us in.

Many churches today are filled with too many spectators who cannot move outside the boundaries of their comfort zones and into the comfort zone of the Holy Spirit in order to seek and save the lost or the love of God to others through the ministry and service of God living in and through us by the power of the Holy Spirit.

Fear or indifference are the biggest barriers to overcome in moving out of our comfort zone. We may be lukewarm and satisfied to eat of the crumbs under the table of God's banquet table with no passion for obeying the Great Commandment and Great Commission. We may fear ridicule, rejection, or persecution.

"So we take comfort and are encouraged and confidently and boldly say, The Lord is my Helper; I will not be seized with alarm [I will not fear or dread or be terrified]. What can man do to me?"
Hebrews 13:6 AMP

. When we find ourselves looking for reasons not to step out of our comfort zones to serve the Lord, we need to remember "perfect love casts out all fear", that the Holy Spirit is always with us and will protect us and give us the strength to overcome our fears. He even promises to give us the words to say when we have opportunities to witness.

Father, give me the strength and will to move outside of my comfort zone and more fully love and serve you and others. In Jesus name, Amen

Maxed Out Life
"I am using an example from everyday life because of your human **limit**ations. Just as you used to offer yourselves as slaves to impurity and to ever-increasing wickedness, so **no**w offer yourselves as slaves to righteousness leading to holiness." Romans 6:18 NIV

Credit Card debt has brought a whole new meaning to millions of card holders who find themselves over their credit limit on one and often times several credit cards.

"Grab your bags, all you who are under attack. God has given notice: "Attention! I'm evicting Everyone who lives here, And right now—yes, right now! I'm going to press them to the limit, squeeze the life right out of them." Jeremiah 10:17 MSG

The buy now and worry about paying for it later mindset seems to be one of the most prevalent life styles in our country. It has been promoted too well by businesses marketing easy payments on just about everything.

Credit is not the only thing that characterizes that characterizes the maxed out life. Doctors and Hospitals are filled to overflowing with the long term effects of maxed out drugging, boozing, smoking. Eating, and other excesses.

The prodigal son is a good example of a bad maxed out life. Those who choose to lose by believing that this life is all there is have every reason to "go for the gusto" and seek all pleasures they can and reject God's wonderful offer of salvation to their peril.

"But the Holy Spirit produces this kind of fruit in our lives: love, joy, peace, patience, kindness, goodness, faithfulness, gentleness, and self-control. There is no law against these things!" Galations 5:22.23 NLT

We can never get maxed out by bearing the love, joy, peace, patience, kindness, goodness, faithfulness, gentleness, and self-control that the Holy Spirit is continually producing within us. When we live our lives maxed out in Christ, re will experience more and more of God's love maxed into us.

Father, help me to live a better life maxed out to You. In Jesus' name, Amen

An Interesting Question

"Now it is required that those who have been given a trust must prove faithful"1 Corinthians 4:1 NIV

If God were to give to us on the basis of what we give to Him how would we feel? Any among us who would be complaining about the stinginess of God should be looking in a mirror and reflecting on our own stinginess towards God.

**"Should people cheat God? Yet you have cheated me!But you ask, 'What do you mean? When did we ever cheat you? You have cheated me of the tithes and offerings due to me."
Malachi 3:9 NLT**

Based on the national average of church members giving around 3% of what they have been given a vast majority of us would be in big financial trouble if God were to short change us as we short change Him.

Thanks be to God that He is not a stingy God. He lavishes His love, relational, spiritual, and financial blessings upon all His Children. All He really asks is that we lavish on others.

In Malachi 3 God actually asks us to test Him by bringing our tithes to the storehouse and promises to bless us richly when we do this. If we really trusted God, we would all become richer by giving more than just 10% to Him.

When God finds that He can trust us with little, He will give us more. When we selfishly hoard or recklessly spend what we have been given we are choosing to live in selfish spiritual poverty that will keep us from experiencing the abundant life Jesus came to give us.

**"When someone has been given mer4 uch, much will be required in return; and when someone has been entrusted with much, even more will be required."
Luke 12;48b NLT**

When we stagnate God's grace by selfishly withholding and hoarding instead of letting it freely flow in and through us we are going to find ourselves cruising on the river of life without a paddle and missing out on God's best.

Father, let my giving reflect my thanks living in every area of my Life. In Jesus' name, Amen

Criticality

"Don't pick on people, jump on their failures, criticize their faults— unless, of course, you want the same treatment. That critical spirit has a way of boomeranging." Matthew 7:1 MSG

"Criticality" or finding fault sometimes seems to be the favorite past time of many Christians.

"That our oxen may be strong to labour; that there be no breaking in, nor going out; that there be no complaining in our streets."
Psalm 144:14 KJV

The conduct of the Scribes and Pharisees that brought Jesus' severest reprimand is often all too obvious in churches. Church members are too good at finding fault with the pastor, the choir, the carpet, the temperature, the conduct of children, and even those who raise their hands or cross their hearts in worship.

We are especially good at criticizing fund raising campaigns forgetting how often we conduct our own fund raising campaigns with God as we ask him for material blessings and prosperity.

While we are all called to hold each other accountable, and should expect our pastors to preach God's Word and our church to do things decently and in order, we need to speak the truth in love in these matters but never fall into the habit of complaining to others.

When we concentrate on being critics of ourselves we will have less reason and time to be so critical of others and find ourselves being more affirming and less critical of them.

"Eventually, we're all going to end up kneeling side by side in the place of judgment, facing God. Your critical and condescending ways aren't going to improve your position there one bit"
Romans 14:10 MSG

We should develop the habit of giving positive reinforcement and encouragement to our pastors and fellow members, and radiate a sweet spirit that reflects our love for Christ and each other.

Instead of people saying: "see how they critcize one another" they should be saying: "see how they love one another". This is what the real communion of Saints is all about.

Father, by the power of the Holy Spirit, take away my critical spirit and replace it with appreciation and affirmation. In Jesus' name, Amen

Getting More than We Bargained For

"There's a way of life that looks harmless enough; look again—it leads straight to hell. Sure, those people appear to be having a good time, but all that laughter will end in heartbreak." Proverbs 14:11 MSG

Among the many complications life are the unforeseen consequences that often accompany actions.

"To deliver you from the way of evil and the evil men, from men who speak perverse things and are liars," Proverbs 2:11

Are there many prison cells occupied by people who want to be there?. Most are there because they got more than they bargained for when they committed the crime.

Are sexually transmitted diseases that can keep on giving for a lifetime ever anyone's purpose in seeking instant gratification through promiscuity? These diseases, along with unwanted pregnancies, broken homes, and a host of other consequences are examples of getting more than bargained for.

No cigarette smokers smoke to get cancer, heart disease, and any number of other ailments, and yet they continue to smoke and get more than bargained for.

The truth is that in spite of outward appearances sin will bring a lot more consequences than were bargained for.

Jesus tells us that we should count the cost. We are told to be prepared to share in His suffering if we are going to share in the joy of our salvation.

When we receive God's gift of heaven through faith in Jesus Christ we always get a lot more than we bargained for when we trust and obey Him.

"Now all glory to God, who is able, through his mighty power at work within us, to accomplish infinitely more than we might ask or think." Ephesians 3:20 NLT

We get the abundance of His grace more than sufficient for our every need for today, direct access through prayer any day, and all of the other blessings of this life promised to those who trust and obey.

Father, Thank you for giving me so much more than I could ever earn or hope for. In Jesus' name, Amen

The Servant's Reward

"For the Son of Man is going to come in his Father's glory with his angels, and then he will reward each person according to what they have done." Matthew 16:27 NIV

There is perhaps more confusion and misunderstanding about rewards in heaven than any other understanding of our Christian faith.

> **"For we all must stand before the judgment seat (bema) of Christ, that each one may receive the things done in the body, according to what he has done, whether good or bad."**
> **2 Corinthians 5:10**

Part of the confusion comes with many viewing the eternal life as a reward even though it is a gift we are given because of what Jesus Christ did on the cross and not a reward for something we have done.

Scripture teaches that rewards will be given when we serve, help the needy, suffer persecution, are generous, and do good.

Part of the failure to believe the biblical concepts of rewards is an overkill from the reformation teaching that we are saved by grace and not by works. Good Works have nothing to do with our destination, but may well have a lot to do with what we will be privileged to do when we get there.

Jesus promised His disciples a servant rulership reward in heaven. For those who truly love God, what greater reward could there be than being given an expanded capacity to serve Him more in heaven?

When we give Jesus an account of what we did with the lives we were given at the Resurrection of believers, we will receive His "well done" if any good works are left after all the wood hay and stubble of our imperfect lives is burned away.

> **" I saw the dead, both great and small, standing before God's throne. And the books were opened, including the Book of Life. And the dead were judged according to the things written in the books, according to what they had done."**
> **Revelation 20:12 NIV**

We all have to face God, regardless of our conditions. We will appear before Christ and take what's coming to us as a result of our actions, either good or bad.

We would all do well to remember Hebrews 6:10: "God is not unjust; he will not forget your work and the love you have shown him as you have helped his people and continue to help them."

Father help me to remember that the greatest among us will be the servant of all in heaven and help me to be faithful in my life here so that I can be great in heaven. In Jesus' name, Amen.

Getting Stalked by Our Past

"But if you will not do so, behold, you have sinned against the Lord; and be sure your sin will find you out." Numbers 22:23 AMP

Our sins have a way of stalking us wherever we go. Our misdeeds of life will often be found out and used against us.

> "Finally, I confessed all my sins to you and stopped trying to hide my guilt. I said to myself, "I will confess my rebellion to the Lord." And you forgave me! All my guilt is gone."
> Psalm 32:5 NLT

Many political career aspirations have been nipped in the bud or cut short when dark deeds are dug up and brought to light. The higher the political, judicial, or other job sought the more comprehensive the fault searching becomes.

A felony or sexual predator conviction will follow us wherever we go in spite of the forgiveness received from God!

The deceiver of our souls is also the master stalker of our souls. Even though God has forgiven our confessed and repented sins and remembers them no more, the devil will sometimes bring up our past failures to discourage and cause us to doubt even whether we are really saved.

Some times a chance encounter with someone out of our past will remind us of past sins. Some times the devil will call them to mind out of nowhere to create doubt and discouragement in our hearts. God can and will use this to draw us closer to Him and celebrate the wonder of His love.

Guarding our thoughts, hearts, tongue, and conduct will give us fewer sins to come back and haunt us.

If our conscience is burdening us with an unconfessed and unrepented sin, we need to go immediately to God's throne of grace with a broken spirit and contrite heart and His forgiveness. Sometimes we need to confess to someone we have sinned against and ask their forgiveness.

For guilt and shame over any sin that God has forgiven and forgotten that seem to keep on stalking us, we need to replace remorse with praise and thanksgiving to God for the reminder of His great love and mercy in forgiving us.

> "God's free gift leads to our being made right with God, even though we are guilty of many sins."
> Romans 5:16b NLT

We must never let confessed and forgiven sins rob us of the joy of our salvation.

Father, help me to let my river of regrets flow into your sea of forgetfulness. In Jesus' name, Amen

355

Dying Better than Changing?

"Tell them, 'As sure as I am the living God, I take no pleasure from the death of the wicked. I want the wicked to change their ways and live. Turn your life around! Reverse your evil ways! Why die, Israel?'"
Ezekiel 33:10 MSG

Most people don't like change away from something comfortable. many seem to prefer death rather than quit smoking, overdrinking, over eating or overdosing.

"But those who wait for the Lord [who expect, look for, and hope in Him] shall change and renew their strength and power;"
Isaiah 40:30-31a AMP

Our call to eternal life calls us to die in order to change. We must die to sin so that we can be born again to a new life in Christ.

Although we are changed instantly into sons and daughters of God and receive the righteousness of Christ in God's sight the hour we first believed, the process of Holy transformation is a life long, ongoing process.

We still live in a fleshly body that is under the curse of sin and under the influence of spiritual forces of darkness doing every thing possible to prevent us from being transformed into the image of Christ.

The truth is that we are never going to be able to make all the changes needed except by the supernatural power of the Holy Spirit living within us.

The often radical change we need to make in our hearts, our thoughts, our speech and conduct is not often easy. Even with this power, we often seem to be falling backwards into moving forward into renewing our minds with the mind of Christ..

Thank God, that we have his unconditional love and forgiveness when we stumble or fall back into sin. We need to thank by putting on His full armor to say no to temptation.

"Bring forth fruit that is consistent with repentance [let your lives prove your change of heart];"
Matthew 3:7-9 AMP

The Holy Spirit Who was given as a deposit and guarantee of our safe arrival in heaven will help us make whatever changes are necessary as we renew our minds by growing in the knowledge and love of God by growing in His Word and being obedient to it.

Father, let my repentance and change be real as I seek to become more like Jesus. In Jesus' name, Amen

The Ultimate Additive

"But the **fruit** of the [Holy] **Spirit** [the work which His presence within accomplishes] is love, joy (gladness), peace, patience (an even temper, forbearance), kindness, goodness (benevolence), faithfulness," Galatians 5:21-23

The power from on high we receive when we invite Jesus into our heart and lives gives us God's strength to overcome our weaknesses and leads into all truth as we surrender to the Holy Spirit.

"[Growing in grace] they shall still bring forth fruit in old age; they shall be full of sap [of spiritual vitality] and [rich in the] verdure [of trust, love, and contentment]."
Psalm 92:14 AMP

As we pray, study, fellowship, and grow in God's Word, and put our added power into action by bearing the "*love, joy, peace, longsuffering, gentleness, goodness, faith, and self control*" of the Spirit. the ultimate additive of all surpassing peace fills our lives with gladness.

The same power that turned weak and timid disciples into bold champions of the faith, that turned the murderous zealot Saul into Saint Paul, is still being poured out today on those who come with a broken spirit and contrite heart and lean on Jesus.

When we dump the fruit of our sinful flesh nature at the cross through confession and repentance we leave that much more room for the Holy Spirit to fill us with the fruit of righteousness and the accompanying love, joy, and peace.

"[That you may really come] to know [practically, through experience for yourselves] the love of Christ, which far surpasses mere knowledge [without experience]; that you may be filled [through all your being] unto all the fullness of God [may have the richest measure of the divine Presence, and become a body wholly filled and flooded with God Himself]!"
Ephesians 3:19 AMP

When the dangers, toils, and troubles of this life threaten to overcome us we need to drink deeper from the well of goodness, grace, and mercy of God by standing firm in the full armor God has provided, and trust in His promises that He will always supply grace sufficient for our every need when our hearts are right with Him.

May we never cease to praise and thank God for the ultimate additive of love, joy, and peace that makes this life worth living.

Father, continue to fill my cup to overflowing with the fruit of Your spirit that you have created me to bear. In Jesus' name, Amen

357

Read Romans 2, Psalm 85

Whose Will

"An undisciplined, self-willed life is puny; an obedient, God-willed life is spacious." Proverbs 15:30 MSG

There is a battle for control raging in every area of life. The will we submit to will condemn us to sin and death or empower us to live above it forever.

"I will listen [with expectancy] to what God the Lord will say, for He will speak peace to His people, to His saints (those who are in right standing with Him)--but let them not turn again to [self-confident] folly." Psalm 85:8 AMP

Today's world of enlightenment is all about self will. The world teaches that we can will our happiness adhering to the world's standards by our own intellect and reason.

We have the secular humanism religion of relative truth, and man being the master of his own fate being taught in our schools and trapping millions in bondage to this self will.

Exercising self will under the influence of our sin nature will assure that we live down to our worst. Selfishness, lust, greed, pride and envy will be our motivators and the consequences will eventually be bad.

Submitting control of our lives to the Will of God by the leading of the Holy Spirit will empower us to live up to God's best. When God is in control good things will happen in both this life and the next.

As simple as the explanation of these two wills may be, the truth explained has a great bearing on our quality of life for now and forever.

When we try to make the world revolve around us and our will the more frustrated we will become when things don't go our way.

As we continue to live in the selfishness of self will, we will continue to live full of ourselves and our pleasure and purposes and miss out on the abundant life Jesus came to give us all.

"But for those who are self-seeking and self-willed and disobedient to the Truth but responsive to wickedness, there will be indignation and wrath." Romans 2:7-9 AMP

Scripture made it very clear that we were created to do the will of God in accomplishing the purposes for which we were created. We should all be seeking to be controlled by this good and gracious will.

Father, help me to pray and live like I really mean "Thy will be done". In Jesus' name, Amen

Faith of Our Father
"O Lord God of Heaven's Armies! Where is there anyone as mighty as you, O Lord? You are entirely faithful." Psalm 89:8 NLT

We generally think of faith in terms of the faith of family, friends, and

> "Because of the LORD's great love we are not consumed,for his compassions never fail. They are new every morning; great is your faithfulness."
> Lamentations 3:22,23 NIV

ourselves in terms of salvation. Scripture hails the heroes of the faith and gives the examples of their faith that encourages us all.

As big as our faith may be, it is miniscule compared to the faithfulness of Our Father God and all of the blessings His faithful love showers on us.

We praise the sovereignty, omniscience, and presence in celebrating the greatness of God but sometimes overlook his faithfulness.

To know the faith of our Father is to know our God Who never fails to keep a promise, Who is always working all things (including our worst) for our good transformation into the likeness of Christ.

Sometimes this faithfulness of God is all that we have to cling to in time of trouble for ourselves and those we love. Millions have found that it was all they needed.

There are literally millions living among us who have been restored and renewed by God's faithfulness in answering our prayers for ourselves and also for those we love.

> "God is faithful (reliable, trustworthy, and therefore ever true to His promise, and He can be depended on); by Him you were called into companionship and participation with His Son, Jesus Christ our Lord."
> 1 Corinthians 1:8-10

We access the faithfulness of God by being faithful. Although He is faithful even when we are not, our faithfulness gives us the assurance and hope for today and bright hope for tomorrow.

How comforting and encouraging it is to know the unconditional love and faithfulness of God we have through faith in Jesus Christ.

Father, Great is your faithfulness! In Jesus' name, Amen

359

Read Luke 2, Zephaniah 3:11-20

What's Under Your Tree?

"Many, O Lord my God, are the wonderful works which You have done, and Your thoughts toward us; no one can compare with You! If I should declare and speak of them, they are too many to be numbered." Psalm 40:5 AMP

If you are one of the thousands mourning the absence of a departed loved one this Christmas, be of good cheer? If you are experiencing financial fallout, be of good cheer? If you are experiencing the depression that seems to be so common this time of year, be of good cheer? The answer to all of these and any other problems is YES!

"The Lord your God is in the midst of you, a Mighty One, a Savior [Who saves]! He will rejoice over you with joy; He will rest [in silent satisfaction] and in His love He will be silent and make no mention [of past sins, or even recall them]; He will exult over you with singing." Zephaniah 3:17 AMP

Jesus Christ has not come to make us sad or depressed. He came to bring salvation and the comfort of God's love to us all. He came to bring us the future and hope that God promised, and God has never been known to break a promise.

We might do well to take all of these unwanted presents out from under our tree and dump them at the Cross. We are promised that when we rejoice, we will receive the all surpassing peace of God that is beyond understanding.

When we sing "Joy to the World" and mean it, how can we not be of good cheer? When we rejoice in the wonder of God's love and know that nothing we are going through can separate us from it, we can be cheerful in the worst of circumstances.

"but the angel reassured them. "Don't be afraid!" he said. "I bring you good news that will bring great joy to all people." Luke 2:9-11 NLT

When we find the joy of the Lord through rejoicing and counting the blessings He has put under our tree of life, we can be of good cheer this Christmas and every day of our lives.

Father, I pray the comfort of your love and the joy of your birth for all who read this devotion. In Jesus' name, Amen

In Search of Wisdom

"Good friend, take to heart what I'm telling you; collect my counsels and guard them with your life. Tune your ears to the world of wisdom; set your heart on a life of Understanding. Proverbs 2:1 MSG

The *"wise attitude, belief, or course of action"* that defines wisdom is

"And unto man he said, Behold, the fear of the LORD, that is wisdom; and to depart from evil is understanding." Job 28:28 KJV

something we should be seeking every day of our lives. It is apart from and often contrary to knowledge.

Scripture makes it clear that all wisdom comes from God. He gave exceptional wisdom to Joseph, Solomon, Daniel, The apostle Paul. and a host of others.

Just as we are told to "seek the Lord where he may be found" we need to concentrate on seeking wisdom where it may be found. "

An abundance of wisdom can be found in God's preached or written Word. Proverbs and Ecclesiastes can be a well spring from on high with the shared insights of King Solomon, reportedly the wisest man of all time.

Isaiah was told that that the "spirit of wisdom and understanding" would rest on Jesus. The more we abide in the words of Jesus, the more wisdom we will acquire.

We can also receive wisdom by praying for it. James tells us that our generous God will not rebuke us for asking.

It takes discernment to distinguish between the wisdom of God and the wisdom of man. *"Since God in his wisdom saw to it that the world would never know him through human wisdom, he has used our foolish preaching to save those who believe."* 1 Corinthians 1:20-22 NLT

"In Him all the treasures of [divine] wisdom (comprehensive insight into the ways and purposes of God) and [all the riches of spiritual] knowledge and enlightenment are stored up and lie hidden. Colossians 2:2 AMP

It also takes discernment to recognize and use the wisdom God gives us for Our good and His glory. The more we discern how little we know, the harder we should search for wisdom where it can be found.

Father, give me the spiritual wisdom and discernment I need to live a life fully pleasing to You. In Jesus' name, Amen.

Read 1 Timothy 4:1-8, Hosea 2:5-14
Liberty and Justice for All
"He is the Rock, his works are perfect, and all his ways are just. A faithful God who does no wrong, upright and just is he." Deuteronomy 32:5 NIV

This inspirational phrase from America's pledge of allegiance was the principle on which this country was founded and has

"So now, come back to your God. Act with love and justice, and always depend on him."
Hosea 12:6 NLT

more or less pursued ever since. These principles have both been abused and often perverted.
Many have taken the liberty of burning our flag, rioting in the streets,and bashing faith in our schools, courts, and media. Justice has often seemed to have become based on how to outsmart the law rather than abide and administer justice by it.

We can all be thankful that there is still liberty and justice in Christ. The price He paid for the penalty of our sin God's justice demanded was high. We too often use what we received as though we were not worth it.

God did not give us liberty from the power of sin to keep sinning more. He gave us the freedom to be and do all that He purposed us to be and do before we were even born.

Jesus dying on the cross to fulfill the righteous demands and justice of God's law for us should inspire us all to show our appreciation by "thanksliving" to the praise of His glory.

Before we question the justice of God we had best maintain a proper perspective.

Bad things happen because of the curse of sin brought into the world and upon us all by the disobedience of Adam and Eve. We should never blame or judge God.

Before we begin making judgments about God's judgments we need to remember

"Henceforth there is laid up for me a crown of righteousness, which the Lord, the righteous judge, shall give me at that day: and not to me only, but unto all them also that love his appearing."
2 Timothy 4:8 KJV

that His ways are higher than ours. Even though we may not see God's justice dispensed we can be sure that He will deal with evil in His way and His time.

How we should thank God for the liberty to choose to receive the wonderful justice He has provided by faith.

Father, thank you for the liberty and justice Jesus died to provide for me. In Jesus' name, Amen

Read James 1,12-17, Isaiah 61:1-3 December 28

Standing Fast

"Stand fast therefore in the liberty wherewith Christ hath made us free, and be not entangled again with the yoke of bondage." Galatians 5:1-3

One of the biggest problems of many believers is our inability to stand fast in our freedom from bondage to sin. In spite of believing in Jesus for our salvation, we have a hard time believing that are chains are gone, we've been set free, and that sin has no more dominion over us.;

"The Spirit of God, the Master, is on me because God anointed me. He sent me to preach good news to the poor, heal the heartbroken, Announce freedom to all captives, pardon all prisoners." Isaiah 62:1 MSG

Like dogs returning to vomit, we give temptation permission to hold us in its power and go back into bondage because we do not stand tall and strong in the supernatural strength and power of the Holy Spirit which was given to enable us to resist, flee, or escape temptation.

"The Devil made me do it" can no longer be used as an excuse. The devil might trick and deceive, but he has no power to make us do anything once we are born again believers.

We do have an ongoing battle with our flesh, the world, and the devil, but we can only lose if we choose not to stand fast in our liberty in Christ and lose these battles by failing to wear the full armor God has provided.

Even when we drop our guard and stumble into sin, we don't have to wallow there. When we take our broken spirit and contrite heart to the Lord in sincere confession and repentance, He will forgive, restore, and lift us up and out of the trash heap into which we have fallen.

The key to standing fast is holding fast in the Word of God, and shielded by faith in the promises and power of God.

The power that raised Jesus from the dead lives in the heart of every true believer to cover our weaknesses with His strength when we stand fast in the new life in which we have been born again.

"But whoso looketh into the perfect law of liberty, and continueth therein, he being not a forgetful hearer, but a doer of the work, this man shall be blessed in his deed." James 1:25 KJV

Father thank giving me the power of the Holy Spirit to help me stand fast. In Jesus' name, Amen

363

Whose Best Interest

"I am the good shepherd. The good shepherd gives His life for the sheep."
John 10:11 NIV

We seem to have a great ability to determine what is in the best interest of everyone else. Judges are always looking for the best interest of children in custody cases. Our doctors are always trying to treat and prescribe according to our best interests.

"and to keep the commandments of the LORD and His statutes which I command you today for your good?"
Deuteronomy 10:13 AMP

Some over aggressive salesmen have you gripping your wallet as they seek to convince you that buying their product is serving your best interest. Politicians, lobbyists and spin masters make a living trying to get you to think that their agendas represent your best interest and the best interests of this country.

The deceiver of our souls has been faking a concern for our best interest for centuries. He deceived Eve into thinking that it was in her best interest to have the knowledge of and equality with God by partaking of the forbidden fruit.

When temptation comes knocking at our doors, the big bad wolf dressed up as grandma to trick little red riding hood is a joke compared to the roaring lion who comes promising popularity, prestige, and all sorts of pleasures as though He really were interested in our welfare and best interests.

How many people has the devil been able to ruin the lives of, fill jail cells with, break up marriages and imprison in bondage to alcohol, and drugs, promiscuity, and other disasters by sugar coating the temptation with rationalization and denial as though living in sin is living according to our best interests.

"And we know that God causes everything to work together for the good of those who love God and are called according to his purpose for them."
Romans 8:27-29 NLT

There is only one person who truly knows and has our best interest at heart. There is only one person who died so that we could live forever. God is always working for our best interest. He can even take our worst and turn it into our best.

Father, let me put my self interest under the blood of Jesus, so that you can work all things for my best interest. In Jesus' name, Amen

The Last Hurrah

"And now, God, do it again— bring rains to our drought-stricken lives so those who planted their crops in despair will shout hurrahs at the harvest, so those who went off with heavy hearts will come home laughing, with armloads of blessing." Psalm 126:3 MSG

"When it goes well for good people, the whole town cheers; when it goes badly for bad people, the town celebrates." Proverbs 11:10 MSG

This book is the 7th of a series of over 1800 devotions I have been blessed to share over the past 8 years, and will be the last.

That the Lord has privileged me to share these insights with so many and use them to encourage, strengthen, convict, and teach is one of the great reasons for me to cheer.

The Lord gives all of His children much to cheer about, and I have had more than my share.

I have celebrated 59 years of marriage with a wonderful wife and mother. We have cheered graduations from college by all, and thank God for the strong faith they all have.

Success in business, horse, and church activities have all filled my cup of cheer to overflowing many times.

We all need things to cheer about to help ease the pain of those regrets that we wish had never happened. We need to use these regrets to cheer God for His faithfulness, grace, and mercy in forgiving us and using them to draw us closer to Him.

At age 82+ with CPOD, lung and prostate cancer problems I am seeing the "lights of that city" more clearly every day secure in the faith I have that my last hurrah will be when I hear that final trumpet sound ushering in that wonderful new life awaiting.

Then the seventh angel sounded: And there were loud voices in heaven, saying, "The kingdoms of this world have become the kingdoms of our Lord and of His Christ, and He shall reign forever and ever!" Revelation 11:13 NKJV

My prayer is that all who read this will be as ready for that last hurrah as I. I pray God's blessing upon you.

Father, thank you for your goodness and mercy that have given me so much to cheer about all the days of my life. In Jesus' name, Amen

No Sad Songs for Me

This day is holy to our Lord. Do not grieve, for the joy of the LORD is your strength." Nehemiah 8:10b NIV

I have recently finished 12 months of surviving lung cancer and am absolutely blown away by how much fun I am having dying.

> "This is the day the Lord has made. We will rejoice and be glad in it."
> Psalm 118:24 NLT

The Lord is providing some sort of sacred delight on an almost daily basis and the realization that I am going to be with Him soon anchors the joy that I am experiencing on a daily basis as I seek to follow the advice of "One Month to Live" to "live passionately, love completely, learn humbly, and leave boldly".

It is absolutely amazing that at almost 83, I am having so much fun doing so many new and different things that I hardly have time for my nap practice. The Lord may be tickling me to death!

My passion for writing these grits has returned, and this makes 366 new devotions for Homily Grits 7. I continue to find great joy in sending out daily email grits to my little congregation of subscribers around the world, and posting a daily grit on our homily grits web site and twitter.

The vicarious pleasure of getting dividends from lives I have invested in over the years continues.

As much fun as all of this doing is, the being is even more fun. I am at total peace, no real regrets except that the Lord has had to forgive so much more than he should ever have to forgive one who professes to love Him and lives to please Him.

> And the city has no need of sun or moon, for the glory of God illuminates the city, and the Lamb is its light.
> Revelation 21:23 NLT

So please, no sad songs or feeling sorry for me. My prayer is that you should be so blessed to have so much fun dying as I am when your death sentence is diagnosed.

Father, as I see the lights of Your City getting brighter, continue to fill me with the peace and joy of Your salvation in the time I have left here. In Jesus' name, Amen

10782723R00213

Made in the USA
Charleston, SC
03 January 2012